THE TRUTH ABOUT EMPIRE

ALAN LESTER
(*Editor*)

The Truth About Empire

Real Histories of British Colonialism

With a Foreword by
SATHNAM SANGHERA

HURST & COMPANY, LONDON

First published in the United Kingdom in 2024 by
C. Hurst & Co. (Publishers) Ltd.,
New Wing, Somerset House, Strand, London, WC2R 1LA
© Alan Lester and the Contributors, 2024
Foreword © Sathnam Sanghera, 2024
All rights reserved.

Distributed in the United States, Canada and Latin America by Oxford University Press, 198 Madison Avenue, New York, NY 10016, United States of America.

The right of Alan Lester and the Contributors to be identified as the authors of this publication is asserted by them in accordance with the Copyright, Designs and Patents Act, 1988.

A Cataloguing-in-Publication data record for this book is available from the British Library.

ISBN: 9781911723097

www.hurstpublishers.com

Printed and bound in Great Britain by Bell & Bain Ltd, Glasgow

This book is dedicated to our friend and colleague Lyndall Ryan, whose chapter is published posthumously after she passed away in late April 2024. We hope that it is a fitting tribute to a woman whose career was spent doggedly pursuing the truth about Australia's history.

CONTENTS

List of Contributors   xi

PART ONE
SETTING THE SCENE

Foreword
                                Sathnam Sanghera   3

Introduction: The Truth About Colonial History
                                      Alan Lester   11

PART TWO
THE REALITIES OF COLONIALISM
AROUND THE WORLD

1. What About Slavery?
                                      Bronwen Everill   49

2. Tasmania and the Question of Genocide in the Black War, the History Wars and the Culture War
                                      Lyndall Ryan   55

3. The Misuse of Indigenous and Canadian History in *Colonialism*
   Adele Perry, Sean Carleton, and *Omeasoo Wahpasiw* 73

4. 'When Men Burn Women Alive, We Hang Them': Sati and 'Civilising Mission' in Colonial India
   Andrea Major 93

5. 'Unencumbered by the Scruples of Justice and Good Faith': The Colonial Achievements of Raffles in Southeast Asia
   Gareth Knapman 121

6. My Empire, Right or Wrong: Rhodes, Milner and the South African War
   Saul Dubow 147

7. Written on the City: Imperial Britain and China
   Robert Bickers 171

PART THREE
HISTORIOGRAPHY AND RACE

8. Morality and the History of Abolition and Empire
   Richard Huzzey 187

9. A Short History of a Controversial Comparison: Empire and Fascism in Black Political Thought During the 1930s
   Liam Liburd 213

10. Escape from Empire: Decolonisation as Disentanglement, Erasure, and Evasion
    Erik Linstrum 235

11. No End of a Reckoning
    Stuart Ward 251

CONTENTS

12. *Colonialism*: A Methodological Reckoning
    Margot Finn 275

Notes 297
Index 359

LIST OF CONTRIBUTORS

Robert Bickers is a Professor of History at the University of Bristol. The author of six books, which have ranged widely in subject across the history of modern China and British relations with China since the 1790s, he is currently preparing a new history of Hong Kong. He co-directs the University's Hong Kong History Centre and leads the Historical Photographs of China project.

Sean Carleton is a settler historian and Associate Professor in the Departments of History and Indigenous Studies at the University of Manitoba. He is the author of *Lessons in Legitimacy: Colonialism, Capitalism, and the Rise of State Schooling in British Columbia* (UBC Press, 2022).

Saul Dubow has worked at the Universities of Sussex and London and is now Smuts Professor of Commonwealth History at Cambridge. He is the author of several books and numerous articles about segregation and apartheid in South Africa and has developed interests in the history of race, science, empire and commonwealth. He is currently working on a book about South Africa as a problem for the world.

Bronwen Everill (FRHistS) is the Director of the Centre of African Studies at the University of Cambridge and a Fellow of

LIST OF CONTRIBUTORS

Gonville & Caius College. She is the author of *Not Made by Slaves: Ethical Capitalism in the Age of Abolition* (Harvard University Press, 2020) and *Abolition and Empire in Sierra Leone and Liberia* (Palgrave Macmillan, 2013).

Margot Finn is Astor Professor of British History at University College London and a Fellow of the British Academy. The author of two monographs with Cambridge University Press, she has co-edited four volumes of essays on British and British imperial culture, including two works on the East India Company. She has published widely on the cultural, social, legal and political aspects of Britain's empire in India and its contemporary legacies, including histories of material culture, gender and loot. A former editor of the *Journal of British Studies*, she is a founding-co-editor (with Deborah Cohen and Peter Mandler) of the book series Cambridge Modern British Histories.

Richard Huzzey is Professor of Modern British History at Durham University. His first book was *Freedom Burning: Antislavery and Empire in Victorian Britain* (Cornell University Press, 2012), and he has published a variety of articles and chapters on abolitionism in the period since the later eighteenth century. He co-edited, with Robert Burroughs, a volume on *The Suppression of the Atlantic Slave Trade* (Manchester University Press, 2015).

Gareth Knapman is a Research Fellow at the Centre for Heritage and Museum Studies at the Australian National University. Dr Knapman works across colonial Southeast Asian history and colonial Australian history. His principal work is *Race and British Colonialism in Southeast Asia, 1770–1870: John Crawfurd and the Politics of Equality* (Routledge, 2016). Much of Knapman's research activity is applied research supporting the provenancing for the repatriation of Australian Aboriginal and Torres Strait Islanders' ancestral remains. Dr Knapman's ORCID profile with

LIST OF CONTRIBUTORS

a complete list of publications can be found at https://orcid.org/0000-0003-4431-6659

Alan Lester (FRHistS) is Professor of Historical Geography at the University of Sussex and Adjunct Professor of History at La Trobe University. He has written widely on British colonial history. Previous books include *Ruling the World: Freedom, Civilisation and Liberalism in the Nineteenth Century British Empire* (Cambridge University Press, 2021) (with Kate Boehme and Peter Mitchell); *Humanitarianism, Empire and Transnationalism in the Anglophone World, 1760–1995* (Manchester University Press, 2023) (edited with Joy Damousi and Trevor Burnard); *Indigenous Communities and Settler Colonialism: Land Holding, Loss and Survival in an Interconnected World* (Palgrave Macmillan, 2015) (edited with Zoë Laidlaw); *Colonization and the Origins of Humanitarian Governance: Protecting Aborigines across the Nineteenth-Century British Empire* (Cambridge University Press, 2014) (with Fae Dussart); *The East India Company and the Natural World 1600–1850* (Palgrave Macmillan, 2014) (edited with Vinita Damodaran and Anna Winterbottom); *Colonial Lives across the British Empire: Imperial Careering in the Long Nineteenth Century* (Cambridge University Press, 2006) (edited with David Lambert); and *Imperial Networks: Creating Identities in Nineteenth Century South Africa and Britain* (Routledge, 2001). He is co-editor of the long-established Manchester University Press Studies in Imperialism research monograph series.

Liam J. Liburd is Assistant Professor of Black British History at Durham University. His research focuses broadly on the ongoing impact of the legacies of empire and decolonisation in modern Britain. His current research focuses on Black radical analyses of fascism and on the question of how historians might use these to transform our understanding of the relationship between

LIST OF CONTRIBUTORS

British fascism and the British Empire, as well as, more broadly, of the politics of race in modern Britain. He is in the process of trying to turn his thesis into his first book, under the working title: Thinking Imperially: The British White Supremacist Movement and the Politics of Race in Modern Britain.

Erik Linstrum is Associate Professor of History at the University of Virginia. He is the author of *Age of Emergency: Living with Violence at the End of the British Empire* (Oxford University Press, 2023) and *Ruling Minds: Psychology in the British Empire* (Harvard University Press, 2016), which won the George Louis Beer Prize awarded by the American Historical Association. He has held fellowships from the American Academy in Berlin, the American Council of Learned Societies, the Institute of Historical Research in London, the Kennedy School of Government at Harvard University, and the Kluge Center at the Library of Congress, among others.

Andrea Major is Professor of Colonial History at the University of Leeds. She specialises in British Colonial and South Asian History; the East India Company; sati (suttee); slavery, indenture and abolitionism; social and gender issues; and colonial philanthropy. Her books include *Slavery, Abolitionism and Empire in India, 1772–1843*, Liverpool Studies in International Slavery (Liverpool University Press, 2012) and *Sovereignty and Social Reform in India: British Colonialism and the Campaign against Sati, 1830–1860*, Edinburgh South Asian Studies Series (Routledge, 2010).

Adele Perry is Distinguished Professor of History and Women's and Gender Studies at the University of Manitoba, where she is also director of the Centre for Human Rights Research. She is committed to creating and disseminating critical histories of empire in the lands where she was raised and lives as a settler.

LIST OF CONTRIBUTORS

Lyndall Ryan AM FAHA is Professor Emerita in Australian Studies at the University of Newcastle, Australia. The author of three books on the history of the Tasmanian Aboriginal people, she has also published widely on the history of convict women in colonial Australia and settler violence and genocide of the Indigenous peoples of Australia and the British Empire. She is also the lead investigator of the digital map of colonial frontier massacres in Australia 1788–1930; https://c21ch.newcastle.edu.au/colonialmassacres

Sathnam Sanghera was born to Punjabi parents in the West Midlands in 1976. He entered the education system unable to speak English but, after attending Wolverhampton Grammar School, graduated from Christ's College, Cambridge, with a first-class degree in English Language and Literature. He has been shortlisted for the Costa Book Awards twice, for his memoir *The Boy with the Topknot* and his novel *Marriage Material*, the former being adapted by BBC Drama in 2017 and named Mind Book of the Year in 2009. His third book, *Empireland: How Imperialism Has Shaped Modern Britain* (Viking, 2021) became an instant *Sunday Times* bestseller on release in 2021, was named a Book of the Year at the 2022 British Books Awards, and resulted in *Empire State of Mind*, the acclaimed two-part documentary for Channel 4 for which he earned a Best Presenter shortlisting at the 2022 Grierson Awards. The book also inspired a sequel, *Empireworld: How British Imperialism Has Shaped the Globe* (Penguin, 2024), which became an instant *Sunday Times* bestseller on release in 2024. He was elected a Fellow of the Royal Society of Literature in 2016 and elected a Fellow of the Royal Historical Society in recognition of his contribution to historical scholarship in 2023.

Omeasoo Wahpasiw is a nêhiyaw iskwew living in Anishinaabe territory. She co-wrote the Federation of Sovereign Indigenous

LIST OF CONTRIBUTORS

Nations Women's Commission submission to the National Inquiry into Missing and Murdered Indigenous Women and Girls and 2SLGBTQQIA+ People and is cross-appointed with Carleton University School of Indigenous and Canadian Studies and the Department of History.

Stuart Ward is Professor of History at the Saxo Institute, University of Copenhagen, working on the political, social and economic dimensions of global decolonisation in the twentieth century and the historical legacies of British imperialism worldwide. He recently published *Untied Kingdom: A Global History of the End of Britain* (Cambridge University Press, 2023).

PART ONE

SETTING THE SCENE

FOREWORD

Sathnam Sanghera

In 2021, Oliver Dowden, the then culture secretary, appeared at the History Matters conference organised by the right-wing Policy Exchange thinktank having recently urged museum curators not to 'denigrate' British history, as if history were a fixed, fragile thing, akin to a faltering tower of Jenga, and not something complex, changing, and robust, with fresh discoveries and new arguments forever changing our sense of it.

According to a report in *The Times*, Dowden proceeded to talk about the risk of curators 'being pushed around by unrepresentative campaign groups ... to remove our history, to remove statues and so on',[1] thus equating history with statues when statues are not history: they just offer one view of a historical figure at one particular point in history—and propounding the peculiar idea that history is erased with their removal (our knowledge of Lenin and Hitler continues to grow without their statues).

Incredibly, the inanity had still not peaked. That moment came when Dowden, according to the same report, was asked what he would do if the Mayor of London's Commission for

THE TRUTH ABOUT EMPIRE

Diversity in the Public Realm, which was set up, among other things, to put up a new memorial for the victims of the transatlantic slave trade,[2] sought to remove statues of national heroes Winston Churchill and Lord Nelson. The then culture secretary answered: 'I would happily chain myself to Nelson to stop him being removed.'[3]

Now, I've checked, and while some activists seem to have complained out loud that Nelson, who resisted the abolition of slavery, should not be glorified, I cannot find a single suggestion from anyone with power that Nelson's column should be pulled down. Moreover, in the three years since Dowden's strange offer to chain himself to Nelson, the Commission for Diversity in the Public Realm, which stated very clearly on being founded that it was not established to remove statues or monuments,[4] has taken down precisely ... zero monuments.

Nevertheless, we still had a minister of state suggesting he would climb 160 feet above Trafalgar Square to chain himself to a statue that was not under threat. In his defence, he was not the only person who succumbed to hysterical hyperbole during the statuecide which erupted around the emergence of the Black Lives Matter movement, and which, in Britain, saw the likeness of slave trader Edward Colston being dragged by protestors into Bristol's harbour.

In the midst of a worldwide health crisis, Prime Minister Boris Johnson managed to carve out time to pen a column and issue a string of tweets in which he vowed to defy any attempt to move the statue of his political hero Churchill from Parliament Square (it had been graffitied but faced no real threat).[5] Later, following a demonstration, the statue was observed being guarded by a sizable contingent of Metropolitan Police officers, even though the protest was over and it was still under no threat of toppling.[6]

Then there were the activists who turned up to guard a statue of the nineteenth-century novelist George Eliot. 'I'm purely here

FOREWORD

to protect our history', one military veteran told CoventryLive, apparently unaware that Eliot was a supporter of the anti-slavery movement and that her statue was under no threat whatsoever, unless the country's army of Jane Austen fans had suddenly become dangerously radicalised in an entirely unexpected way.[7]

There's a risk, I realise, in focusing on these incidents, of implying that it's only those on the right who are inclined to excess when it comes to imperial history. This is not true. 'Topple the Racists', an online crowdsourced map of problematic statues and monuments, targets, among many others, commemorations to former prime minister William Gladstone, which feels decidedly unnuanced, given that he opposed the slave trade, as well as defended it at times, while also benefitting from family wealth generated from it.[8] Some of the estimates made for reparations are such colossal numbers that they stop being useful: it feels unrealistic to begin a conversation on the topic with the claim that Britain 'drained' a total of nearly $45 trillion (in today's money) from India during the period 1765 to 1938, or the 1999 claim from the African World Reparations and Repatriation Truth Commission that $777 trillion would be suitable compensation for the enslavement and theft endured by Africa during colonisation.[9]

But the crucial difference is that, in Britain, the left has not been in power for more than a decade. In contrast, the right have in recent years had their arguments adopted by government and amplified by interlinked, opaquely funded thinktanks keen on culture wars, and the consequences have been serious.[10] At least, it felt serious when, in June 2020, Gavin Williamson, the then education secretary, rejected proposals to add more about Britain's involvement in slavery and colonial past to the history curriculum with the words 'we should be incredibly proud of our history'.[11] Studying history should never be about instilling pride or shame; it should be about encouraging understanding. We don't need to look far in the world, only to Ukraine, for an extreme illustration of what can happen when imperial history and patriotism blur.

It also felt serious when, in February 2019, Brexiteer Jacob Rees-Mogg referred to one of the darkest episodes in imperial history, the death of around 50,000 South Africans,[12] mostly children, in British-run concentration camps during the South African War and claimed that 'these people were interned for their safety'. He added that '[t]he death rate was exactly the same as Glasgow',[13] claims I cannot recall being made by any historian in years of reading on the subject. Indeed, the consensus among imperial historians who have been studying the subject for their professional lives has long been that General Kitchener authorised the construction of 'concentration camps' in South Africa with the intention of dividing the families of Boer commandos and severing their access to supplies, comfort, and food.

These incidents demonstrate how imperial history is no longer confined to libraries, classrooms, and tutorials. It plays out in frontline politics and on the front pages of newspapers, with imperial historians regularly being vilified, and their work being wilfully misunderstood, in public. What has been driving the government's involvement in this culture war? *The Economist* has suggested it does it simply because it comes easily—'As the pandemic recedes, the government will have to make choices about the future role of the state and how to steady the nation's finances, which cannot please both camps. How much easier, then, to put off such thorny decisions and play a little more Elgar.'[14] Tim Shipman of *The Sunday Times* has argued that some Conservatives see it as a way of appealing to voters who are left wing on spending and public services but 'culturally conservative'.[15] Meanwhile, historian Michael Taylor has proposed that historians are handy hate figures now there's not much to be

FOREWORD

gained from attacking the European Union: 'After all, we cannot just hate Jean-Claude Juncker for ever.'[16]

I suspect that Conservative politicians have been motivated by a combination of all these factors, and behind it all lies a misunderstanding of what history is, and what historians do. British Prime Minister Rishi Sunak revealed as much when he was challenged in the Commons by the Labour MP Bell Ribeiro-Addy on the issue of reparations for slavery and replied that 'trying to unpick our history is ... not something that we will focus our energies on', seemingly not comprehending, or deciding not to comprehend, that 'unpicking' history is exactly what all historians do.[17]

The impact of this culture war on individual historians has sometimes been devastating. It's a matter of record and a cause of national shame that one of Britain's most respected historians, David Olusoga, has to employ a bodyguard at some speaking events.[18] I largely stopped doing events for adults for a period because the abuse had become routine.[19] And then there is Professor Corinne Fowler, who co-authored a report for the National Trust in 2019 on its estates' ties to the East India Company and transatlantic slavery and was subjected to a barrage of hate.[20]

Her entirely measured report concluded that a third of the National Trust's properties had links to British colonialism, and, initially, the media reporting was reasonable. But then the report was condemned by Cabinet ministers, and a gathering of MPs within the Conservative Party, who call themselves the Common Sense Group, turned the spotlight on Fowler and her colleagues. In a speech to Parliament, Rees-Mogg claimed the report denigrated Churchill by mentioning his home, Chartwell (the report recalls, factually, that Churchill was Colonial Secretary and voted against Indian Independence). Despite the National Trust Act of 1907 clearly stating that the Trust 'may acquire property ... for purposes of public recreation resort or instruction', *The Daily Telegraph* claimed that the Charity Commission could look into the National Trust on the grounds that the report was outside the Trust's charitable remit.[21]

From this point on, the onslaught expanded to Fowler's other research project, *Colonial Countryside*, a child-led history and writing project steered by historians. The book was the focus of several attacks, including inaccurate reporting (*The Daily Telegraph* falsely claimed that she wrote in her book that 'gardening is racist') and *The Daily Mail* claiming incorrectly that the National Trust report was 'error strewn'. Another inaccurate report claimed she had likened Japanese treatment of POWs to British colonialism (*The Daily Mail*), an article that provoked an avalanche of hate mail and threats. Fowler was denied the opportunity to respond in most of these articles. Senior government ministers and members of the 'Common Sense Group' briefed against her, and she says the whole experience made her feel as though she was passing 'through the valley of the shadow of death'. Her safety was compromised; she occasionally needed to call the police and was, at times, unable to walk alone.[22]

It feels absurd to have to say it, but it's not acceptable that historians should be terrorised in this way simply for doing their work. Discussion and free speech are essential. But threats, wilful misrepresentation of people you may disagree with, and intimidation are not. Equally concerning has been the intensifying enthusiasm among the imperially nostalgic to break the basic rules of conducting history in order to make their case. There are countless illustrations in this volume of the tactics employed, from the erection of straw men to attack, highly selective quoting, cherry-picking evidence, dismissing some witnesses to events but not others, and making false accusations, to ignoring context.

But for me the single most troubling development has been the denial of the Tasmanian genocide, as outlined by Lyndall

FOREWORD

Ryan in Chapter 3. There is no one single truth about the British Empire, and as Stuart Ward explains in Chapter 11, there is nothing new or illegitimate about British historians wishing to justify and defend imperialism. Niall Ferguson and Jan Morris are among them. But while the former describes how 'the Aborigines in Van Diemen's Land were hunted down, confined and ultimately exterminated', as 'one of the most shocking of all the chapters in the history of the British empire' and 'an event which truly merits the now overused term "genocide"',[23] and while Morris cites the episode as the 'cruellest' illustration of the fact that 'empire *was* race',[24] we now live in an era where bestselling authors try their best to absolve Britons of responsibility.

It's depressing beyond belief that imperial nostalgia has become so extreme that its advocates feel the need to deny killing that has, through the consensus of experts, long been accepted as deliberate and largely tolerated, if not condoned, by the empire's governmental and legal structure at local level. An episode which the celebrated art critic Robert Hughes has described as 'the only true genocide in English colonial history',[25] and which was employed as a case study by the lawyer Raphael Lemkin when he shaped the concept of 'genocide' after the Second World War.[26] History is argument. But the arguments have to be based in facts. The arguments also have to acknowledge the overwhelming consensus, when it exists, among people who have studied the subject for decades. It has become highly unfashionable to say it, but the work of experts counts, and this volume demonstrates why.

INTRODUCTION

THE TRUTH ABOUT COLONIAL HISTORY

Alan Lester

The contributors to this book are all academics who specialise in histories of colonialism.[1] Lately, our field has become a battlefield in a culture war, but we have not come together to fuel the divisions. We doubt that many committed participants in the culture war will change their minds about Britain's colonial past because of the historical evidence we supply and our interpretation of it. The culture war is about politics rather than historical understanding. For its most avid participants, interpretations of the past are simply a weapon to be wielded in a struggle between progressive and reactionary philosophies and instincts.[2] The pitch and intensity of that social, cultural and political struggle, first identified by political scientists in the United States of the 1960s, has intensified since the financial crisis of 2008, with the resurgence of simplistic, populist 'solutions' to structural inequalities. In this politically charged context, our craft—colonial history—has been woven together with gender, sexuality, abortion, religion, race, environmentalism, migration and other potentially weaponised demarcations of difference.[3] For culture warriors, where one stands on Britain's colonial history is determined by one's political orientation, not by serious research or even interest.

The differences between the approaches we adopt as professional scholars of colonialism and the inclination of those engaged in culture war politics will never be absolute. None of us is capable of a God-like detachment from political affairs or unadulterated objectivity. But there are significant differences of degree. We became interested in the colonial past for a variety of reasons, but the main motivation we share is genuine curiosity about it. This is a different motivation from entering the fray directly to promote or defend political claims. There are significant differences among us, since academic history is still about questioning, debating, discussing and disagreement. But for us, interpretations of the past are not simply a battlefield on which one has to be aligned with one army or the other. The other main difference between us and those who comment regularly on colonial history as culture warriors is that we have spent our careers immersed in study of the subject. Collectively, the time dedicated to poring over archival documents, most of them left by British colonists and officials, and discussing one another's interpretations of them, amounts to decades.

The first aim of this book is to make the fruits of this historical work on aspects of British colonial history, many of them key points of contention in the culture war, more accessible.

The second is to show how the work that we do, and that many of us have been doing for decades, is being misrepresented in the culture war. Gareth Bacon, a member of the Common Sense Group of Conservative MPs, for instance, claims that 'traducing' the 'reputation of key figures in our country's history' calls 'the very sense of what it is to be British ... into question'.

INTRODUCTION

Our work, which inevitably entails examining the actions and beliefs of such figures, means for him and his colleagues that 'Britain is under attack.'[4] Nigel Biggar's bestselling book *Colonialism: A Moral Reckoning*, granted welcoming publicity by *The Daily Telegraph* and *The Spectator* among other media outlets upon its publication in 2023, alleges that an unthinking 'anti-colonialism' is 'fashionable' in academia, 'opening doors to posts, promotions and grants'. It argues that scholars like us are brainwashed by Frantz Fanon's 'preference for "barbarous" vitality and irresponsibility over civilised reason and restraint' and even speculates that a 'degenerate Christian sensibility' results in 'a perverse bid for supreme self-righteousness', which in turn drives critiques of colonialism.[5]

Biggar's *Colonialism* is by no means the first popular defence of British colonialism's morality. Historians and journalists set about rationalising the idea of empire in the late nineteenth century, and, as we will see, moral defences have resurfaced during times of imperial anxiety, for instance during the First World War and at the end of empire.[6] Biggar, however, was explicit that his moral assessment arose from the contemporary culture war context. He explained that his interest in colonialism stemmed from being publicly criticised for defending the statue of Cecil Rhodes in Oxford against the Rhodes Must Fall movement. Academic specialists in colonialism vehemently opposed a research project he set up to debate (although critics suggest to reassert) the morality of colonialism, and his publisher Bloomsbury decided not to proceed with his book, which was instead published two years later by William Collins.[7] This all indicates an intolerant cancel culture emanating from those who insist upon British colonialism's innate and indefensible violence and racism.[8] It seems to justify the allegation that disinterested scholarship has been overtaken by a shared 'anticolonial' predisposition.

THE TRUTH ABOUT EMPIRE

Biggar had a precedent. An article by Canadian American Bruce Gilley calling for voluntary recolonisation, published in the journal *Third World Quarterly* in 2017, was withdrawn after threats were made against the journal's editor. Gilley had presented data which appeared to show that formerly colonised countries had fared better in the long run than those which had remained independent. He blamed stalled progress on the nationalists who led many countries to independence, condemning them for turning their backs on the advantages of European colonial governance. Academics criticised Gilley's methods, data and findings, but it was the threats from some activists that resulted in the article's withdrawal.[9] Those threats did the cause of academic freedom and debate tremendous harm. Refusing to engage with the lawful arguments of those with whom we disagree rarely helps to further knowledge and understanding, while of course personal threats to academics are unacceptable from any quarter.

As Sathnam Sanghera indicates in this volume's foreword, though, the pressure to 'cancel' academic research on colonialism now seems to come mainly from the populist right wing of the culture war, including Bacon's colleagues in the Common Sense Group. Academics like Corinne Fowler, who led the National Trust report on its properties' colonial connections, and the researchers at last uncovering evidence of institutional involvement in slavery, are targeted and their work declared 'anti-British'.[10] While *The Daily Mail* and *The Daily Express* wage a populist 'war on woke' with attacks on colonial scholars, *The Daily Telegraph* provides a platform for a clique of retired Oxbridge professors to write repeatedly about scholars of colonialism supposedly undermining history.[11] At the time of writing, it is the historian of technology Jenny Bulstrode who is receiving serious personal threats, as well as some more disinterested scholarly critique.[12] Much of the animosity against

INTRODUCTION

Bulstrode arises not from the intricacies of her well-publicised article itself (which argues that the British industrialist Henry Cort's patented process of rendering scrap metal into valuable bar iron was stolen from enslaved African metallurgists) but from a furious response to the very idea that Black people may have played any kind of role in Britain's Industrial Revolution and a manufactured outrage that such an analysis amounts to a criticism of all White Britons today.[13]

Biggar and I have published our exchanges and engaged in a school debate.[14] This book allows other specialist historians to engage specifically with Biggar's popular moral defence of British colonialism and consider what has happened to their fields of research more broadly in recent culture war discourse. It gives us an opportunity to present the work of experts on some of the most controversial aspects of colonial history. We are intent on telling the truth based on the evidence we have analysed and debated over many years. We leave it to readers to judge the strength of our analysis and decide how those truths should be deployed in the dilemmas facing society today.

Writing colonial history

As Hilary Mantel wrote, history is

> no more 'the past' than a birth certificate is a birth, or a script is a performance, or a map is a journey. It is the multiplication of the evidence of fallible and biased witnesses, combined with incomplete accounts of actions not fully understood by the people who performed them. It's no more than the best we can do, and often it falls short of that.[15]

But if there is no objective and comprehensive basis for history writing, what is it that distinguishes academic writing seeking impartiality from mere polemic?

The answer lies in the guidelines academics use to assess credibility through peer review and scholarly debate. They should try to read the work of all other scholars who have written on their topic and reflect honestly upon their evidence and arguments. This means reading beyond only those scholars with whom they are disposed to agree. They should try to reflect equally upon the evidence at their disposal. For the most part, this takes the form of texts written during the period they are studying and retained in various archives and collections. Whether qualitative or quantitative, this evidence is very different from the 'data' that repeatable experimental observations can yield for most scientists.[16]

Historians need to consider Mantel's point that their sources of evidence are the writings of 'fallible and biased witnesses'. Not only that, but also the point that these witnesses' records were the ones selected by institutions and individuals for preservation. Equally valid insights from other witnesses were never written down or never preserved. Writing about most people in the past who were illiterate, and about whom we have only scraps of evidence, mainly from the perspective of their social 'superiors', is an especially different proposition from conducting an experiment and recording one's observations. A loose analogy would be a chemist able to see only a tiny fraction of the periodic table, and that fraction compiled by someone with a preference for certain elements and a prejudice against others.

This question of a far-from-neutral selectivity for document storage and preservation is especially acute in colonial contexts. A disproportionate number of the documents now available to colonial historians were generated by colonial officials, responsible for maintaining order over disenfranchised colonised people. They tended to look upon those people as potential sources of disorder. Their writings are redolent with stereotypes and infused with anxieties. While those anxieties and stereotypes are telling in themselves, historians cannot necessarily take their sources at their word.[17] As Antoinette Burton puts it, 'strategic antagonism toward sources is, or should be, the hallmark of all historians interested in a critical engagement with the past'.[18]

INTRODUCTION

While being healthily sceptical of the 'evidence' upon which they rely, competent and conscientious historians nevertheless try to develop their arguments as they engage with it through archival study and debate. They do not set out with an idea they intend to 'prove' and stick with it stubbornly in the face of contradictory evidence. Whether they trust a text's version of reality or not, they should never ignore it or misrepresent what its writer was seeking to convey. They try not to cherry-pick words or sentences to make it seem that witnesses were saying one thing when they were saying another. Rather, they try to work out why witnesses recorded things in the way they did, often through triangulation with other sources.

All these guidelines, ideally, inform how academic historians judge each other's work through peer review, although they sometimes fall short. The referees to whom editors send papers for peer review may be arbitrary in their judgement, they may have a vested interest in defending a particular approach, their egos may be bruised by criticism of their work and they might even discriminate against authors whose backgrounds they consider 'suspect'. Editors' responsibility is to mitigate these risks. Historical scholarship is an imperfect system, but in Mantel's words, it is 'the best we can do'.

Honesty and diligence in a historian are not the same thing as objectivity. Fastidious historians might read different sources, or even the same sources, and come to very different conclusions because they ask different questions of them or interpret them differently. It is impossible to remove the historian from their work. The starting point for credible historical research is not the supposition that the researcher is impartial. It is the recognition that they are prone to bias and attempt to address it, sometimes even using it to uncover new truths to be set alongside established accounts that are equally biased in other directions. What may be surprising is how recently historians of colonialism have set about implementing these practices of reflection, mitigation and inclusion, albeit imperfectly.

Between J. R. Seeley's founding the sub-discipline of imperial history as a teaching subject with *The Expansion of England* in 1883 and the 'subaltern studies', Marxist, feminist, postcolonial and 'cultural-turn' approaches of the 1970s to 1990s, most practitioners considered the experiences of colonised people and women to be relatively unimportant.[19] In part, this was because of the relative exclusion of sources from women and people of colour in the archives themselves. A survey of historians conducted in the 2010s yielded this response: '[A]nybody who spent the late 1970s and early 1980s looking for hints that women were recorded in the documents they were reading learned to read carefully and problematise as they went. You had to think about what was there and what wasn't there at the same time.'[20] The same goes for the voices of most colonised people, with Gayatri Spivak famously pondering the ethics of trying to speak for those 'subaltern' peoples who bear no archival trace.[21]

But the biases of imperial history were also influenced by the characteristics of most of its practitioners. Along with many other professions, academic history was hard for women and people of colour to break into. The leading historian of empire, Catherine Hall, notes that 'none of my generation of feminist historians started off in the universities—we had to wait for years to be accepted, working outside in adult education etc. And eventually things shifted.'[22] Things have still not shifted much in terms of the representation of people of colour in the upper echelons of the academy, with only a handful of Black professors.[23] It is not so much, then, that imperial history has suddenly been hijacked by people of a certain race, class and gender orientation; more that it has always had that mantle, albeit unacknowledged and for a long time uncontested.

The backlash that some historians are facing today is, in part, a reaction against the recognition and rejection of the

INTRODUCTION

unacknowledged assumptions that have long shaped our discipline. Recent interpretations of colonial and imperial history have added women, colonised and racialised people to the cast of characters whom the social historian of the working classes E. P. Thompson wished 'to rescue ... from the enormous condescension of posterity'.[24] This work tends to attract opprobrium from those who favoured the older perspectives. At the same time, it is evident that historians who want to swing the pendulum away from more exclusive, established perspectives raise hackles among some conservatives, with what the latter see as over-correction.

Undoubtedly, some historians have extracted moral parables from the overwhelming evidence of colonial violence and racism encountered in their research. 'In their zeal to dispel the lingering spirit of colonialism', some focus almost exclusively on those characteristics rather than the arenas of cooperation, collaboration and mutual benefit which also characterised colonialism and to which I will return below.[25] Perhaps the most often-cited recent example is Caroline Elkins, who makes her concern to set the record straight clear when she cites a 2014 poll indicating that nearly 60 per cent of Britons thought that the empire was 'something to be proud of'. In response, her *Legacy of Violence* concentrates on 'the ways in which state-directed violence in the British Empire ... shaped large parts of the contemporary world' and concludes that 'those who have lived the experiences of liberalism's "inhuman totality" must demand universal rights and unfettered inclusion, sometimes peacefully and other times forcefully'.[26] Many of her critics prefer to return to longer-established, more self-congratulatory perspectives that may or may not be more 'balanced'.

British colonial history: a summary

According to the Oxford Online Dictionary, colonialism means 'the policy or practice of acquiring full or partial political control over another country, occupying it with settlers, and exploiting it economically'. I will first take each of these core features of the 'official' definition—political control, occupation and economic exploitation—in turn, assessing the ways that most professional historians of colonialism now explain them in the British context. But there is something important missing from this definition, which applies particularly to modern European, including British, colonialism. That is racial stratification, and especially anti-Black racism. So I will discuss this too.

Political control

Different British government offices established diverse forms of political control over other parts of the world, and they changed considerably through time. The Colonial Office in London governed the Crown colonies, appointing autocratic governors to take decisions on the spot, although those with large, White settler populations later attained qualified democratic self-governance as Dominions, and some governors consulted with executive and legislative councils composed overwhelmingly of British colonists. The East India Company governed India and other territories until 1858, when the government established the India Office to replace it, with a Viceroy assuming overall control within the subcontinent. The Princely States within India retained their own Indian aristocratic rulers, but they were subject to oversight and occasional replacement by the British authorities. The Foreign Office governed some colonies, including Protectorates such as those in the Mediterranean, with a relatively 'light touch', but others received far more intervention from the Colonial and War Offices.

The British Empire was never a unitary entity, each of these various offices of governance having their own agendas, located far from the reality of colonial relations on the ground and being

INTRODUCTION

lobbied continually by competing interest groups. Varying degrees of accommodation with Indigenous agendas were as important as British intentions in determining the way that colonial rule worked out in different places. Too often, generalisations about the whole are made based on a familiarity with one part of the empire, especially India, whose governance was actually very specific.

The Caribbean colonies were seized from prior colonial occupants—mainly Spanish and French—after they had already overseen the wholesale destruction of the region's Indigenous peoples and their replacement by enslaved captives from Africa. British colonists took control of Barbados in 1625, after Portuguese and Spanish slave raiding had led to its complete depopulation. Spanish slaving had also all but eradicated the Taino of Jamaica before the British conquered the island in 1655 and the 'Arawaks' and 'Caribs' of Trinidad before the British invaded in 1797. During the eighteenth century, the relationship between British planters in the Caribbean colonies and Britain conditioned the mercantilist system of trade between them. As Hall explains: 'This was a system rooted in the "Guinea Trade", the capture of Africans and the utilization of their lives and labour on Caribbean cane fields to produce sugar for export to Britain. Its mercantile base, the source of credit, was in London, [and] its plantation regime was shored up by a colonial state designed to fix racial hierarchies' between enslaved people who were Black and owners who were overwhelmingly (though not exclusively) White.[27]

Emigrant Britons established political control over what became the Dominions in North America, Australia and New Zealand through the displacement, dispossession and frequent killing of Indigenous peoples. Indigenous nations, who had signed treaties with the British to fight the French during and after the Seven Years War (1756–63), found the terms of those treaties breached as waves of British settlers displaced them in the nineteenth century. While the legal status of most Aboriginal people in Australia remained inconsistent, somewhere between foreign aliens and subjects of the Crown, small parties of settlers backed by the military used violence to 'clear' them from the land where disease had not already done the job. With the assistance of some Māori *iwi*, British forces progressively conquered others, despite the provisions of the 1840 Treaty of Waitangi, in the New Zealand Wars of the 1840s to 1860s.

The East India Company obtained political control of India with a combination of actual and threatened armed force as well as negotiation, its governors exploiting the chaos of the disintegration of Mughal rule to conquer Bengal, the Marathas, the Punjabi Sikhs, Nepal and Burma from the 1750s onwards. In the Princely States, the Company's Resident Agents withheld the use of force only as long as their guidance was followed, and rulers were supplanted by more compliant men where they stepped out of line. When Britain seized Hong Kong from China, it was part of the punishment exacted from the Qing dynasty for defying British traders smuggling opium illegally into Canton. The Chinese Empire was forced to sign a treaty ceding the territory, among other provisions, after a British force had destroyed the Chinese fleet and marched on Nanjing in 1839–42. The use or threat of violence continued to secure British interests across China well into the twentieth century, even though it was never formally colonised.

In the second half of the nineteenth century, British forces launched around sixty-five colonial wars to establish either direct or indirect political control over regions that were not already part of the empire: Southern, Western and Eastern Africa, Afghanistan and parts of the Middle East. In 1886, the artillery officer Colonel Charles Edward Callwell, who had served in the Second Anglo-Afghan War (1878–80) and the First Anglo-Boer War (1881), wrote a treatise on 'small wars' against 'savages ...

INTRODUCTION

deficient in courage and provided with poor weapons', which was adopted as a British Army field guide. His advice on 'campaigns of conquest and annexation and their characteristics', which would later inform *The United States Marine Corps Small Wars Manual*, advocated the scorched earth tactics deployed, for example, against the amaXhosa in Southern Africa. There, 'rigorous treatment was meted out to the enemy in crushing out disaffection, and with good results; the Kaffir villages ... were burnt, their crops destroyed, their cattle carried off'. Callwell explained that 'uncivilized races attribute leniency to timidity. A system adapted to La Vendée [by which he was referring to Europe in general] is out of place among fanatics and savages, who must be thoroughly brought to book and cowed or they will rise again.'[28]

Britain's governing authorities, like those of other empires, issued prohibitions on making unjust war. Despite the enormous wealth that people like Robert Clive, Stamford Raffles and Charles Napier gained through plunder, both the War Office and the East India Company told their officials and soldiers that they were not to wage wars of expansion just for their own cupidity. Accordingly, 'a narrative confirming self-defence' generally came to accompany most of these wars of expansion.[29] If it was not a case of 'they started it', the pretext tended to be 'we had to intervene on humanitarian grounds'. Such legitimations for unprovoked attacks supply much of the archival evidence relied upon by defenders of Britain's colonial record. Professional historians generally try to triangulate them with other evidence.

To give an example, those resisting calls for the repatriation of the Benin Bronzes from the British Museum today recycle the pretexts supplied for the expedition that seized them in 1897.[30] These were twofold. The first was that the expedition was punishment for the massacre of an unarmed British diplomatic party led by Acting Consul General James Phillips of the Niger Coast

Protectorate, which had entered Benin to negotiate with its ruler, the Oba. The second was that the invasion was a humanitarian intervention to stamp out slavery and human sacrifice in the kingdom. Historians who have researched the episode using the full range of sources, however, tend to place more emphasis on factors not mentioned in these justifications. British palm oil traders had been clamouring for the removal of the Oba for years because he insisted on the payment of tariffs which dented their profit margins. Phillips' supposedly unarmed 'diplomatic' party was responding to these demands, entering the kingdom despite the Oba's warning to stay away. Phillips had informed the Foreign Office that he did intend to negotiate, but that if the Oba refused his terms, he would overthrow him. Although he and the other White men on the expedition carried only their pistols, thus declaring themselves 'unarmed', they were accompanied by 400 armed African troops who would be called upon if necessary to achieve this usurpation. This 'diplomatic party' was attacked and Phillips killed because the Oba assumed its ulterior motive, having seen British officials carry out similar manoeuvres against African rulers in the region. The idea that the ensuing British 'retaliatory' invasion, which burnt Benin to the ground and seized the Bronzes, was motivated by the need to save the Oba's subjects from the cruelties of human sacrifice and slavery seems to have been articulated only as an afterthought.[31]

Some of the most concentrated wars of British imperial expansion were launched in 1878–9 to unify the various colonies and kingdoms of Southern Africa as a confederation, for the Colonial Office's administrative convenience and Britain's economic advantage after the discovery of diamonds at Kimberley.[32] The High Commissioner appointed to achieve this outcome, Sir Henry Bartle Frere, launched an intense burst of wars against the Xhosa, Griqua, Pedi and Zulu peoples. In the case of the Zulu Kingdom, his pretexts were King Cetshwayo's border dispute with a group

INTRODUCTION

of Afrikaners, the rough treatment of two colonial surveyors and a Zulu man's murder of two wives on the territory of Natal. As the liberal family of Archbishop Colenso in Natal protested, it was inconceivable that British officials would normally see such things as cause for the invasion and overthrow of a foreign power. But with an imperative to find 'just cause' for a war of confederation, Frere declared that 'it will be necessary to send to the Zulu King an ultimatum which must put an end to pacific relations'.[33] He told Cetshwayo that he must disband his army and surrender his sovereignty. Once his deadline had passed, the invasion began.[34] Yet it is still common to hear the 'Zulu War' explained in Britain as one of defence, fought to protect the colonists of Natal from a bloodthirsty Zulu kingdom to their north.

There were exceptions to conquest as the means of taking political control. Some local rulers signed treaties with British officials for protection from other European colonists, especially during the late nineteenth-century 'Scramble for Africa'. This was done mainly in the hope that they could continue to govern themselves internally, in exchange for surrendering their external relations to sympathetic British officials. In 1892, the Nama leader Hendrik Witbooi, for instance, appealed for protection from genocidal German colonialism in German South West Africa (Namibia). He was seeking to emulate King Khama III, who had negotiated for the retention of most of his autonomy in Northern Bechuanaland (now Botswana) under a British Protectorate. Khama achieved this feat to protect his people from the fate of neighbouring chiefdoms: incorporation into the Cape Colony as a labour reservoir for Cecil Rhodes' diamond and gold mines.[35]

Occupation

The second part of the definition of colonialism is occupation. We have seen how the occupation of the Caribbean colonies was predicated on the prior displacement or eradication of the region's Indigenous peoples and their replacement by captives brought from Africa from the seventeenth century. After initial settlement in 1607 by English immigrants hoping to find resources and free land, the Puritans established colonies in New England during the 1630s, as places in which they could conduct their religion free of a state church that they found too Catholic. They were accompanied by immigrants from the British Isles in search of land and commercial opportunities, amounting to some 20,000 by the 1640s. Half of these were indentured servants, some of them transported convicts. Colonists from Barbados developed plantations using African captives, modelled on those of the Caribbean, from the 1670s. Despite the defeat of the French in Quebec in the 1770s, a drastic expansion of British occupation in North America occurred only after the American colonists had gained their independence, from the early nineteenth century.

Between 1815 and 1914, 22.6 million people left the British Isles to settle in the United States and the remaining British colonies of North America in what is now Canada, Southern and Eastern Africa and Australasia.[36] The culture war has brought reassertion of their justifications for expelling Indigenous peoples and occupying their lands, including the claim that where no treaties existed, no international law was broken, and the Lockean idea that the cause of humanity was best served, since the prior inhabitants were incapable of cultivating land productively.[37] In Australia and in each of the other settler colonies, the occupation of settlers, however, resulted in the decimation of Indigenous peoples.

There were twin causes: newly introduced disease and violence. Smallpox spread through south-eastern and south-western Australia in advance of the wave of British settlement and claimed up to 90 per cent of people in some societies. Its origins lay, most likely, in the British settlement in Sydney. It arrived in Tasmania only after British settlers had seen to the destruction of Aboriginal society overwhelmingly through violence.[38] As a result of Lyndall Ryan's meticulous research, sparked by Australia's own 'history wars' of the 1990s and 2000s, we know that British settlers displaced Aboriginal Australians from their land with hundreds of separate, small-scale massacres.[39] These killings and displacements exacerbated disease, since groups who had lost valuable hunters and food sources developed nutritional deficits and reduced immunity.

Despite a governor who sought to avoid it, Tasmania was the clearest-cut case of genocide inflicted by British colonialism. But massacres continued to be carried out in Queensland well into the twentieth century, with Aboriginal police brought in from elsewhere to 'clear' land on behalf of settlers.[40] Very few cases of murders committed by settlers against Aboriginal people reached the courts, and in all but one case, those that did resulted in settler juries and magistrates acquitting the suspects. By contrast, 'several thousands of Aboriginal people were killed outright in defence of their land'.[41]

Once British settlers were in occupation of Indigenous lands, their societies and economies boomed (although with many vicissitudes) under representative governments elected by settler men.[42] Their policies towards Indigenous people, most of whom were excluded from the vote by property and other qualifications, or simply by the refusal of local electoral officials to admit them, settled upon the goal of assimilation. In Australia, Protectors of Aborigines had first been appointed by the British government, at a time when the Colonial Office was especially influenced by antislavery reformers, to protect Aboriginal people and reserve small parcels of land.[43] By the 1880s, their priority was to take Aboriginal children away from their families. These children were placed in White-run residential schools or foster homes, not on the grounds of any parental abuse or neglect but because they were Aboriginal. The outcomes for them varied, with some of the 'Stolen Generation' declaring that it improved their life chances and prospects in what had become settler nations.[44] Many Australian Aboriginal families, however, are still paying the price of these 'Stolen Generations', with disproportionately high rates of alcoholism and child neglect and abuse.[45]

Similar to Australia's anti-Indigenous policies, Canada used the residential school system as 'a key plank' of its 'Indian policy'.[46] Between 1883 and 1996, Canada's federal government and various Christian churches created a school system that separated more than 150,000 Indigenous children from their families. Some went with their parents' consent, but as in Australia, many others were removed by force. The system was described as a 'national crime' by a government official of the time. It is now known that more than 4,000 children died in the schools, and many more have spoken of widespread abuse. In 2008, the federal government officially apologised to survivors and agreed that the residential school system constitutes a form of cultural genocide. Despite some culture war-driven denial, 'most Canadians now know the truth about the damaging history of residential schooling for Indigenous Peoples and generally support the strengthening of Indigenous–settler relations, a process known as reconciliation'.[47]

Whether such reconciliation should be an objective of contemporary governments in the former settler colonies is of course a political decision, but we suggest it is one that should be made in the light of as complete a knowledge as possible of Indigenous peoples' experiences of British colonialism, rather than attempts to deny or diminish them.

Economic exploitation

The third part of the definition of colonialism is exploiting another country economically. This took various forms in the

INTRODUCTION

British Empire. Perhaps the most notorious was the capture and trafficking of around 3.1 million people on British ships, out of a total of 12.5 million, to be used as enslaved labour in the commercial plantations of the Americas.[48] The sugar, tobacco, cotton and other commodities this chattel workforce produced was part of a process that transformed three continents and laid the foundations for today's global economy.

Between the sixteenth and the mid-nineteenth centuries, much of Africa was destabilised as African polities either participated in the slave trade by selling captives to European slave traders or succumbed to raids themselves; the ecology and demography of the Americas was fundamentally altered as commercial plantations replaced indigenous plant species, and Indigenous peoples were displaced by enslaved Africans, while Europe embarked on its Great Leap Forward with the assistance of the capital acquired through the use of enslaved labour in the Atlantic plantation economy.[49]

'What was new about Atlantic slavery was the way that enslaved people began to function as a capital asset that could be used to finance investments in other sectors of the economy *and* could themselves be investments, financed through debt.'[50] By the late eighteenth century, the trans-Atlantic, slave-based plantation economy was supplying around 10 per cent of Britain's national income, much of it invested in the regions undergoing rapid industrialisation. Along with the consumer demand for the products of the plantations, and the technological and administrative know-how that was generated through slave trading and plantation management, the Atlantic slave-based economy helped fuel the transformation in British fortunes and power known as the Industrial Revolution, although it is impossible to quantify exactly how much relative to other factors.[51]

Although they were never embraced as equals and many of their arguments were overlooked, the testimony of Ignatius

THE TRUTH ABOUT EMPIRE

Sancho and the 'Sons of Africa' Ottobah Cugoano and Olaudah Equiano vitally assisted the efforts of British reformers including Thomas Clarkson and William Wilberforce to shift public opinion against the slave trade, securing its abolition in 1807.[52] The British government in turn was assisted in implementing the policy by African polities that had already turned against it. Critics of current scholarship complain that British abolition attracts little attention compared to slavery itself, yet it is proving as fascinating to the current generation of historians as it ever was.[53] Between 1808 and 1860, over 1,500 British sailors died in the Royal Navy's effort to capture 1,600 slave ships and free 150,000 captives from the Middle Passage. Research has shown that these 'liberated Africans' rarely achieved freedom or were able to return home. Most were either impressed into the military in the Caribbean or taken to ports including Freetown, Cape Town and St Helena, to be assigned as unpaid labour to colonists (including free Black colonists in Sierra Leone) for ten to fifteen years. Historians tend to refer to them now as 'recaptive' rather than 'liberated'.[54]

While the trans-Atlantic trafficking of captives was outlawed in 1807, the ownership of already-enslaved people continued within the British Empire until outlawed in 1833. Emancipation, enacted the following year, was not unprecedented. British abolitionists prepared legislation based on discussion of the gradual emancipation laws that had been passed by the northern states of the USA and in the Bolivarian republics and Mexico, since 1780.[55]

At the time a reformed Parliament carried the vote for emancipation, over 40,000 Britons distributed across virtually every British city and town—and including a surprising number of clergymen and widows—owned around 800,000 enslaved people in the Caribbean and other colonies. It was these owners, rather than their captives, who were paid compensation upon abolition.

INTRODUCTION

The value of the people they owned was calculated depending on the market rate in each colony, and a sum of £20 million in total, equivalent to 40 per cent of national governmental revenue, was handed to them. The government borrowed the funds in such a complex way that the last vestiges of the debt, along with a host of other historic debts, were paid off only in 2015.[56]

While the slave trade and slave ownership are the best-known, and probably most controversial, examples of economic exploitation across the British Empire, there was also the exploits of the East India Company. Once it had ceased to be a monopolistic trading entity after its Charter renewal in 1813, its business model consisted in large part of extracting rent from Indians to send to British shareholders as dividends and enforcing the production of opium in India. This was smuggled into China by licensed traders who then bought tea for the European market.[57]

These forms of colonial economic exploitation forged global connections. The tea brought from China with narcotics from India was consumed in Britain sweetened with the sugar grown by enslaved captives in the Caribbean. Around a third of the cloth brought by the East India Company to Britain was re-exported immediately to swap for these captives along the West African shoreline.[58]

When Britain's enslaved captives in the Caribbean were emancipated, the shortage of labour was resolved by resorting to India again for the recruitment of over a million British Indian subjects under indentured labour contracts.[59] As Philip Harling puts it, in the effort 'to advance a global system of commodity exchange from which metropolitan Britain would chiefly benefit', the 'minimal state committed itself to remarkably ambitious social-engineering projects that sought to mobilise and direct' Black and Brown people's 'labour to where it was (supposedly) most needed'.[60]

Well after the abolition of slavery, British colonists continued to see African people as units of labour. Part of the job of colonial governments was to place this labour at Britons' disposal. Whether it be for domestic service, deep within South Africa's gold and diamond mines, or as levies exacted for colonial building schemes, they developed policies to police African mobility and education to ensure a continued supply.[61] As Under-Secretary of State for the Colonies in 1906, Winston Churchill explained to Parliament that 'in West African colonies and Protectorates, in which there is legal power to demand labour on roads and waterways, the Governor or High Commissioner alone can make an order that such work shall be done'.[62] A colonial officer in the British Protectorate of Nyasaland wrote to his mother in 1929:

> One chief has to bring me 200 men to work for nothing and he brings me some every day, but he has to bring me a lot more yet. The hatred on his face when I tell him he has to bring more still or I will make war on him is intense, but he's got to do it, or I'll burn all his villages and crops down.[63]

While grand totals of the 'drain' of wealth from India to Britain, such as the $45 trillion figure used by politician Shashi Tharoor, rely upon estimates and assumptions, the principles of Britain's economic exploitation of the subcontinent were noted by both Indian and British contemporaries. The East India Company charged Indians rent and used it to buy their produce. Indian farmers and manufacturers effectively paid the company to take what they produced. The company then sold the produce overseas, retaining the profit for its British shareholders. 'Home Charges' were also taken out of the taxes paid by Indians and sent back to Britain, over 70 per cent of them used to subsidise Britain's overseas military campaigns.[64] Yet those determined, for whatever reason, to defend Britain's imperial record seek to deny there was any 'drain' at all, or indeed claim that 'improving' India came at an overall cost to Britain. Certainly, Indian elites came to rely upon British innovations for their own enrichment. One

INTRODUCTION

of the few academic defenders of Britain's economic record in India, Tirthankar Roy, argues that 'The Company's legacy was greater inequality between capitalists and skilled workers on the one side and unskilled or manual workers on the other. Merchants ... gained; the south Indian farm servant did not gain much ... The colonial state had neither the will nor the money to make a significant difference to peasants and labourers.' Most historians of colonial India go further, however, to argue that British rule generally made the conditions of poorer Indians worse. The extent to which British policies caused the repeated and devastating famines of the nineteenth century is contested, but scholars tend to agree that they rendered millions more people vulnerable when local food shortages struck.[65]

Large-scale schemes to improve 'normal' Indian subjects' welfare generally came very late in the period of colonial rule and as concessions to nationalist criticism. For most of the colonial period, the British government of India lacked the money, even if it often had the intention, to improve the conditions of the masses. This was in part because the British Treasury itself was still subsidised by funds extracted from India. In 1884, Richard Temple presented the 'General Statistics of the British Empire' to the Royal Statistical Society, noting that of the £203 million at the disposal of the British state for general government within the United Kingdom, £89 million came from the UK itself (including Ireland), £74 million from India and £40 million from territories and colonies in the rest of empire.[66]

Economic exploitation was a key reason for colonialism, although it was never the only one. Narrowly materialist Marxist interpretations are as flawed as any other 'model' seeking to isolate one key driving force. When the commercial interests of some Britons clashed with the agendas of others, such as those of the humanitarian and missionary lobby to 'civilise', those of the military to avoid overstretch or those of strategists to maintain a balance of power with other empires, it was up to colonial governments to tease out the contradictions. They would seek compromise between different agendas or overrule some Britons in favour of others.[67] But whenever and wherever governmental imperatives facilitated it, Britons proved just as capable, if not more so, of enriching themselves with the land, resources and people of their colonies as the representatives of any other empire have done through recorded history.

Colonialism and racism

As they established political control, occupation and exploitation of most other parts of the world, the modern European empires fostered a phenomenon that was quite novel in the broader history of empires: an entrenched association between status and racial difference. The association first developed with the trans-Atlantic slave trade, since it was the first in which only Black people were enslaved.[68] While, in the seventeenth century, European travel literature had tended to describe non-European peoples as 'nations', and artists had represented them as occupying a variety of statuses, as the slave trade became the dominant form of interaction between Europe and Africa, so representations changed. Non-Europeans became organised into 'tribes', while '"nation" came to signify the distinctive social and political systems of European countries', and 'race' came increasingly to be associated with physiognomy. By 1753, the philosopher David Hume suspected 'the negroes, and in general all the other species of men (for there are four or five different kinds) to be naturally inferior to the whites. There never was a civilized nation of any other complexion than white, nor even any individual eminent either in action or speculation.'[69]

In every European colony, settlers and their governments maintained racial hierarchies, although they were never impermeable and were not necessarily legislated. The abolition of slavery did nothing to change the dominance of racial thinking. As

INTRODUCTION

Nancy Stepan put it, 'just as the battle against slavery was being won by abolitionists, the war against racism in European thought was being lost'.[70] Indeed, 'abolition redeemed racism from the odour of slavery'.[71]

Part of the reason for this apparent contradiction was many Britons' almost immediate disillusionment with the results of emancipation. Persuaded by prominent commentators like Thomas Carlyle and Charles Dickens, who mocked the 'telescopic philanthropy' that had led sentimental Britons to identify more with the fate of 'savages' overseas than the domestic poor, many Britons came to feel by the 1850s that emancipation had failed to 'improve' African people.[72] In British public discourse, slavery was still morally wrong, the Britons of the 1830s were celebrated for abolition and Britain prided itself as the leading antislavery nation. But, perhaps, many Britons reasoned, their confidence that Africans were the potential equals of White Europeans was misplaced?

African American antislavery campaigner Frederick Douglass explained the disillusionment in 1857:

> All our tests of the grand measure [the British abolition of slavery] have been such as we might look for from slave-holders themselves. They all proceed from the slave-holders' side, and never from the side of the emancipated slaves. The effect of freedom upon the emancipated people of the West Indies passes for nothing. It is nothing that the plundered slave is now a freeman; it is nothing with our sagacious, economical philosophers, that the family now takes the place of concubinage; it is nothing that marriage is now respected where before it was a mockery ... it is nothing that the whipping post has given way to the schoolhouse; it is nothing that the church stands now where the slave prison stood before; all these are nothing.[73]

The measure of emancipation's success, or rather lack of it, was instead plummeting sugar production, as formerly enslaved people left the plantations to reconstitute families broken up by the sale of husbands, wives and children. Men like Carlyle represented the outcome as the inevitable result of innate African laziness rather than the strength of family bonds with which most Britons could potentially have identified.[74]

By the late nineteenth century, most Britons felt that other races were potentially improvable, but over generations. The failure of idealistic humanitarians like Thomas Fowell Buxton to 'redeem' Africans through free trade with the Niger Expedition of 1841 was explained as the result of Africans' deficiencies rather than those of the utopian planners. The prevailing notion among Britons was that racial improvements would take place only with a glacial gradualism.[75] The even more pessimistic ideas of racial scientists like Robert Knox, that 'inferior' races were biologically incapable of 'improvement', were the outcome of their search for scientific 'proof' to rationalise existing racial hierarchies. Although such racial science was never mainstream, ideas of biologically inherited traits continued to shape colonial rule.[76] In some cases, they built upon social hierarchies that British rulers inherited after conquest. An example is the codification of entire Indian 'tribes' and castes as inherently criminal under the Criminal Tribes Act of 1871. It was not the British who first saw these groups as hereditarily inclined to criminality, but it was British administrators who classified everyone born into them as inherently a criminal, restricting and policing their movements accordingly.[77]

Once the theory of social Darwinian evolution came to be broadly accepted, popular British understandings were that White people had evolved further than non-White people, with Africans and Indigenous people closest to their primate ancestors.[78] In most Britons' view, it would take more than just educating Africans alongside White children to render them equals. Indians were generally positioned above Africans in a hierarchy of civilisation, with some Britons believing their culture had degenerated from a higher plane in the past, rather than having never attained anything beyond primitivism.[79]

INTRODUCTION

Such a hierarchical view of race was compatible with the notion that the empire's job was to civilise people of colour, assisting them to catch up with the British or European race over an indefinable, evolutionary, timescale. As Kipling put it when exhorting the United States to colonise the Philippines: 'Take up the White Man's burden—And reap his old reward—The blame of those ye better—The hate of those ye guard.'[80] In the meantime, the 'primitiveness' and exoticism of certain colonised people rationalised their exhibition in the human zoos which toured Europe until the 1950s.[81] It is difficult to conceive of how European rulers could have blithely assumed the right to carve up Africa among themselves during the Scramble for Africa of the 1880s to 1900s without an overriding sense of *racial* entitlement.[82]

By around 1900, for all the accommodations with Indian princes and merchants, for all the recognition accorded to African chiefs under indirect rule, and for all the reliance upon locally recruited or imported Indian troops and police, White men were in charge in every British colony. Those referred to as 'natives' were expected to show deference to any White person they might encounter. Periodically, moral panics would break out over rumours of Black and Brown men threatening White women's 'purity'.[83] Even the poorest White colonial families generally had Black and Brown servants to do the domestic work. When Black or Brown servants sought prosecutions for masters and mistresses who abused them, their chances of success were tiny in the face of White juries and judges, no matter how 'colour blind' the law was in principle.[84] 'Ordinary' Black people could find themselves physically abused on the streets by even the lowest status White person, without any recourse to justice.[85] Across the British Empire, racial discrimination was the everyday norm, with the degree of insult sometimes finely graded according to ethnicity or skin shade.[86] Access to jobs, the law, health care, education, democracy, justice and even the railways was generally conditioned by race as well as wealth.[87]

Most British authorities used property qualifications (to vote), or territorial distinctions in rights and privileges, or simply trusted to informal distinctions of wealth to create a de facto regime of White supremacy, without specifically mentioning race de jure. For example, A. M. Rendel, consulting engineer of the East Indian Railway Company, submitted to its Board of Directors in 1868 that 'Third class passengers, who are chiefly natives, should not be run in the same trains with the First and Second class, who are chiefly Europeans; and the trains for the former should make longer stoppages at the stations and not run so fast', since 'natives' would not mind slower journeys.[88] Similar assumptions that class segregation would suffice to ensure racial segregation existed on Southern Africa's railways, although catering facilities were explicitly segregated by race. As Gordon Pirie pointed out,

> discussion of and preparation for ... enforced physical separation of black and white passengers in compartments and carriages on the railways occupied considerable time, engaged the attention of senior politicians and government officials and, on a daily basis, aroused the emotions of many ordinary South Africans, both white and black.[89]

Despite well-crafted informal means of ensuring segregation, British imperial officials known as Milner's Kindergarten also helped develop the most formal, extreme and sophisticated form of racist governance in the modern world, apartheid. They reconstructed the Southern African region after the South African War according to coherent precepts of racial segregation, consolidating pass laws, 'native' reservations, segregated cities and job reservation to protect White colonists' racial privilege.[90] After 1948, an Afrikaner nationalist government retained and entrenched these features of White supremacy while attuning them more specifically to the needs of White Afrikaans-speakers.[91] The pre-apartheid practices of racial segregation

INTRODUCTION

installed by British administrators were mirrored to a greater or lesser extent in the colonies of Rhodesia and Kenya.[92]

The benefits of colonialism

Despite its fractured and inconsistent nature, the British Empire is often seen as having been uniquely liberal, and the relationship between liberalism and colonialism has been a major preoccupation of its historians.[93] Never a coherent programme of governance, liberalism emerged in modern Europe and its offshoots during the late eighteenth century as an expression of the rights of individuals against arbitrary, absolutist governance, but it has always been so contested as an analytical term that it obscures or conflates a range of distinct elements. While it clearly indicates freedom, the questions of freedom of what and for whom, to do what, are crucial and can only be addressed contextually. What is certain is that the key characteristics often ascribed to liberalism developed through colonial relations operated highly unevenly, with race a key determinant of the freedoms allowed.

The prosperity that Britons involved in industry and commerce enjoyed as a result of privileged access to colonial resources, labour and markets was as much a cause of Britain's 'liberal' political dispensation as the Reform Act of 1832 or the agitation against the Corn Laws. It provided a major claim for the greater representation of commercial interests alongside the established aristocratic and mercantilist elites in Parliament, and for the cause of free trade, which liberals invoked to justify the Opium Wars. By the mid-nineteenth century, many British liberals believed in free trade as the appropriate response to colonial famines, first in India, and then in Ireland and the Cape Colony, undoubtedly exacerbating their disastrous effects. The 1867 Reform Act was Disraeli's tactical concession to a more liberal form of governance, extending the franchise again within Britain at the very moment that the Morant Bay rebellion led the White planters of Jamaica to abandon self-governance for fear of too many freed, propertied, Black people voting under a non-racial franchise.[94] As this coincidence suggests, the 'liberalism' that reformers were fighting for in Britain was not the racially qualified 'liberalism' of its colonies.

By the 1880s, the officials governing the empire were agreed that Britain's was the best of all possible political dispensations and that, in an ideal world, its benefits should be spread to colonial subjects regardless of race. However, they tended to share the view that what was appropriate for Britons at home and in the settler colonies was not suitable for other races.[95] Colonial subjects (other than White British emigrants and their descendants) needed to be 'civilised' before they could exercise the responsibilities that came along with the rights of liberalism. At present, they were rather like children, whose demands for equal rights with adults would be accommodated only for the sake of expediency. The Secretary of State for India, Lord Salisbury, conceded that '[i]f England was to remain supreme ... she must tolerate the political role of Indian princes and of participation by Indians in the administration'. He added later, however, 'that if the number of well-educated Indians ... should increase, the government would face the indecent and embarrassing necessity of closing that avenue to them'.[96] The Colonial Secretary, Henry, 3rd Earl Grey, put it more bluntly—'the principal bar' to self-government in most colonies was 'their being inhabited chiefly by a population of which a large proportion is not of European race'.[97]

Many highly educated Indians themselves were persuaded of the advantages of Britain's domestic political dispensation. Inspired by the doctrines of Bentham, Mill and Macaulay, men like Raja Rammohan Roy and Syed Ahmad Khan, who sought to explain to the British why the Indian Uprising had taken place

INTRODUCTION

in 1857, asked to become active participants in the governance of their own country, not instead of, but alongside Britons. Nonetheless, White British men retained an almost exclusive right to govern. Only a decade or so before independence did elected Indians earn the right to govern the provinces and, even then, subject to the British Viceroy's veto. In the meantime, Viceroys might be fundamentalist adherents of some aspects of 'liberalism', such as free trade as a panacea for famine, but not so enthusiastic about others, such as a free press or free speech.[98]

Although selective, British administrators' more liberal principles often benefitted certain colonial subjects. From 1879, Indians sentenced to execution in Mauritius would not, at least, be publicly beheaded, for example. Relatively small numbers of Indigenous men could exercise the vote in the self-governing colonies provided they passed certain hurdles that included dissociating from their First Nations communities in Canada, while enslaved people benefitted from the crusades of David Livingstone and Frere against Arab slave trading in Central and East Africa. Wealthier Indian businesspeople could use the railways that British investors had funded with guarantees of underwriting from Indian rent to move freight, and in later famines they could be used to deliver relief. Hundreds of thousands more gained an education in British-derived institutions and employment in the Indian government's bureaucracy, despite Salisbury's threatened prohibition. Many of their descendants are staunch defenders of the Raj's reputation.

Reconciling liberal aspiration with the reality of colonial White supremacy, however, was a thorny issue for those attempting to oversee the empire from London. Even a revitalised late nineteenth- and early twentieth-century cadre of eager, liberal, often Eton-educated men, some of whom had the best intentions to render the British Empire a force for good, found it impossible to square the rhetoric of liberalism with the reality of colonial rule, as colonial legislatures insisted on racial discrimination by one means or another. When the imperial government tried to prevent the settler Dominions from policing migration from Asia with explicitly racist legislation, for example, settler parliaments simply got around the prohibition by using indirect measures such as language tests.[99]

Wherever the basic premise of British control was secure, and whenever British public opinion was mobilised against governmental hypocrisy, 'liberalism' could gain a purchase in empire. However, liberal rhetoric would never override basic economic or geopolitical self-interest. While Britain, as an advanced industrial power with emerging traditions of effective and liberal governance, had much to offer its colonies, the intrinsic nature of colonialism mitigated against all but a grudging sharing of these benefits. Indeed, the rule, occupation and exploitation of its colonies was a key reason that Britain was becoming the prosperous, efficient, internally tolerant and liberal society that it was. Sharing the rights that Britons were coming to expect, especially those of democratic governance, with subjects overseas would mean the loss of that colonial advantage, and it would not be contemplated until there was no other choice.

If the British Empire helped spread the often rather vague *idea* of liberalism—ultimately to its own cost as nationalist leaders pointed out its hypocrisy—but was only selectively liberal in practice, in what other ways did it bring benefits to its subjects? Even if colonial historians, as we will see in this volume, have been somewhat equivocal about the most loudly proclaimed beneficiaries of British colonialism, including captives liberated from slave ships, Indian widows saved from immolation (see Andrea Major in this volume) and peasants brought into agricultural modernity, they do tend to agree on the demonstrable benefits that British colonial regimes brought to certain groups. Most of these were British. They include the emigrants who forged the

INTRODUCTION

prosperous new nations of Canada, Australia and New Zealand. Their descendants share some of the world's highest standards of living, effective state apparatuses and stable democracies. The owners of enslaved people, some of whose descendants are now intent on reparations, were not the only beneficiaries of their trafficking.[100] Most Britons, who have never seen a colony in their lives, have benefitted from the infrastructures, physical and financial, that were funded in part through colonial activities, although the 'trickle down' of resources from those actively involved in colonial wealth extraction to working-class Britons was slow, uneven and indirect.[101] Colonialism's benefits at home were filtered powerfully by class.

Colonised people too could benefit from the institutions and infrastructures that Britons developed to facilitate their rule, and many became as heavily invested in empire as most Britons were, some much more so. As we have seen, British governance facilitated long-term prosperity for Indian merchants, investors and middle classes, while hundreds of thousands of colonised people sought alliances and worked on behalf of colonial authorities. The British colonies in East Africa were governed with the assistance of Indians who migrated there as soldiers, policemen, civil servants, labourers and traders, forming a middle-strata between colonised Africans and their British rulers. With much to lose if their status was reduced to that of Africans, virulent anti-African racism could be the result.[102]

Millions of colonial subjects served in the British military's auxiliary as well as regular units, and their local deployment was critical in the success of most colonial campaigns.[103] The controversies over the differences between White soldiers' commemoration and those of soldiers of colour from around the empire after the World Wars point to the investments of many colonised subjects in imperial defence, whether their motives were secure employment and remittances, personal status and pride in a martial identity, comradeship, the avoidance of other aspects of their colonised condition such as slavery (in the case of the British West India Regiments) and famine, or loyalty to empire. From the letters sent home by wounded Indian soldiers convalescing in Brighton Pavilion during the First World War, we can discern all of these motivations, as well as British censors' anxiety that only positive associations with the British metropolis be transmitted back to India.[104]

Sometimes the positive colonial legacies credited to Britons are rather more complex than we might imagine given these widespread investments in imperial power. Public health initiatives against smallpox and malaria, for instance, were begun in India during British rule but often pushed by Indian government employees in the face of resistance from British officials. They took off on a large scale only once India had become independent. In most countries, drastic improvements in public health occurred only when post-independent governments focused scarce resources more on the welfare of the masses than the imperatives of colonial rulers.[105]

One figure that has cropped up more than once in recent attempts to highlight that Black people were beneficiaries of empire too is the Nigerian novelist Chinua Achebe, best known for his trenchant critique of British colonialism's impact on African societies in the novel *Things Fall Apart*.[106] Bruce Gilley, the Canadian political scientist who had advocated a resumption of colonialism in the withdrawn *Third World Quarterly* article, first suggested that Achebe later came to endorse colonialism's 'positive' legacies, and his assessment is echoed by Nigel Biggar.[107] Gilley's argument focuses on Achebe's last book, *There Was a Country*, in which he reflected mournfully upon the Biafran War that tore Nigeria apart seven years after its independence. Gilley emphasises Achebe's reflections that at least the British brought 'the experience of governing and doing it competently'. They instituted educational institutions that gave Achebe his ability to write and an efficient postal system, which enabled him to send off his manuscript. Gilley's conclusion is that

> Achebe made a clear statement about the positive legacies of colonialism, praising the British project of state formation and nation building ... Achebe was never the simple anti-colonial figure that most assumed, and ... his seeming reversal could be read as the culmination of a lifetime's meditation on African history and politics.[108]

However, it is the qualifications to Gilley's argument that do most to highlight the complex nature of colonial legacies. Far from enacting a 'seeming reversal' of his prior anti-colonial position, Achebe was insistent in *There Was a Country* that 'I am not justifying colonialism.'[109] In fact, he wrote, '[w]e were considerably damaged by colonial rule ... Colonial rule means that power, initiative is taken away from you by somebody else who makes your decisions.'[110] At the same time, Achebe bemoaned the decisions of Nigeria's postcolonial leaders, which led to the Biafran War. Gilley's pro-colonial inference is that they failed because they abandoned the stable and efficient governance that Britain had provided. But Achebe's criticism of them is quite different, and very far from an endorsement of prior British rule. Achebe was well aware that it was British administrative convenience that had created the conditions for the Biafran War by bringing disparate northern and southern polities together within the new nation state of Nigeria.[111] He quoted the British Commonwealth Office attitude once war had begun: 'The sole immediate British interest is to bring the [Nigerian] economy back to a condition in which our substantial trade and investment can be further developed.'[112] Both Gilley and Biggar encourage us to indulge in a rather selective reading of Achebe as an advocate of 'positive' colonial legacies. More realistically, he was a critic of self-interested alien rule, who recognised that certain of its characteristics, such as an efficient postal system, could serve to benefit local people. It was up to Nigeria's leaders to make of independence what they could:

45

THE TRUTH ABOUT EMPIRE

> [W]e could no longer pass off this present problem simply as to our complicated past ... for the second time in our short history we had to face the disturbing fact that Nigeria needed to liberate itself anew, this time not from a foreign power but from our own corrupt, inept brothers and sisters![113]

The moral reckonings of colonialism

Trying to weigh up the costs of empire to some and the benefits to others is a fruitless and rather naïve endeavour, indulged in mainly by those who want to defend the colonial past rather than understand it. Even in a single day, colonial rule could mean different things to a single individual. In mid-twentieth-century Nigeria, a hypothetical African woman intending to post a letter might benefit from the postal system that Achebe appreciated and yet suffer the humiliation of being forced to the back of the queue each time a White customer approached the counter. It is absurd to claim that we can come to anything other than a politically pre-determined conclusion when we presume to weigh up such experiences for millions of colonial subjects over 300 years, especially given that most of these mundane experiences were never recorded or preserved.

However, if professional historians of colonialism tend to avoid moralising about its benefits and costs, that does not mean that they avoid questions of morality. Rather than casting their own judgements, they analyse the moral sentiments expressed by contemporaries in order better to understand the ways they shaped the past. Historians have plenty to grapple with when it comes to the ethical agonies that empire presented, both to those who facilitated, resisted or simply lived through British colonial control, and to Britons themselves.

PART TWO

THE REALITIES OF COLONIALISM AROUND THE WORLD

1

WHAT ABOUT SLAVERY?

Bronwen Everill[1]

Since the beginning of the nineteenth century, British abolitionists have been using the existence of slavery somewhere else as a forceful tool for exerting moral imperialism. The argument is approximately, "yes, everyone had slavery in the past, because it was morally acceptable; then the British decided that slavery was bad and, having worked this out, had a moral responsibility to abolish slavery throughout the rest of the world".

Did everyone have slavery, as this argument asserts? No. *Wealthy* people in a lot of societies around the world in different times held people in bondage. What was new about Atlantic slavery was the way that enslaved people began to function as a capital asset that could be used to finance investments in other sectors of the economy *and* could themselves be investments, financed through debt. An enslaved person could be purchased by a slaveowner in the West Indies using credit on a future crop.[2]

THE TRUTH ABOUT EMPIRE

They could then finance the construction of a new wing on their country house in Britain, or purchase a share in another enterprise by offering their enslaved people as part of their collateral.[3] In other words, where enslavement had historically been about labor, in the Atlantic system it became a mortgage, a credit card, and a passive income stream. Slave traders—in Europe, in Africa, and in the Americas—benefited from the ways that the slave trade commodified people, and although the scale of this trade was much larger than anything that had come before, the trade itself was not the innovation: it was the way that the trade facilitated the use of people as not *just* laborers whose work produced wealth, not *just* commodities for sale, but *also* as assets that could be turned into financial instruments. These developments in finance were at the heart of how Atlantic slavery helped to create new forms of wealth for investors in enslavement.[4]

So Atlantic slavery, in which the British Empire participated, was different from other forms of slavery in both its scale and its contributions to financial development. Was abolitionism also unique to Britain? No. In many African societies, people resisted enslavement and pushed back against governments that enabled enslavement. For instance, in 1789, Thomas Clarkson, the British abolitionist, wrote about "the wise and virtuous" Abd al-Qadir Kane, leader of a revolution in Futa Toro on the Upper Senegal River. Despite "having been trained up in a land of slavery" and having to "sacrific[e] part of his own revenue," he had abolished the Atlantic slave trade in his country. Clarkson declared that, decades before the British abolition of the slave trade was passed by Parliament, Kane "has done more for the causes of humanity, justice, liberty, and religion" than "any of the sovereigns of Europe."[5]

Nor was Kane the first African leader to push back against the Atlantic trade. Lourenço da Silva Mendonça brought a case against the slave trade all the way to the Vatican in the seventeenth

WHAT ABOUT SLAVERY?

century.[6] Other African states fortified themselves or made themselves unattractive to slave traders.[7] One British slave trader complained in the 1770s that south of the River Congo, the people were "piratical" and "often cut off ship's boats and are therefore not much resorted to."[8]

In fact, it was only by allying themselves to people who already opposed the slave trade in West Africa that British abolitionists managed to accomplish anything in the way of enforcement. Did abolitionism facilitate the expansion of British imperialism and domination overseas? Unfortunately, yes. Not least in the actual first imperial settlement that Britain possessed in Africa—not the Cape Colony in 1814 as Nigel Biggar writes, but Sierra Leone in 1808.

In 1787, the first group of Black Britons arrived on the Sierra Leone peninsula as part of a project in self-government with the support of the London-based abolitionist leaders Granville Sharp and Olaudah Equiano. The first settlement faced hardships and lacked support among the Temne whose land they were renting.

In 1791, another group arrived in the colony and sought out a new treaty of settlement. This group chose to immigrate to Sierra Leone from Nova Scotia (Canada), where they had been settled by the British government as "Black Loyalists" after fleeing from slavery to the British line during the American Revolution (1776–83). A new organization, the Sierra Leone Company, took over the management of the colony from London. Their records show that by the early 1790s, the Temne and Susu saw the arrival of these colonists as an opportunity.

One British official commented of the Temne that "their mouths were full of proposals to trade with us and plant Cotton and Coffee."[9] And a neighboring Susu leader's deputy launched a verbal attack against the slave traders, telling them that

> [i]t is you slave traders who cause all our palavers. It is you who set the people in this country one against another. And what do you

bring us for this? We have Cloth of our own if you were gone tomorrow we should not be naked. If you were gone we should want but little guns and powder.[10]

There is a misconception that Britain was the first to abolish the slave trade. Sierra Leone shows that, in order to enforce that abolition, the British had to rely on the support of African states and polities that had already turned against the slave trade.[11] This support of the Susu and Temne around Sierra Leone for the colony, its trade, and its African diaspora population meant that the colony seemed like a natural fit for the British when they were looking for a way of enforcing their Slave Trade Act in 1807. The British based an antislave trade naval patrol in the colony, as well as a Vice-Admiralty Court for processing captured slave ships. The Sierra Leone Company, which had not found a way to be commercially profitable, was happy to hand over control to the British government.[12]

But it was also by framing their work as absolutely necessary to the rescue of African victims that Britain began to create a role for itself in the nineteenth-century world as a moral policeman.

While the Temne and Susu may have been pleased to have new trade partnerships based on non-slave trading commerce, the arrival of the British naval squadron tipped local power away from these groups and towards the British government at Freetown, which was responsible, first and foremost, to Parliament and British interest. Local leaders signed treaties agreeing not to trade in enslaved people but also guaranteeing trade with British merchants.

Pushing out from Sierra Leone, antislavery became British actors' rhetorical justification for dispossession and violent campaigns against other West African states—whether or not local populations knew they needed rescuing—from the bombardment of Lagos in 1851 to the sacking of Benin in 1897.[13] Some of these campaigns undoubtedly derived from genuine antislavery

WHAT ABOUT SLAVERY?

feeling. But Britain's sense of its place in the world in the nineteenth century arose from the idea that Britain, and Britain alone, had acted against slavery while others let it persist. And this blinded London. Despite evidence to the contrary, they believed that without them, no one else would have been able to abolish the slave trade. Yes, there was certainly violence that was unpopular at home and among antislavery activists as well, but at least sometimes the British state was using that force for good, right?

The better question is, what if they hadn't needed to use it at all?

Further reading

Diouf, Sylviane A., *Fighting the Slave Trade: West African Strategies*, Athens, OH: Ohio University Press, 2003.

Everill, Bronwen, *Not Made by Slaves: Ethical Capitalism in the Age of Abolition*, Cambridge, MA: Harvard University Press, 2020.

Nafafé, José Lingna, *Lourenço da Silva Mendonça and the Black Atlantic Abolitionist Movement in the Seventeenth Century*, Cambridge: Cambridge University Press, 2022.

Ware, Rudolph T., *The Walking Qur'an*, Chapel Hill, NC: University of North Carolina Press, 2014.

Williams, Eric, *Capitalism and Slavery*, London: Penguin, 2022.

2

TASMANIA AND THE QUESTION OF GENOCIDE IN THE BLACK WAR, THE HISTORY WARS AND THE CULTURE WAR

Lyndall Ryan

The Black War in Tasmania (1826–32) is one of the most controversial aspects of both Australia's and the British Empire's histories. It lay at the heart of Australia's 'history wars', which in many ways foreshadowed today's UK-centred culture war over the past. The 1988 bicentenary of the Botany Bay settlement, which initiated the British colonisation of the continent, proved a point of contention which generated similarly binary approaches. Colonial and Aboriginal scholars were derided as 'Black Armband' historians by those who wished only to celebrate the overwhelmingly White nation's progress, for pointing to the violence entailed in the colonisation of Tasmania, and in the British conquest of Australia more generally, and for empathising with Aboriginal activists' calls for the bicentenary to be an occasion for mourning rather than celebration.[1] The criticisms of Australia's historical scholars have been picked up and aired again, with broader targets across the Anglophone world, in the last few years. In this chapter, I indicate the current state of specialists' understanding of the Black War among the historians who have conducted primary research on it. I then examine the ways in which it has featured in right-wing revisionist narratives, first by Keith Windschuttle within Australia, and then by Nigel Biggar, writing of it as part of the broader canvas of the British Empire.

The Black War

The Black War in Tasmania officially began on 29 November 1826, when the governor of the island, George Arthur, published a government notice that enabled settlers, soldiers and police to kill with impunity Tasmanian Aboriginal people who attacked settlers, their property and their workers. The Aboriginal people of Tasmania were no longer considered as British subjects. Rather they were now designated as hostile 'subjects of an accredited state'.[2]

First settled by Britain in 1803 with about 500 British convicts and soldiers to forestall a possible French claim, Tasmania, then known as Van Diemen's Land, is an island similar in size to Sri Lanka and in 1803 supported an Aboriginal population of at least 8,000. In 1817, about 1,500 cashed up retired defence force officers from the Napoleonic Wars and their families began arriving in Tasmania to take up free grants of land on the Midlands Plain, which the British called the Settled Districts, comprising the 125-mile stretch of open land between the major towns of Hobart and Launceston, the Clyde River valley and a strip of the East Coast. Their purpose was to raise sheep for raw wool for export to the textile mills of northern England, and for labour

TASMANIA AND THE QUESTION OF GENOCIDE

they relied on British convicts transported to Tasmania. The new venture had an immediate impact on the Tasmanian Aboriginal people. By 1830, when the British population reached 23,500, and the sheep population about one million, the Aboriginal population had plummeted to about 100, with most of the rest killed in the Black War.[3]

Most settlers and their convict servants held the Tasmanian Aboriginal people in contempt. In response to the government notice of 29 November 1826, the Tasmanian newspaper *The Colonial Times* wrote: 'With the murder of a Colonist still fresh in their memory, the people will kill, destroy, and if possible, exterminate every black in the island, at least so many as they fall in with.'[4] It could be argued that Governor Arthur implemented extreme measures to force the Aboriginal people in the Settled Districts to surrender. Then, as he later said, possibly in defence of his extreme actions, he intended to negotiate with their chiefs and relocate them in a designated reserve in the island's north-east, where no settlers then resided.[5] However, this never happened, and he defended himself by pointing out that the Aboriginal people did not cultivate the land.[6]

Three Aboriginal nations, the Oyster Bay, the Big River and the North Midlands peoples and later the North nation, were the most impacted by the government notice. Their homelands, or 'country', included the Midland Plain, which supported a large kangaroo population. They crossed the plain each autumn and spring to feast on kangaroo and hold major ceremonies. When they encountered settlers and vast numbers of sheep, they were shocked when convict shepherds kidnapped Aboriginal women for sex. This is not surprising, for there were at least five British men for every British woman in the colony. Aboriginal men retaliated by killing the kidnapper, and by the end of 1826, they had killed at least thirty-five convict shepherds. When they killed the son of a leading settler, however, the governor was forced to take action. The government notice of November 1826 formalised the war.[7]

British soldiers were now despatched on regular patrols in the Settled Districts, along with police and armed convicts, to track down Aboriginal 'insurgents'. In 1827 and 1828, they carried out at least seventeen massacres of more than 400 Aboriginal people in reprisal for Aboriginal people killing more than sixty British men. However, the Aboriginal killing of a settler woman and her children in October 1828 led Governor Arthur to declare martial law across the Settled Districts on 1 November 1828. Soldiers, settlers and police as well as convict shepherds could now kill any Aboriginal person they encountered with impunity.[8] Over the next two years, they killed more than 350 Aboriginal people in reprisal for the Aboriginal people killing ninety British people including women and children. Still unable to control Aboriginal resistance, on 7 October 1830, Arthur established what is now known as the Black Line. He ordered the assembly of more than 2,000 colonists and soldiers and the formation of a military line across the northern part of the Settled Districts. Over the following three weeks, the Line moved in a south-easterly direction until it reached East Bay Neck at Tasman Peninsula in the expectation that Aboriginal people corralled on the other side of the Line would surrender.[9] Although only two Aboriginal boys were captured and two others killed, a further 100 were killed in mopping up operations over the following year.[10] In December 1831, when the remaining twenty-six Big River and Oyster Bay people were captured near Lake Echo, the Black War was formally concluded, and the survivors were deported to a detention camp on Flinders Island in Bass Strait.

When Charles Darwin visited Tasmania in February 1836, he observed that 'Van Diemen's Land enjoys the great advantage of being free from a native population.'[11] In fact, there is still a vibrant Aboriginal population in Tasmania called the Palawa,

TASMANIA AND THE QUESTION OF GENOCIDE

who are mainly descendants of White male sealers who cohabited with Aboriginal women, many of whom were abducted, on the Bass Strait Islands.

The Black War is the best-known settler war in the British Empire. It was widely reported in the contemporary British press, the subject of a British Parliamentary Paper in 1831 and a key issue in the House of Commons Report on British Settlements in 1837.[12] At the height of the war, the Secretary of State for the Colonies warned the governor of Tasmania that the outcome could lead to the extinction of the Tasmanian Aborigines and leave a 'hated stain' on Britain's reputation as a benign coloniser.[13] In 1870, the war was considered by historian James Bonwick as more dreadful in the number of massacres and overall brutality than the shocking violence of the Spanish in Latin America.[14] As Biggar notes, the Australian scholar Robert Hughes called the Black War 'the only true genocide in English colonial history'.[15]

The question of genocide

In 2002, the question of whether the war was an act of genocide became the central focus of the Australian history wars, or, more accurately, the Tasmanian history wars.

The leading combatant, the polemicist Windschuttle, is now editor of the conservative magazine *Quadrant*. In 2002, he self-published *The Fabrication of Aboriginal History: Volume One, Van Diemen's Land 1803–1847*, which, he contended, was a 'contra account' of the recent texts on the Black War by historians Henry Reynolds and me. His book, he said, would show how we had purportedly invented massacres of Aboriginal people in the Black War to argue that genocide had been committed.[16]

The key purpose of my book, first published in 1981, was to demonstrate that the Tasmanian Aboriginal people did not die out in 1876 nor in any other period of Tasmania's history, and that in each historical period from the Black War to the present, they sought justice for their dispossession.[17] In focusing on the Tasmanian Aboriginal people as the traditional owners of the land, I investigated their side of the Black War by following their acts of resistance to the settler invasion of their country that were recorded in the journals of the conciliator, G. A. Robinson, the colonial press and the seventeen volumes of incidents, known as 'The Depredations', located in the Tasmanian archives in Hobart.[18] I also recorded the violence of the settler response cited in Robinson's journals and described three gruesome incidents of settler massacres of Aboriginal people in northern Tasmania.[19]

In *Fate of a Free People*, Reynolds, the leading exponent of Aboriginal resistance, argued that in defence of their country, the Tasmanian Aboriginal people waged a devastating guerrilla war against the settlers and successfully resisted the might of the British Army, police and settlers, martial law and the Black Line. He claimed they would have won the war had they not been outnumbered by the settlers and their endless capacity to increase by immigration. When the Aboriginal people realised they could not hold out against them, they surrendered to the government 'conciliator', Robinson, who negotiated on their behalf a verbal treaty with the governor, Arthur. The terms included recognition that they were a free people who would voluntarily relocate to Flinders Island until it was safe to return to their country. When the colonial government failed to observe this part of the treaty, the Aboriginal leaders on Flinders Island sent a petition to Queen Victoria, requesting their return to their country. The petition was accepted by the Queen, and the community returned to mainland Tasmania in 1847. Reynolds reached four conclusions: that Governor Arthur recognised that settler colonialism is never a peaceful business; that a treaty should have been signed

TASMANIA AND THE QUESTION OF GENOCIDE

with the Tasmanian Aboriginal people at the outset of colonisation; that they should have been compensated for the loss of their country; and, finally, that as an autonomous people, the Tasmanian Aborigines always understood the injustice of their dispossession and continue their campaign for justice and compensation in the present.[20]

I would argue that, in his 'contra account', Windschuttle set up Reynolds and me as straw men to deny that genocide of the Tasmanian Aborigines ever took place, even though we were not concerned at that time with the application of the term, merely with recording what had actually happened. Indeed, Reynolds published a book on the subject in 2001.[21] Windschuttle drew on the long-outdated work of nineteenth-century scientists imbued with the doctrine of Social Darwinism, to claim there were only 2,000 Aboriginal people in Tasmania at the outset of British colonisation in 1803, rather than at least 4,000 estimated by the archaeologist Rhys Jones and then increased to 8,000 by Brian Plomley, the editor of Robinson's journals.[22] He then claimed that the Tasmanian Aboriginal people were an 'internally dysfunctional society' that survived for tens of thousands of years (at least 40,000 years) 'more from good fortune than good management', and that when the British arrived in 1803, 'this small, precarious society quickly collapsed under the dual weight of the susceptibilities of its members to disease and abuse and neglect of its women'.[23] As 'agents of their own demise', he said, they were politically incapable of conducting a guerrilla war with the settlers in defence of their homelands and were more like 'black bushrangers' who attacked settlers' huts for plunder. He then made the extraordinary claim that more than twice the number of settlers were killed in the war than Aboriginal people and disputed the massacres cited by Robinson and others reported in the colonial press. Indeed, he asserted there was only one genuine massacre in the entire war, and even then, he was the first to identify it.[24]

However, the real purpose of his book, he said, was to defend the honour of the British Empire and the settlers who came to Tasmania during the Black War. They were imbued with respect for the rule of law and the ideals of humanitarianism and so could not have acted in the violent and cruel way depicted by Reynolds and me. Further, as Australian historians, we were part of a "degeneration of standards within our universities" that began in the 1970s to attack the British Empire and the ideals that it stood for. In demonstrating that we had fabricated the worst excesses of the Black War, he was restoring the empire to its true position.[25]

Windschuttle's book found a ready audience with the Rupert Murdoch-owned Australian press and in particular their national masthead *The Australian*. Their right-wing columnists and commentators, known to Australian historians as the 'Pretorian guard', promoted the book by attacking Reynolds and me as 'fabricators of the past'. Among the raft of attacks, I was accused of inventing footnotes about massacres.[26]

In the United States, Roger Kimball, the editor of the conservative American magazine *The New Criterion*, hailed Windschuttle's book as a 'scholarly masterpiece ... destined to become an historical classic, changing forever the way we all look at the opening chapter of Australian history'.[27] In another review in *The New Criterion*, and republished in *The Australian*, conservative Australian historian Geoffrey Blainey congratulated Windschuttle for his detailed research in the Tasmanian archives.[28]

It was clear that *The Australian* expected Reynolds and me to engage with Windschuttle, and in August 2003, we contributed chapters to a major riposte, *Whitewash: On Keith Windschuttle's Fabrication of Aboriginal History*, edited by prominent Australian political scientist and former editor of *Quadrant*, Robert Manne. In his chapter, Reynolds argued that by claiming the Tasmanian Aborigines had no 'mental universe' nor word for 'property',

TASMANIA AND THE QUESTION OF GENOCIDE

Windschuttle's purpose was to claim that when the British arrived in 1803, Tasmania was 'terra nullius'.[29] Tasmanian historian James Boyce pointed out that, in relation to Windschuttle's claim of a low Aboriginal death toll, he relied on a source that was designed to estimate White casualties, not Black.[30]

In my chapter, 'Who Is the Fabricator?', I outlined the tactics Windschuttle deployed in relation to the primary sources to make accusations of fabrication. They included rejecting a military report on the grounds the soldiers could not have killed the Aboriginal people listed; relying on outdated research to claim a pre-invasion Aboriginal population that was too small to be sustained in a hunter-gatherer society; mis-reading and relying on sources that any scholar with a knowledge of the Tasmanian archives would have readily found to be incomplete; denying the existence of an entire Aboriginal nation so that he did not have to admit they were virtually dispossessed by settler massacres; and stubbornly refusing to accept evidence of killings of Aboriginal people from credible White informants.[31]

Tasmanian historian Boyce, in responding to Windschuttle's claim that the Tasmanian Aboriginal people were incapable of conducting a war against the settlers, noted that Windschuttle simply ignored the translations of the extensive journals of the French explorers, who thrice visited Tasmania immediately before the British invasion. They recorded a society that held an acute political understanding of their rights as a people and were certainly capable of defending their country. Put together with the contemporary accounts of the war found in the colonial press, the despatches of the governor, Arthur, the journals of the conciliator, Robinson, the account by the contemporary historian of the war, Henry Melville, along with settler testimonies, none was in any doubt that the Tasmanian Aboriginal people were fighting for their country. Boyce concluded his chapter by turning Windschuttle's attack on historians on himself: 'There is a world of difference between historians who go to the past to *investigate* the evidence about the subject and those who go to *vindicate* a stand they have already taken.'[32]

Rather than shutting down the investigation of settler massacres as Windschuttle and the Murdoch press had expected, the history wars encouraged Australian historians to explore new methods of approach to the subject, drawn from international scholarship in the aftermath of the massacre at Srebrenica in 1995.[33] It was clear that settler massacres of Tasmanian Aboriginal people were widespread during the Black War, that a greater number of Aboriginal people were killed overall than previously realised and that their population in 1803 was probably closer to the estimate of 8,000 made by Plomley.[34] Along with *Whitewash*, the publication of Boyce's *Van Diemen's Land*, Tom Lawson's *The Last Man: A British Genocide in Tasmania* and the online map of Aboriginal massacre sites in Tasmania which identified at least thirty massacre sites in the Black War with an estimated Aboriginal death total of more than 400, that is, about 40 per cent of the number of Tasmanian Aboriginal people estimated killed in the war overall, the new texts considerably enlarged our understanding of the extreme violence of the Black War and clarified the debate about whether it constituted genocide.[35]

Colonialism and the Tasmanian genocide

How, then, does Biggar's *Colonialism* apply a moral reckoning to Tasmania's Black War? It appears to take an even-handed approach to the subject, but with each issue discussed, it prefers Windschuttle's account. Apart from the texts by Lawson and myself, to which it makes only cursory reference, *Colonialism* returns to the Tasmanian history wars of more than twenty years ago and deploys Windschuttle's tactics of deflection and guilt by association as props to its 'moral reckoning'.

TASMANIA AND THE QUESTION OF GENOCIDE

Colonialism readily acknowledges that the fate of the Tasmanian Aboriginal people is 'highly contested territory, containing controversies over the number of aborigines [sic] who died, the reasons for their dying and whether their near extinction amounted to "genocide"'.[36] However, Biggar's efforts to seriously engage with the questions seem driven by a devotion to Windschuttle's account.

On the question of the Aboriginal population in 1803 and the number killed in the 'so-called "Black War" of 1825–32', Biggar considers Windschuttle's lower estimate of 2,000 Aboriginal people in Tasmania in 1803 and fewer than eighty Aboriginal deaths in the war as more reliable than my estimates on the grounds that Windschuttle 'has argued with considerable cogency that the scale of aboriginal deaths has been exaggerated by recent historians'.[37] Yet six pages later, he admits there could have been 6,000 Aboriginal people in 1803.[38] Biggar then attempts to find support for Windschuttle from other Australian historians such as Ann Curthoys, who according to Biggar says that Windschuttle's book is 'one of the key works on this aspect of Tasmanian history'.[39] Biggar's claim, however, is a clear misreading of Curthoys, who was referring to the combatants in the history wars rather than Windschuttle's status as a historian of Tasmania.

In further support of the lower number of Aboriginal casualties, Biggar cites Canadian political scientist and conservative activist Tom Flanagan, who 'contends that aboriginal oral history, uncorroborated by original documents, is "completely unreliable, just like the oral history of white people"'.[40] Windschuttle is the only historian to reject White people's testimonies of massacre in the war, so Biggar appears to take an even-handed approach to the issue:

> That does not mean, of course, that oral testimony of the killing of aboriginals by settlers is necessarily untrue, but it does mean both that we cannot be sure that it is true and that it is likely that some of it is not. And most of the allegations of the killings of aboriginals

are based on testimony, not documentation. On the other hand, given that the settlers had an interest in under-reporting how many aboriginals they had killed, it is also very likely that the number of documented deaths is too low.[41]

The initial attempt to deny accounts of massacres recorded by settlers seems ridiculous. The official sources only record Aboriginal deaths as acts of self-defence. Nor does Biggar's account acknowledge that during the long period of martial law, Aboriginal people were killed with impunity and their deaths not recorded. To overcome the silence in the official sources, historians have relied on Robinson's journals, settler diaries and colonial newspapers. *Colonialism*'s apparently even-handed approach ends up as a deflection from a genuine consideration of the Aboriginal death toll.

In further justification of low Aboriginal casualties, *Colonialism* turns to Blainey's claim that Windschuttle's research was carried out 'with impressive thoroughness' and that 'many of the errors, made by historians on crucial matters, beggared belief. Moreover, their exaggeration, gullibility, and what [Windschuttle's] book calls, "fabrication", went on and on.' Reinforcing the dominating theme of his book, Biggar also follows Blainey and Windschuttle in stating that the evidence for 'genocide' or deliberate 'extirpation' appears 'frail or false'.[42] Biggar continues: 'Although some of the settlers may have killed the Tasmanian Aboriginal people', 'probably in the mid-to-low hundreds', disease and inter-tribal war 'were to blame for many others'. Further, even before the arrival of the British, Blainey argues that, according to 'a strong oral tradition' from the Aboriginal people themselves, they had been struck by a 'catastrophic epidemic', which 'annihilated entire tribes'.[43] Apparently, it is acceptable for Blainey to rely on oral testimony, but not the historians under fire.

Blainey appears to argue that having experienced an epidemic before the British invasion, the Aboriginal survivors were vulnerable to 'inadvertently introduced disease' and thus destined to die out. This view is promoted by some historians in other parts of Australia as an explanation for the dramatic Aboriginal population decline in the aftermath of settler conquest.[44] In Tasmania, however, the colonial statistics reveal that until 1820, colonial deaths were from old age or misadventure rather than exotic disease, suggesting that the Tasmanian Aborigines enjoyed better health in the early decades of colonisation than their counterparts on the Australian mainland.[45] Indeed, Tasmanian Aboriginal people only appear to become susceptible to British diseases such as influenza and tuberculosis after 1828 and after they were captured and placed in detention. Neither Biggar nor Windschuttle acknowledge this important fact. It would certainly not suit their argument to do so.

Colonialism then addresses Windschuttle's claim that during the first twenty-five years of invasion, the Tasmanian Aboriginal people never made 'any political approaches to the British' and were only interested in 'the criminal theft of goods'.[46] On the other hand, neither Windschuttle nor Biggar question why the British did not approach the Tasmanian Aboriginal people for a treaty. Indeed, Reynolds points out that Governor Arthur lamented on several occasions that a treaty should have been signed with the Tasmanian Aboriginal people at the outset of the British invasion.[47]

Avoiding further discussion on this issue, Biggar endorses Windschuttle's account of an alleged attack on a settler in 1829 by the Port Davey Aboriginal people as clear evidence of his claim that settlers never occupied the Port Davey people's hunting grounds, and that the Aborigines attacked the settler because they were savages.[48] The account comes from the journals of Robinson, who at that stage knew little about the Aboriginal nations in Tasmania. Plomley's *Aboriginal–Settler Clash in Van Diemen's Land, 1803–1831*, a compilation of every known Aboriginal attack on settlers, and the key source for Windschuttle's claim that more settlers were killed in the war than Aboriginal people, reveals that the attack was not made by the Port Davey people but by the Big River people, whose homelands were long occupied by the settlers.[49]

Windschuttle failed to make the connection, using the incident as a segue to a discussion of tribal boundaries. Biggar follows suit. He says that Windschuttle considers the boundaries as 'very fluid and changed with the seasons', although the Tasmanian people did have an 'emotional affinity' to certain territories, 'and a notion that game and other fruits of the land belonged to them'.[50] The statement exposes a limited understanding of the subject, since the pioneering work on tribal boundaries by archaeologist Jones is dismissed on the grounds that he had deliberately inflated the Aboriginal population at the time of the British invasion in 1803.[51]

Colonialism's attempts to represent the Black Line can at best be described as limited too. The Black Line, surely, is the great moral reckoning of British colonial policy. In October 1830, more than 2,200 White men, including 500 soldiers, set out across the south-eastern part of the island on a carefully planned military operation lasting several weeks, with the sole purpose of hunting down fewer than 200 Tasmanian Aboriginal people. How, then, does Biggar's *Colonialism* consider this horrifying event?

Once again, it turns to Windschuttle for guidance. The Line, Windschuttle says, was not intended to exterminate the Aboriginal people but to herd them into a closed reserve 'well suited for the purpose of savage life'.[52] Reynolds however, considers the Line a manifestation of ethnic cleansing, similar to that carried out by the British in other parts of the empire.[53] No, says Biggar, Windschuttle considers that Governor Arthur could not think like that, because he was 'a convinced humanitarian'.[54] What then of the settlers? Biggar acknowledges that Reynolds and

TASMANIA AND THE QUESTION OF GENOCIDE

Plomley consider that the settlers were 'extirpationists almost to a man', and that Reynolds cites as evidence the statements that twelve settlers made to a government inquiry several months before the Line. Reynolds claims that eight of these were clearly in support of extermination.[55]

According to Biggar, Reynolds is misleading, for Windschuttle says that he only cited bits of the settlers' testimonies. It does not occur to Biggar that Windschuttle could also have been selective, even though he devotes almost an entire chapter of his book to the subject. Even so, Biggar accepts that 'a clear majority' of the respondents to the committee 'thought that the whites—especially remote stock-keepers and bushrangers—were to blame for causing aboriginal hostility'. Yet he slips and slides around the issue. 'Windschuttle', he says, 'does not claim that the exterminationist sentiment was entirely absent from the settlers, but rather that it was kept in check by the evangelical humanitarianism that was unusually influential among the founders of the colonies of New South Wales and Van Diemen's Land', as Tasmania was then known.[56]

The guiding principle of humanitarian thought in Tasmania during the Black War was that Aboriginal people should be removed from the settlers' and soldiers' guns and deported to an island in Bass Strait, where they would benefit from the twin gifts of Christianity and civilisation. This view was advocated by Robinson and Arthur and the Quaker missionaries James Backhouse and G. W. Walker. Boyce considers that deportation to Flinders Island was 'the easiest administrative and political path to follow' and is puzzled that all of the men mentioned above, as well as the settlers generally, fell for the 'psychological appeal' of a 'native free' Tasmania.[57] In the 1840s, leading humanitarians such as the newspaper editor John West firmly opposed the return of the Tasmanian Aboriginal people to their homeland after more than fifteen years in detention on Flinders

Island. West was fearful that even this small group of forty-seven elderly people would re-engage in the Black War.[58]

Neither Biggar's nor Windschuttle's book appears to understand the humanitarian impulse in Tasmania. Rather the term is used as a convenient cover to assert that the settlers could not have advocated the extermination of the Tasmanian Aboriginal people in the Black Line.[59] Biggar's disquisition on the topic on page 142 is another example of appearing to consider both sides of the question only to conclude that Windschuttle's view is 'probably correct'. 'The historic record shows that this prospect (i.e. extermination) divided the settlers deeply, was always rejected by government and was never acted upon.'[60] Yet the Black Line was not a failure, as Windschuttle claims. The Line determined the location of the remaining Aboriginal people in the Settled Districts, enabling police and soldiers in the immediate aftermath to track down and kill more than 100 of them. It also enabled Robinson to force the twenty-six Aboriginal people remaining in the war zone to surrender and face deportation to Flinders Island.[61]

The final question Biggar addresses is whether the Black War was an act of genocide by the colonial state. He is relieved to find that neither Reynolds nor Windschuttle claim that it was, enabling him to assert that '[t]he virtual, if not quite actual, annihilation of the Tasmanian aboriginals was far more tragedy than atrocity'.[62] Nevertheless, he cannot ignore the claim of genocide made by Lawson's *The Last Man*, which was published in 2014.

Biggar addresses the question by placing it within the context of nineteenth-century British colonisation and the ideology of human progress. So many colonists benefitted from the ideology, he asserts, and if the Aboriginal people in Tasmania were to be saved by preventing colonial expansion, then Britain would have been faced with a settler revolt, much like that in the

TASMANIA AND THE QUESTION OF GENOCIDE

American colonies, resulting in the loss of Tasmania: 'It would have been a highly hazardous undertaking and British officials can be forgiven, I think, for not contemplating it. And if the British had succeeded in vacating Tasmania, the vacuum would likely have been filled ... by the French or even the Americans.' He concludes, 'I do not think, therefore, that the British as a whole can be fairly blamed for what befell the Tasmanian aboriginals, although no doubt individual Britons committed grave crimes against them.'[63]

He then changes tack. 'However, even if the British were not culpable, they were responsible, in that their presence (largely) inadvertently caused the aboriginals' demise.'[64]

There was no inadvertent behaviour by the British. They killed Aboriginal people from the outset, as demonstrated by the massacre at Risdon Cove on 3 May 1804, which took place eight months after the first British settlement was established.[65] The digital map of massacre sites in Tasmania shows that settlers and soldiers took part in at least twenty-five massacres of Aboriginal people during the Black War with the loss of several hundred lives.[66] The perpetrators knew they would never be arrested, let alone charged and convicted of murder. It is hard to accept that the colonial government was unaware of these shocking events. The Aboriginal people were subjected to martial law for more than three years, at the end of which very few of them were still alive. Those who were suffered deportation to Flinders Island and were not expected to survive. None of these actions was inadvertent. They were deliberate. When Darwin declared that the island was at last 'native free', this was the outcome the settlers had always wanted.[67]

Despite its subtitle, *Colonialism: A Moral Reckoning* has applied no moral reckoning to the deliberate killings and violent dispossession of the Aboriginal people of Tasmania. It simply does not face the fact that in the case of Tasmania the British

THE TRUTH ABOUT EMPIRE

Empire failed the test of protecting its Indigenous subjects. The rule of law was never applied, let alone upheld, and no genuine attempt was made, despite Reynolds' assertion, to negotiate a treaty. It's more than time, surely, that Britain accepts that the Tasmanian Aboriginal people were victims of its deliberate policy of genocide.

3

THE MISUSE OF INDIGENOUS AND CANADIAN HISTORY IN *COLONIALISM*

Adele Perry, Sean Carleton, and *Omeasoo Wahpasiw*

Introduction

In the final pages of Chinua Achebe's novel *Things Fall Apart*, an unnamed "District Commissioner"—a British official in charge of upholding colonial laws and defending Christian missionaries in West Africa—wrests control of Umuofia, a Nigerian village. This is a fictional account, but the book's conclusion reveals an important truth about the role of "storying" in justifying the colonial project. "In the many years in which he had toiled to bring civilization to different parts of Africa," Achebe explains, the Commissioner "had learned a number of things ... Every day brought him some new material." To share his lessons with other colonial officials throughout the empire, the Commissioner plans to write a book. He wants to call it *The Pacification of the*

THE TRUTH ABOUT EMPIRE

Primitive Tribes of the Lower Niger. Like many writers, however, the Commissioner is faced with the difficult decision about what to include and what to omit. He confesses, "There was so much ... to include, and one must be firm in cutting out the details."[1]

The ending to *Things Fall Apart* confirms one of Frantz Fanon's observations about imperialism and history: that imperialists make history, and they know it.[2] Indeed, there is an established record of colonial officials deliberately concealing or destroying damning documents and of imperialists writing whitewashed histories to justify colonial policies and politicians, in Canada and other parts of the empire.[3] To the victor go the spoils; but congratulatory accounts of the past, complete with flattering footnotes, help to protect the victor's power and control.

Cheerleaders for colonialism such as Nigel Biggar, Bruce Gilley, and Keith Windschuttle (see Lyndall Ryan's chapter in this volume), like Achebe's Commissioner, take up the work of imperial apologetics enthusiastically. They seem to see themselves as stewards of Britain's imperial legacy. Like *The Pacification of the Primitive Tribes of the Lower Niger*, the work of such apologists is shaped by selective representation of reality, of choosing to emphasize positive details while "cutting out" or misrepresenting unflattering ones that contradict a certain worldview. The stated objective is to defend the colonial project as a way of sticking up for the West and Christianity. A less clearly stated goal seems to be to shore up the power, privilege, and profit Britain amassed during the age of empire of which many Britons are continuing beneficiaries.[4] Moralistic defenses of empire help the conservative cause of rallying around the status quo and warding off any kind of radical reckoning or redistribution of the spoils of empire. While many may agree with this politics, it should be recognized for what it is: politics and not history.

Biggar's book *Colonialism: A Moral Reckoning* is a salutary example of the common techniques used by imperial myth-

INDIGENOUS AND CANADIAN HISTORY

makers, past and present, to justify empire. In this chapter, we consider the selective representation of Canada's and Indigenous history specifically, arguing that it is certainly "firm" in the "cutting out" or misrepresentation of many important details. In its heyday, the British Empire relied on the exploitation of its colonies for resources; imperial apologists extract and manipulate Canada's and Indigenous peoples' histories and historiographies to defend the empire's legacy.

The Canadian context

When readers first crack open Biggar's *Colonialism*, they are greeted in the early pages by a Mercator map showing British possessions around the world circa 1910. These maps, often created by imperialists such as Canadian George R. Parkin to promote imperial unity, were standard features of many school classrooms in Britain and the colonies. The maps were used to deliver important lessons to students about colonial legitimacy and the greatness of an empire so vast that the sun never set on its acquired territory.[5] The reader's eye is immediately drawn to the top left-hand corner where they first encounter "Canada," the largest land mass in the British Empire. Canada, as Biggar reminds readers, was the first British colony to be granted Dominion status in 1867.[6]

Despite its geographic size and importance as a settler colony and Commonwealth country, Canada is afforded only a small role in Biggar's account. Many histories that would generally be registered as significant, both trans-imperially and within the local context of Canada, receive no mention at all in *Colonialism*. The Hudson's Bay Company, granted a royal charter in 1670 and serving as a kind of de facto colonial government for a substantial part of northern North America until 1870, receives not even a cursory mention, even in Chapter 6 with its focus on trade and political economy. Canada's Indian Act was first passed in 1876, and a version of it remains in effect today. In Biggar's account, however, this crucial piece of race-making and colonial administration receives three mentions, two relegated to the notes. The Indian Act appears in the body of Biggar's book only to be explained away as a "mistake."[7] In short, much is missing from Biggar's treatment of colonialism in Canada.

The word "Canada," or a variation thereof, appears 165 times in *Colonialism*. That is more appearances than Sudan (seventeen), Palestine (forty-one), Ireland (seventy-six), and Australia (119) but not as many as Egypt (172), South Africa (192), India (343), or Africa generally (885). Almost half of the 117 notes dealing with Canada reference just two contemporary authors. Thirty-six reference controversial historian J. R. Miller, and nineteen cite the infamous far-right ideologue, political strategist, and retired University of Calgary professor Thomas Flanagan.[8] Some of *Colonialism*'s arguments are also drawn from untrustworthy or illegitimate sources, including a number from non-peer-reviewed publications credited to far-right think-tanks and magazines sustained by conservative counterparts in Canada. In common with some of these sources, *Colonialism* simply does not add up to a meaningful engagement with Canada or Canadian historiography.[9]

Along with the colonial cheerleaders upon whom it relies, *Colonialism* uses and misuses Canada—and Indigenous peoples—in specific ways that have serious implications for how the colonial past and present are understood. What follows, then, is an examination of the key rhetorical devices employed, especially but not exclusively in *Colonialism*, to misrepresent Canada and Indigenous peoples as well as our responses as historians, as a team composed of a nêhiyaw iskwew scholar and two Canadian settler scholars.[10] Building on Alan Lester's analysis, we take up Biggar's handling of the Canadian context and its sources.[11] We

INDIGENOUS AND CANADIAN HISTORY

focus on six overlapping techniques: (1) turning an Indigenous leader into a defender of dispossession; (2) distorted historiography; (3) ignoring context; (4) refusing Indigenous knowledge; (5) justifying colonialism; and (6) collusion in denial.

Turning an Indigenous leader into a defender of dispossession

Louis Riel (1844–85) was a Métis leader and politician who led two powerful, if very different, movements that resisted Canadian colonization of Indigenous territories to its north and west.[12] The Red River Resistance of 1869–70 was a response to the unilateral transfer of Indigenous lands from the Hudson's Bay Company to Canada, without consultation let alone consent. The immediate result was that Manitoba entered Canada as a province with limited tools of self-governance and with some recognition of Métis rights to land, language, and religion.[13] Following the Resistance, Riel went into exile and moved around Métis communities on both sides of the Canada–US border, three times prevented from taking up his seat as an elected member of Canada's parliament in Ottawa, Ontario. In 1884, Riel returned to help lead the North-West Resistance, which saw Métis and First Nations allies—mostly nêhiyaw—engage Canada in five months of armed insurgency. Riel surrendered to the newly formed North-West Mounted Police in May 1885. In the summer of that year, the Métis leader was tried for high treason, one of eighty-four Indigenous men tried for their roles in the Resistance. Riel's trial was highly politicized, and it is an enduring example of the extent to which the Canadian state was willing to bend its own rules to establish authority over the Northwest. Riel was found guilty and hanged in the fall of 1885.[14]

Riel meant and continues to mean many things to many people and communities in Canada, both past and present. As historian Max Hamon notes, Riel is "likely the most written about person in Canadian history," and he has been assigned numerous roles: "Catholic martyr to Protestant violence, a French patriot crushed by English fanatics, a spiritual leader, a deranged lunatic, the father of a nation and an Indigenous hero."[15] In *Colonialism*, Riel is given an altogether different meaning. Biggar argues that Riel "recognized the cogency" of European philosophers' argument that it is morally legitimate to take the land of people who use it differently.[16] The evidence cited is drawn from the second of two speeches Riel made at his trial for treason. Riel's speech is quoted at length, and in a book with little textual engagement with archival sources, particularly those produced by Indigenous peoples, this passage is an outlier. It is also one that steps badly wrong, distorting Riel's layered discussion of the processes of dispossession in the Northwest as evidence of his support for arguments that underpinned dispossession here and elsewhere in the British imperial world.

Note 24 in Chapter 4 cannot show us why the discussion of Riel goes off course, but it does show us how.[17] It references Riel's address to the court published in a collection of documents, in turn quoted in Flanagan's 2000 book that "reconsiders" Riel's legacy. Introducing a longer version of the same passage, Flanagan notes that this part of Riel's speech "must be read carefully, for his English phrasing was awkward, even though the ideas were clear."[18] Biggar does not offer this care to Riel's words, or to the context in which they were made. In his response to Lester's review, Biggar offers a partial admission of Riel's words. Biggar returns to his one secondary source, Flanagan, and admits that he was not sufficiently clear in his argument that Riel recognized the "cogency" of the moral justification of dispossession, rather than supporting it.[19] That Riel well understood the legal and intellectual arguments that accompanied the loss of Indigenous lands and governments to imperial and settler regimes is without doubt, and to note this is an odd place for any scholar of colonialism to land. The poor handling of Riel's speech reflects a lack of contextual knowledge, thin research, and, above all, a commitment to harnessing the historical record in defense of the British Empire, no matter the intellectual damage done.

Distorted historiography

Colonialism is a sporadic and controversy-driven treatment of colonialism in Canada, and it is one that leans heavily on a handful of secondary sources. When it selectively engages the work of serious historians, it often distorts their nuanced conclusions or the body of scholarship that has developed over decades. Historian Sarah Carter has produced a substantial corpus of work analyzing the gendered history of colonialism in the nineteenth- and twentieth-century Canadian west.[20] *Colonialism* draws on only one of her short essays: a chapter on Indigenous peoples and the British Empire. In these twenty pages, useable quotes are found that bolster the book's case but also examples of history to be distrusted, disagreed, and quarreled with. This includes Carter's willingness to take oral sources seriously when she argues that Annishinaabeg and Crown understandings of treaty were at odds during the negotiations of treaties, in this case in Upper Canada during the late eighteenth and early nineteenth century.[21]

Carter's extensive research on the dispossession of Plains Indigenous peoples and the development of the reserve system and settler agriculture in late nineteenth- and early twentieth-century Canada receives no mention in *Colonialism*. Exploring this work would lead to a different and more contextualized understanding of James Daschuk's prize-winning *Clearing the Plains: Disease, Politics of Starvation, and the Loss of Aboriginal Life*, which is one of the few books that comes under Biggar's sustained scrutiny and attention, with Daschuk accused of "some tendentiousness."²² *Colonialism* treats Daschuk's research like it is *sui generis*, an island unto itself undermining readers' faith in Canada's first prime minister, John A. Macdonald, and the policies he is most associated with. Reading Daschuk alongside work like Carter's, John Tobias's article "Starvation and the Subjugation of the Plains Cree, 1879–1885," and Maureen Lux's prize-winning monograph *Medicine that Walks* would put it in a line of scholarship that has carefully documented the impact of federal policy on Indigenous lives.²³ Instead, Biggar argues that Daschuk misunderstands Canada's failure to live up to its treaty promises and the magnitude of Canada's humanitarian response to Indigenous peoples in crisis.²⁴ In the notes, Biggar characterizes Daschuk as a "politically hostile witness," confirming that for Biggar this is all a trial, and historians sit on one side or the other.²⁵ To make his case, Biggar draws on what is by now a predictable set of suspect sources—Flanagan's work, a post by Ged Martin, and Patrice Dutil's essay in *The Dorchester Review*, enlivened by email correspondence with a professor at a private Christian university.

Cree scholar Robert Alexander Innes suggests a different set of concerns with the available historiography, most of it written by non-Indigenous scholars. Why, asks Innes, have historians not been more willing to engage the language of genocide? Why have they not utilized all the available archival resources or offered a clearer numerical accounting of Indigenous loss in the late nineteenth-century west? In the cases of Cowessess First Nation in what is now Saskatchewan, research conducted for the Treaty Lands Entitlement process indicates that around 320, or 33 per cent, of Cowesses citizens lost their lives to federal starvation policies.²⁶ Read in the context of a long-standing scholarship, and with Innes' concerns in mind, what stands out is that Biggar portrays Daschuk as an unreliable outlier and a hostile witness in an effort to downplay the conclusions of generations of careful historical scholarship that have demonstrated the impact of Canadian policies on prairie Indigenous people in the late nineteenth century.

Ignoring context

While a closer examination of the notes in *Colonialism* reveals obvious distortion of certain Canadian historians' work, what is also striking is what is omitted. Indeed, elision is another key strategy employed to misrepresent. *Colonialism* selects just a handful of contemporary historians to stand in for the field of Canadian history as a whole and give the (false) impression that the field's consensus on the colonial past confirms colonial cheerleaders' view of Canada, and by extension the empire, as peaceful, benevolent, and even humanitarian. The perception of Canada as a "Peaceable Kingdom" is, as Cree scholars Gina Starblanket and Dallas Hunt have shown, colonial mythology.[27] In the case of Canada, many have illustrated how mythology operationalizes elision—the omission of contradictory evidence—as a strategy to create and maintain the legitimacy of Canada's settler capitalist society on an ongoing basis.[28]

In recent years, historians have challenged the view that Canada's colonial project was—and still is—peaceful, but *Colonialism* does not reference any of this contemporary literature, which gives readers the impression that the field agrees with this assessment, and it is only woke and "hostile witness" scholars who are the outliers. This is a misrepresentation of the field. Since 2003, the Canadian Historical Association—the largest organization of historians and history professionals in Canada—has awarded its best book prize to authors offering critical, nuanced assessments of colonialism seven times.[29] *Colonialism* cites only one of these studies—Daschuk's *Clearing the Plains*—and then only to distort and downplay its critical findings about the loss of Indigenous life. None of the other major studies, produced by a range of scholars, that on balance have demonstrated the negative consequences of Canada's colonial policies and accented ongoing resistance by Indigenous peoples, are cited.[30] Moreover, *Colonialism* elides all scholarship on colonial violence and Indigenous resistance, which, again, misrepresents the historiography.[31] This kind of argumentation might be seen as disingenuous by anyone familiar with the literature, and *Colonialism* seems to rely on most readers not paying close attention to the source material, or even being willing or able to access it. The "cutting out" of these details will be obvious to any specialist historian but may not be detected by the general reader.

Refusing Indigenous knowledge

In its limited engagement with Indigenous authors' intellectual work, *Colonialism* alters and denigrates their meaning through an epistemological lens that is foggy at best and self-serving at worst. Like other defenses of colonialism, it is steeped in an obvious ethnocentrism that refuses and rejects Indigenous knowledge.

Colonialism's section on Indigenous land rights suggests that newcomers could not comprehend "whose freedom to land use obliged respect [sic]."[32] In this vein of dismissiveness, seemingly sarcastic quotation marks are placed around the description of Indigenous scholar Tracey Lindberg as a member of the "Cree 'First Nation,'"[33] indicating immediately the author's own moral relationship to the Nations of Turtle Island and, further, ignorance of them. The quotation marks subtly signal a skeptical position concerning Indigenous peoples' original connection to land in North America, an undermining discursive tactic he may have adopted from Flanagan's controversial book *First Nations? Second Thoughts*. Biggar continues to describe Lindberg's cogent description of nêhiyaw law as "fanciful."³⁴ Perhaps greater knowledge or a reading of the article in full might have enabled a more appreciative assessment of Lindberg's claims, including recognition of her as a nêhiyaw iskwew, and her people's deep appreciation for metaphor, in the terms "mother earth" and "inherent right" to the land.³⁵ Lindberg warns the reader of their own interpretational limits in the very next sentence, "our meanings, philosophies, world views, and laws cannot be detailed fully in a manner which approximates their meaning in English ... concepts run over the top like spring water in a barrel."³⁶ *Colonialism* is marked by a non-attempt to comprehend Lindberg's words and point: nêhiyaw relationships to the land cannot be easily explained in an alien system of ownership and laws to protect ownership, and furthermore cannot be denied, regardless of the latter system's attempted dominance.

Another problem is Biggar's over-reliance on Flanagan, whom he describes as someone who "writes with authority."³⁷ The latter is the problem. Biggar and Flanagan describe Indigenous peoples as "taking control of land, just as earlier aboriginal settlers did."³⁸ Flanagan tries to position Indigenous peoples as the original settlers in a sleight of hand that serves to alleviate the guilt and responsibility of European settler colonizers. Based upon even *Colonialism*'s own limited retelling of Lindberg's discussions of nêhiyaw law, this is the opposite of what nêhiyaw ancestors did. Where Biggar and Flanagan see "control," Lindberg describes a relationship of reciprocity, humility, and sharing of space that cannot be owned or violated. "Peoples belong to the land"³⁹ as much if not more so than vice versa. Instead of recognizing the discrepancy between these two perspectives on land and belonging, *Colonialism* opts to denigrate a sophisticated and nuanced nêhiyaw ethic to justify European settler colonization and the creation of Canada as commonsensical.

Embedded in the refusal of Indigenous knowledge is the strong commitment to a narrow ethnocentrism that normalizes white supremacy. In Chapter 5, "Cultural Assimilation and 'Genocide,'" *Colonialism* provides only three options for culture clash: domination, assimilation, or segregation. This is akin to the saying "there are two types of people in the world," meaning there is no room here for ethical choices, despite the book's overall claims. The number of throwaway sentences that seem to belie an unconscious white supremacy are countless, including the use of quotation marks to refer to First Nations and genocide throughout the book. Another example is where the reader is reminded that "[t]he view that native peoples were essentially equal to Britons, possessed of the potential to become equally civilised, predominated in the imperial metropolis, even when some settlers on the colonial periphery doubted it."[40] Definitions of civilization abound, and it does not seem that the statement "British colonial settlement did sometimes cause the annihilation of a native people" would fit into any of them.[41] This particular paragraph ends by suggesting that the people closest to the action in "the colonial periphery," and therefore the ones with the most intimate knowledge of Indigenous peoples, "doubted" their "essential" equality to Britons. These sentences and comments are easy to edit out, and yet they stand as evidence of a larger project that seems to us rooted in ethnocentrism, white supremacy, and a steadfast refusal to acknowledge Indigenous knowledge and perspectives.

Justifying colonialism

In its discussion of Indigenous territorial control and concomitant violence, *Colonialism* focuses on the latest possible conflicts. The effect is to contrast and elevate the non-violence of the British as they invaded Indigenous territories. By contrast, drawing again on Flanagan, the most violent of Indigenous existence is remembered and elevated as justification for a new colonial order. Like Flanagan, Biggar uses an Indigenous politician, famed Dene activist George Erasmus, who, like many, romanticizes a pre-settler colonial past, as if his claim to the truth was itself responsible. Among these three figures, not one is beholden to an academic truth.[42] Either way, *Colonialism*'s paragraphs belie the fact that the cited genocidal violence on Turtle Island followed decades or more of introduced diseases among Indigenous populations, disrupting any previous forms of stability for nations, their territories, and their worldviews.

Settler greed for land is justified in the following way: "It is true that settlers, eager to better their lives and knowing what could be achieved with land associated with native peoples, were often frustrated with the latter's failure to make it more productive and by the apparent squandering of resources."[43] An inference is that the author agrees with this assessment of land and its so-called "proper" use, which as mentioned above, is antithetical to how nêhiyaw people, at least, describe the purpose of land. In addition, the settlers are represented as more "knowing," more knowledgeable, and therefore, superior in their understanding of the world and their purpose, through this desire to turn the land into something "productive." A review of various philosophies follows that suggest "superiority" is not a good reason to steal land, but the natural conclusion to which the reader is drawn is still that land theft was broadly honorable.

The misinterpretation of Riel's speech, mentioned earlier, takes on special meaning within this context of refusing to recognize Indigenous knowledge and justifying colonialism. Biggar, following Flanagan, mobilizes a portion of Riel's final speech, again out of context and missing entirely what is seen by other Métis scholars as "irony."[44] Biggar erases Riel's treatises on tribal sovereignty and treaty making. He reads, "I think it is a fair share to acknowledge the genius of civilization to such an extent as to give, when I have seven pairs of socks, six, to keep one"[45] as a statement alone, where in context, it is sandwiched within Riel's reiteration of Indigenous sovereignty. This points to a failure to appreciate epistemologies outside of and beyond the author's own. Furthermore, Riel's interpretations and descriptions of Métis and First Nations land rights coincide with those elaborated by nêhiyaw scholar Lindberg. In Lindberg and Riel, just beyond Biggar's own reading, lie similar arguments of the inviolability of Indigenous peoples and their territories, as well as an ethic to share those riches. *Colonialism*, an ethical analysis, was an opportunity to interpret this ethic just as easily and more accurately, but instead it reiterates Flanagan's ideological perspective as unquestionable fact.

Collusion in denial

The misrepresentation of Canada's and Indigenous peoples' histories in *Colonialism* and its main sources is perhaps most obvious—especially to Canadian and Indigenous readers—in the book's sections dealing with Canada's Indian residential school system. The Indian residential school system was a key plank of Canada's Indian policy. Between 1883 and 1996, Canada's federal government partnered with various Christian churches to devise, deploy, and defend a school system that separated, often by force, more than 150,000 Indigenous children from their families. The goal was to undermine Indigenous lifeways and assimilate Indigenous peoples into Canadian society to facilitate Canadian nation-building and settler capitalist development as part of the expansion of the British Empire. Recent research has shown how this school system, described by one official during the height of its operation as a "national crime," meets the definition of genocide, with more than 4,000 children dying and many more testifying to being mentally, physically, and sexually abused.[46] In 2022, the federal government officially apologized to Survivors and agreed that the system constitutes genocide.[47] The Pope even traveled to Canada in 2022 to apologize directly to Indigenous peoples and acknowledge the system as genocide.[48]

Most Canadians now know the truth about the damaging history of residential schooling for Indigenous peoples and generally support the strengthening of Indigenous–settler relations, a process known as reconciliation.[49] History and historians have played and continue to play an important role here. Mary Jane Logan McCallum and Erin Millions write that

> [h]istorians are and will be an important part of piecing this history together, bringing names to places where they have been forgotten or never cared about, bringing numbers to "masses" who starved, teaching topics and research methods that were never considered "real" history, and making meaning of this for the kind of place we want to live in going forward.[50]

Still, there are some people—including a handful of historians—that are engaging in what is known as residential school denialism to twist, distort, and misrepresent basic facts about the system's history to shake public confidence in the emerging public consensus and protect Canada from a reckoning with its colonial past. Notably, some denialists use false balance—a form of bias that wrongly suggests an issue is more balanced between opposing views than the evidence suggests—to argue that the "good" and "bad" need to be understood as equal parts of the whole residential school story.[51] This is the same kind of misrepresentation of evidence that *Colonialism* relies on to balance the "good" and "bad" of the British Empire, so it should come as no surprise that the book's engagement with Canadian writing on the subject of residential schooling largely draws on those advancing residential school denialism. The pattern of misrepresentation that develops should, by now, be clear.

Two obvious points can be made in this regard. First, *Colonialism*'s treatment of residential schooling draws mostly from one book: J. R. Miller's *Shingwauk's Vision: A History of Native Residential Schools*. Miller's book, published in 1996, is recognized as an authoritative history of the system alongside John S. Milloy's *A National Crime: The Canadian Government and the Residential School System, 1879–1986*, published in 1999. In the field, both books are usually credited together as helping Canadians begin to understand the history of residential schooling, though Milloy's book is more critical and is based on church and state sources that Miller did not have access to. Milloy's book was recognized by *The Literary Review of Canada* as one of the 100 most important books in Canadian history, but it is not cited in Biggar's book.[52] Though Miller's work is still used, he has recently been criticized—but feted by right-wing commentators—for challenging descriptions of the system as genocide and signing a public letter organized by right-wing writers decrying the so-called "'genocide' myth."[53] That Biggar only cites Miller, and emphasizes his most sympathetic points at that, and ignores all of the contemporary scholarship on the subject to construct his "defense," can be seen as an egregious example of cherry-picking and elision and commitment to engaging mostly right-wing perspectives. Second, the notes on pages 345–51 regurgitate known denialist talking points from questionable sources, like the right-wing outfit *The Dorchester Review*, to justify a lack of engagement with the Truth and Reconciliation Commission of Canada's (TRC) final report. This will be a red flag for most Canadian readers. The TRC was an independent commission appointed to investigate church and state records and gather Survivor testimony to establish the truth. *Colonialism*, like many denialists it cites, tries to delegitimize the TRC because it concluded that the Indian residential school system was genocidal, and it frequently tries to undermine the credibility of Survivor testimony.[54] Its reliance on suspect sources reproduces a problematic political logic and thus renders the treatment of residential schooling specifically and Canadian colonialism generally shallow and untrustworthy. The relationship between residential school denialism and empire denialism is symbiotic.

Conclusion

As *Colonialism* was making waves in the UK, one right-wing commentator, Peter Shawn Taylor, tried but failed to capitalize on the momentum in Canada. Taylor interviewed Biggar and published the transcript for C2C—a right-wing "conservative to conservative" outlet—hoping to spread *Colonialism*'s ideas across the pond.[55] Taylor also wrote an opinion piece based on the interview for Canada's right-wing daily national newspaper *The National Post*, arguing that "[c]olonialism contained 'good things as well as bad.' Why can't we just accept that?"[56] In these articles, Taylor cherry-picks Biggar's arguments that he thinks redeem a reactionary defense of Canada's colonial status quo, from apologies for conservative Prime Minister Macdonald to the argument that "the motivation for establishing residential schools was basically humanitarian."[57]

In regurgitating *Colonialism*'s apologetics, Taylor reproduces the same six discursive techniques outlined earlier. Perhaps most revealing is Taylor's manipulation of Chinua Achebe to frame his defense of Biggar, just as *Colonialism*, taking its lead from Gilley, twists Achebe to frame its own defense of empire. Taylor borrows Biggar's quote of Achebe, saying "[t]he legacy of colonialism is not a simple one but one of great complexity with contradictions—good things as well as bad."[58] The problem is that, like much of Biggar's work and that of his politically inclined interlocutors, this is an example of cherry-picking and distortion. Nevertheless, Taylor doubles down on Biggar's misrepresentation of Achebe.

The original quote comes from an interview Achebe gave in 2012 about the enduring relevance of *Things Fall Apart*. His interviewer asks: "Over 50 years have passed since you wrote the book *Things Fall Apart*. Have your viewpoints and approaches toward the presence of a colonial power in the soil of your country changed since that time?" In his response, before noting that colonialism's legacy was complicated, Achebe explains:

> Every thinking person, if you consider yourself a serious intellectual grows ... Intellectual evolution and growth does not mean, however, that all of a sudden horrendous things in our shared history appear less appalling. It means that greater knowledge and understanding help place the best and worst of events in clearer perspective.[59]

His evaluation of "good" and "bad" here is *not* actually proof of his overall reconsideration of colonialism's legacy, as Biggar and Taylor suggest. Rather, Achebe is reflecting on the positive changes he has seen in the past fifty years in Africa—regarding "women's rights" and "race relations"—that prove "the world is a much different place today than it was in 1958 when *Things Fall Apart* was published." The "good," then, is not about straightforwardly defending the colonial project but is rather Achebe's reference to the struggles to change certain aspects of the colonial condition in Africa since his book was published. *Colonialism* cuts out this context, and Taylor follows without question. Achebe's "Commissioner" would be proud of the firm "cutting out" of the details on display.[60] This proves, yet again, that cherry-picking and misrepresenting evidence is at the heart of imperial apologetics and illustrates the dangerous consequences of flawed ideas spreading and being used in different contexts.

Fortunately, Taylor's attempt to start a "Biggar" debate about Canadian colonialism failed. In part, this can be explained by the obvious misrepresentation of Canada and Indigenous peoples' histories in *Colonialism*. The book's attempts to force Indigenous and Canadian histories awkwardly into a moral defense of empire will be seen through by most Canadians, certainly by serious historians. Moreover, the needle on issues of Indigenous–settler relations and truth and reconciliation have moved far enough in recent years that silly arguments—for example that residential schooling was "humanitarian" in its effects—hold up poorly in the face of careful, exhaustive, and compelling research done by scholarly researchers and commissions like the TRC. Such simplistic assertions might seem convincing to those unfamiliar with the Canadian context, but many Canadians are becoming aware of truths about empire and its consequences for Indigenous peoples in ways that make them more immune to this obvious misinformation and disinformation. But there is more work to do. In the words of Achebe, from his 2012 interview: "So the struggle to make the world a better place must continue!"[61] This seems to be exactly what those promoting imperial apologetics are afraid of most of all.

Biggar's *Colonialism* offers a confident, genial view of the British Empire. Canada plays a modest and episodic role. *Colonialism* is a story of empire where the intentions of colonizers and logic of colonizers are what matter and what drive the story, and where Indigenous experience and archives are distrusted, minimized, or ignored altogether. For those of us who attended state-funded schools in twentieth-century Canada—whether the residential schools aimed at Indigenous children that existed until 1996, or the public schools where settler and some Indigenous children were taught—the kind of one-sided, self-congratulatory mythology dressed up as "history" will likely be familiar, maybe painfully so. In the last two decades, however, Indigenous peoples have profoundly unsettled and challenged these familiar narratives of Canada's past and its relationship to Britain. Whether in the reports of inquiries, prize-winning scholarly monographs, or Canadian best-seller lists, historical research has played an important role in this process of unsettling and truth-telling about colonialism and empire.

THE TRUTH ABOUT EMPIRE

It is the unsettling of imperial mythology, in Canada and across the former empire, that is the real anxiety at the core of the curious book *Colonialism*. Cherry-picking Canadian examples to help stop the unraveling of empire's legitimacy, it is clear that the book does not rest upon a great knowledge of Canada and its histories. Nevertheless, it finds common cause with a modest number of Canadian researchers and writers, most of them not professional historians, who have taken to open letters and online fora to decry these critical histories of Canada's past, too. In fifty years, *Colonialism: A Moral Reckoning* will make a revealing and powerful record of what was at stake in reframing histories of the British Empire in the 2020s.

4

'WHEN MEN BURN WOMEN ALIVE, WE HANG THEM'

SATI AND 'CIVILISING MISSION' IN COLONIAL INDIA

Andrea Major

In popular debates about empire, certain moments, policies, and events are often foregrounded as standing for a larger but less tangible whole. Charles Napier's oft-reported actions on encountering sati (widow-burning) in India are one such example.[1] On hearing of an intended immolation during his controversial conquest of the north-west region of Sindh in 1843, Napier apparently 'made it known that he would stop the sacrifice'.[2] When local priests argued that it was a religious practice and therefore sacrosanct, he replied:

> Be it so. This burning of widows is your custom; prepare the funeral pile. But my nation has also a custom. When men burn women alive, we hang them, and confiscate all their property. My carpenters shall

therefore erect gibbets on which to hang all concerned when the widow is consumed. Let us all act according to national customs.[3]

Napier himself is, of course, best known for the one-word telegram he reportedly sent to his superiors in the East India Company (EIC) on annexing the formerly independent region: 'Peccavi' or 'I have sinned/Sind.' 'The story of that pun might earn Napier an appreciative footnote in any imperial history', Michael Gove remarked in 2008, apparently unaware that the story was apocryphal and the pun itself originated in *Punch* magazine.[4] Napier's supposed intervention to suppress sati is similarly widely shared and just as often misrepresented. 'What secures him a more substantial presence in any chronicle of Britain's past is his response to the suggestion that the practice of suttee be allowed to continue', Gove goes on, before recounting Napier's famous remarks.[5] The story appears with predictable regularity in popular histories of the British Empire, where it functions as a symbol of supposed British imperial benevolence and moral clarity. In *Empire: What Ruling the World Did to the British*, for example, Jeremy Paxman uses it to illustrate the supposed newfound confidence of the British to intervene on 'moral' issues. Sati was not widespread, Paxman admits, but its prevalence was not the point—'its suppression was a dramatic and emotional demonstration of the ethical purpose of empire'.[6] Likewise, Jacob Rees-Mogg—who presents Napier as one of 'Twelve Titans Who Forged Britain'—comments of the episode: 'This was Napier's imperialism, moral, liberal, just, and implacable. This was the good that not merely could be done with power but the good which must be done, in order to justify possessing that power.'[7]

Perhaps even more intriguing than its problematic but predictable prevalence in accounts of British Empire in India is the life the Napier story has acquired beyond the history books. It has been mobilised repeatedly in the press and on social media

SATI AND 'CIVILISING MISSION' IN COLONIAL INDIA

in a wide range of contexts, most notably in debates about multiculturalism, cultural relativism, and the dangers of 'wokeness'. As far back as 2001, in the wake of the 9/11 terror attacks, Polly Toynbee used the story to attack 'the fuzzy idea on the soft left' that 'Islamic cultural otherness' could supersede basic human rights. 'No moral or cultural relativism here', Toynbee remarked approvingly of Napier's response to sati, 'a burning widow feels the same pain whatever her culture'. Toynbee was using the example to uphold the position of what she refers to as 'hard liberals', who she claimed

> hold basic human rights to be non-negotiable and worth fighting for. They do not turn the other cheek, understand the other guy's point of view, or respect his culture when it comes to universal rights. Promoting liberal values everywhere ... is not neo-colonialism, but respect for a universal right to freedom from oppression.[8]

More recently, the story has appeared repeatedly in the right-wing press. I'll give just a few examples from the last fifteen years. In 2008, Matthew Parris deployed it when criticising Rowan Williams' views on Sharia law in *The Times*—both Toynbee and Parris seemingly oblivious to the fact that sati was a Hindu rather than Muslim practice.[9] In 2015, Jonah Goldberg referred to it in *The National Review* when discussing American troops' behaviour in Afghanistan. 'Yes, yes, let us all note that imperialism is an ugly thing', Goldberg remarked. 'But this is still a glorious example of might and right working in tandem.'[10] Discussing the controversy over the Rhodes Scholarship in 2016, *The New Criterion* commented: 'We've always regarded the PC attack on British Imperialism—and by extension, on Cecil Rhodes—as slightly preposterous', before going on to use a paraphrased version of Napier's remarks to support philosopher George Santayana's assertion that '[n]ever since the heroic days of Greece has the world had such a sweet, just, boyish master'.[11]

More recently still, in a piece called 'The Harry Potter Publisher and the Cancelled Professor', Chris McGovern takes a swipe at the supposed 'woke witch-finders and inquisitional heresy-hunters' whose criticisms of Nigel Biggar's 'Ethics and Empire' project led Bloomsbury to decide against publishing the resulting book. 'I suspect that Biggar's book is unlikely ... unconditionally to condemn colonial interference, from time to time, in local culture', McGovern remarks, before going on to tell the ubiquitous Napier story. 'Paxman was allowed to quote such British imperialist heresy in 2011 when his book was published by Penguin to accompany a BBC TV series', he concludes. 'Would he get away with it today?'[12]

To his credit, Biggar does not discuss Napier's supposed intervention on sati in *Colonialism: A Moral Reckoning* (which was eventually published by William Collins in 2023).[13] As McGovern anticipates, however, he does offer a predictably problematic defence of imperial intervention as 'civilising mission', which will be discussed in the next section. For now, suffice to say that McGovern's suggestion that historians of empire might no longer be 'allowed' to talk about sati or speak positively about its prohibition is peculiar. Few aspects of colonial encounter in India have received such prominent, extensive, and sustained attention from both historians and popular commentators as the abolition of sati. New publications on sati in colonial and postcolonial India appear almost every year, and the custom still looms large in the popular imagination.[14] Despite only affecting a tiny proportion of the population of British India—Anand Yang has estimated that even at its height, the rite only affected 0.2 per cent of widows in Bengal—sati has received disproportionate attention in western depictions of India, both at the time and since.[15] 'The British obsession with sati was boundless', the celebrated historian of colonial India Christopher Bayly remarked: 'Thousands of pages of Parliamentary Papers were

SATI AND 'CIVILISING MISSION' IN COLONIAL INDIA

given up to 4,000 immolations while the mortality of millions from disease and starvation was only mentioned incidentally.'[16] Often touted as an unproblematic example of the so-called 'civilising mission' in action, sati frequently appears alongside railways and cricket in Monty Pythonesque iterations of what the British did for India. Even in this wider context of preoccupation with sati, the Napier anecdote has gained unprecedented prominence, however, prompting us to ask why this story has caught the popular imagination from among the vast corpus of British writing on sati before and after its abolition. With its origins in a notorious case of territorial aggression, and its suggestion of extrajudicial violence, it is a peculiar example to choose to illustrate the supposed moral basis of British imperialism. Moreover, the events in question took place over a decade after the prohibition of sati in British India and are hardly representative of the complex ways the colonial state dealt with the custom, before and after its abolition.

Perhaps it is precisely because it depicts British action to prevent the widow-immolation as clear-cut and decisive, rather than the messy affair that it was, that the Napier story is so popular. After all, the implication that the British saw an irrefutable evil and acted decisively to prevent it is useful if the aim is to assert ideas of British moral clarity trumping cultural relativism or 'wokeness'—however far removed that interpretation might be from the more complex reality. There are darker implications in the popularity of this story too, however, in the tacit assumption that a certain amount of arbitrary violence—in this case, the threat of extrajudicial lynching, without recourse to the due process of law—should be considered not only acceptable but positively laudable if 'the natives' are doing something we do not like. It is also worth noting the unspoken intention behind deployment of the Napier story in these debates, which is to silence criticism of western imperial and neo-imperial interventions around the world by implying that opposition to empire amounts to support for—or at least indifference to—violence against women. Given this latter subtext, it may be worth stating clearly at the outset that I am categorically against burning women alive under any circumstances—whether in the context of sati, witchcraft, religious martyrdom, judicial punishment, war crimes, or domestic violence.[17] There is an extensive literature on how sati functioned as a tool of patriarchal oppression of women in both colonial and postcolonial India, to which I ascribe and to which I owe a considerable intellectual debt.[18] The intention of this chapter is neither to defend sati nor condemn its suppression. With that said, however, it is both historically inaccurate and logically unsustainable to conclude—as many commentators who invoke the Napier story do—that the British abolition of sati provides irrefutable evidence of the moral purpose of British imperialism as 'civilising mission'. To do so overemphasises the social, cultural, and statistical significance of sati in India, exoticises specific forms of violence against women while erasing other forms of gender-based inequality and oppression (including in contemporaneous western culture), and fundamentally misunderstands the complex nature of the British encounter with sati before and after abolition.[19]

This chapter seeks to move beyond persistent representations of the abolition of sati as the archetypal example of 'empire as civilising mission' epitomised by the Napier story and instead explore how the eventual British prohibition and suppression of sati actually came about. In doing so, it seeks to move beyond simplistic approaches to weighing up the supposed 'pros' and 'cons' of empire and think instead about the complex ways in which the colonial state functioned in practice. The chapter will contextualise the Napier story within the longer history of British encounters with sati and consider what its persistent popularity tells us about attitudes to empire today. The next

SATI AND 'CIVILISING MISSION' IN COLONIAL INDIA

section will provide some reflections on the wider theme of 'empire as civilising mission' and how this discourse has functioned to shape debates about empire, both in the nineteenth century and more recently. It will then go on to provide some more detailed context for understanding Napier's intervention on sati, in the contexts both of British colonial expansion in India and of the trajectory of the sati debate before and after 1829. Finally, it will look in detail at how the British dealt with sati in their territories after prohibition. A close look at the colonial record on sati suggests that contrary to Napier's assertion, the British occasionally convicted but never actually hanged anyone for burning women alive.

Empire as 'civilising mission'

The question of how far British colonial expansion can be understood as a vehicle for positive change is a controversial one. Many popular assessments of empire take what has been described as a 'balance sheet' approach, weighing up the positive benefits of the imposition of colonial modernity against the violence and dispossession often inherent in colonisation to determine whether empire was 'a good thing'. It is an analytical framework that has more in common with W. C. Sellar and R. J. Yeatman's seminal *1066 And All That* than serious historical scholarship but is one that has become increasingly entrenched in the popular framing of debates about empire and its legacies. Biggar has recently courted controversy by taking a similar approach in *Colonialism: A Moral Reckoning*, but he is only the most recent to do so. School textbooks, television talk shows, and YouGov polls have all sought to understand empire through simple binaries of 'good' or 'bad', exploitative or benevolent, something of which to be proud, or something that should elicit shame. In practice, of course, history can rarely be reduced to such neat binaries, and the case of the British prohibition of sati is no exception. As this chapter will demonstrate, the prohibition of sati was far from the straightforward act of British moral certitude and decisive action that those deploying the Napier version of its suppression would imply. Indeed, while few would argue that legislation to prevent burning women alive was anything but a social good, the story of how the British abolition of sati came about is an instructive example of how ambivalent even supposedly clear-cut examples of beneficial colonial social reforms could be.

Ideas of 'civilising mission' were an important component of nineteenth-century colonial discourse and have continued to shape debates about empire today. Carey Watt describes it as 'an ever-shifting set of ideas and practices that was used to justify and legitimize the establishment and continuation of overseas colonies, both to subject peoples and to citizens or subjects in the homeland'.[20] Influenced by Enlightenment ideas about classification of races, stadial theory, and the resulting hierarchy of nations, ideas of 'civilising mission' were embedded in assumptions of difference and posited that the supposedly superior societies of Europe had a duty to bring the benefits of western modernity to the 'backward' populations they colonised. In some parts of Africa, North America, and Australia, this difference was described simply in terms of the 'primitive' nature of indigenous or tribal groups. In others, especially those perceived as having more sophisticated precolonial polities, the case was made in terms of moral and material difference. As Watt puts it: 'A fundamental difference between colonial subjects in India and their British overlords was posited, with Indians and other subject peoples placed at lower or "inferior" positions in new "scales of civilization", and the British (and Europeans generally) at the top.'[21] Faced with the sophistication, wealth, and dynamism of the Mughal Empire and its successor states, the British could hardly argue that Indians were 'primitive'. Instead, British impe-

SATI AND 'CIVILISING MISSION' IN COLONIAL INDIA

rial officials, historians, and commentators posited a moral difference. They characterised India's mostly Muslim rulers as tyrannical 'oriental despots', depicting the subcontinent as sunk in a chronic state of warfare and disorder that could only be resolved by Pax Britannica. Meanwhile, missionaries and others criticised Hindu socio-religious life, pointing to the supposed degeneracy of idolatry and sensationalising such practices as religious self-mortification (especially hook-swinging), infanticide, human sacrifice, and sati in a virulent attack on the Hindu character. British rule, it was argued, would disseminate the 'civilised values' of British liberalism, utilitarianism, and evangelical Christianity and thus 'improve' India's supposedly backward population, eradicate barbaric practices, and ready Indians (eventually) for good self-government. As Watt notes, 'Indians were thereby condemned to continually try to catch up to their British rulers' in what Partha Chatterjee has described as 'the rule of colonial difference': the idea that while empire was justified on the basis it 'improved' Indians by making them more like their British colonisers, in practice this process could never be completed, as success would remove the rationale for British presence.[22]

There is considerable debate among historians about how far British colonial officials believed in and were motivated by the ideals of 'civilising mission' described earlier, both individually and collectively. While some argue that they were little more than window-dressing for the more hardnosed economic, political, and strategic motivations for empire, others see more complex interactions between the incentives of exploitation and improvement. It would be as reductive to suggest that these ideas had no influence on individual and collective attitudes as it would be to claim that they were the primary motive for colonial expansion. Suffice to say, while some colonial officials certainly did believe they were doing good, colonial records suggest that in practice ideas of 'civilising mission' had at best an uneven and inconsistent influence on imperial policy and frequently ran up against more pressing, or indeed more mundane imperatives of colonial rule.[23] Of course, even if we accept that some colonial officials were motivated by ideas of civilising mission, there is no escaping the fact that it is a deeply problematic ideology. The discourse of civilising mission was grounded in chauvinistic assumptions about British superiority, the primacy of western models of 'progress' over all others, and the inadequacy of non-western civilisations and cultures. Other societies were frequently measured, assessed, and represented in ways that reaffirmed this belief in western superiority and encoded the supposed individual and collective failings of others as essential characteristics rather than reflecting the more complex realities of diverse and sophisticated societies and cultures. The various assumptions, issues, and power dynamics that shaped western representations of colonised cultures have been the subject of extensive study over the last fifty years, with historians, literary theorists, historical anthropologists, sociologists, human geographers, and other scholars around the world exploring the opportunities and challenges posed by the 'colonial archive' from a wide range of disciplinary perspectives and regional contexts. The result is an extensive body of literature exploring why western accounts of other cultures were constructed in the way they were, how they related to the lived reality of colonised societies, how to read 'against the grain' of colonial sources, and why we need to think more critically about nineteenth-century representations of the colonial encounter in general.

It is disappointing, but perhaps not surprising, to find that many recent defences of empire have chosen to simply ignore the methodological and conceptual issues raised by decades of scholarship. Biggar, for example, claims to offer 'a more historically accurate' account of the British Empire but sees no need to question the self-representation of powerful elite white men such as

SATI AND 'CIVILISING MISSION' IN COLONIAL INDIA

Rhodes, Lord Cromer, and Alfred Milner, upon whom he relies—largely uncritically—for much of his supposed evidence base. The result is a restating of nineteenth-century discourses of civilising mission for a twenty-first-century audience, complete with the assertions that 'sometimes the sense that imperial Britons had of their own superiority was justified', sometimes 'native people needed help', and sometimes Britons had a duty 'to try to stop them oppressing each other'.[24] Biggar attempts to reinforce this idea of a moral imperative for imperial intervention by drawing comparisons with today's human rights activists, who, he argues, 'inadvertently mirror the Christian missionaries and humanitarians of the nineteenth century, when they protested against such things as slavery, female infanticide and child marriage, and appealed to the British government to use its imperial power to suppress them'.[25] Leaving aside the cognitive dissonance involved in drawing a moral equivalence between human rights organisations lobbying international institutions today and an imperial power invading another country and expropriating its resources in the past, it is worth stressing that there is nothing 'inadvertent' about the links between twenty-first-century human rights discourse and that of the nineteenth-century colonial reformers, especially when it comes to the position of women. Biggar may be unaware of the vast corpus of scholarly literature on precisely this subject, but most serious human rights activists are not so ill-informed about the contributions of postcolonial feminism. To take an example directly relevant to this chapter, the connections between the nineteenth-century abolition of sati, its twentieth-century reincarnations, and its wider relevance for the status and treatment of women in India has been the subject of extensive study by scholars in South Asia and beyond. Among the many issues they explore is the relationship between colonial debates about sati and its postcolonial manifestations, and particularly how Indian feminists can challenge patriarchal oppression without reproducing unhelpful colonial tropes and stereotypes. A first step towards this, as Lata Mani, Ania Loomba, and Vasudha Dalmia, among others, have shown, is to understand the complexity of the colonial debate itself.[26] To do this, we need to move beyond simplistic depictions of British horror at sati as an indicator of western moral superiority and its abolition as an emblem of British colonial benevolence. Instead, we need to consider the range of British responses to sati, question why they chose to intervene on this issue when they did, and explore how effectively they enacted this intervention once it was passed.

Burning issues: the British debate on sati

The question of sati became a major political and moral issue in both Britain and India in the early nineteenth century. As Bayly notes, the EIC state dedicated thousands of pages of correspondence to it, while in Britain missionaries and other evangelical groups petitioned Parliament for its abolition. As noted previously, sati became a highly emotive issue in the early nineteenth century in ways that contrast sharply with the muted response to other more devastating forms of mortality in India.[27] The salient question then is not whether historians of empire should view the prohibition of sati as a 'good thing' but rather why the issue of sati and its prohibition has been so elevated in the discourse. The first point to make is that British observers did not immediately intervene to prevent sati when it came within their power to do so. The EIC was granted the Diwani of Bengal in 1765 and expanded its territorial and political control in the region over nearly a century thereafter. It took them more than forty years to start debating sati and a further twenty-five before they finally prohibited the rite in their territories in 1829. The EIC thus spent two-thirds of their time in power in India tolerating sati and almost as long debating whether to prohibit it as they did presiding over its abolition. Nor was the unequivocal condemnation of sati that predominated in the 1820s the only, or even the normative British response to the rite. Accounts and depictions in the eighteenth century, though lamenting the cruelty of the custom, often also found space for admiration of the widow's bravery and conjugal devotion. 'Why should I think this woman has done wrong?', footman John MacDonald remarked of a sati he witnessed in 1771. 'She has done this to obtain heaven and God's favour; and have not the greatest and most learned men in England and other Christian countries done the same, who had the Bible to direct them?'[28] Likewise, John Zephaniah Holwell, writing in 1767, maintained that if sati was viewed 'without prejudice, and without keeping always in sight our own tenets and customs', then the impartial observer would have to 'confess they act upon heroic, as well as rational and pious principles'.[29] Late eighteenth-century paintings reflect this tendency to see the virtuous elements of the sacrifice, with works by Tilly Kettle and John Zoffany portraying a heroic image of the sati that contrasted sharply with later nineteenth-century depictions. While there was still plenty of scope for criticism and condemnation in eighteenth-century British accounts, abhorrence was not an automatic response that intrinsically separated British colonisers from their Hindu subjects but rather one that emerged out of shifting political imperatives and reflected changing social-cultural norms across the period. I have written extensively elsewhere about how changing British attitudes to issues such as suicide, mental health, gender relations, and public spectacles of pain contributed to reshaping European responses to sati, as well as on how the rise of liberalism and evangelicalism more generally underpinned new frameworks for interpreting the custom in the early nineteenth century.[30] For now, it is enough to note that the implication drawn from the Napier story—that the British saw what they deemed to be an obvious and intrinsic wrong, and acted decisively to prevent it—does not match the reality of their often ambivalent relationship with sati over more than seventy years between their accession to political authority in Bengal and their eventual prohibition of the rite in 1829, or the implementation of that prohibition in the decades thereafter.

The EIC first started seriously debating what to do about sati in 1805, when the Acting Magistrate for Bihar placed the matter before the Nizamat Adalat (the branch of the High Court in Calcutta with revisionary powers over criminal matters) in the wake of the intended immolation of a twelve-year-old widow in Gaya. At the request of the girl's friends, the local *daroga* (head policeman) was sent to the site 'to ascertain if it was voluntary on the part of the girl and at the same time to endeavour to dissuade her from being guilty of such a rash act'. When he arrived, he found an intoxicated child being pressured into mounting the pyre by her in-laws amid a large crowd. As a result, the magistrate decided to prevent the immolation, even though there were no specific rules against the performance of sati at that time. 'I am since given to understand that the girl and her friends are extremely grateful for my interposition', he informed the Secretary of Government, but he also asked that the matter be put before the Governor General and that orders be given for the guidance of colonial officials, 'as the prejudices of the natives may be affected by the interference on the part of a magistrate'.[31] In this example, then, it is the girl's friends who instigate her rescue and an Indian police officer who carries it out. The British magistrate, while giving the order to prevent the immolation, is concerned that his actions will be censured by his British superiors as an unwarranted interference in local religious custom given the EIC's stated position on socio-religious issues 'to consult the religious opinions, customs and prejudices of the natives in all cases in which it has been practi-

SATI AND 'CIVILISING MISSION' IN COLONIAL INDIA

cable, consistently with the principles of morality, reason and humanity'.[32] While the case described above would clearly seem inconsistent with the latter principles, the magistrate's question prompted not a decisive response but a long drawn out debate. Instead of ruling on the matter, the Governor General put it before the Nizamat Adalat, asking them to determine how far 'this unnatural and inhuman custom' was grounded in religion, whether it could gradually be abolished, and if not what measures could be adopted to prevent abuses such as drugging or coercing women into the sacrifice and to 'rescue from destruction such females as, from immaturity of years or other circumstances, cannot be considered capable of judging for themselves, in a case of so serious and awful a nature'.[33]

Despite this early foray into the question of how to deal with sati in their territories, no further action was taken by the EIC until 1812, when the Nizamat Adalat was once again asked to investigate the matter. The result was the first formal policy on sati in 1813, when the EIC decided not to abolish but to regulate the practice. The regulations of 1813 stated that a government official must be present at all potential immolations, that detailed records of the number of widow-burnings must be kept, and that only those that conformed to certain principles should be allowed to proceed. Criteria for a 'legal' sati included that the widow be over sixteen years of age, be childless (or at least have made suitable arrangements for the future care of any infants), be of an appropriate caste, and—importantly—be acting of her own volition and not under the influence of any intoxicants.[34] This was intended to ensure that only immolations that conformed to Hindu religious scriptures took place, thus allowing the EIC to maintain its stated policy of religious non-intervention. Mani has referred to the process of differentiating between 'legal' and 'illegal' sati on scriptural grounds as a 'textualization of tradition', as EIC officials gave precedence to certain written forms of religious authority over local custom in framing their legislation.[35] In practice, these rules were unevenly enforced and prosecutions were rare, however, as local religious belief was claimed in mitigation of even obviously non-compliant immolations. Moreover, far from curtailing the custom, the number of recorded widow-burnings increased dramatically in the wake of these measures. Whether this was the result of better record keeping, the sense that sati was legitimised and authorised by the official EIC presence, or because the custom had, as Ashis Nandy suggests, become a vehicle for Indian self-assertion against a colonial state that was increasingly encroaching on socio-religious issues, is unclear.[36] What is apparent from the detailed records kept by the colonial state is that between 1813 and 1829 British colonial officials were more likely to watch and record an immolation taking place than they were to intervene to prevent it, or to punish the perpetrators afterwards. Meanwhile, they continued to debate whether prohibition of sati was feasible, or even desirable in the context of their stated commitment to non-intervention in religious matters and their vested interest in maintaining the support of key groups, and especially the loyalty of the sepoys of the EIC army.

If the colonial state found itself in a quandary about how to square its distaste for sati with its desire to avoid unnecessary (and unprofitable) agitation of the population, other sections of British society were becoming more decided on the matter. The emerging missionary movement saw sati as an indicator of Hindu religious degeneracy and used sensationalised and exaggerated accounts of the rite's prevalence to mobilise British public support for proselytisation and conversion. Baptist missionary William Carey discussed sati in detail in a letter from Serampore in 1793. This was published in the *Periodic Accounts of the Baptist Missionary Society* in 1800, and accounts of sati became a staple of missionary publications thereafter. Although the movement would grow in popularity, it is worth noting that at the turn of the nineteenth century missionaries did not represent mainstream opinion either in Britain or India. EIC officials viewed them with suspicion, concerned that their proselytising would cause unrest and discontent among the Hindu population. Back at home, Enlightenment ideas of religious toleration precluded interfering with the belief systems of others. Charles James Fox believed that 'all systems of proselytisation are wrong in themselves', while Sydney Smith famously referred to missionaries as 'little detachments of maniacs' in *The Edinburgh Review* in 1806.[37] It was not until 1813 that the missionary movement garnered sufficient mainstream support to see 'the Pious Clause' inserted in the EIC Charter, and not until the late 1820s and the tenure of Governor General Lord William Bentinck that evangelical sentiment started to have a noticeable influence on EIC policy. As late as the 1820s, some British colonial officials still objected to the prohibition of sati on the grounds that it would be an infringement of the right to religious freedom. As E. A. Kendall put it in a letter to the *Asiatic Journal* in 1822, 'it is solely because the burning of widows has its foundation, whether erroneously or not, in the religion of the country, that the British laws do not and ought not to interfere'.[38] For Kendall and others like him, this was a matter of principle, and religious toleration should not be dependent on British approbation for the customs tolerated. The prominence of the anti-sati campaign conducted in evangelical circles in the 1820s has tended to overshadow other more equivocal or ambivalent engagements with the rite in the early nineteenth century, but taking their vitriolic criticism of the custom as reflective of a shared British national response would be an over-simplification of a complex debate.

Far from acting decisively to prevent sati, the EIC prevaricated on the issue for nearly a quarter of a century between 1805 and 1829. Criticism of the EIC's failure to prevent sati in the 1810s and 1820s is reflected in artwork of the time. Thomas Rowlandson's satirical cartoon, 'The Burning System', published in 1815, suggests financial incentives for non-interference, depicting British political and religious leaders standing aside as an immolation takes place, while Brahmins surreptitiously press sacks of rupees into their hands. Rowlandson's satire suggests both personal corruption and the bigger collective moral failing of an organisation that prioritised its profits over potentially disruptive socio-religious reform. The frontispiece of Baptist missionary James Peggs' influential work *India Cries to British Humanity* (1830) makes a similar point, depicting British men—recognisable by their bowler hats and tailcoats—turning their faces away from the funeral pyre as the sati burns. While the composition of the image suggests British horror at the custom, the covered faces of the European men also imply turning a blind eye, a criticism of the EIC's failure to intervene decisively to prevent the burnings. Meanwhile, Indian progressives such as Raja Rammohan Roy had taken up the issue, and there was growing support for prohibition in reformist circles. The debate over abolition that took place in the 1820s saw a division not between Britons and Indians but rather between British and Indian progressives and reformers on one side and non-interventionist EIC officials and more orthodox Hindus on the other. When prohibition finally came, two petitions against the regulation were presented to Bentinck from the orthodox community, with just over 1,000 signatures between them, but there were also letters of thanks supporting the prohibition, organised by Roy and his friends, that carry upwards of 300 signatures. In Calcutta, agitation was pursued along constitutional lines, and an organisation—the Dharma Sabha—was formed to 'protect Hindu religion' and raise money for an ultimately unsuccessful appeal to the Privy Council in 1832. The orthodox newspaper *Samachar Chandrika* warned in 1832 that the Hindus 'are now rebelling in

SATI AND 'CIVILISING MISSION' IN COLONIAL INDIA

heart because of the injury done to their religion', but the anticipated public backlash failed to materialise.[39] The government of India stopped keeping formal records of sati cases after abolition, so it is difficult to say with certainty how successful the prohibition was, but it seems to have been effective in the areas into which it penetrated. This did not amount to the whole of the subcontinent, however, as the prohibition only related to areas directly governed by the EIC. In the semi-independent Princely States (which until 1843 included Sindh), sati continued to be legal for decades after 1829.

'Give the axe of justice such a sweep': Napier and the pacification of Sindh

To fully understand the implications of Napier's reported pronouncement on sati, we must turn our attention to the situation in Sindh, as well as to the wider British policy towards sati in the semi-independent Princely States. General Sir Charles James Napier was born in 1782 and in 1839 was made Commander of Sindh, an area then in the north-west of India (now in Pakistan) directly above the Rann of Kutch and Gujarat. In 1843, using the pretext that local resistance needed to be crushed, Napier invaded the territory and incorporated it into British India. 'We have no right to seize Sind,' Napier himself admitted on first being posted there, 'yet we shall do so and a very advantageous, humane, and useful piece of rascality it will be.'[40] It certainly proved a most lucrative venture for Napier, who received £70,000 as his share of the spoils and was knighted in recognition of his victory.[41] The conquest of Sindh was controversial even at the time, however. Beyond the clever wordplay, the satirical power of 'Peccavi' relies on the fact that the double-meaning—'I have sinned'—would have resonated with sections of the British public who were already questioning the conquest's morality. The

British press at the time described events in Sindh as 'infamous' and 'harsh and barbarous', while former Governor General Lord Elphinstone commented that coming after the EIC's defeat in Afghanistan, the conquest of Sindh 'puts one in mind of a bully who had been kicked in the street and went home to beat his wife in revenge'.[42] Indeed, the backlash over Sindh was such that the British government produced 'Blue Books' to defend the process of annexation. These compilations were supposed to alleviate controversy by putting official correspondence in the public domain, but as Sarah Ansari has demonstrated, in the case of the Sind Blue Books this evidence was first 'laundered' to paint a more positive picture of events.[43]

Anxiety about events in Sindh related to both how the conquest came about—by imposing impossible terms on the Balochi amirs and then annexing the area on the pretext of suppressing resistance when they refused to comply—and the brutality with which the region was subsequently pacified. Military historian Byron Farwell reports that the British lost about 270 men at the pivotal Battle of Miani, while their Balochi opponents lost an estimated 6,000. After the battle, most of the local amirs had little choice but to surrender. 'Come here instantly', Napier reportedly told one local ruler. 'Come alone and make your submission, or I will in a week tear you from the midst of your tribe and hang you.'[44] Napier, by his own admission, was not averse to using violence to achieve results: 'The best way to quiet a country is a good thrashing, followed by great kindness afterwards', he is reported to have said. 'Even the wildest chaps are thus tamed. The human mind is never better disposed to gratitude and attachment than when softened by fear.'[45] The following account gives an idea of the way in which colonial violence was deployed to pacify the newly conquered region, as Napier and his men set about bringing the local Balochi clans under British rule:

SATI AND 'CIVILISING MISSION' IN COLONIAL INDIA

Death however he inflicted only for murder, a restriction which did not prevent his rule being at first more stern and life-taking than comported with his natural benevolence; giving him constant care and anxiety, which combined with other vexations affected his health. For the habits of the Beloochee race had been so barbarous, their customs so ferocious, and the worst examples of cruelty and all odious vices had been so constantly given by the ameers, that a general depravity of feeling prevailed and could only be corrected by fear.[46]

The extract is taken from *History of General Sir Charles Napier's Administration of Scinde*, which was written by Sir William F. P. Napier and published in 1851 with the specific intention of defending his brother Charles's reputation. Yet even in this deliberately sympathetic account, it is impossible to escape the implication of judicial violence being used for political ends. By his brother's admission, Napier was meting out capital punishment at such a rate that it made him ill, declared himself as 'resolute to hang as they were to murder', and believed that the gallows should eventually 'overbalance Mahomet' in shaping the attitudes of the people he had been sent to subdue.[47] It is, however, the way in which this excess of judicial violence was justified that is of most relevance to the current discussion. The prevalence of female infanticide, violence towards women, and domestic slavery were all emphasised in this account, implying that the excessive use of capital punishment was motivated solely by the desire to suppress these customs rather than being designed to bring about the political submission of the recently dispossessed Balochi leaders. While some of the abuses listed certainly had a basis in local reality, the sensationalised account of gendered violence as a specifically Balochi vice also served an important discursive purpose. The way in which the annexation of Sindh had effectively been 'engineered' was considered controversial and morally dubious even at the time, and there was considerable public sympathy for the deposed amirs.[48] An emphasis on the Balochi debauchery and the mistreatment of women in their society offered a way to reassert British moral superiority in the wake of a violent and immoral annexation. It would, however, be stretching credibility to suggest that improving Balochi gender relations was the main motivation for the opportunistic land grab, or the only reason Napier felt it necessary to mete out the 'sternest repression'.

When considered in this context, Napier's famous pronouncement on sati offers a more problematic example of British imperial masculinity and 'civilising mission' in action. The earliest source we have for Napier's supposed intervention in sati is the account in *History of General Sir Charles Napier's Administration of Scinde*, which as we have already seen was far from neutral in its objectives. This text states explicitly that Napier's comments were made in direct response to 'hearing of an intended burning', suggesting that his decisive action prevented a specific sati case. A later telling in William Napier Bruce's *Life of General Sir Charles Napier* (1885), however, suggests that the comments were made not in response to an imminent immolation but in response to complaints about his plans to suppress the custom more generally.[49] Given the prominence of the 'rescue fantasy' in British accounts of sati—what Gayatri Spivak has referred to as the trope of 'white men saving brown women from brown men'—the difference between the two versions of the story is significant.[50] Sati was not a universal custom across India and was primarily practised in Bengal (where it was outlawed in 1829) and in the Princely States of what is now Rajasthan, where it continued to be legal in some states well into the 1850s, though primarily as an elite practice associated with royal households. Though not unknown outside those two areas, it was extremely rare in other parts of India and was almost unheard of in the Muslim-dominated region of Sindh. In fact, having been through all the

SATI AND 'CIVILISING MISSION' IN COLONIAL INDIA

EIC Foreign Department records on sati in the Princely States (among which Sindh would have been included until 1843), I have not found any examples of sati cases being reported there. Thus, although both accounts imply that the suppression of sati in Sindh was Napier's personal initiative, the emphasis is very different. In the original, Napier is framed as an imperial hero intervening to save a widow at the point of immolation. In the other, it is a hypothetical intervention, which while discursively interesting is unlikely to have had a significant impact on women's lived experiences given the rarity of sati in Sindh. Moreover, with the incorporation of the region into British India, the 1829 prohibition would have automatically come into force there regardless of Napier's personal intervention.

Prosecuting sati in British India

As noted earlier, the EIC stopped keeping detailed records of sati cases after its prohibition in 1829, so it is difficult to glean concrete information about how suppression was handled in the years immediately after this. The index to the Board's Collection of East India Company Records at the British Library contains intermittent references to illegal sati cases in the years after 1829, but unfortunately the accompanying collections of documents to which they relate have largely been destroyed, making it hard to track the implementation of the prohibition or the punishments meted out for its infringement in the decades between 1820 and 1858. To find out more about how the colonial state implemented the prohibition of sati in Bengal, we need to turn to the Home Department Records of the Government of India, held in the National Archives of India in Delhi, which contain a record of sati cases that were prosecuted under various sections of the Indian Penal Code after 1860. While it is unlikely that these records contain comprehensive accounts of all the illegal sati cases that took place between the institution of Crown governance in 1858 and independence in 1947, they do give us a significant body of archival material on sati cases and their handling in the late nineteenth and early twentieth centuries.

The first thing to note in relation to the prosecution of illegal sati cases is that despite Napier's much vaunted threat of capital punishment, there is not a single example of the death penalty being awarded in relation to a sati. The most severe penalty I have been able to find was a sentence of transportation for life, awarded to a Brahmin named Sitaram in 1870 for officiating at the sati of his daughter-in-law. Other active participants, who included family members and local Brahmins, were sentenced to between five and ten years' hard labour, with 'all the rents and profits of their land, where they own land' being forfeited to the government during the period of their transportation and imprisonment.[51] A local *lambadar* (a powerful local estate-holder) who had reportedly 'entered the widow's house to ascertain whether she really intended suttee' and forced her to 'prove her determination' by drinking boiling milk and burning her little finger in a lighted *chirag* was not prosecuted. Nor were several other *lambadars* who were aware of the intended sati and refused to assist the local policeman in preventing the rite. 'The sentences appear to have been very severe,' the Commissioner of the Sitapur Division remarked on reviewing the case, 'but I suppose it is necessary.'[52] The severity of the punishments on this occasion seem to have been outliers, however, and sentences for involvement in a sati—where the accused were prosecuted at all—were more likely to be in the region of two to five years' hard labour.

Unevenness in the penalties applied for sati reflected differences in the circumstances attending each case, and some slippage in official attitudes to whether sati was best understood as suicide or murder. Reporting on a sati in Gaya in 1903, the local District Superintendent of Police, J. D. Berrington, reflected on

SATI AND 'CIVILISING MISSION' IN COLONIAL INDIA

the procedural difficulties in securing sati prosecutions, noting that in sati cases there were usually two offences committed, one under section 302 of the Indian Penal Code (culpable homicide) and one under section 306 of the Indian Penal Code (abetment of suicide). 'The former relates to those persons who actually placed fire, or in any way helped while the woman was still alive, and the latter to those persons who made no attempt to stop the woman burning on the funeral pyre.' In the case to which Berrington refers, twenty-one people were initially accused, of whom sixteen went to trial and seven were convicted under section 306 of the Indian Penal Code and sentenced to three years' hard labour.[53] On appeal, the High Court upheld the sentence, 'which they did not consider a heavy one', but altered the section under which the accused were convicted from 306 (abetment of suicide) to section 304 of the Indian Penal Code (culpable homicide not amounting to murder).[54]

The change in section under which the accused were prosecuted in the case above is indicative of a wider problem in determining who was culpable for sati. While Napier may have been confident that he would know whom to hang in the aftermath of an immolation, where due process of law was applied things were rarely so clear-cut. Even leaving aside the contentious issue of female agency in sati (of which more shortly), the question of who should be prosecuted for an immolation in which a whole village could potentially be considered complicit was a complex one. As Berrington noted of the sati in Gaya in 1903,

> it is extremely hard to decide who to send up under section 306 of the Indian Penal Code. In this case there is no doubt that the whole village was present, that there was tremendous excitement and that no attempt was made to prevent the woman from becoming a sati, it must be remembered that the village is a Hindu village and that the fact of a sati having occurred makes the village both holy and famous for ever after.[55]

Prosecutions often faltered when villages closed ranks to hamper investigations, and disparity between the legal status of sati and the popular sense of the merit it bestowed created local tensions. 'It is reported that the sympathy of the whole community is with the sutti [sic]', the Commissioner of Patna reported of a sati in his district that took place before an estimated crowd of 2,000 in October 1904, 'and that no one is willing to give evidence against the accused.'[56] Nor was there clarity about how far efforts to prevent a sati on the part of individuals could be expected, or how far inaction amounted to complicity. Of the local police officer in the Gaya case, Berrington commented:

> [T]here is no doubt that his position was a difficult one. He is Muhammadan and as he said to me that if he had actually tried to stop the sati by force, he would have been killed. This is perfectly true and though theoretically he should have sacrificed himself rather than let the woman be burnt, this is more than can be expected.[57]

Thus, while it could sometimes be proved that the accused were present, determining who was directly involved and gathering the evidence necessary to prove guilt beyond reasonable doubt was more problematic.

Legal distinctions in the law between culpable homicide and abetment of suicide—and their respective punishments—help to explain striking similarities between the narrative of events that emerge after illegal sati cases. While these narratives also reflect the influence of 'traditional' ideals of sati as a self-determined and sometimes even miraculous sacrifice, they also demonstrate an understanding of the legal implications of the widow's volition.[58] The widow's unilateral decision and insurmountable determination to perform sati were frequently invoked as a defence in sati cases and were often accepted as indicating 'a pure case of sati' (as opposed, presumably, to one where the widow was subject to foul play).[59] While early nineteenth-century debates had ques-

SATI AND 'CIVILISING MISSION' IN COLONIAL INDIA

tioned whether the widow could ever really be considered a 'free agent' in sati, prosecutions in the early twentieth century usually assumed she was acting of her own volition, unless coercion could actively be proved. As a result, many prosecutions centred not on discovering which men were complicit in her murder as Napier implies, but rather on whether the onlookers could reasonably have been expected to prevent her suicide. In extreme cases, this could even result in the prosecution of widows who survived sati, as under the Indian Penal Code she could be liable to up to one year's simple imprisonment for attempted suicide. Such was the case in the Hazaribagh district in 1930, when a widow was sentenced to three months' simple imprisonment because she 'deliberately attempted to destroy herself by ascending the lighted pyre and staying there until her clothes caught fire and her body was scorched'.[60] Of the male accused in this case, seven were convicted of abetment and sentenced to six months' simple imprisonment on the grounds 'they assisted the woman in making the necessary preliminaries to the act of sati and made no attempt to stop her climbing onto the pyre'.[61] Thus while discourses of empire as civilising mission tend to present sati as a barbaric act perpetrated against an unwilling victim, in practice the colonial state's problematic willingness to accept female volition as a mitigating factor frequently hampered decisive action to punish sati cases as culpable homicide.

Conclusion

'Sati must be one of those things that look quite different from different viewpoints', former Deputy General of Police R. J. Hirst remarked of a controversial sati case that took place in Barh, Bihar, in 1927. 'If we cannot see it from the orthodox Hindu's side, we cannot know what aspect it shows to him. Nor can we expect to persuade him that our view of it is clearer or truer than his.'[62] Hirst's comments are not well known and rarely appear in popular defences of empire, though they are arguably based on a more direct personal experience of policing sati than Napier's famous remarks. It would, of course, be misleading to suggest that Hirst's attitude epitomises British responses to sati any more than Napier's does. Hirst's comments do not prove that cultural relativism was a defining feature of British colonialism any more than Napier's remarks prove its moral certitude. Juxtaposing the two does give us some sense of the complexity of the British response to sati, however, and reminds us of the challenges involved when selecting and evaluating historical evidence. As the preceding exploration of the British encounter with sati over 200 years has hopefully illustrated, the reality of colonial social reform was uneven, ambiguous, and problematic, and it was rarely completely separable from the more coercive aspects of empire. Thus while Napier's remarks may be impactful in making certain political points today, they do not help us to understand the complex history of the British encounter with sati in any meaningful way. Rather, they function as a warning about the dangers of taking such anecdotes out of their historical context and extrapolating sweeping value judgements from limited or problematic source material; doing so only obscures our understanding of the complex ways empire functioned and was experienced in practice.

5

'UNENCUMBERED BY THE SCRUPLES OF JUSTICE AND GOOD FAITH'

THE COLONIAL ACHIEVEMENTS OF RAFFLES IN SOUTHEAST ASIA

Gareth Knapman

In *Colonialism: A Moral Reckoning*, Nigel Biggar uses the British Empire as a case study to 'understand and reflect on the ethical terms in which empires have been viewed historically'.[1] One of the examples Biggar uses to portray the positive agency of the British Empire is the figure of Sir Thomas Stamford Raffles, Lieutenant Governor of Java (1811–14) and Bencoolen (1818–24), and finally founder of Singapore (1819–23). Biggar declares that Raffles

> established an EIC [East India Company] trading post at Singapore in 1819. Raffles so appreciated the value and beauty of Java's indigenous culture and its pre-Islamic Hindu heritage that he sought to

recover it from oblivion by collecting antiquities and by writing *The History of Java* (1817). In 1823 he founded the Singapore Institution, partly to enable the company's employees to learn the native languages. This still flourishes—renamed in 1868 as the 'Raffles Institution'—in the form of a secondary school that gained the highest number of admissions to the University of Cambridge in 2019.[2]

Raffles' orientalist scholarship was an example for Biggar of how historians over the last fifty years have unjustly critiqued the British Empire as morally bankrupt and racist. The intellectual assault on the memory of the British Empire Biggar blames on 'academic "post-colonialists", whose bible is Edward Said's *Orientalism* (1978)'. Biggar's critique, however, was that Said's *Orientalism* was a 'post-colonial caricature of Western attempts to understand eastern cultures as exercises in imperial control that violate their subject'.[3] To support his argument that Said had produced a caricature of British colonialism, Biggar relies on a long quote from historian David Gilmour's observation that orientalists were scholars 'who had no colonialist agenda of their own, men motivated by pure curiosity and a desire to learn'.[4] Although that was the case for some 'orientalists', Raffles' scholarship was interconnected with colonial administration, justifications for colonial expansion and self-promotion.

Biggar uses Raffles to illustrate how colonial officials pursued policies of anti-slavery and freedom of labour. One of Biggar's key arguments is that '[f]or the second half of its life, anti-slavery, not slavery, was at the heart of imperial policy'.[5] Raffles therefore becomes an illustration of that commitment, with Biggar writing:

> Shortly after the Slave Trade Act was passed in 1807, in the person of Sir Stamford Raffles it summarily abolished the importation of slaves and slavery itself on the island of Penang. Subsequently, Raffles banned slave importation in Java, and in 1818–19 he emancipated the slaves in Bencoolen and established a school for their children.[6]

THE COLONIAL ACHIEVEMENTS OF RAFFLES

The above portrayal constitutes Raffles as a benign orientalist colonial administrator who pursued information on the peoples of Southeast Asia as a result of a benevolent enquiring mind. He did introduce ideas that we can label liberal policies of reform, such as individual rights to property, anti-slavery and free trade. Together, they are often presented as the humanitarian aim of empire.

The problem with using Raffles is that he was, in today's political terminology, a 'hollow man'. He appealed to superiors, blamed subordinates when things went wrong, had few consistent beliefs and generally reneged on any agreement he made. His administration was an illustration of colonial corruption, disobeying orders and deliberately misinforming or lying in his despatches, as well as being duplicitous to all the native states he had dealings with. Raffles' despatches and sanctioned histories present an image of a seamless reformist government. It is only through cross-checking his writings, his fellow officers, despatches and treaties with Javanese and Malay princes that the venal corrupt practices endemic to the brief British occupation of Java and, by extension, Singapore, become apparent.

Raffles was a career East India Company (hereafter Company) servant, who had some form of vision of an expansive British Empire in Southeast Asia supporting the China trade. In 1795, at the age of fourteen, he became a temporary clerk in East India House (the Company's London office) and was despatched to Prince of Wales Island (Penang) as Assistant Secretary in 1805. In 1810, he proposed a plan to Lord Minto (the Governor General of Bengal) in which Raffles would persuade Javanese and Malay states to ally with the British against the Franco-Dutch colonial regime in Java. Raffles became Minto's diplomatic agent in the Malay states.

In 1811, during the Napoleonic Wars, a British force defeated the Franco-Dutch colonial army in Java. As Governor General,

Minto made Raffles the Lieutenant Governor of Java. With the Peace of Vienna in 1815 that ended the Napoleonic Wars, Java was returned to the Netherlands. Raffles however had already been recalled in 1814 over concerns about his administration after the commander of British forces in Java, Major General Gillespie, had accused Raffles of corruption in 1813. Gillespie died before the inquiry was concluded, and consequently Raffles was exonerated for lack of information. Returning to England, Raffles published his account of Java to wide acclaim, and his fortunes recovered. After dedicating his book to the Prince Regent and gifting the Prince a collection of Kris (Southeast Asian swords) that Raffles had taken from the plunder of Yogyakarta, he received a knighthood and became the toast of London society. He was conferred in the position as Governor of Bencoolen, Sumatra (1818–24), an unremunerative backwater in the Company's Asian empire.

In 1818, Raffles tried to reinvigorate the idea of the British ascendance in Southeast Asia. Lord Hastings, the Governor General of Bengal, had rejected most of Raffles' schemes for colonial expansion in Sumatra but agreed with the idea of building a base in the Malacca Straits. After finding the Dutch had already occupied the Port of Riau, part of the Riau–Johor Sultanate, Raffles made a deal with the Temenggong, a renegade Riau–Johor official, who had fled with his followers to Singapore and had access to a claimant for the Sultanate. In 1819, Raffles established a Company settlement in Singapore and then proceeded to disempower the Malay rulers who had supported him in doing so. Raffles left the colony in 1823, by which time it was on the verge of civil war, with murders and political assassinations occurring daily.[7]

This essay explores the history of the British Empire in Southeast Asia through the career of Raffles, examining his diplomatic engagement with the Southeast Asian native states to whom he promised independence and his diplomatic duplicity

THE COLONIAL ACHIEVEMENTS OF RAFFLES

and contrived wars of occupation and plunder of native treasuries. The essay then examines the establishment of Singapore and the tension that Raffles created, which left the colony on the verge of collapse, before looking at his achievements as a colonial humanitarian in the areas of freedom of property, slavery and the promotion of free trade. Finally, it shows how Raffles has been portrayed as a figure of nostalgia divorced from the historical reality.

Raffles' promises of independence to the native states

In the leadup to the British invasion of Java, Raffles was engaged in facilitating the cooperation and assistance of native states to support the British against the Franco-Dutch forces in Southeast Asia. From December 1810 to June 1811, Raffles wrote to the Rajas for Riau–Lingga, Siak, Pontianak, Banjarmasin, Sambas, Jambi, Palembang, Cirebon, Banten, Bali, Madura, Sumenep, Surakarta and Mataram. From the surviving letters, most of the Rajas agreed either to support the British invasion or not to intervene.

In 1811, British government policy was to give Southeast Asian states independence after destroying the Dutch. The British government's Secret Committee—the overriding government body coordinating British and Company policy—authorised the invasion force to remove French power and then organise 'for the abandonment of Java' and 'hand the island over to the Javanese'.[8] Raffles' correspondence with the native states prior to invasion was consistent with this message that the British were not going to colonise Southeast Asia. In early 1811, Raffles wrote to the Susuhunan ('Emperor of Java'), giving hope that the British would be their liberators:

> Great Governor General of Bengal and of all India has heard with Concern of the Conduct of the Dutch on the Island of Java and of their having broken through and destroyed long established Customs

and the rights and dignity of your Majesty and that he is in consequence inclined to expel from the island of Java and from the Eastern Countries all the Dutch and French authority ... I now write this letter with the authority of the Governor General of Bengal to inform your illustrious Majesty that the English will not act as the Dutch have done.[9]

In Palembang, Sumatra, a Dutch commission of inquiry from the 1820s concluded that Raffles had promised independence to native states.[10] The surviving correspondence between Raffles and Sultan Ratu Mahmud Badaruddin in Palembang points to Raffles recognising the independence of Palembang. On 5 January 1811, Raffles' envoy, Tunku Radin Mahomet, promised the Sultan of Palembang that 'the English and Palembang, who are on friendly terms as are all rajas of dark complexion, straightforward and without any ulterior motive whatsoever' and went on to declare that Raffles 'does not intend to take the revenues of Palembang at all, but only for brotherly love and affectionate protection of the English dignity'.[11] In return, for this promise of 'straightforward brotherly love', Raffles' envoy conveyed a request from Raffles to 'expel' the Dutch.[12] Palembang was initially reluctant to get involved, writing to Raffles that 'we do not want, in any circumstances, to be involved in the feud between the Dutch and the English'.[13] The Raja went on to say he would only go to war in self-defence: '[I]f the Dutch were to become mean, in an instant we would act with force.' But he could not go to war 'without any reason'.[14] Raffles persisted, and the Raja responded by stating that with 'regard to the enemy of the English dignity, the Dutch in Palembang, to the best of our ability we shall expel them', but, keeping in mind the idea of a just war, the raja wrote 'in a manner that will not incur censure, blemish or curse among friends in the future'.[15]

Between January and May, Raffles continued to pressure Palembang to get rid of the Dutch and sent weapons to

THE COLONIAL ACHIEVEMENTS OF RAFFLES

Palembang to evict them.[16] At Raffles' urging, by 5 May 1811, Palembang devised a plan for a just war against the Dutch: '[W]e have now sent an emissary to Batavia requesting that the Dutch in Palembang be withdrawn with speed',[17] adding that '[i]f they are not withdrawn promptly they will inevitably be accursed'. The Sultan concluded that from that point 'we are not at fault in the matter'. The Sultan took the British at their word and attacked and killed all Dutch forces, including their families in Palembang. This slaughter would later be used by Raffles to justify the attack and removal of the Sultan of Palembang, for the sake of taking 'half of his treasure'.[18]

The actions of Minto and Raffles in Java and Sumatra prior to the invasion gave every indication to the native states that the British were equal allies and were planning on leaving after the destruction of the Franco-Dutch forces. On 3 September 1811, after defeating the French and Dutch forces, Minto informed the British government that he was going to disobey his original orders and make Java a permanent colony.[19] He reasoned that Java 'was a place of much greater consequence' and argued that if the British left it 'would have been inevitably followed by general massacre and ruin' of the island's European population.[20] Minto then made Raffles the Lieutenant Governor of Java.

Turning on allies: Raffles and colonial expansion

British colonial expansion in Southeast Asia is a story of regulations which aimed to prevent colonial expansion and the subsequent evasion of those regulations by colonial officials. Prize money from plundered treasuries was a major inducement for colonial expansion. The personal gain from prize money represented a major inducement for military commanders to advocate military action. It is not clear how much prize money Raffles was able to claim, but Colonel Gillespie, who commanded the British forces attacking Palembang and Yogyakarta, received a final allocation of £12,000 in prize money.[21] In 2022 values, Gillespie's share was the equivalent of £10,500,000.[22] After the attack on Yogyakarta, the *Batavia Government Gazette* joyfully reported the rewards the British troops would receive:

> We are happy to hear that the exertions of the gallant troops ... will be rewarded with the richest booty which has been shared of late years. The property captured at Jogyacarta amounts in silver coin to eight lacs of Spanish dollars, and the gold and jewels are valued at from eight to twelve lacs more making in all 4 or 500,000 pounds.[23]

When looking at the reason for colonial expansion, we need to read the protests of British innocence and justice present in the despatches against the personal wealth that these same commanders gained from looting Asian treasuries.

The India Act of 1784 made it unlawful for the Company to pursue wars of aggression. The Act stated 'it shall not be lawful for the said Governor General and Council of Bengal to invade, or enter with any armed force, or in any hostile or offensive manner, into the territory of any native, independent Prince or State'.[24] Not only did the Act outlaw aggressive wars, but the House of Commons actively attempted to enforce the non-aggression principle behind the India Act. In 1788, the former Governor of Bengal, Warren Hastings, had faced an impeachment trial for engaging in wars of aggression.[25] We can add to these regulations that Enlightenment political discourse was also opposed to colonial wars of aggression.[26] Consequently, the Company operated under legal conditions not too dissimilar to modern states under the post-1945 United Nations Charter. Despite these regulations and norms, the Company continued to expand.

Although aggressive war was unlawful, wars of self-defence were permissible. The India Act maintained that a war in self-defence was possible if 'intelligence' indicated that 'such Prince

THE COLONIAL ACHIEVEMENTS OF RAFFLES

or State is about to attack and make war upon, or actually making preparations to attack and make war upon the territories' of the Company.[27] The consequence was that colonial officials could launch a war of expansion if they developed a narrative confirming self-defence.

The need to demonstrate self-defence required colonial officials to produce curated narratives of events which demonstrated that their actions were just. These narratives were written and despatched to higher colonial authorities retrospectively. A condition of the authorisation of the occupation was that Raffles should transform Java into a commercially viable colony, if it was to be retained by the British.[28] The state of Mataram with its capital in Yogyakarta was a wealthy native state—the capture of its treasury would provide capital to support the fledgling colonial government as well as economically secure the pensions of colonial officers.

Raffles and his officers developed a carefully worded narrative for the destruction of both Palembang and Yogyakarta. In the official history, Major William Thorn wrote that Raffles used the Sultan of Palembang's 'plunder of their [Dutch] property and demolition of their fort' as the *casus belli* to legitimise the British seizure of the Sultan's *kraton* (palace) and treasury, because 'plunder of property' was 'contrary to the law of nations'.[29] Consequently, the Company's despatches are full of the horrors that Palembang unleashed on the 'civilised' Dutch, despite Raffles being complicit in requesting those actions by Palembang.

When Raffles' men arrived in Palembang on 14 November 1811 to take possession of the Dutch fort and Dutch trade monopoly, the Sultan was perplexed with his officials, telling the British: '[I]n compliance with the wish and upon the suggestion of Mr. Raffles to make a free port of Palembang, they had ... freed[?] themselves from their ties with the Dutch and expelled their Resident, razing the fort to the ground.' And that 'the

Sultan had complied [with Raffles' directions] and that they could not conceive any object still remaining for adjustment'.[30] Contrary to Raffles' previous assertions of opening Palembang for free trade, he actually wanted to secure all trade for the Company.

Palembang continued to demand that Raffles kept his word, telling the British 'there is here no place, the former Dutch Residence being completely removed from the ground where it stood. I must therefore beg to be excused upon that, not that I have any apprehension the English would ever become oppressors like the Dutch' and went on to call British soldiers pirates.[31] Palembang's refusal to yield was a deciding factor in Raffles' decision to attack it. Raffles was always of the belief that Palembang had a large treasury, and according to a history written for the Company Directors, 'the resolution which Mr Raffles had formed [was] of dethroning the sultan and exacting the disposal of the half of his treasure'.[32] Therefore, taking the Sultan's revenues—which Raffles had explicitly said the British would not do—was the reason for the attack on Palembang. By the time Raffles' army reached Palembang, the Sultan had disappeared into the jungle with the treasury, and the British found an empty palace.[33]

In making the case for an attack on Mataram and Yogyakarta, Raffles continued to maintain in his despatches that the Sultan, Hamengkubuwono II, was preparing for war, and that the British attack on Yogyakarta was in self-defence. The narrative relied on declaring Javanese actions as barbaric and presenting British actions as just.

British accounts maintain that tensions escalated soon after the signing of the 28 December 1811 treaty between Raffles and Hamengkubuwono, which according to Major Thorn (the Deputy Quarter-Master-General to the Forces in Java and first historian of the invasion) 'transferred' from the Sultan to the British 'the sole regulation of the duties and collection of tribute with the dominions of the Sultan, as well as the general administration of justice in the cases where the British interests might be concerned'.[34] The history written for the despatches, however, merely stated that the treaty 'bound [the Sultan] to fulfil all the Engagements contracted with the late Government'.[35] Thorn presented Hamengkubuwono as signing in bad faith so that he could 'violate his engagements, and to exercise the most savage tyranny'.[36]

The history in the despatches emphasises Hamengkubuwono's brutal execution of Javanese elites as the reason for war, with Raffles declaring they were 'protected' people.[37] The 28 December 1811 treaty, however, made no mention of protected persons, and Article 4 gave responsibility for policing and justice to the Sultan, with no controls over the Sultan's interpretation of justice.[38] Hamengkubuwono, who was responsible for police and justice, had every right under the terms of the treaty to exercise justice according to his own interpretation.

Using the argument of self-defence, Thorn's account of the lead-up to the conflict was full of emotive language with little detail of actual political events. He wrote that the Sultan had 'ambitious views of aggrandizement' and pursued a 'racial hatred' and that the 'European settlers extended along a coast of more than seven hundred miles ... looked to the British Government for protection.' After these emotive accusations followed by no detail, Thorn wrote 'the magnitude of the threatened danger, therefore, calling for immediate action, no procrastination could possibly be admitted'.[39]

On 19 March 1812, Raffles wrote in his dispatch that 'the powers of the Sultan of Mataram should be reduced',[40] followed by the reason for war being the Sultan's 'crimes and infractions of [the] treaty', with no reference to what those infractions were other than the execution of Javanese courtiers. These 'crimes and infractions' according to the British Resident of Yogyakarta John Crawfurd's rendition of Raffles' opinion, 'rendered him [the Sultan] altogether unfit to be further entrusted with an administration'.[41]

The account for the Directors stressed that Raffles was 'anxious to avoid the horrors of war'. This was for the benefit of the readers in London; however, Raffles offered no mechanism of conciliation. On 18 June, 'Raffles announced to the Sultan his arrival for the purpose of placing the hereditary Prince on the throne and gave him two hours to determine whether he would admit this arrangement quietly.' After no response in two hours, the British proceeded to bombard the Sultan's *kraton* for a day and a half. Raffles maintained the bombardment would facilitate peace because it was 'with the view of giving the Sultan an opportunity to negotiate', but he also noted it 'afford[ed] time for a considerable detachment under colonel MacLeod' to arrive and enable a successful British attack.[42]

At face value, Raffles' actions were procedural; however, his own words suggest that he preferred war. In February 1813, sensing colonial corruption, the editor of the *Examiner* newspaper in Britain included an implied rebuke: 'We should like much to know the reasons which led to the overthrow and Captivity of this Eastern Sovereign.'[43]

Twenty years after the attack, when most of the British officers who had participated were dead, Crawfurd provided a moment of reflection on British responsibility for the war. While giving evidence to the House of Lords, he declared that before he became Resident of Yogyakarta, the 'sultan of Java, had a fertile territory, and about a million and a half of subjects'.[44] He saw his time as Resident of Yogyakarta as a failure, with the culpability lying with the British: '[W]e exercised, during our possession of Java, the same kind of interference which we exercise in the administrations of' independent Indian states.'[45] This interference began 'after a quarrel with him [the Sultan of Mataram], which followed almost immediately on the conquest of the island, and which arose out of a desire to throw off the yoke of the European supremacy'. Crawfurd noted it 'terminated in hostilities' and that 'the same meddling, indeed, with the other native princes of Java, had, on previous occasions, produced exactly similar effects'.[46]

A Javanese account of the attack on Yogyakarta maintained that the British tricked the Sultan into war. The account is the *Babad Bĕdhah ing Ngayogyakarta*, a Javanese chronicle written by Pangeran Arya Panular (*c.*1772–1826), a prince of the Yogyakarta court.[47] In the scene after the fall of the *kraton*, Hamengkubuwono wonders 'why the British are doing this to me, for I have already submitted with all my army and I am prepared to follow whatever the Lieutenant-Governor wishes', and that 'it was Raffles himself who had reappointed me as Yogya ruler [six months earlier in December 1811]'.[48] The Javanese narrative depicts Hamengkubuwono as a loyal colonial partner of the British whom Raffles tricked into conflict as a pretext to plunder the treasury.

The retrospective British accounts show that Raffles barely followed British legal procedures for declaring war on Hamengkubuwono. The British accounts rely on stereotypes of a despotic sultan who did not follow British systems of justice—despite the British never insisting on those systems in their treaties with the Javanese. The careful narrative of events written by Raffles suggested he was knowingly making a case for the legitimacy of his actions to circumvent the clauses in the India Act of 1784. Raffles' manufacturing of pretexts along with the fact that the original invasion was meant to hand power back to Pakubuwono IV and Hamengkubuwono II meant that even within the conventions of the time, Raffles was following a course of action of questionable legitimacy.

Raffles turned on his previous allies despite promising that British rule would give them their independence. As a diplomat,

Raffles' words were meaningless. He did not honour any of the treaties he signed. Despite the questionable legitimacy of his action, Raffles had to report to Minto. Minto, who had been a judge in his earlier career and who had already disobeyed orders from London by keeping Java as a European colony rather than 'hand the island over to the Javanese', brushed the probity of Raffles' actions aside. He complimented Raffles, writing 'the superiority of European power was exerted, unencumbered by the scruples of justice and good faith'.[49]

Founding and then leaving Singapore on the verge of civil war

Modern Singapore originated as a deal between Sultan Hussein, the Temenggong and the Company, represented by Thomas Stamford Raffles and William Farquhar. The deal vested sovereignty with the Malays and gave management of the Malays to the Sultan and the Temenggong and the management of the Europeans to the British. Raffles left the colony in 1823 in a state of open hostility and on the verge of civil war. The conflict was resolved by Raffles' replacement, Crawfurd, who negotiated to purchase sovereignty from the Malay rulers.

The treaty between the Company and Sultan Hussein and the Temenggong of 6 February 1819 only enabled the British to establish a commercial factory with an annual land rent that the Company paid to Sultan Hussein, and the treaty's wording made it clear that sovereignty continued to rest with the Malay aristocracy, with the Company creating a factory and paying annual land rent of $5,000 Spanish dollars for the privilege, as well as explicitly stating that the Company is 'to be considered in no way bound to interfere with the internal politics of his [the Sultan's] States, or engaged to assert or maintain the authority of His Highness by force of arms'.[50]

Farquhar abided by the spirit of the treaty and worked with the Malay rulers in governing and developing the colony, but

THE COLONIAL ACHIEVEMENTS OF RAFFLES

Raffles was not happy with the situation. Raffles castigated Farquhar for enabling the continuous Indigenous sovereignty of the Island, calling Farquhar's approach an 'extraordinary principle' and that Farquhar 'maintained ... in opposition to my authority, that the disposal of the land was vested in the native chiefs, that the government of the country was native and the port a native port'.[51] Despite Raffles' desire to remove any vestige of Indigenous sovereignty, the original arrangement set out in the 1819 treaty gave Farquhar little option. Raffles took control of the colony from Farquhar and used administrative regulations and town planning to increase the size of the settlement and reduce the power of the Malays. The consequence was an outbreak of violence between different ethnic factions, with the colonial forces outnumbered and powerless to stop the events occurring all around them.

The Company archive provides glowing accounts of the colony's growth but with very little reference to the violence that was rife in the colony. Abdullah bin Abdul Kadir, the Malay translator who worked for Farquhar, Raffles and later Crawfurd, painted a picture of a very violent settlement. Abdullah outlined a number of different types of violence. It was divided between two distinct groups—the original inhabitants who were the Temenggong's followers, and the new settlers:

> All the inhabitants were dismayed by frequent incidents, houses catching fire, robberies taking place in the high noon, people getting stabbed. When morning came people would be found stabbed and wounded to death. The Temenggong's men, the Sultan's men and the foreigners of all races went about fully armed; some of them robbed people in broad daylight, some broke into houses and stole people's property, for they were afraid of nothing.[52]

Abdullah emphasises the impotence of the colonial forces, writing that 'the number of white men was not yet large' and that the 'Indian troops had not come and there were only four or five policemen'.[53] Abdullah's account is reaffirmed by a Dutch observer, Baron Huibert Gerard Nahuys van Burgst, who also saw the British as powerless observers when it came to resolving the tensions in the settlement and there was an expectation of war:

> Many of the residents are not without anxiety that a man like the Malayan Tommagung, tempted by the large treasure, could easily be induced with the underlings and a great many of his friends the pirates, to attack the weak garrison and citizens unexpectedly and then clear off with his booty to places where he could not easily be traced.[54]

Crawfurd described the violence as politically motivated 'assassinations' 'committed by the followers of the native chiefs, who claimed exemption from our jurisdiction'.[55] As the man in charge, Raffles was to blame for creating the situation. War was only averted because his successor bought Singapore from the Malays, a simple solution that Raffles could also have achieved but never bothered.

Raffles as a humanitarian hero

Despite Raffles' contrived wars of expansion, he has continually been upheld as an example of colonial humanitarianism. Raffles' self-promotion is the source of this initial interpretation. The dedication to the Prince Regent in his book *History of Java* declared that colonialism was a humanitarian duty. The purpose of the empire, Raffles lectured, was 'to uphold the weak, to put down lawless force, to lighten the chain of the slave, to sustain the honour of the British arms and British good faith'.[56] He argued that the Malayan nation had 'degenerated' and proposed that the British Empire should revive it through colonisation:

> [H]ad Java remained permanently annexed to the British crown, the redress of these evils would have been, in a great measure, in the power of the English nation: the undertaking would have been worth

THE COLONIAL ACHIEVEMENTS OF RAFFLES

of their general character, and there was no other nation that could have possessed the means in an equal degree, even if it had indeed possessed the inclination.[57]

Colonialism through humanitarianism continued, with later writers looking to Raffles' words as an inspiration. James Brooke—whom Joseph Conrad would reinterpret as Lord Jim—created a private empire in Sarawak and saw himself as following in Raffles' footsteps.[58] Raffles' wife, Lady Sophia Raffles, created the beginning of colonial nostalgia of Raffles as a benign imperialist concerned with the rights of others. We see three ideas presented as the means of reinvigorating what Raffles decided to label as degenerate society: individual property rights, anti-slavery and free trade.

Freedom of property

The first is the idea of individual rights to property. The focus was systems of government revenue, in which peasants became responsible for paying land tax rather than the elites. In traditional Javanese and Malay culture, government revenue or tax was collected by the various levels of aristocratic elites and paid to the government, with each level taking a cut of the revenue. In Java, Raffles wanted to make the elites police, rending them paid employees of the state. He tried to cut out the elites' role in collecting land rent and instead develop direct relationships between peasants and government:

> With respect to the persons to whom the lands should be let, there can be no doubt that the greatest amount of revenue to the state would be derived, were the higher class of natives excluded; because such people, if allowed to have estates, derive their income from the rents and revenues of the land, which would otherwise come directly to Government.[59]

The government therefore needed to create leases directed at the 'head man of the peasanty' to 'rent a small lot, parcel or ground'. Raffles believed the Javanese peasants had to learn 'some knowledge of the right of property', and what property right was, and therefore saw his reforms as work in progress.[60]

His reforms in Java failed because of a shortage of money in the colony. The peasants refused to farm commercial crops, preferring to farm rice, and therefore the peasants did not have the money to pay the rent.[61] Consequently, Raffles did not raise the capital to pay the elites (Regents, *demangs*, *bupati* and *bekel*, who were the feudal Javanese ranks that governed the conutry).[62] In Sumatra and Singapore, Raffles looked to create European and/or Chinese colonisation, selling land rights to Europeans and Chinese to settle and farm the land after deciding the local populations were not productive enough on their own.[63] Therefore we see in Raffles a link between the settler colonialism that would develop in Australia and the economic colonialism that existed in India.

Slavery

The second recurring theme was the belief in an individual's right to their labour in a monetary economy and a corresponding rejection of slavery. The idea of rights to individual labour and the monetisation of the economy was a key part of liberal thinking in the late nineteenth century—often reflected in the impassioned rejection of slavery. Although there was a shifting scale between slavery and forced labour in Southeast Asia, Malay elites often described their followers as slaves. The Temenggong in Singapore described and likened his followers to slaves in the sense that a follower was 'in no respect master of his own property or actions'.[64]

In contrast to Biggar's claim that Raffles ended slavery in Penang in 1807, Raffles was a mid-ranking colonial official at the

THE COLONIAL ACHIEVEMENTS OF RAFFLES

time—he had no power to end slavery in Penang.[65] The Company had outlawed the sale of slaves in 1811. In March 1823, at the end of his time in Singapore, Raffles legislated that 'all persons' living in Singapore 'under the protection of the British authorities at Singapore, cannot hereafter be considered or treated as a slave, under any denomination, condition, colour or pretence whatever'.[66] He left Singapore on 9 June 1823. Soon after, he wrote to another friend boasting of Singapore's role as a bastion of freedom in the region: 'Singapore is now perhaps the only place in India[67] where slavery cannot exist.'[68] Despite ending slavery, Raffles allowed and regulated the condition of 'bond-debtors' as a means of controlling labour.[69] Under Raffles' regulations, the difference between 'bond-debtors' and slaves was that the bond-debtor could not be transferred to a different owner, and therefore the sale of bond-debtors was not allowed.

Although Raffles ended slavery at the close of his career, he had a very different relationship with slavery during his career. In 1810–11, while acting as Minto's agent with the native rulers of Southeast Asia, Raffles was in receipt of nine enslaved people.[70] These were given to him as diplomatic 'gifts'. Although they were gifts, in each instance the gifts occurred in the context of native rulers' requests for return gifts of 'guns', 'cannons', 'gun powder' and 'warships'. The request of return gifts meant that Raffles trafficked in slaves—he traded weapons for people. Five of the slaves Raffles received were young women, and one of them was only eight years old.[71]

As the Lieutenant Governor of Java between 1811 and 1814, Raffles enjoyed the service of enslaved people in his household and did not attempt to end the policy of slavery.[72] Raffles wrote to Bengal protesting his impotency to change the system. He first argued that he was in no position to comment on the morality of slavery, then that the problem was too big and finally that freed slaves were unreliable and immoral:

139

> It is not for me to say, whether this system was either necessary or proper, it may be sufficient to state, that it has been uniformly persevered in, and that on the arrival of the English, there was no class of domestic servants in Java, but slaves thus reared in the families of the Dutch. There are many of these who have been emancipated by the masters, and who occasionally hire themselves out to strangers, but they are little to be depended upon; the sudden change of condition from actual slavery to unlimited freedom, has no doubt, in many instances, tended rather to destroy than improve the morals.[73]

There were 27,142 slaves owned by Europeans in Java, and thus, though both Minto and Raffles chose to end the importation of slaves, they kept slavery intact.[74]

Raffles outlawed slavery in Singapore. However, before he did so, his translator, Abdullah Bin Abdul Kadir, came to Raffles distressed, telling him that people were being sold at the docks and families were being separated. Raffles placated Abdullah, telling him 'that business will not last much longer for the English are going to put a stop to it', and that 'if we live to be old we may yet see all the slaves gain their freedom and become like ourselves'.[75] The Company's regulations of 1807 had already made slavery illegal in Company settlements, and Raffles could have gone down to the markets and ended the slave sales immediately, but he chose not to and gave Abdullah some placating words instead.[76] Raffles therefore ended slavery when doing so was politically convenient for him—he was not the anti-slavery crusader that Biggar claims him to be.

Free trade

The third theme was free trade. After Adam Smith published *The Wealth of Nations* in 1777, free trade became a liberal shibboleth.[77] In Southeast Asia, it was popular with the country traders—private British merchants who traded between India

THE COLONIAL ACHIEVEMENTS OF RAFFLES

and other Asian ports. These country traders believed that trade should be open to competition with little or no regulation and argued for a reduced role for the Company. Free trade became an 'elastic' term in British Southeast Asia that could be stretched to mean not only country traders but any freedom from taxation, especially port and harbour fees, and reduced oversight and government interference.

Free trade in British Southeast Asia became linked especially to Raffles. This linkage was only strengthened after his death, thanks largely to his widow, Sophia, who with the publication of her late husband's *Memoir* in 1830 'at once established his public reputation as one of the most liberal and enlightened of all British governors in the East'.[78] Her curated collection of Raffles' letters and documents emphasised that free trade was the goal of her late husband in establishing Singapore.

However, compared to other British Company officers, such as Crawfurd, Raffles' attitude to free trade was mixed. In Palembang, the Sultan had opened his port to free trade. Raffles' use of free trade in his letters had been a misnomer: he wanted mercantilist Company control of the tin trade, not open free trade. Soon after establishing Singapore, he derided free trade for sponsoring 'speculations' and 'indulgences'.[79] Tze Shung has argued that Raffles' critical approach to free trade was 'consistent with a long-held distrust of what Raffles had, as early as 1811, impugned to be the "commercial adventure" and "interference" of "individuals", which were "injurious" and "by no means scrupulous"'.[80] Throughout his career, Raffles vacillated between free trade and mercantilist ideas of Company control of trade and land. Although he made reference to Adam Smith in his letters and book, it is not clear he understood what free trade was. The focus on Singapore being a free trade port was a consequence of events after 1823, when Crawfurd took control of management of the settlement—as he was a committed believer in free trade.

THE TRUTH ABOUT EMPIRE

Conclusion: the legacy and memory of Raffles

In life, Raffles was a self-serving colonial official. He reneged on most of the important agreements he made and only supported reforming ideas if politically convenient. Raffles does not appear to have been a man holding any convictions; rather, all decisions were made with an eye to career advancement. He was a sycophant whose publications were full of humanitarian slogans aimed at capturing the attention of real liberal reformers in India and London, but there is very little consistency in any of his ideas. At the time of his death, the Company took most of Raffles' estate to cover unpaid debts that the Company argued were a consequence of not following orders.[81]

We owe the memory of Raffles, as a humanitarian reformer, to his wife Sophia, who published the selective memoirs in 1830 and in 1832 organised for a statue to be erected in Westminster Abbey.[82] The sculpture is seated with a scroll (representing scholarship) at his feet. The inscription emphasises conquest, science and scholarship but is carved with ambiguous humanitarian references:

> To the memory of Sir Thomas Stamford Raffles, L.L.D. F.R.S. Lieut. Governor of Java and first President of the Zoological Society of London. Born 1781 Died 1826. Selected at an early age to conduct the government of the British conquests in the Indian ocean, by wisdom, vigour, and philanthropy, he raised Java to happiness and prosperity unknown under former rulers. After the surrender of that island to the Dutch, and during his government in Sumatra he founded an emporium at Singapore, where in establishing freedom of person as the right of the soil, and freedom of trade as the right of the port, he secured to the British flag the maritime superiority of the eastern seas. Ardently attached to science, he laboured successfully to add to the knowledge and enrich the museums of his native land, in promoting the welfare of the people committed to his charge, he sought the good of his country, and the glory of God.[83]

THE COLONIAL ACHIEVEMENTS OF RAFFLES

The inscription does not mention the abolition of slavery. It does note that he 'established freedom of person as the right of the soil', which refers more to the creation of private property in land rather than the freedom of labour. Conveniently, however, the next sculpture along the north choir aisle of the abbey is the statue of William Wilberforce (erected in 1840), who was a real abolitionist.[84] Consequently, Raffles' ambiguous inscription to freedom receives something of the abolitionist glow of Wilberforce's proximity.

By the mid-nineteenth century, Raffles was largely a forgotten colonial figure. His memory was only reinvigorated because of a history-writing campaign in *The Straits Times* in the 1880s and 1890s.[85] Many people wrote letters to *The Straits Times* in Singapore, exclaiming that they had no idea of Raffles until reading the paper's articles. In 1884, probably as a consequence of the articles, Sir Frederick Weld, the Governor of the Straits Settlements (Singapore, Malacca and Penang), decided to pick Raffles from obscurity and proposed a statue honouring him. For want of a better name, the Raffles Hotel was named in December 1887 a few months after the statue was erected.[86]

Weld proposed the Raffles statue as part of a speech in which he announced he would not grant self-government and representative democracy to Singaporeans because it would mean giving the Chinese subjects voting rights. Weld had instigated limited representative self-government when he was governor of the West Australian colony in the 1860s but believed democracy was only for Englishmen. The British 'capacity for governing is a characteristic of our race', he maintained, while the Chinese were 'created to get rich and enjoy the good things of the earth'.[87]

Raffles fitted Weld's view of a visionary governor-leader supporting commerce rather than democracy. He was according to Weld one of 'the best and ablest men of those to whom England owes her Imperial position in the East, and whose memory the natives still revere'.[88] Freedom was merely freedom of property and not participation in the body politic. Weld maintained 'the genius of Sir Stamford Raffles selected it [Singapore] as a British settlement, which he rightly judged would one day be ... placed at the crossroads of the central highway of commerce'.[89] Consequently, the Singaporeans received a statue that they could 'revere'—and birds could defecate on—rather than the vote.

In 1897, two biographies emerged of Raffles, both as part of rival retrospective series on the heroes of the empire. The biographers both noted that Raffles had fallen into obscurity. They opened with similar declarations of Raffles' importance, with one noting that the empire 'owes her position in the Far East' to Raffles, while the other stated 'among the men who have established the political and commercial power of this country in the seas of India and China, no one would deny a foremost place to Stamford Raffles'.[90] The 'Great Man' view was further reinvigorated in 1972, when the postcolonial Singaporean government erected a new 'white' polymarble reproduction of the bronze Raffles monument with the label: 'On this historic site Sir Thomas Stamford Raffles first landed in Singapore on 28th January 1819 and with genius and perception changed the destiny of Singapore from an obscure fishing village to a great seaport and modern metropolis.'[91] The sentiment has become one of cultural memory, in which Raffles' more recent biographer, Victoria Glendinning, wrote: 'The name delivers an instant message: exclusive, probably expensive, uniquely Singaporean, "heritage".'[92] The memory of Raffles has overtaken the inconvenient history of Raffles, a man who Minto said extended the empire 'unencumbered by the scruples of justice and good faith'.

Further reading

Herzog, Shawna, *Negotiating Abolition: The Antislavery Project in the British Straits Settlements, 1786–1843*, London: Bloomsbury Academic, 2021.

THE COLONIAL ACHIEVEMENTS OF RAFFLES

Knapman, Gareth, *Race and British Colonialism in South-East Asia: John Crawfurd and the Politics of Equality*, New York: Routledge, 2017.

—— 'Settler Colonialism and Usurping Malay Sovereignty in Singapore', *Journal of Southeast Asian Studies*, 52, 3, 2021, 418–40. doi:10.1017/S0022463421000606.

Knapman, Gareth and Sadiah Boonstra, 'Plunder and Prize in 1812 Java: The Legality and Consequences for Research and Restitution of the Raffles Collections', *Art Antiquity and Law Quarterly*, 28, 3, 2023.

Knapman, Gareth, Anthony Milner and Mary Quilty (eds), *Liberalism and the British Empire in Southeast Asia*, Abingdon: Routledge, 2019.

Tiffin, Sarah, *Southeast Asia in Ruins: Art and Empire in the Early 19th Century*, Singapore: NUS Press, 2016.

6

MY EMPIRE, RIGHT OR WRONG

RHODES, MILNER AND THE SOUTH AFRICAN WAR

Saul Dubow

In 1889, an article in the *Financial Times* titled 'South African Muddles' opened with the observation that there was no part of the British colonial world that was of 'such absorbing interest'. South Africa's 'wonderful' gold mines offered huge potential. Yet Britain, the *FT* advised, should be wary of repeating past mistakes in South Africa. One problem was the 'enormous concession' of mining rights rumoured to have been made by the Matabele king, Lobengula, to a 'single London company' (the British South Africa Company). Was it in Britain's national interests, the paper asked, 'to allow a native barbarian to hand over the entire mining rights to companies or adventurers for a song?'[1]

Published a decade before all-out imperial—and civil—war would engulf South Africa, and a decade after the British destruction of the Zulu kingdom, *The Financial Times* was expressing disquiet over Cecil John Rhodes' buccaneering capitalist enterprise in the sub-continent. More than a century later, in 2015, Rhodes re-emerged as the locus of political and moral outrage when the 'Fallist' movement removed a statue honouring his legacy at the University of Cape Town. The removal of the statue and the empty plinth that remained soon became the defining symbol of the gathering storm to 'decolonise'. This had global ramifications, not least when protestors mobilised in Oxford to remove a statue honouring Rhodes at Oriel College, Oxford. The controversy in Oxford drew Nigel Biggar into the fray, launching him on a trajectory that would lead to his vigorous defence of Rhodes and the record of the British Empire as well.[2]

Controversies around Rhodes and the lengths to which he and other mining magnates went to promote their interests in Southern Africa are not new. Indeed, they have been central to debates about the motives and morality of British imperialism for nearly a century and a half. When I was a student at the University of Cape Town in the late 1970s, the memorials to Rhodes and Jameson were not specifically targeted; they were seen as part of the furniture of empire. But Rhodes was nevertheless fully in the sights of radical opponents of apartheid. He was identified as one of the most important shapers of the cheap labour system that underlay the mining economy and the system of exploitation that underpinned apartheid. The claim that control over access to gold and diamonds lay behind the South African War (1899–1902) and other colonial conflicts loomed large in intellectual and political discussion and was at the centre of the animated 'race–class' debates of the time. So, too, the relationship between capitalist interests and jingoistic imperialism, which was argued over passionately during and after the South African War. In this chapter, I outline the significance of these debates and note Biggar's surprising reluctance to give full account of them.

We might surely expect a historian and ethicist to be equipped to assess and contextualise the past in the light of past moral standards, yet Biggar's moral accounting in his book, *Colonialism: A Moral Reckoning*, privileges his own personal views above all. His cause is not always helped by his selection of heroes, men like Rhodes and Alfred Milner, who were not short of loyal devotees and followers but were also heavily censured by contemporary detractors. Reputations rise, fall, and sometimes rise again, so there is reason to relitigate their careers. But it's a tough ask to do so in the case of Rhodes and Milner which requires a full appreciation of how such figures were understood by their contemporaries as well as by succeeding generations. Here, Biggar misses a trick.

Cecil Rhodes and Alfred Milner

Rhodes first made his fortune on the diamond fields of Kimberley in the 1870s. He saw the growth of his business empire, his political career, and that of the British Empire as co-dependent. The fulfilment of his plans relied upon the employment of tens of thousands of African men to work for low wages under harsh industrial conditions in dedicated labour compounds. Placing pressure on Africans to enter into migrant labour contracts in order to pay colonial taxes entailed limiting their access to land and constraining their freedom of movement. Rhodes played a key role in shaping the migrant labour system and the development of racial capitalism. This, rather than his stated views on race and civilisation, underpinned his politics and actions.

Rhodes saw industrial labour as an essential part of the 'civilising mission'. It was an outlook that brought him into conflict with those of a more liberal and humanitarian disposition who maintained that the civilising mission could best be realised by allowing Africans to be left substantially in possession of their land: Africans should be encouraged to accumulate capital as peasant farmers and to benefit from Christian enlightenment and modern education. Commerce and Christianity were central to the civilisational creed propounded by missionaries like David Livingstone as well as later missionaries like John Mackenzie, who ministered to the Batswana near the Kimberley diamond fields. By contrast, Rhodes wanted the Batswana to be taxed as colonial subjects, their labour made available for his mines, their territory used to facilitate northward colonial expansion. In 1883, as member of the Cape parliament for Barkly West, Rhodes got himself appointed to the boundary commission examining the Cape colony's contested frontier. Ignoring the Batswana's own arguments for a protective British colonial force to help retain their independence from encroaching Boers, Rhodes told the Cape parliament, 'I look upon this Bechuanaland territory as the Suez Canal of the trade of this country, the key of its road to the interior.'[3]

Rhodes had to wait a while for his vision to be realised, since the local British official, Charles Warren, initially established a Crown Colony for the Southern Batswana where 'native interests' were prioritised over 'colonial ambition'. As Kevin Shillington has claimed, Warren (a military man who trained as a Royal Engineer) 'sought to find a moral imperative within the imperial project'.[4] Rhodes also began the negotiations with Khama and other Northern Batswana chiefs that would eventually lead to the northern Bechuanaland Protectorate, forerunner of modern Botswana.

Warren had once been an admirer of the young, energetic Rhodes but became increasingly critical of him once Rhodes' political schemes came to light. Like other liberal-inclined officials, Warren voiced his explicit opposition to Rhodes' brand of colonial expansionism. Dispossessing Africans and allowing white settlement on their lands would 'cause strife and disturbances', bringing destruction and ruin.[5] Southern Bechuanaland was finally absorbed into the Cape, as Rhodes had demanded. By that time, Rhodes was engaged upon his British South Africa Company-led conquest of the Ndebele and Mashona to the north as well as his scheme to remove President Paul Kruger of the South African Republic (Transvaal), the heart of the newly discovered gold fields.

In 1886, gold was discovered in present-day Johannesburg. The mining encampments in Johannesburg and the surrounding Witwatersrand now became the focus of an intense international gold rush: waves of speculative investment flowed in from Britain and Europe. Rhodes and his partner, Charles Rudd, had missed out on the initial gold boom, but in 1887 they formed a limited company, pinning their hopes on finding a 'second Rand' in present-day Zimbabwe (Rhodesia). In 1888, as alluded to at the start of this chapter, the pair negotiated the mining concession with Lobengula, who repudiated the agreement once he realised its implications (likely without the benefit of having read the *Financial Times*). Rhodes and his associates duly occupied Mashonaland in 1890 in the name of the British South Africa Company with the support of London financiers and the promise of opening central Africa up to British settlement. The British government hastened to award the Company a royal charter. Hercules Robinson, who had arrived in South Africa in 1881 to take up the governorship of the Cape as well as the office of high commissioner, came under Rhodes' magnetic and mercurial sway. Robinson identified with the 'colonialist' interests—and also had a substantial personal investment in Rhodes' British South Africa Company. Together with his influential private secretary, Graham Bower, Robinson backed Rhodes as the leading powerhouse of settler nationalist expansion. Bower, who learned of Rhodes' schemes in advance, hoped that English-speakers and Afrikaners might be guided towards unity, with Britain holding the ring as the paramount regional power.[6]

While prime minister of the Cape, Rhodes conspired to topple Kruger's government so as to modernise the administration and secure effective control of the gold fields. This took the form of a scandalous (and failed) 1895–6 conspiracy known as the Jameson Raid which ensnared Bower (who took the hit for the colonial secretary and the high commissioner). Whereas Rhodes' invasion of African lands north of the Zambezi was welcomed enthusiastically by many in Britain and at the Cape as a bold act of colonial sub-imperialism, the attempt to conquer Kruger's republic was condemned on account of its blundering invasion of a sovereign territory and also because it destroyed the political alliance that Rhodes had developed with the Afrikaner Bond, the main party in Cape politics representing Afrikaner interests. In the parlance of the day, colonialism and imperialism were not coterminous: the former referred to local initiatives by settler-colonial citizens who thought of themselves as rooted in South Africa; the latter denoted unwanted interference by the 'imperial factor' in London. The 1897 British South Africa Committee of Inquiry set up at Westminster to investigate the affair placed Rhodes directly in the spotlight and became a cause célèbre in Britain. It stretched over five months and aroused enormous public interest.

An unrepentant Rhodes used the occasion of the parliamentary investigation to present himself as a 'visionary empire-builder and a defender of the liberties of British subjects'.[7] Rumours of involvement by figures like Joseph Chamberlain, the Colonial Secretary, were deflected by evasive, dissembling testimony on the part of Rhodes and others. This encouraged a view that the committee was determined to conceal rather than reveal the truth.[8] Rhodes, the mercurial shape-shifting 'colonial imperialist', turned the furore over the hearings to his own advantage:

the follies of the Jameson Raid did nothing to halt the enthusiasm for the reinvigorated 'new' imperialism and populist jingoism. With Chamberlain at the colonial office and Milner as high commissioner for South Africa, the determination finally to resolve the South African problem by breaking down internal resistance hardened rapidly.

Milner's recent experience in Egypt, where he worked on government finance under Evelyn Baring in the Khedivate government and then as chairman of the Board of Inland Revenue, disposed him to use systematic administrative and technocratic reforms to achieve his ends. A former journalist, Milner was also a skilled publicist. Milner's appointment to South Africa in 1897 was received well by the press. Heading to Cape Town, he declared: 'S.A. is just now the weakest link in the Imperial chain, and I am conscious of the tremendous responsibility which rests upon the man who is called upon to try and preserve it from snapping.' Soon after his arrival, he became keen to 'work up to a crisis' with the Transvaal by presenting a 'strong *cumulative case*'.[9] British grievances included inadequate civil and voting rights for *uitlanders* (foreigners) resident in the Transvaal (Milner memorably said they were regarded as 'helots'), the treatment of Africans and 'Cape Boys' ('Coloureds'), as well as Kruger's monopoly over the production of dynamite—an important cost factor in gold mining. A supportive loyalist press in South Africa and Britain helped to weaponise these complaints into *casus belli*. Although not necessarily bent on war at all costs, Milner made constant demands which Kruger, despite some willingness on his part to compromise, could not deliver on without (as he saw it) losing sovereign control of his country. Milner's pressure tactics sought to impress on the Boers 'the *danger* of defying us'. He held out the prospects of conciliation but only on his terms: it was imperative to 'put our foot down' and 'keep it there'. We cannot afford to be seen as 'weak'.[10]

Despite Biggar's insistence that Milner was in favour of protecting African rights, he was also well aware that the racial views of the British and Boers in South Africa were not so antithetical.[11] He wrote that it might be possible 'to unite Dutch and English by protecting the black man' but that would mean uniting them 'against yourself and your policy of protection. There is the whole *crux* of the S. African position.'[12] Instead, Milner sought to bring the different elements into line by exerting direct imperial control. The key, to his mind, was firm, judicious governance. Hence Milner's well-known statement of his war intentions just before hostilities began: 'The *ultimate* end is a self-governing white Community, supported by *well-treated* and *justly governed* black labour from Cape Town to Zambesi. There must be one flag, the Union Jack, but under it equality of races and languages.'[13]

By 'races', Milner was referring to whites. His reference to equality of languages also presupposed that English would become predominant. Although blacks should be justly treated—an easy assurance to make, and one that was necessary to alleviate the qualms of 'colour-blind' liberals in Britain and in the Cape parliament—Milner did not wish that blacks should enjoy equal rights as citizens, though he appreciated the political risks of ruling this out explicitly. As the war progressed, Milner and his supporters were coming to the view that a new imperial dispensation—in the form of a federation led by the metropole—might be achieved if Boers and Brits could only settle their differences and agree the terms of white supremacy. This is indeed what happened in the era of post-war reconstruction (1902–10), when racial segregation was engineered as part of the process of 'reconciliation' between Boers and Britons.

The South African War

The South African War between the British Empire and the Boer republics that broke out after Milner's successful provoca-

MY EMPIRE, RIGHT OR WRONG

tion in 1899 was perhaps the greatest colonial conflagration involving Britain in the interval between the Napoleonic Wars and the Great War of 1914–18.[14] Boer deaths in battle were considerably exceeded by civilian casualties, rendering the conflict an early instance of humanitarian concern and outrage. In all, nearly 28,000 Boer women and children perished from disease and malnutrition while imprisoned in the concentration camps constructed by the British army to deprive Boer fighters of refuge and support on their farms and homesteads. It is less well known that as many as 20,000 African refugees, fully a fifth of those interned by the British in separate concentration camps, perished in conditions that were even worse than those endured by Boer civilians. The convenient fiction that this was a 'white man's war' was subscribed to by Boer and British combatants alike in order to ensure that black political rights formed no part of a future political agenda.

The South African War did a great deal to generate modern understandings of imperialism, anti-imperialism, and colonialism. Participation on the side of the British by Australian, New Zealand, and Canadian troops was indicative of strong colonial support of imperialism. But it also induced a palpable sharpening of colonial nationalist sentiment in the white dominions on the basis that loyalty to the empire should be rewarded with greater political autonomy. Internationally, the war evoked powerful sentiments and moral outrage against rapacious British imperialism. Volunteers from around the world, including prominent Irish republicans, expressed their disapproval of British imperialism by rallying to support the Boers.

The war proved controversial within Britain too, providing the key point of division in the 1900 'Khaki election'. Most Liberals were supportive—whether stemming from core beliefs in the inevitability of progress and patriotism (the advance of 'civilisation') or hopes that the interests of Africans were best secured within the framework of benevolent British governance. A 'Stop the War Committee', founded by W. T. Stead in 1899 with leading political figures like Keir Hardie and Lloyd George in support, straddled the liberal–socialist divide.[15] It also intersected with vocal 'pro-Boers' and pacifists who inclined to the view that the war was inherently unjust and corrosive of British values, or that it functioned as a cloak for sectional interests and capitalist enrichment.

Emily Hobhouse's on-the-spot reports on the suffering of Boer women and children in the concentration camps were eagerly taken up by Liberal leader Henry Campbell-Bannerman. Hobhouse's charges were subsequently investigated by Millicent Garrett Fawcett, feminist and suffragist. Fawcett opted to spread the blame by being critical both of pro-Boers and of Boer sanitary habits and their alleged medical ignorance, a clear case of victim blaming. She excused some of the maltreatment experienced in the camps as 'part of the fortune of war', a stance oddly echoed by Biggar and others today.[16]

The Boer War helped to precipitate the formation of the Labour Party in 1900. Ramsay MacDonald was opposed to the South African War on moral grounds, but he did not venture into extended critiques of capitalism and recoiled from the advanced views of the Fabians. Hardie, a forthright opponent of the war and an internationalist, declared in 1900 that the war was 'a Capitalists' war, begotten by capitalists' money, lied into being by a perjured mercenary capitalist press, and fathered by unscrupulous politicians, themselves the merest tools of the capitalists'.[17] By contrast, the Conservative/Unionist perspective appealed to patriotic duty and the need to defend British supremacy through military might if necessary. Joseph Chamberlain and Milner were of this persuasion.[18] The Aborigines' Protection Society, established voice of humanitarian interests, found itself in the difficult situation in 1899 of not being able to take a clear position: sympathy for the Boers clashed with their members' predisposition to speak up for African interests; Chamberlain, long a supporter of the society, was now one of the principal protagonists in favour of war.[19]

The South African War also brought long-running tensions within the Liberal Party and liberal conscience into sharp focus. Lord Rosebery, who succeeded Gladstone as prime minister in 1894 and returned to opposition a year later, now attached himself to the cause of 'Liberal Imperialism', a term of his own coinage referring to a new imperial 'spirit' that was both 'sane' and compatible with a 'larger patriotism'.

One aspect of the conflict's modernity, which was amply recognised by both sides, was 'the power of public opinion' and propaganda. The conflict was covered by British journalists and war correspondents of very different political sympathies, including Winston Churchill, Flora Shaw, Sarah Wilson, G. W. Steevens, Leo Amery, and J. A. Hobson. It gave a conspicuous boost to the campaigning journalism of W. T. Stead and the liberal newspaper editor C. P. Scott at *The Manchester Guardian* as well as pro-imperialists Charles Moberly Bell and George Buckle of *The Times*. Crude jingoism was encouraged by the populist 'yellow' press, especially Alfred Harmsworth's *Daily Mail*.[20] The reporting and literature emanating from writers and press correspondents served to define the war as a contest between nationalism, patriotism, imperialism, and republicanism.

Significantly, the war encouraged intellectuals and propagandists to define imperialism in terms of systemic economic rapacity and exploitation. Hobson, the radical liberal English journalist and economist, was developing an underconsumptionist theory of capitalism. As *The Manchester Guardian*'s correspondent in South Africa during the South African War, Hobson refined his ideas by drawing on his own direct experience as well as informants like Olive Schreiner.[21] In a chapter titled 'The

Economic Taproot of Imperialism', he concluded that in the United States, Britain, and Europe imperialism was the result of 'economic pressure of a sudden advance of capitalism which cannot find occupation at home and needs foreign markets for goods and for investments'.[22] Income inequality within Britain, Hobson explained, tended to exacerbate the problem of underconsumption because it had the effect of concentrating wealth in the hands of the few.

As is widely appreciated, Hobson's ideas were taken up and adapted in a more theoretical manner by European Marxists as well as by Lenin in his landmark study *Imperialism, the Highest Stage of Capitalism*. For Hobson, the period from the Jameson Raid to the Boer War vindicated both his theory of finance-led imperialism and his belief in the power of jingoistic nationalism. Hobson's embrace of conspiracy theories to explain how specific interest groups—the capitalist-controlled 'yellow' press, 'foreign' Jewish financiers, *uitlander* lobbyists—directed self-serving imperialism has attracted ridicule.[23] Yet, Peter Cain and Tony Hopkins make a good case to distinguish between the original insights of Hobson's analysis about the nature of the British economy and his polemical, prejudiced journalism.[24] Rhodes certainly articulated an expansionist vision by pointing to the likely dividends accruing to the domestic British populace:

> My cherished idea is a solution for the social problem, i.e., in order to save the 40,000,000 inhabitants of the United Kingdom from a bloody civil war, we colonial statesmen must acquire new lands to settle the surplus population, to provide new markets for the goods produced in the factories and mines ... The empire, as I have always said, is a bread and butter question.[25]

This was the basis of his appeal to 'social imperialism'.

Hobson offered some penetrating remarks about how the generation of wealth was dependent on the exploitation of black labour: 'Put in a concise form, it may be said that this war is being waged in order to secure for the mines a cheap adequate supply of labour.' Or, Africans 'do the work and don't count'.[26] Yet, these denunciations remained secondary to his primary purpose, which was to identify the evil machinations of the imperialists, who bore the greatest responsibility for the war. In stirring up British politics and evoking tub-thumping slogans, acrimonious debates about ultimate responsibility for the war had the effect of marginalising the predicament of black South Africans, the ultimate losers from the conflict.

Milner, the Kindergarten, and segregation

One of the first priorities of the post-war British government in the Transvaal was to reopen the gold mines, but with many Africans reluctant to resume work as migrant labourers (some were able to take advantage of the destruction of the Boer homesteads to re-establish themselves on the land), Milner instead resorted to the importation of Chinese indentured mineworkers. This proved to be highly controversial in South Africa and in Britain. White workers were worried that their wages and conditions would be undercut; the Liberal government in Britain deplored the ill-treatment and flogging of Chinese indentured labourers. Milner relinquished his position as high commissioner, returning under a cloud to Britain in 1905. The following year there was a motion in the British Parliament to censure him for the punitive treatment of Chinese 'slaves'.

The new Liberal government in Britain turned towards conciliation, compromise, and the promise of responsible government for the defeated Boer republics. In elections, newly formed Dutch-led parties came to power in the Transvaal and Orange River colonies. In the Cape, Prime Minister Leander Starr Jameson, a visible reminder of Rhodes' tainted imperialism, was replaced by a coalition of colonial parties led by John X. Merriman. This was therefore also a victory for parliamentarians, who greatly resented Milner's dictatorial suspension of the Cape constitution in 1901. The revival of domestic politics was soon accompanied by enthusiasm for national reconciliation among whites. 'Closer Union' societies were constituted around the country to explore the potential for federation at a national level. Unitary solutions were as yet not considered feasible in the light of deeply entrenched regional, cultural, and political differences. At a national convention called in 1909, political representatives from the four white colonial governments agreed to constitute South Africa as a unitary state with strong elements of decentralisation built in through provincial legislatures and rights.

The creation of a unitary state of South Africa in 1910, led by the Boer general Louis Botha, was an extraordinary and mostly unanticipated outcome given the country's recent conflict and the longer history of failed efforts at confederation which extended back half a century. It was made possible through a spirit of political cooperation and renewal led by senior politicians like Botha, Jan Smuts, Merriman, and the Cape's chief justice, Henry de Villiers, who chaired the convention. Much of the 'new South Africa's' governmental template had been set out by the group of young men Milner appointed to head up reconstruction after the war, known as his 'Kindergarten'. The commissions they appointed to advise on policy agreed that overall white supremacy should be secured within the context of imperial belonging, that colonies and ex-republics should be integrated as far as possible, and that the future of industry and agriculture was dependent on a regular supply of pliant black labour and an integrated railway and customs system. Racial segregation and white unity were abiding themes.

From 1905, 'segregation' was increasingly deployed as an ideological keyword by British planners and thinkers based in South

Africa. They envisaged a systematic solution to the 'native question' premised on the fundamental and permanent distinction between blacks and whites. Lionel Curtis, a key member of the Milner Kindergarten, discoursing on 'The Place of Subject People in the Empire' to a group of like-minded experts in the Fortnightly Club, rejected arguments based on individual rights or personal standing. It was a 'false criterion' to take men like Gandhi or Dr Abdurahman and point to their educational superiority over the mass of white voters. Individual potentiality, from a social and political point of view, 'can only be measured by the potentiality of the race as a whole'.[27]

The revived defence of Rhodes' imperialism

Biggar's interest in Southern Africa and in what he refers to as the Second Boer War (more commonly known today as the South African War) may have something to do with his having been taught as an Oxford undergraduate in the 1970s by G. H. L. Le May, one of several historians at the time who questioned the good intentions of British involvement in South African affairs. Biggar remembers Le May with fondness in his acknowledgements and quotes him in the text of *Colonialism*.[28] When Le May's *British Supremacy in South Africa, 1899–1907* was published in 1965, Eric Stokes remarked that it 'makes up a measured indictment of the collision course along which Chamberlain and Milner set British policy'.[29] Biggar does not indict Milner or Chamberlain. On the contrary, he defends them.

There is no reason why Biggar should not act as counsel for the defence. But why no acknowledgement of the prosecutorial case? The Jameson Raid is relegated to a single footnote with the adjective 'infamous'.[30] That Rhodes was arraigned by a British parliamentary committee in 1897 for his role in the raid does not rate a mention in Biggar's work. Nor does Biggar mention the wave of controversy, in which Milner was directly implicated on account of his role in sanctioning the flogging of Chinese indentured workers. Coming shortly after the anti-imperialist Boxer uprising (1899–1901), which was suppressed by an alliance of British, American, French, Russian, Austro-Hungarian, German, Italian and Japanese troops, the treatment of indentured Chinese labour in South Africa had reverberations throughout the empire.[31] In the British elections of 1905, controversies arising out of the Boer War concentration camps and 'Chinese slavery' featured as serious moral and political issues, contributing to the Liberal landslide victory. There is no discussion in Biggar's moral reckoning of the ethical debates these aroused other than the briefest assurance that 'Liberal metropolitan indignation was overwrought.'[32]

Biggar does mention the concentration camps constructed by the British military—how could he not in a book about ethics?—but *Colonialism* fails to consider the extent to which they aroused public outrage or contributed to the rise of modern Afrikaner nationalism. It was as a result of the findings by brave investigators like Hobhouse that Campbell-Bannerman famously spoke up against 'methods of barbarism'. This phrase is recorded in *Colonialism* but only to make the point that the huge proportion of civilian deaths were not intentionally caused and, further, to defend the use of the concentration camps in terms of 'just war' ethics.[33] Muscular theology. Biggar mounts an argument against those who called the Boer War concentration camps a 'holocaust', citing Thomas Pakenham's 1979 book as his sole reference.[34] Few if any serious historians claim that it was the British intention to kill civilians, much less that the British aims were genocidal. Neglect, maltreatment, and brutality towards civilians are the more usual charges. But *Colonialism* apparently sets the record right merely by rejecting accusations of genocide that even the most strenuous Afrikaner critics of British conduct avoid.

MY EMPIRE, RIGHT OR WRONG

As for the causes of the South African War, these have long been debated. Biggar is wholly opposed to the idea of a capitalist conspiracy, and here he finds himself in good company—including even Marxist historians. There is a sophisticated literature on topics such as the technical requirements of deep-level gold mining, the role of the stock market and speculation, short- and long-term political thinking, the class interests and racial views of British workers, as well as rampant political manipulation and propaganda in the new age of mass journalism. Yet, Biggar's account deals with none of this. In respect of the economic motivations for the war, no smoking gun has been found in the archives. But there is a lot of circumstantial evidence.[35] It is safe to say that had the South African Republic not contained huge seams of gold in which British and European financiers had enormous investments, it is unlikely that Milner and Chamberlain would have risked blood and treasure to overthrow President Kruger. The strategy in *Colonialism* is to reduce complex economic motivations and calculations to the capitalist conspiracy theory propounded at the time by Hobson, whose wilder flights of fancy were supercharged by anti-Semitism—and his economic arguments weakened as a result.

No account is taken of the impact of Hobson's work on opinion at the time, nor of the refinements of Hobson's work undertaken by a generation of Marxist thinkers including Rosa Luxemburg, Rudolf Hilferding, and Lenin. Nor is there any mention of the serious re-evaluation of Hobson's work in Hopkins' and Cain's influential concept of 'gentlemanly capitalism' and the role of the City of London.[36] Theories about capitalist imperialism were widely current at the time of the South African War, as were discussions about the appropriate response of organised labour or the role of the 'yellow' press in sustaining jingoism.[37] Anguished discussions such as these had profound ethical and political implications bearing on the meaning and legitimacy of the civilising mission and of imperialism. They were crystallised in the British 'Khaki' election of 1900. Sidney Webb came up with the compelling slogan reflecting divisions in the liberal-left: '[T]he war is *wholly* unjust but wholly necessary' (by which he seems to have meant unavoidable for the progress of civilisation), surely an interesting formulation for a historian interested in the morality of empire. All this is, however, entirely overlooked in *Colonialism*.[38]

Biggar's book makes fleeting mention of black South Africans supporting the British during the war and of Irish nationalists who supported the Boers.[39] In the former case, it does not tie the support given by black South Africans, like Sol Plaatje, to their profound sense of disillusionment and abandonment when, in 1910, the British government acceded to the terms of union and effectively reneged on previous promises of citizenship in order to secure the accord between English- and Afrikaans-speakers.[40] In the latter case, it makes no mention either of worldwide sympathy for the Boers in their fight against British imperialism. As indicated earlier, this included Irish volunteers fighting on the behalf of the Boers, as well as Scandinavians, Americans, Dutch, French, and Russians. Their varied ranks included socialists, republicans, monarchists, and romantic adventurers.[41] What they agreed upon was that British imperialism was in the wrong and ought to be opposed. As British imperialism was subjected to scrutiny in the court of international opinion, new understandings of the meaning of imperialism, capitalism, and racism were developed and refined. These raised complex intellectual and moral questions. *Colonialism*'s binary ethical approach has no place for any of this.

Biggar's extended discussion of franchise rights in South Africa is deeply flawed because of its insistent oversimplification. He feels obliged to defend Rhodes throughout as a proponent of 'equal rights for all civilised men'. In doing so, he ignores good evidence that Rhodes really meant 'white' men but was enjoined to drop the racial qualifier when challenged by coloured voters. More broadly, Biggar seeks to defend Rhodes from charges of racism, wriggling over the meaning of 'barbarians' in a speech by Rhodes of 1894.[42]

Biggar engages with William Beinart in the endnotes of *Colonialism* but does not take account of Beinart's quotation from Rhodes, speaking in 1887:

> Either you have to receive them on an equal footing as citizens, or to call them a subject race. Well, I have made up my mind that there must be class legislation ... and that we have got to treat natives, where they are in a state of barbarism, in a different way to ourselves. We are to be lords over them ... Treat the natives as a subject people as long as they continue in a state of barbarism and communal tenure.[43]

For most readers, and for the parliamentarians to whom this speech was delivered, what Rhodes meant is amply clear. Lest there be any doubt, we should note that Rhodes supported further restrictions on the franchise in 1887, and he was prime minister when the 1892 Franchise and Ballot Act was passed. These measures resulted in an absolute reduction of the numbers of Africans registered to vote. Just how much this reduction amounted to on a district-by-district basis is not clear, but one might expect *Colonialism* at least to acknowledge Rhodes' complicity in the narrowing of franchise rights—not least because he cites a recent article by Farai Nyika and Johan Fourie which tackles the numbers.[44] True, pressure to reduce African voter numbers did come from the Afrikaner Bond party, but Rhodes was in agreement that Africans should not be in a position to decide elections.[45]

We can debate whether Rhodes meant that blacks should be treated as a subject race in perpetuity. But Rhodes was not given to much serious or personal reflection, and when he did think he had little original to say. Rhodes was a consummate politician, an opportunist with a cynical view of human frailty (he was always happy to offer bribes), as well as a brilliant entrepreneur and industrialist. He used his position as prime minister of the Cape to attempt to differentiate blacks into a small class of mission-educated Christians and men of property, on the one hand, and a much larger class of exploitable workers on the other. This was exactly what he intended in his 1894 Glen Grey Act, sometimes known as his 'Bill for Africa'. The closed compound system which Rhodes and others developed in Kimberley was used to control and discipline migrant black labour. Patrick Harries—who taught me African history at the University of Cape Town—would be horrified to see how Biggar has misused his sophisticated analysis, with its emphasis on African agency, to justify the compound system.[46]

The free pass granted by Biggar to Rhodes is echoed by the virtue he makes of the Cape's achievement of representative government in 1853. This created a colonial legislature and introduced racially blind voting for all men, subject to an educational and property qualification. Biggar sees this as an imperial gift. In fact, the progressive constitutionalism introduced at the Cape in 1853 was not the result of British imperialism. Rather, it was the outcome of concerted pressure on the part of locally based Cape citizens—including a boycott of government institutions in 1848–9—who were fighting for recognition of their status as respectable free-born Englishmen and against what they saw as unrestrained gubernatorial authority. As well as representing a ripple of the European liberal 'spring' of 1848, about which Chris Clark has written so illuminatingly, it was also a response to the 1851–2 Kat River rebellion which shook the colonial government and led the liberal attorney-general William Porter, a supporter of an inclusive voting system, to declare: 'I would rather meet the Hottentot at the hustings voting for his representative, than meet the Hottentot in the wilds with his gun upon his shoulder.'[47]

Cape liberals who continued to defend (to a greater or lesser degree) equal rights for blacks as well as whites included figures like Porter, Saul Solomon, John Molteno, Merriman, and South Africa's first great novelist, Olive Schreiner. They drew also on the support of leading Afrikaners like J. H. Hofmeyr and the Afrikaner Bond. This alliance was shattered by the Jameson Raid, and Rhodes, who up to this point was believed to be an ally of moderate colonial nationalism, now emerged as the incarnation of rampant British imperialism and moral corruption. There is a large literature on this.[48] It is not to be found in Biggar's book.

It is conspicuous, too, that *Colonialism* omits any discussion of the role of the pumped-up militarist British imperialism that led to destructive war against the Zulu nation in 1879—let alone the preceding half-dozen wars of dispossession against the Xhosa where evidence of British arrogance and cruelty is in plentiful supply.[49] If imperial violence and conquest is underplayed, so is the morally questionable basis of reconciliation between whites after the South African War which was brokered through broad white agreement around the idea of racial segregation (as explained earlier). Biggar's take is that 'Milner wanted to give South Africa the benefit of ... virtuous government, and to secure regional peace, first between Afrikaner and British, and then between white and black.'[50] Why, then, does his account fail to mention the key role of Milner's deputies in contributing to the theory and practice of racial segregation between 1902 and 1910?[51]

The selection of sources in *Colonialism* is questionable. The readable popular work of Pakenham (mentioned over forty times) on the Boer War and the Scramble for Africa is pilloried. But Pakenham's genial refutation of the assumptions of British imperialism hardly represents the state of modern scholarship—and in fact was never at the forefront of historical knowledge. Conversely, the moral authority of Margery Perham (1895–1982) is cited approvingly on multiple occasions. Discussed also in the chapter in this volume by Stuart Ward, Perham was a respected academic at Oxford and a public figure known for her deep knowledge of colonial Africa as well as her personal admiration for district officers and governors. An articulate and passionate defender of principles of indirect rule, she subscribed to benevolent colonialism. In the latter part of her career, she welcomed decolonisation as the culmination of the colonial project. Perham's judicious approach to the 'transfer of power' flattered late colonial sensibilities. Even as she criticised reactionary settlers and lent cautious support to African nationalism, she remained loyal to the imperial establishment, reminding audiences of its best intentions.[52] *Colonialism* does not present Perham as a product of her time or as the conscience of the colonial office but offers her instead as an oracular figure, a living authority of unimpeachable, objective, 'discriminating judgement' with 'expert eyes'.[53]

Reliance on old and dated secondary sources is one thing. The manner in which *Colonialism* takes issue with more modern, scholarly critiques in the endnotes is another. Many of its endnotes are hundreds of words in length. They relegate Beinart, who wrote a lengthy submission to the Oriel College Commission assessing Rhodes's career, to several very long notes.[54] Hundreds of words are devoted in the endnotes to explaining why Biggar disagrees with a short letter of mine published in *The Daily Telegraph* ('Britain's Inglorious Tactics during the Boer War', 11 August 2021) without noting that this was written in reaction to a newspaper article written by his History Reclaimed colleague, Robert Tombs.[55] Decontextualised in this way, but giving me my full academic title, Biggar makes out that my letter was a work of scholarship rather than a sharp rejoinder to a rebarbative op-ed in *The Telegraph*.[56]

Why does Biggar do this? Perhaps he was persuaded by his publisher that the text should be free of qualifications and complexities in order to reach and satisfy a general audience. Indeed, Biggar states in his 'Introduction' that he has 'consigned most of [his] skirmishes with historians to the endnotes'. It's a tricky manoeuvre that effectively says trust me, no need to read the fine print. Yet the fact that more than a third of the book takes the form of often rambling endnotes serves a purpose: it allows Biggar to simplify the arguments in the main body of the text while maintaining the appearance that his is a work of deep scholarship. Biggar has every right to take issue with scholars who are critical of the British Empire, and I am not altogether unsympathetic to some of his assertions, including the rejection of any notion that there was a unitary 'imperial project'. But readers should be aware that today's culture-war apologists for empire are themselves involved in a deeply partisan project and that Biggar is one of their tribunes.

This chapter has argued that, for much of the nineteenth and twentieth centuries, South Africa aroused great public interest. Political debate was led by humanitarians and their antagonists, imperialists and anti-imperialists, pan-Africanists and African nationalists, feminists, labourites, socialists, passive resisters, as well as supporters and opponents of racial segregation. Such discussions vividly illuminate the moral quandaries and political assumptions of their day. Why, one wonders, are those who defend imperial morality now so reluctant to engage with controversies as they were framed at the time? Their preference, instead, is to inflame the culture wars through a highly selective and ill-informed view of the past.[57] This desire to court public controversy contrasts with a surprising lack of curiosity about the courts of public opinion of the past. Unfortunately, Biggar's

THE TRUTH ABOUT EMPIRE

Colonialism misses the opportunity to investigate ethical and moral questions in both senses of the word 'contemporary': of *its* time and in *our* time.

Further reading

Bright, Rachel, *Chinese Labour in South Africa, 1902–10: Race, Violence, and Global Spectacle*, Basingstoke: Palgrave Macmillan, 2013.

Jeeves, Alan, 'The Rand Capitalists and the Coming of the South African War 1896–1899', *South African Journal of Economic History*, 11, 2, 1996, pp. 55–81.

Kubicek, Robert V., *Economic Imperialism in Theory and Practice: The Case of South African Gold Mining Finance 1886–1914*, Durham: Duke University Press, 1979.

Le May, G. H. L., *British Supremacy in South Africa, 1899–1902*, Oxford: Clarendon, 1965.

Lowry, Donal (ed.), *The South African War Reappraised*, Manchester: Manchester University Press, 2000.

Lukasiewicz, Mariusz, *Gold, Finance and Imperialism in South Africa, 1887–1902*, Cham: Palgrave Macmillan, forthcoming.

Magubane, Bernard, *The Making of a Racist State: British Imperialism and the Union of South Africa, 1875–1910*, Trenton: Africa World Press, 1996.

Omissi, David, and Andrew Thompson, *The Impact of the South Africa War*, Basingstoke: Palgrave Macmillan, 2002.

Rotberg, Robert, and Miles F. Shore, *The Founder: Cecil Rhodes and the Pursuit of Power*, Oxford: Oxford University Press, 1990.

Smith, A., and M. Bull (eds), *Margery Perham and British Rule in Africa*, London: Frank Cass, 1991.

Willan, Brian, *Sol Plaatje: A Life of Solomon Tshekisho Plaatje, 1876–1932*, Auckland Park: Jacana Media, 2018.

7

WRITTEN ON THE CITY
IMPERIAL BRITAIN AND CHINA

Robert Bickers

The violence of British imperial power is not often found explicitly acknowledged in public at the heart of the empire. Usually, it is clothed in metaphor. Simple words stand for bloody deeds—the names of battles, the posts great men held, or the names of those honourable men, but only if you recognize any of these as you walk London streets. Here is Clive, and there is Gordon. The facades of the building now housing the Foreign and Commonwealth Office are crowded with two score such figures, among them James Bruce, the Eighth Lord Elgin. British losses are acknowledged and mourned clearly and explicitly, with sacrifice and valour caught in stone or bronze, but the fact of great pain once inflicted on others must be gleaned by reading between the lines of a list. Sometimes the violence of subjugation is represented, usually through some sort of visual metaphor where gendered subordination is portrayed and is easily read.¹ It is startling, then, to stand with your back to Admiralty Arch on the Mall, with Buckingham Palace in view at the other end of that thoroughfare, and to look closely at the bronze relief on the north-east face of the Royal Marines National Memorial. It is not easily picked out from a distance, and your gaze is likely to be diverted by the life-size figures that surmount the pedestal, but stand close and you can see clearly a marine run his bayonet deep into the chest of a Chinese soldier who has been knocked clean off his feet by the impact of the thrust. You can run your hand over it.

The British enterprise in China was steeped in violence. It began with one war, was consolidated through another, and defended in a third—that last, in 1900, the occasion of the encounter caught in bronze on the Mall. British forces used bayonet, bullet, and cannon repeatedly from 1839 onwards with the onset of the First Anglo-Chinese or 'Opium' War. They were able to do so with ease because an elaborate military infrastructure was developed after 1841 that oversaw garrisons in Chinese cities and gunboats on China's coasts and along its rivers, secured intelligence that would pave the way for victory if or when war came, and which supported and armed British clerks and traders who formed volunteer units as a second line of defence against threat after large squads of Sikh policemen.²

The whole was backed up by the full force of British imperial power, for reinforcements were only a few days' sailing away. And sail they did: the single largest deployment of British forces between the two World Wars, for example, formed a Shanghai Defence Force, assembled in 1926–7 at the height of the Chinese nationalist revolution led by the Guomindang under Chiang Kai-shek. Marines, soldiers, ships, and aircraft were sent to China. This was exceptional, but more routinely down to the Communist Party's victory in the Chinese civil war in 1949 the flag was flown, sometimes high above a fusillade or a bombardment, mostly above warships deployed in silent threat in China's harbours and along its rivers.

One hundred and seven years after it had first fought its way up the river, the Royal Navy was embroiled in a final engagement on the Yangtze when central China fell to the forces of the Chinese Communist Party in the spring of 1949. HMS *Amethyst* raced under cover of darkness downriver on 30 July, having been trapped by communist artillery 150 miles from the sea three months earlier. Its successful escape was achieved at the cost of a Chinese civilian vessel it shadowed, and the lives of some of the passengers and crew as that ship caught fire and sank after being hit by communist shells.[3] The escape seized the British imagination, stoked by the press and the Admiralty, and through martial theatre. On the morning of 16 November, the crew of the ship marched to a thanksgiving service in London at the Church of St Martin-in-the-Fields in Trafalgar Square, before parading to the Guildhall through streets lined with cheering crowds. They mustered in Horse Guards Parade, were then inspected by Prime Minister Clement Attlee, and then marched off, their route taking them directly past the Royal Marines Memorial. It was a raw, cold misty day, but the connected violence of the long arc of Britain's Chinese century was crystal clear, if you wanted to see it.

You have to want to see it, but it often gets overlooked. Nigel Biggar's Colonialism has not overlooked it, not entirely, but it has downplayed it, quite substantially, corralled it, and has turned the facts of violence around, for his verdict is that while it was immoral for the British to go to war in China over the opium trade in 1839–42, the impact of this was dwarfed by the 'evils culpably inflicted on China within living memory by Chairman Mao'. As a result, 'those inflicted by the British pale into insignificance'.[4] Elsewhere in the book, Biggar uses China as one of his examples of a country that had historically practised slavery,

THE TRUTH ABOUT EMPIRE

and a culture in which ethnic chauvinism could be found. His account of the British Empire does not much include China, but a history of the projection of British power overseas needs to, not least because little mattered more in China's foreign relations before the First World War than the unequal relationship with British power exercised within, on, and beyond its borders. What I will do here is focus on the fact that his book mostly ignores the wider history of China's century-long experience of what many far beyond the 'Chinese Communist Party' frame as the 'Century of Humiliation'.

Biggar's account of British bellicosity is restricted to the First Opium War; he does not trouble to note the second, or third, or the latent violence embodied in the Royal Navy's China Station, its Yangtze and West River flotillas, and the army's China Command. British violence in China did not end with the Treaty of Nanjing that ended the opium war in 1842, and critiques of the British presence in China were not and are not restricted to those uttered by any single Chinese political formation. They lie at the heart of understandings of modern China's history across the worlds of the Chinese, inside and outside China.

Here I will take the history of that image of violence on the Mall and suggest how that specific history of violence in China has been smothered today by a socially and politically uncontentious story of the memorialization of British sacrifice in modern conflict. It has become a war memorial; it no longer represents imperial violence, regardless of what it actually depicts, which is coldly and precisely that.

China was never a British colony, but its sovereignty was compromised in many different ways by many different powers after the first British invasion in 1839–42. France and Japan went to war with China in 1884–5 and 1894–5 respectively. Eight powers invaded North China in 1900 and occupied the capital. 'Punishment' columns in the northern and north-eastern provinces exacted a terrible revenge well into 1901. After 1841, territory was annexed or leased, some for fixed terms, some in perpetuity. Huge swathes of what now form Russia's Siberian provinces fell under its control; at the other end of the scale, Belgium took 120 acres of the city of Tianjin as a concession in 1902. The agents of various colonial or foreign ministries, the German navy, banks, and corporations, among others, took on the administration of larger or lesser plots of territory where the Qing emperors once ruled. China's historical satellites in Southeast or Northeast Asia—the Nguyen dynasty in Vietnam, the Joseon in Korea—fell under French or Japanese control, and the British pushed up against the borders of the Qing from India.

Important central state agencies were captured in part or in full by foreign interests. Foreign advisors sat in government ministries in the capital. An Englishman, Sir Francis Aglen, all but controlled the finances of the Republic of China in the early 1920s. Treaties instructed the state what terms might be used to describe foreigners, mandated the changing of laws and removal of prohibitions on Christian evangelization, and subordinated foreign nationals in China to the jurisdiction of their own states, which was exercised in law courts built in China's cities. As railways were built, they were controlled by different foreign powers. Sun Yat-sen, the great revolutionary apostle of the first quarter of the twentieth century, argued that China's position was worse than that of other territories subjected to imperialist control: no single power among the many which subjected it to degradation had any responsibility for it.[5] A single colonial sovereign would at least have to pay some lip service to the duties of possession.

Across the century after 1842, China was always, despite all this, recognized as a sovereign and independent state. Its continued independence and overall territorial integrity were considered vital to the peaceful balancing of foreign interests, within and beyond China.[6] This balance sometimes broke down, for example when Japan went to war with Russia in 1904, a conflict mostly fought on Chinese soil. It became more fragile and then broke down steadily and comprehensively after 1931, when the Japanese seized Manchuria and created a puppet state and then exercised greater and greater pressure more widely in China, leading to the outbreak of the Sino-Japanese War in 1937. The Japanese invasion also involved an increasingly fraught cold war with the British in China, in particular.

The complexities of this Chinese century always take some explaining (and Qing China was also, of course, a conquest empire); but the politics of modern anti-imperialism relied on simpler rhetoric.[7] The idea that China was facing 'national extinction' was a refrain that had developed by the end of the nineteenth century: it was suffering from 'unequal treaties' imposed on it by the powers, young scholars argued, as they took advanced degrees in law or international history overseas, leaving it in a position that could not be justified under the international law that they studied in New York or London.

The deployment of the national humiliation narrative today is one that certainly invites analysis as to its purposes, and it needs contestation too. But these concepts predated the emergence of the Chinese Communist Party, which is exclusively associated with this narrative in Biggar's text and which therefore invalidates it in his mind, because of the party's own record of atrocities and its policies at home and abroad in the 2020s. Yet, non-communists and anti-communists alike debated the nature of China's predicament; the pro-Japanese collaborationist regime led by Wang Jingwei did so too. All argued that the underlying problem China faced was its subordination to foreign power. Chinese nationalism is grounded in anti-imperialism. The specific language of 'national humiliation' itself dates to at least 1915 and popular opposition to the wartime Japanese assault on Chinese sovereignty known as the 'Twenty-One Demands', but the idea was older.[8] The restoration of China's sovereignty had been achieved by the time the Communist Party seized power. The intellectual case had been more and strongly and effectively made; and the Guomindang's National Government, established in 1927—the Shanghai Defence Force notwithstanding—had been able to abrogate all the remaining treaties by 1943, but others too had perceived existential threat: many Chinese worlds were turned upside down. Popular disquiet exploded more than once after 1842, with the presence and activities of Christian evangelists generally, although not exclusively, the incendiary spark; legal disputes and individual instances of violence sometimes prompted extensive popular protest, while opposition to foreign privileges in railway development, for example, was a powerful factor in mobilizing elite opposition to the Qing on the cusp of the republican revolution in 1911 that overthrew it.[9]

Scholars have taken the evolution and deployment of the language of Chinese nationalism seriously, but this does not mean that they accept its premises uncritically. Identifying precisely how, when, where, and in what ways China was subjected to foreign power, an injunction to the field issued by US China historian Paul A. Cohen in 1984, reacting against a simplistic mode of writing about China as a victim of imperialism, has informed my own work and that of many others.[10] This has also been informed by the need to acknowledge Chinese agency and power throughout the period during which it was a party to these treaties. The central Chinese state, whether under the Qing or its republican successors, did not collapse. It was able mostly to manage the impact of these intense pressures, and it survived their associated challenges, such as the Taiping Civil War in 1850–64. There were spectacular failures, such as its defeat in the 1894–5 war with Japan, but, given that it was assailed by multiple powers, sometimes explicitly in concert, but routinely implicitly supporting each other, it is analytically productive to examine how, and in what ways, it retained its integrity. This was also, as the 2023 British Museum exhibition 'China's Hidden Century' showed, a period of rich and diverse innovation and creativity in Chinese culture and society.[11] But this does not mean that we can ignore the fact that China was subjected across just over a century to sustained foreign violence or the threat of violence. The bayonet, sheathed or unsheathed, was always there.

Soldiers commissioned, and an ex-soldier designed, the monument on the Mall, which perhaps explains the starkness of what you see. Unveiled on 25 April 1903 by the Prince of Wales, the future King George V, it had been commissioned by a committee of senior officers from Adrian Jones, who turned to sculpture after retiring from the army, where he had served as a veterinary surgeon. Surmounted by the figures of two Royal Marines, one stricken, the other standing over him, rifle ready, it commemorated Marine casualties in the South African and the Boxer Wars.[12] Two figurative bronze reliefs by Jones were mounted on each of the longer sides of the plinth, designed by Thomas Jackson, which portrayed two engagements, the Battle at Graspan (also known as Enslin) in South Africa in November 1899, and an incident at Peking just under a year later. These two reliefs, together with a third that lists the names and ranks of the dead, and a fourth, which shows the crest of the corps, provide the eye-level explanation and amplification of the meanings of the sculpture mounted above, which was a necessary feature of such memorials. Without these details, the monument lacks narrative coherence, and so the choice of the scenes presented was quite deliberate.[13] In his address to the crowd assembled around the monument, the Prince commented that he had 'especially desired that it should occupy a prominent place in the capital of the Empire'. He went on:

> The annals of few corps could record deeds nobler than those enacted on the slopes of Graspan and in the grounds of the British

Legation in Pekin ... in the former place the Marines, shoulder to shoulder with their comrades, the bluejackets, bravely carried the position in the face of a withering fire with the loss of nearly half their number; and in the latter, the gallantry and indomitable pluck of a handful of Marines successfully maintained the arduous struggle of those long and anxious days at Pekin.[14]

For the committee, the initial design had an admirable 'artistic effect ... as a work of art', but it was 'not considered suitable to the purpose in view, being not sufficiently true to fact'.[15] The facts of war and the incidents chosen to foreground the experience of the corps in the two campaigns were paramount. The installation of this monument in the heart of London close by the Admiralty and the War Office (and in one of the Royal Parks, St James's) was a deliberate political act, part of a wider bid to demonstrate the continuing relevance of the corps in a new age of naval warfare, sealed with royal approval. After all—and the question was asked in the aftermath of the battle in which they took such high casualties—what were Royal Marine units doing at Graspan, hundreds of miles from the sea?[16]

The battle at Graspan took place on the British march north from Cape Town to relieve the besieged town of Kimberley in the first weeks of the South African conflict.[17] The Admiralty had sanctioned the landing of a sizeable Naval Brigade composed of sailors as well as a contingent of Royal Marines to strengthen the forces available for the expedition. At Graspan, on 25 November 1899, they were deployed in a frontal assault on Boer commandos who had prepared positions on higher ground, on a ridge of small hills ('kopjes', in Afrikaans). As Arthur Conan Doyle wrote of this and related engagements in his official history of the war, 'We won the kopjes, but we lost our men.' The scale of the slaughter of marines and sailors not trained in infantry warfare was ghastly. Questions were asked afterwards in Parliament and in the press about this 'misuse of marines', and to add insult to the injury, not only did newspaper reports routinely omit mention of the corps (instead simply referring to the Naval Brigade) but there was to be no Graspan clasp for the South African War medal. In that sense, the battle never happened, even though over 100 men were killed. The memorial was designed to put that right; and to do that effectively, it showed the fight.

There was more logic in their presence in Peking. A lethal combination of first flooding, then drought set the scene against which farmers across north China rose in despair and rage in 1899–1900, prompting what became a multinational invasion of north China. This rising, characterized by the practice of a set of rituals that earned them the soubriquet the 'Boxers', bears comparison with other risings of the powerless in the face of existential crisis.[18] As news and rumours of disorder and violence spread, seventy-nine marines had been mustered from scattered detachments in north China and Shandong province and sent with other British military personnel to reinforce the modest guard usually stationed at the British Legation at Peking in late May 1900.

Three weeks later, the foreign legations entered a state of siege that would last fifty-five days before the arrival of relief forces that had landed at Dagu, seized Tianjin after a bloody battle, and fought their way north. The incursion, unsanctioned by the Qing authorities, prompted them to declare that a state of war existed and to commit their forces to the conflict alongside the insurgents. During the intermittent fighting that took place at the legations in Peking across those eight weeks, three marines lost their lives among almost seventy foreign combatants killed, and a Victoria Cross and a Distinguished Service Cross would be awarded to men of the corps. Mid-way through the siege, in the early morning of 3 July, a party of American and British marines, and Russian sailors, led by an American officer, stormed and cleared a Chinese-held barricade on the city wall overlooking the American legation. This is the incident caught in bronze in London.[19]

WRITTEN ON THE CITY

It is not the only memorial in Britain marking British lives and British sacrifice in China. They can be spotted on church walls and in cemeteries across the country, usually for the military dead—especially casualties of the Second Opium War—but also to commemorate missionary martyrs. Perhaps the angriest is the inscription on a Norfolk tombstone in memory of William de Normann who 'Perished in captivity / In the cruel power of the heathen / After a captivity of sixteen days' during the invasion of north China in 1860. Rooted in profound maternal grief, the tomb had a companion in a huge granite cross shipped to China in 1862 that eventually stood in the British consulate gardens at Shanghai for a century.[20] But if not the starkest in language, the memorial on the Mall is the most explicit. There is much else by way of other mute evidence of the British wars in China. Lord Elgin looks out across a city that houses in its museums a great deal of Chinese artifacts seized during the invasion of 1860 that he oversaw as High Commissioner and Plenipotentiary to China. The Royal Marines Memorial can be paired with the loot gathered in 1900 that now sits alongside those in museums, galleries, and libraries, such as the 1,500-year-old 'Admonitions Scroll', the earliest surviving Chinese scroll painting. Many of these institutions are less than explicit about the origins of such holdings, just as the statues of great men remain tight lipped.[21]

The Mall itself grew more and more important in the years after Jones' monument was unveiled. With the memorial to Queen Victoria unveiled outside Buckingham Palace at the southwestern end in 1910, and Trafalgar Square having been opened up with Admiralty Arch close by the statue as part of the same project, the Mall became what has been described as a 'great stage set' for imperial and royal processions and ceremonial. Securing a site within this had been the hope of the committee that had commissioned the memorial from the very start.

THE TRUTH ABOUT EMPIRE

Trafalgar Square itself was already the site of statues of several military figures associated with the British Empire.[22] Like many memorials, that to the Royal Marine dead in 1899–1901 has not been fixed in place since its installation, neither physically, nor in terms of its meaning and associations. In December 1940, it was removed from its original site to a builder's yard in Battersea on the south bank of the Thames to make way for the building of the Admiralty Citadel, the concrete bunker alongside the Admiralty building that still stands today.

It is worth pausing to note the anxiety about the fate of London's statues in wartime that can be tracked in the press, especially in the columns of *The Times*, in the winter of 1940–1. A small number of monuments had been removed by the end of October 1939, but the vast majority remained in place, some sandbagged, others left exposed, and damaged: John Milton was knocked off his pedestal outside a City of London church in August 1940. Some correspondents pointed out that in peaceful times there was rarely much consensus in London on the subject of statues, and that 'no form of art focuses so much passion and disagreement as sculpture', or else that they should wear their wounds with pride, as Londoners were doing. But the 'weeping and wailing' of patrician voices in favour of safeguarding these public monuments appeared to win out. They were 'memorials of the immortal activity of the men of our race', it was argued, that could 'teach the wayfarer ... so many gracious and instructive lessons in English history'. Some were indisputably works of art, Rodin's 'Burghers of Calais', for example, and, it was argued, should have been made safe as artworks if national galleries and museums had been made safe. In early 1941, despite competing priorities, some statues were moved to the grounds of Berkhamsted Castle, north-west of London, their safeguarding—the Rodin included—reassuringly recorded in photographs published in *The Illustrated London News*.[23] Clearly, statues mattered, or to be more precise, mattered to enough of those with influence sufficient to prompt the diversion of scarce resource to protect them in wartime.

An Office of Works civil servant noted pointedly in December 1940 that the Royal Marines memorial was not removed 'because of artistic merit' or for reasons of safety: it was simply in the way. Most statues were reinstalled after the end of the war, but this was a slow process; some were re-sited: General Gordon was moved out of Trafalgar Square to the Embankment. Some, such as the Royal Marines Memorial, had no home to go back to. In 1943, it had been moved to the grounds of the Royal Hospital Chelsea. Might it stay there, or be moved to the Royal Marine barracks at Chatham, mused officials, although that could 'offend the corps'? Eventually, in November 1948 it was re-erected on a site across the Mall from its original location.[24] The memorial had provided a focus for a commemoration of the Battle of Graspan in November 1925, when wreaths were laid, and on its thirtieth anniversary in 1929.[25] But it was only later in the twentieth century that a commemoration involving serving Marines and veterans at the monument became an annual event, with the first 'Graspan Memorial Parade' taking place in 1976.[26] In October 2000, after renovations, the monument formally assumed a new identity, as the Royal Marines National Memorial. Unveiled by Prince Philip, the Duke of Edinburgh, in his role as Captain General Royal Marines, the renovations were funded by the Royal Marines Charity, which had appealed for funds to augment the memorial to mark the 10,000 Royal Marines who lost their lives in the twentieth century. This took the form of a bronze ring on the ground around the plinth, which records that '[t]his memorial was rededicated in October 2000 in honour of all Royal Marines who have served their country by land and sea and who are forever remembered by their friends'. With this addition, and through the 'Graspan Parade' in May, which commemorates

Royal Marine losses, the monument's meanings shifted shape again. It was now a national war memorial, the fine and pointed politics of its installation lost in time.

There was always more to the history of the British presence in China after 1839 than violence of course. As well as conflict, misunderstanding, and arrogance, there is plenty of evidence of collaboration, profound intellectual engagement and exchange, admiration, humanitarian enterprise, love, and friendship. Stories of all can be found and should be and have been told. But the foundation was violence, in thought, word, and deed. There were countless daily humiliations inflicted wittingly and unwittingly in China and on the Chinese across the worlds in which they lived under British flags. It is written across the City of London in church, museum, and on the streets. This caused concern to those who looked. Just as Royal Marines in the Shanghai Defence Force were about to land in Shanghai in 1927, an anxious civil engineer contacted the Foreign Secretary about the 'menace' the portrayal of a 'marine spitting a Chinaman in midair on the end of his bayonet' presented. It was 'fraught with possibility' as a subject for 'Red propaganda', and it ought to be removed. Civil servants brushed the suggestion aside.

Commenting on the debate about monuments in early 1941, *Tatler* journalist Oliver Stewart, tongue a little in cheek, wrote that 'I personally would rather have a tree—any tree—than a Wren church, a few flowers rather than all the architecture in England, and any weed you care to name than a battalion of London statues.' Perhaps, he continued, those that had been encased in sandbags might remain that way after the war camouflaged with 'a graceful awning of green', and nothing but the flowers whose seeds had blown on to them and sprouted.[27] Instead, the telling of 'gracious and instructive' tales, of the bayonet thrust to the Chinese stomach, resumed on London streets as it continues today, if you want to hear it.

PART THREE

HISTORIOGRAPHY AND RACE

8

MORALITY AND THE HISTORY OF ABOLITION AND EMPIRE

Richard Huzzey

By considering the role of anti-slavery politics in the history of the British Empire, this chapter highlights distinctions between the historical study of moralities in the past and presentist judgements about morality in our society. As we shall see, academics associated with the website History Reclaimed—here dubbed 'Reclaimers'—have claimed to be defending historicism—meaning the faithful understanding of past worlds and historical contexts. These authors charge mostly unnamed scholars with the perjury of presentism—meaning the subservience of historical truth to contemporary politics and concerns. The Reclaimers have simultaneously criticised recent research into slavery and empire for failing to promote moral exemplars of national pride. As well as considering historical research into anti-slavery moralities and imperialism, the chapter argues that the Reclaimers misapply the very principles of empirical research and open-minded historicism that they avow.

Understanding the past on its own terms means analysing—and not accepting as uniform or uncontested—the very terms of that past, which encompass the dominant narratives and voices in the sources available to us and the unarticulated assumptions and contexts they bear. Arguments over the relative perspective, insight, or relevance of particular sources or extrapolations are the bread-and-butter of historical debate—not the monopoly of a particular group of historians. The leading Reclaimer, Robert Tombs, denounces unspecified recent scholarship as 'ideology, propaganda and often careerism', from which he and his fellow Reclaimers are purportedly immune.[1] Founded by Tombs to defend theologian Nigel Biggar from criticism of his 'Ethics and Empire' project, History Reclaimed publishes blogs and newspaper columns—mostly reacting to questions of contemporary memorialisation and policy today regarding the legacies of slavery and empire. Contrary to their stated desire to defend historicist research methods, the Reclaimers conflate their contemporary political opinions with fidelity to historical truth in ways that diminish the latter by insisting it has a singular politics in the present.

Histories of slavery and abolitionism have occupied a growing share of attention in both academic research and public interest in the years surrounding the 2007 bicentenary of abolition of the slave trade under British law and following the rise of the Black Lives Matter protests.[2] New scholarship has arisen from new research questions and fresh interpretations of evidence, rather than a disregard for historical truth. Undoubtedly, twenty-first-century ideas shape the questions we pose about our history, if only by destabilising the assumptions taken for granted about what is natural and determined in past societies: historians have sought to historicise gender, race, or national identity as their own societies became conscious of the contingencies forging

MORALITY AND THE HISTORY OF ABOLITION

each. The answers to new questions still require evidence, analysis, and historicist sensitivity—even if historical questions and understandings of the past expand and change.

Acknowledging the distinctive roles for historical investigation and for present-day citizenship is likely to make us better at each and encourage good faith debates on the proper relationship of one to the other. Public and political consideration of international development, racism and racial inequalities, Britain's role in the world, and humanitarian interventionism have all drawn on the facts, meaning, and implications of the British Empire's leading roles in both slavery and then suppression of the slave trade. Public, moral, and spiritual deliberation by citizens over a society's present and future should always be informed by historical research and scholarly debate, in addition to popular memory. Yet a presentist question—entirely centred in the ethics and politics of our own times—spurs public debate on what that history means for our society's heritage and obligations today. A distinction between historicising moralities in the past and debating political obligations in the present might avoid making them interdependent. This chapter therefore begins by establishing how historians have engaged with the question of morality in investigating the emergence of abolitionism up until emancipation in the British West Indies; in doing so, it shows how historians can analyse morality historically rather than, as Biggar proposes, judging historical institutions as morally instructive or repulsive to us today. Secondly, the chapter considers the ways scholars have researched Victorian anti-slavery policies and the naval suppression of the slave trade, highlighting how Biggar and the History Reclaimed authors risk overlooking the complexities of the relationship between abolition and empire.

The ability to pose new questions about the past need not reduce historical research to partisan warfare over contemporary politics. The final section considers the differences among scholars, including among the Reclaimers themselves, on the proper relationship of historical research to present-day society: it proposes one way to understand the virtues of historical particularism as complementary, rather than identical, with contemporary debates about how the past should inform present-day politics. Many historians will accept the impossibility of fully detaching ourselves from our own times yet remain committed to evidence-based argument that seeks to understand truth. An empirical humility can leave historians aware of the impossible task and unimaginable scale and unlimited scope of their task to historicise—and still bequeath a better vantage point into past worlds than a retreat into partisan polemic. If historians may glimpse the truths of the past obscured from prior scholars' viewpoints, generating new interpretations and questions, then we cannot imagine that we can fully escape our own present, provide the final word on any period, or avoid errors from which successive generations will surely correct us. If our own times prompt new research questions about the past, the quality of our answers depends on historical evidence, not those answers' value or relevance as ammunition in a culture war. In conflating historicism with particular research conclusions, or with a particular politics of heritage in the present, the Reclaimers undermine the very research practices they profess to defend.

Historicising abolitionist moralities (1783–1838)

The proper relationship of history to morality has been—though sometimes unacknowledged—at the heart of histories of abolitionism in the British Empire. The transformation of British social attitudes and political policies towards slavery in roughly fifty years from the 1780s to 1830s has proved fascinating to historians because it was so abrupt—given Britain's world-leading role in the eighteenth-century slave trade—and because it was so quick—at least from a historian's perspective of cultural change.³ In 1808, the abolitionist Thomas Clarkson wrote his own 'History' of the deep origins and proximate course of the campaign to abolish slave trading under the British flag. His emphasis on abolition as a fruit of God's Providence and unfolding civilisational progress reflected much of the theology and rhetoric of abolitionist campaigning.⁴ Within a generation of emancipation in the British West Indies, the Irish historian William Lecky judged abolitionism one of the few 'perfectly virtuous' acts in his history of European morals.⁵ The first challenge to the supposed self-evident logic of humanitarianism arose in 1944, when Trinidadian historian Eric Williams argued that what mattered most in securing anti-slavery policies was economic interests—though, interestingly, he questioned the causal influence more than the personal sincerity of the 'Saints'.⁶ Since then, historians of abolitionism have paid attention to the variety, contexts, and complexity of abolitionism, answering the question set by Williams even when disagreeing on the balance of popular pressure and elite calculation in parliamentary victories.⁷

Critics of Biggar's 'Ethics and Empire' project have pointed out that '[g]ood and evil may be meaningful terms of analysis for theologians' yet are 'useless to historians'. He characterised this as the common claim of historians 'that the making of moral judgements was professionally beneath them'.⁸ Yet he misses the point that historical questions would typically analyse 'good' to analyse 'good for whom?' and 'good to what end?' and 'good in whose judgement?' Scholarship on slavery and abolition certainly has been interested in historical moralities as causal explanations or as an object of study. Indeed, the latest generation of scholarship on abolitionism has tended to take moralities extremely seriously—seeing moral arguments or appeals as crucial to the popularisation of abolitionism.

Research into abolitionist campaigning, for example, has emphasised the breadth and variegation of personnel and beliefs, focusing on empirical investigation of the religious, commercial, and cultural networks behind local committees or their rhetorical, emotional, and entrepreneurial skill.[9] Influentially, Christopher Leslie Brown applied the concept of 'moral capital' to explain how various abolitionist leaders sincerely supported abolition as a good in itself but also as part of their wider religious and social vision. He argues that the transatlantic rows over the American Revolution crystallised the question of responsibility for slaving, politicising the moral quandary of Parliament's potential responsibility for continuing or ending it. Brown shows how Claphamite evangelicals saw abolition as the first—colonial—target in a wider reformation of manners in Great Britain. Crucially, he analyses how Clarkson conceived of himself as a romantic hero acting as the instrument of God's Providence—shifting the earliest self-explanation of abolition into a historical subject of why abolition emerged as a political cause when it did.[10] A critical rather than cynical approach to the religious, political, and social history of British abolitionism suggests a rich, complex, and often conflicted range of views, applied in different contexts and periods of time, united only in the broadest opposition to slavery.

Greater understanding of British slavery before its abolition has also improved the understanding of anti-slavery politics with the United Kingdom. For example, research into the slavery-related wealth of institutions, families, and individuals can illuminate the strength of pro-slavery views or the silences of some politicians during the controversy. The expanding quantitative and qualitative investigation of the slavery business, the productive and reproductive labour of enslaved people in particular colonies or plantations, and the dynamics of resistance provide not just a fuller picture of what the abolitionists were up against but what they did *not* seek to challenge in their attack on chattel slavery. Rather than diminishing our understanding of abolitionism, research in these fields offers a richer and fuller picture—by helping to explain how the costs of imperial defence in the Caribbean, the frequency of risings, and the pro-natalist reproduction of the enslaved population figured in the elite and popular politics of empire.[11] While present-day rejection of racialised difference has spurred scholars to take the experiences and agency of enslaved people seriously, historians such as Gelien Matthews carefully trace the process by which resistance emerged as an argument for, rather than against, abolition in British debates. This historicises the impact of resistance, acknowledging it as the earliest source of opposition to slavery without demanding its causal supremacy over other political pressures bearing on Parliament.[12] To fear that interest in the history of slavery is to risk displacing, erasing, or obscuring our understanding of abolition is to assume a zero-sum game of attention. Indeed, we understand abolitionism within the British Isles better for knowing more about slavery and emancipation in colonial or comparative contexts.

As Biggar notes, John Wesley and other preachers quoted scripture to condemn Christians' participation in slavery before the American Revolution. However, demands for Parliament to interpose legal restraint on slaving only crystallised in the 1780s.[13] Moreover, for many years Christian teachings had been used as a bulwark to justify slavery.[14] This points to historical changes in attitudes towards slavery, the place of metropolitan subjects in regulating colonial policy, and the role of the state in addressing perceived vices. David Richardson, in his final book, argues that multiplying reports about the ship-board resistance by enslaved Africans in the middle passage—and hence the conditions that provoked them—helped to fuel the changing concerns about British traders' role in the traffic, more than any Enlightenment philosophy.[15] To this may be added the developing deliberation of judicial and ordinary providentialism in evangelical and natural theology, respectively, which Granville Sharp, Ottobah Cugoano, Olaudah Equiano, and Thomas Clarkson all applied to the relationship between the immorality of slavery and the national interest.[16] Considering the religious and cultural contexts for the emergence of abolitionism, however, is to seek historical explanations of this change rather than to validate or praise it. Even an atheist can recover and study the historical role of Christian theology, popular religiosity, and cultural authority without passing judgement on its spiritual truth.

Crucially, anti-slavery policies emerged in the context of—not in rejection of—anxieties about the prosperity of the British Empire. Indeed, Lawrence Goldman's survey for History Reclaimed incorporates this scholarship to highlight many of the complexities that forged abolitionist fortunes.[17] Most abolitionists imagined a more pliable and fecund Black peasantry in the West Indies after abolition and emancipation.[18] Resistance in Demerara (1823) and Jamaica (1831–2), as well as the ghosts of the Haitian revolution, would slowly be redefined as proofs of the dangers of slavery, not the risks of emancipation.[19] The dynamics of maritime and colonial warfare during the Napoleonic Wars changed the balance of realpolitik in Britain's unilateral renunciation of the slave trade in 1807, as Roger Anstey—himself no cynic about evangelical sincerity—argued long ago.[20] To place abolitionist morality in these contexts is to historicise 'a Christian ideal of basic human equality', highlighted by Biggar as historically particular rather than universal, without avowing or denying it.[21]

Moralities must be seen as worldviews that incorporate the question of when, whether, and how virtue and prosperity relate to each other. Biggar posits that 'there is nothing at all wrong with pursuing our own *genuine* interests', and 'the fact that national interests are among the motives for a government's policy need not make it immoral'.[22] He is right to note that economic determinism has proved insufficient explanation for the overwhelming majority of scholars explaining popular abolitionism, but he does not engage scholarship evaluating the complexities of anti-slavery moralities and ideologies. Abolitionists themselves proved contrary, inconsistent, and vague on the relationship between morality and prosperity much of the time, although they had rich answers to it. The prayer of a 1792 petition from Newbury insisted that 'no considerations of either gain or policy can exculpate this nation from the foulest guilt' of slaving, but that abolition 'would not ultimately be inimical to the political or commercial advantages of our country' since it would 'avert the indignation, and have a rational ground to hope for the blessing, of the Benevolent Creator'.[23] Political economists and abolitionist theorists searched for evidence of the exact means by which, as Adam Smith predicted, free labour would prove more profitable 'in the end'.[24] Indeed, as Olaudah Equiano's 1789 *Narrative* suggested, trading with—not in—Africans would yield to Britain 'immensely rich' raw materials from Africa 'in return for manufactures'.[25] To point to the relationship between moral and material interests is not to suggest the former is a cloak for the latter, but that each might forge perceptions and definitions of the other. Rather than discerning the value of abolitionist moralities (plural) as transcendental motives, historians have sought to recover the values individuals and groups expressed publicly or shared privately. This underscores the historical question of how individuals and states might construe their interests and morals converging or conflicting in particular contexts.

Historicising the morality of abolitionism within the British Isles helps to clarify the complex interplay of political, material, and cultural forces that changed attitudes to slavery. The popular mobilisation of abolitionist petitioning also helps explain the wider transformation of political culture within the United

Kingdom in the half-century after the 1783 Treaty of Paris.[26] Analysis of the rhetoric of leading abolitionists demonstrates their general use of moral over policy-related arguments in public debates—especially compared to pro-slavery opponents—but this is not to make normative claims for their morality.[27] Rather than upholding abolitionism as moral, historians have sought to historicise moral understandings of slavery as an enemy rather than an engine of human progress.[28] As we shall see in the next section, this has implications for the translation of abolitionist politics into anti-slavery policies after the 1834–8 experience of emancipation in the British Caribbean.

The morality of anti-slavery and empire (after 1838)

Having considered the cultural shift in attitudes to slavery within the British Isles, this section considers the roles of anti-slavery policy, morality, and ideology at the frontiers of Victorian imperialism. History Reclaimed founder Tombs suggests, in response to public discussion of the royal family's links to the slavery business, 'that Britain, and hence its monarchy, were the leaders of a long global campaign to end the slave trade and then slavery itself'.[29] For the period after 1838, Biggar emphasises how 'anti-slavery, not slavery, was at the heart of imperial policy'—but the complexity of anti-slavery policies challenges the Reclaimers' desire for clear moral lessons from the past.[30] While leading abolitionists and wider publics might share pride in their anti-slavery nation, they differed in what policies and obligations that should actually dictate. Notably, anti-slavery activists as well as party politicians divided over whether preferential tariffs for sugar from the West Indies should be retained after emancipation.[31] In fact, while the boycott of sugar had been a means of protesting slavery in British colonies before 1834, many Britons saw no contradiction in consuming the produce of enslaved labour from the United States, Brazil, or other foreign economies.[32]

The moral condemnation of enslavement did not necessarily unsettle the ethnic essentialism and civilisational hierarchies that informed ideas about racial difference in the period. Noting this fact does not seek to censure past practices by the standards of contemporary morals but rather historicises and decouples our present expectation that opposition to racialised slavery must imply opposition to racism. Tombs' claim that 'mass petitions and boycotts of slave-grown products' are 'sufficient proof that Britain has long been one of the least racist societies' risks ahistorical conflation of the two.[33] Rejecting the legal institution of slavery as the most extreme form of human exploitation could—but did not necessarily—challenge racialised thinking. In fact, Colonial Office plans for apprenticeship, as part of the 1833 Abolition Act, and then policies in colonies such as Jamaica to force Black labourers back to the plantations, sought to rig the forces of supply-and-demand to ensure that freedom would sustain a cheap, peasant economy.[34] Indeed, the disappointment of anti-slavery expectations for free-labour productivity in the Caribbean seems to have encouraged rising racist pessimism and essentialism in the decades after emancipation—unshackling racism from its pejorative association with slavery in the press.[35]

Over many decades, Britain's Foreign Office pursued diplomatic treaties authorising the interception and adjudication of slaving vessels flying other nations' flags, attacking illegal slaving by Britons but also policing the traffic by other countries' nationals. In this campaign, Biggar sees that 'the history of British involvement in slavery had a virtuous ending, albeit one that the anti-colonialists are determined we should overlook'.[36] In contrast, scholars have sought to examine the Atlantic—and latterly Indian Ocean—suppression campaigns in order to understand their aims, policies, and realities for officials, sailors, and enslaved Africans.[37] The Royal Navy's international responsibility for maritime slave-trade suppression arose from the specific politics of the wartime Abolition Act of 1807 and the Concert of Europe after the Napoleonic Wars. The Duke of Wellington and other British leaders did not intend to make European abolition one of their goals in the 1814–15 Congress of Vienna, but a wave of popular mobilisation opposed complicity in permitting the resumption of foreign slave trades. Both anti-slavery and pro-slavery supporters could unite, for very different reasons, in seeking to curb the traffic in enslaved Africans to rival powers' colonies.[38] British diplomats translated decades of naval interception during wars with European powers of foreigners' prize cargoes, including enslaved Africans, into a legal-military regime of suppression.[39]

In his analysis of the Royal Navy's suppression campaign, Biggar largely relies on an article by international relations theorists who argue for the value placed on national prestige and reputation arising from the diplomatic and naval campaign. These may not be direct economic motives, but they point to the ways in which the determination of moralities and national interests remained intertwined in ways that point to moral complexity.[40] In Biggar's consequentialist assessment of slave-trade suppression, it might be pertinent to consider the treatment of the 'liberated Africans' aboard slavers intercepted at sea. As a new generation of scholarship has shown, the legal and bureaucratic process of condemning slaving vessels treated 'liberated Africans' as a dispossessed workforce entitled to papers of freedom and apprenticed labour.[41] While some scholars trace the origins of international human rights law to Britain's web of anti-slave-trade treaties and courts, the zeal and boldness of naval interception clearly reinforced hierarchies of national sovereignty and realpolitik.[42] Indeed, the Foreign Office demarcation of sovereignty treaty-making between 'civilised' and African states helped to establish, as historian Robin Law argues, the legal doctrines for colonial annexation in subsequent decades.[43] To highlight these complexities is to historicise moral values.

In fact, Victorian Britons themselves debated the morality of violence and military power in enforcing suppression of the slave trade. An important strand of abolitionist activists within the British and Foreign Anti-Slavery Society, particularly influenced by Quaker ethics, opposed the naval suppression in the 1840s and 1850s. In this, they found strange bedfellows in some Cobdenite free traders and West Indian protectionists who disliked the military expense, and each looked to their rival trade policies to see free labour triumph.[44] The unlikely composition of this group of anti-suppressionists offers its own evidence of the ongoing contests over the heterodox priorities and policies arising from the British Empire's renunciation of slavery as a legal institution.

Explaining the popular presumption of a national interest in the suppression of foreign slave trading defies simplistic resort to rational-choice theories of self-interest; as Biggar notes, based on calculations by David Eltis, expenditure on naval suppression represented a sizeable chunk of the small Victorian state's expenditure.[45] However, explaining the multi-generational politics of anti-slavery policy requires something beyond Manichean contrasts between morality and economics given their close association with the complementary expectations of commerce, Christianity, and civilisation. Elleke Boehmer's judgement that 'no empire set out to bring law and order to other peoples in the first instance' because 'motivating forces are profit and more profit' is challenged by Biggar as reductive.[46] Yet, as historians have traced, imperial politics often fused expectations of national interest, commercial prospects, and moral zeal in different examples of colonial expansion.[47] The imperial projections of David Livingstone and his successors in the central African lakes, of the British East African Company's promises to shareholders and ministers, or of Frederick Lugard in the conquest of Nigeria could each summon—by varying degrees of sincerity or priority—the anti-slavery promise of serving morality and prosperity together.[48]

Precisely because anti-slavery doctrines often held that suppression of slaving would unlock the bountiful production of new exports, speculative colonial projects were dreamed up or promoted to a wider public on the premise of future trade, taxation, or cultivation complementing Britain's moral purpose. For this reason, the European division of African territories for commercial and colonial development took place in concert with discussions to suppress inter-societal slaving at the Brussels and Berlin conferences. A focus on the disruption caused by slaving raids led to colonial officials retreating from the responsibility of ending slavery persisting under the British flag in 'protectorates'. The abolition of slavery under British law in the Caribbean colonies had not marked the end of slavery in British territories. In India, British authorities had moved to change the English vocabulary by which they referred to forced labourers and to avoid actively recognising—or, indeed, disrupting—'traditional' customs of coerced and hereditary labour. As Suzanne Miers and others have shown, this model of 'delegalisation' rather than emancipation would be applied in the 'protectorates' developed to exclude British colonial officials from responsibility for emancipating enslaved Africans within African territories claimed for the empire.[49] Indeed, in the period after the First World War, Lugard would promote to the League of Nations and the International Labour Organization his policies in British Nigeria that codified the definitions of slavery and 'native labour'.[50] The anti-slavery policies that tolerated ongoing forms of slavery and forced labour pose challenges to any moral assessment of imperial rule.

MORALITY AND THE HISTORY OF ABOLITION

Biggar's desire to assess the moral example of the British Empire as a talisman for our own times follows in the footsteps of some early twentieth-century studies of slavery and its abolition. The first generation of scholarly enquiry in the twentieth century examined abolitionism as an example of imperial humanitarianism within the British Empire, which then still existed. Reginald Coupland, for example, hoped his history of the antislavery movement would encourage his own generation to live up to his ideals of trusteeship for the British Empire in the interwar years. On the centenary of emancipation, he hoped to revive readers' interest in the 1930s work of the Anti-Slavery Society to tackle the problem of slavery still alive in the world.[51] Ironically, one of the great causes of the abolitionist movement in this period would be support for Mussolini's invasion of Abyssinia, which promised to end slavery in the country.[52] To mention this is not to claim moral superiority to the activists of that time, but to point to the complexities—rather than moral clarity—of antislavery as a facet of imperialism. Indeed, as this section has emphasised, a nation increasingly proud and secure in its antislavery commitments retained stark divisions over what imperial policies this might now oblige.

Here, expert researchers legitimately disagree on the continuities between abolitionism as a reformist movement and the antislavery policies practised by Victorian officials, investors, and missionaries. To some historians, the 'antislavery rationale it [the state] adopted for imperialist policies' should be understood as categorically separate to abolitionism as a social movement aimed at dismantling the state's support for slavery.[53] This chapter has, instead, argued for the complex continuities of ideas and personnel between abolitionist reformers and anti-slavery imperialism.[54] Historians disagree in good faith over the historical question of the extent to which abolitionist moralities informed imperial policies; this reflects scholarly judgement rather than political point-scoring in the present. Biggar's approach—of assuming anti-slavery and empire stand trial jointly for a moral verdict today—sits uneasily with historical enquiry into the causes, motives, rhetorics, logics, and moralities of the past. Indeed, historians as citizens may find the relationship between abolitionism and imperialism disturbs our present-day understanding of the former as much as the latter.

How history should relate to contemporary morality

This section will consider the Reclaimers' arguments about the proper relationship between past and present in historical research and contemporary society before suggesting a practical alternative. The authors writing for History Reclaimed demonstrate intriguing differences among themselves as regards the relationship posited between the past and the present—and hence between history and politics. Tombs has urged 'society to remember accurately, fully and honestly, and to understand the vital differences between the past and the present'.[55] Similarly, Goldman argues that '[h]istory cannot be studied through our eyes and values'.[56] These are pleas for historicism as the denaturalisation of our own logics and the alienation of the present by appreciating the differences of past experience, thought, and deed. Most historians, differing in their methodological training or contemporary politics, will share this desire to avoid finding political validation or comforts in the past.

However, the Reclaimers' core claims to defend empirical research and historical sensitivity sit uneasily with Tombs' lament that 'our younger generation are being told to despise everything about our common past—one of the main foundations on which national solidarity rests'.[57] His condemnation of people 'rewriting our history to fit a new agenda' could just as easily apply to his denigration of peer-reviewed research by historians of the British

MORALITY AND THE HISTORY OF ABOLITION

Empire.[58] In similar terms, Biggar argues that 'at stake is not merely the pedantic truth about yesterday, but the self-perception and self-confidence of the British today'.[59] While a society's understanding of the past clearly shapes national identities, it is not clear why historical truth should be subservient to patriotism. Far from defending historicism against presentism, Tombs in particular appears to advocate a kind of Erastianism for history—where revelation defers to the interests of the nation-state.

Indeed, the historical insight that made Tombs a respected expert on nineteenth-century France is evident when he observes that the 'British Empire was marked by staggering contrasts and it is easy to fashion a narrative to fit an ideological programme.' Such complexity and contrast is precisely what is lacking from the narrative about slavery and empire on which he insists: Tombs attacks uncomfortable evidence as 'nit-picking criticism' that threatens the truth of and pride in 'our common past'.[60] But what is the prioritisation of 'our common past' and pride in it but 'an ideological programme', and one at that which makes the present-day usefulness of our findings the determinant of historical truth?

However, it would be tiresome to simply throw back and forth accusations of partisanship and polemic, claiming devotion to a historical truth superior to that of the Reclaimers. Instead, it may be helpful to tease apart their individual claims about the relationship between empirical research and what histories of slavery and the British Empire ought to mean for the twenty-first century—in the hopes of proposing an alternative. Goldman argues that 'we certainly need to be true and faithful to the history', which should be 'based upon the sources and the facts'. True to his aims, his lecture for History Reclaimed on the history of the anti-slavery movement incorporates much of the complexity of recent scholarship on abolitionism and its international contexts before his audience invites him to comment on what this might mean for national memory today.[61] In moving, however, from the realms of 'a scholarly approach' to consider contemporary implications in society today, Goldman follows other Reclaimers in dismissing unnamed 'ideologists' for whom 'evidence matters far less' than for him.[62] This risks conflating the interpretive role of historians in assaying the relative significance or meaning of different forms of evidence about the past—about which there can be intelligent and good-faith disagreements—with the political and social questions of what the past means for Britons today—about which there can also be intelligent and good-faith disagreements.

Historical interpretation is never finally settled or concluded: while new empirical evidence occasionally changes the 'facts', more often debate involves scholars identifying different answers in the meaning of evidence, or perhaps by simply asking a different question from their predecessors. Historians cannot ever escape our own present circumstances or personal views, but neither could those historians writing before us. Most commonly, scholars seek a historicist understanding of how people in the past imagined their own world and often emphasise the strangeness and alien nature of the past, rather than its simple parallels with our own concerns. It is common to explain the reasons we suspect other scholars have fallen into error—by reference to the assumptions and anxieties of the time in which they wrote or the methodological and ideological commitments we believe them to have held—and scholarly debate rests on the strength of argument from evidence. Just as a stopped clock can be right twice a day, explaining why an author may have been attracted to a particular interpretation does not falsify it. If we cannot escape the present, we might glimpse the past better by seeking to argue on the basis of evidence and interpretation.

Biggar still stands apart from his fellow Reclaimers in both his disciplinary background and his aims. Setting out to evaluate the morality of the British Empire, he proposes both that historians are ill-equipped to offer moral judgements and that they often fail to recognise when they are doing so in their writing.[63] This seems a reasonable, if commonplace, criticism, since historians seek to escape and transcend the assumptions of their present in researching the past but broadly realise they cannot succeed. Just as questions in our present may pose new ones for our past, so the answers we draw about historical realities will be constrained by our conception of human nature or the explanatory power of structure and contingency. While most historians seek to judge historical questions of causation or experience, he proposes that '[w]e cannot help but judge the past by our present ethics'.[64] However, Biggar draws a distinction between such historians and those whose 'moral and political motives refuse to allow themselves to be tempered or corrected by data and reason'.[65] Like many of the principles of scholarship professed by his fellow Reclaimers, this goal is uncontentious. However, detecting scholarly sin in others is often easier than abstaining from it.

The attempt to draw a contrast between scholarly neutrality on the part of Reclaimers against ideological activists, often unnamed, is the fundamental flaw of a project that is really focused on disputing contemporary politics and memorialisation. A challenge for anyone wishing to engage the Reclaimers' arguments is that their outputs are principally unreferenced blog posts on their website or opinion columns in the press. It is to Biggar's credit that his transparent referencing allows us to trace these points—and he admits that many of the theories and interpretations he targets come from literary scholars of postcolonialism.[66] In other cases, the Reclaimers struggle to distinguish between the historical aims and political positions of initiatives they wish to criticise. For example, Tombs describes projects to research historic links to slavery as 'crude propaganda' signalling capitulation to an '"anti-racist" mission to destroy Britain'.[67]

THE TRUTH ABOUT EMPIRE

Some criticisms of History Reclaimed have focused on the fact that the historians claiming scholarly authority on contemporary memorialisation are almost exclusively experts in fields other than the history of the British Empire.[68] However, this scholarly territorialism obscures a wider question of whether any historical researchers focused on understanding the past on its own terms hold particular wisdom as citizens navigating the legacies and memory of slavery and imperialism for twenty-first-century Britain. After King Charles III commissioned research into the monarchy's own history, Goldman noted that 'historians have always known about these links, though they are buried deep in national history'.[69] Popular understanding and public deliberation about 'national history' are not always synonymous with the frontiers of historical scholarship. Goldman's article, headlined 'Leave History to the Historians', suggests that deliberation on the wider legacies or public memory of the past is a distraction from present social ills. Certainly, historians have an important role to play in sharing interpretations, explanations, and evidence about the past in order to inform public history, national memory, and political deliberation with evidence and evidence-based analysis, but historians are not the only stakeholders in what history means to present society. While historical research influences how society remembers that past, it is ultimately an ethical or political debate between citizens as to when and how to extract pertinent lessons for their present—and what they wish to glorify, emulate, or reject in the future. This is not to distort evidence or bury truths about the past but to recognise that arguments—for example about whose statutes to erect, remove, recontextualise, or reposition—are debates about heritage in the present.

It is not clear why historians *as historians* should claim superior wisdom in divining the past's political, social, and moral meanings for our present, whatever their expertise in historical analysis. It is possible and desirable that scholars who vote alike might disagree on the causal analysis of past events or, conversely, that historians who share an interpretive framework for a historical problem differ on what it means for policy, memory, and identity today. The conflation, then, of historical fact with a particular prescription for politics and memory in the present is a sleight of hand that risks doing more damage to the former. This chapter has focused on the authors associated with History Reclaimed because of the particular political conclusions they draw from broader historicist principles—precisely because those historicist aims are worth defending from monopolisation by those with a particular approach to the heritage and legacies of empire. Posing new questions to the past and unsettling the assumptions of existing interpretations is the lifeblood of historiographical practice; indeed, this is demonstrated in the original and insightful contributions that Tombs and Goldman, for example, have made to their own fields of historical expertise, which added new understandings rather than simply re-composing established facts in new prose.

As this chapter has argued, histories of abolitionist campaigns and anti-slavery policies have developed an appreciation of the sources, variety, and limits of past moralities as an object of historical research, developing historical rather than normative judgements about morality.[70] The causal balance of factors in explaining the parliamentary majorities for the 1807 and 1833 Acts, the continuation of naval suppression in 1850, or particular anti-slavery 'bridgeheads' of imperial expansion are open to reasoned debate based on evidence. At the same time, scholars will differ in how they translate shared historical conclusions into present-day imperatives, since identifying the relevance of comparisons and parallels is a political judgement in itself. For example, a historian writing about the moral complexities of anti-slavery imperialism in the nineteenth century may be surprised by the presentist conclusions a columnist draws from his work about contemporary 'activist groups'.[71] However difficult in practice, differentiating the roles of historical scholarship and present citizenship is likely to strengthen each by distinguishing claims about *what* happened in the past from the question of how parallels, legacies, or problems in the present *ought* to be informed by our understanding of that past.

Disagreements over what the imperial past means for contemporary social questions of racial inequalities, racist prejudice, international development, reparation, modern slavery, or public memorialisation are political questions for citizens to debate. If contemporary dilemmas pose historical questions for investigation on the basis of evidence, judgement, and analysis, they do not require comforting, simple, or moralistic answers. When Biggar argues that '[w]e should forgive our ancestors for not perceiving some moral truths quite as clearly as we do, just as we shall surely need forgiveness from our grandchildren for our own moral dullness', he risks eliding the historicist investigation with a presentist ethics of intentionality.[72] As Andrew Roberts notes, while 'it is completely illogical, ahistorical and unfair to natural justice to judge the people of the past by today's morals, it is also very hard not to'.[73] While historians seek to explain the past's morals, citizens will naturally argue for the future's morals on what they admire or reject in history.

The question of how far slavery should be considered an individual vice or a national crime lies at the heart of History Reclaimed authors criticising the contemporary reckoning with the legacies, structures, and memory of slavery. In seeking to emphasise the abolitionist movement or the role of anti-slavery imperialism, Biggar draws contrasts with the 'slavery some British people were involved in'.[74] However, the role of the state in promoting and supporting the slave trade in the eighteenth century lay at the heart of abolitionist demands for the state to act against it. When the Quakers' Meeting for Sufferings appealed to Parliament in 1783, its argument would be founded on the premise that 'the Righteous Judge of the whole earth chastiseth nations for their sins, as well as individuals'.[75] The Quaker Joseph Woods argued for parliamentary interposition against the slave trade precisely because 'the revenue of the government, the profits of the merchants, and the luxury of the people, have involved the whole nation as *participes criminis*'.[76] That abolitionists argued this does not mean that the Reclaimers are bound to follow their lead in what they wish to advocate in the present; they are not obliged to draw political conclusions from these historical facts any more than they can claim that contemporary judgements on the state's payment of £20 million compensation to slave-owners are historically illiterate.[77]

Conclusion

The Reclaimers' fear that historical judgements may be cowed by contemporary politics is not wholly misplaced; rather, their desire for a 'national history' that endorses 'social cohesion' seems to risk just that by diminishing the status of historical scholarship to that of partisanship. As Miranda Johnson has argued, New Zealand's present-day power-sharing with Māori in national life has sometimes seen institutions, including universities, seek to endorse a particular interpretation of the history of the Treaty of Waitangi. While she personally supports the steps towards stronger power-sharing with Māori people in New Zealand today, she argues that this can be pursued as a political good on its own terms rather than grounded in a search for tradition in a particular account of the treaty's true meaning.[78] In making these historicist points—at the risk of her political intent being misconstrued or traduced—she demonstrates the possibility of separating historical truth-seeking from presentist politics in ways far superior to the prescriptions of History Reclaimed. Equally, it should be possible to study a revolutionary change in social attitudes to slavery within the United Kingdom without either reducing abolitionism to pure sophistry and flannel or erasing the complexities and imperial entanglements of anti-slavery politics in the British Empire.

This chapter has argued that the contributions of History Reclaimed risk damaging historical research as a discipline by eliding historicist truth-telling with a particular version of patriotism—and by conflating the historian's role in interpreting the past with a citizen's role in judging the present. Their website describes its members as scholars 'with a wide range of opinions on many subjects, but with the shared conviction that history requires careful interpretation of complex evidence, and should not be a vehicle for facile propaganda'.[79] This part of their manifesto is laudable and should command broad support, but it does not follow that such a pledge dictates any particular set of political commitments regarding memorialisation, anti-racism, or reparations in the present. In prosecuting a culture war against fellow historians, History Reclaimed promotes presentism and damages the very historicism they claim to defend.

Further reading

Hall, Catherine, Nicholas Draper, Keith McClelland, Katie Donington, and Rachel Lang, *Legacies of British Slave-Ownership: Colonial Slavery and the Formation of Victorian Britain*, Cambridge: Cambridge University Press, 2014.

Huzzey, Richard, *Freedom Burning: Anti-slavery and Empire in Victorian Britain*, London: Cornell University Press, 2012.

Matthews, Gelien, *Caribbean Slave Revolts and the British Abolitionist Movement*, Baton Rouge, LA: Louisiana State University Press, 2006.

Oldfield, J. R., *Transatlantic Abolitionism in the Age of Revolution: An*

MORALITY AND THE HISTORY OF ABOLITION

International History of Anti-slavery, c.1787–1820, Cambridge: Cambridge University Press, 2013.

Taylor, Michael, *The Interest: How the British Establishment Opposed the Abolition of Slavery*, London: The Bodley Head, 2020.

Williams, Eric, *Capitalism and Slavery*, New York: Russell & Russell, 1944.

The author is grateful to Laura Channing, Miranda Johnson, Liam Liburd, Irene Middleton, John Oldfield, Jake Subryan Richards, Robert Saunders, Adam I. P. Smith, and Justin Willis for advice on this chapter, but remains wholly to blame for its content.

9

A SHORT HISTORY OF A CONTROVERSIAL COMPARISON

EMPIRE AND FASCISM IN BLACK POLITICAL THOUGHT DURING THE 1930S

Liam Liburd

Introduction

In 1955, the Martinican poet, communist, and anti-colonial intellectual, Aimé Césaire, published a pamphlet entitled *Discourse on Colonialism*. The pamphlet is a philosophical and political critique of European colonialism in which Césaire argues that the violence and authoritarianism of the Nazis was not exceptional but represented a logical development of European civilisation. As he put it:

> Yes, it would be worthwhile to study, clinically, in detail, the steps taken by Hitler and Hitlerism and to reveal to the very distinguished,

very humanistic, very Christian bourgeois of the twentieth century that without his being aware of it, he has a Hitler inside him, that Hitler *inhabits* him, that Hitler is his *demon*, that if he rails against him, he is being inconsistent and that, at bottom, what he cannot forgive Hitler for is not *the crime* in itself, *the crime against man*, it is not *the humiliation of man as such*, it is the crime against the white man, the humiliation of the white man, and the fact that [Hitler] applied to Europe colonialist procedures which until then had been reserved exclusively for the Arabs of Algeria, the 'coolies' of India, and the 'niggers' of Africa.[1]

Césaire refused to be surprised or shocked by the genocidal excesses of European fascism, which, he maintained, resembled the methods of rule that Europeans had spent years 'cultivating' in their colonies. Césaire's argument was by no means new but represented a strain of political critique and, moreover, a movement of sorts, with its roots in the anti-colonial politics of the interwar black diaspora. His argument represented an example of what Black Studies professor Cedric Robinson called the 'black construction of fascism'. By this, Robinson meant a way of conceptualising, analysing, and opposing fascism articulated by generations of political activists and thinkers among the black diaspora that held that 'the occurrence of fascism—that is militarism, imperialism, racialist authoritarianism, choreographed mob violence, millenarian crypto-Christian mysticism, and a nostalgic nationalism—was no more an historical aberration than colonialism, the slave trade, and slavery'.[2]

This essay examines this tradition of anti-imperialist and anti-fascist analysis as developed and articulated by black activists in Britain and its empire during the interwar period, bringing their insights to bear on contemporary debates about the legacy of the British Empire. Before turning to the history of black anti-imperialist anti-fascism, it begins with an exploration of the hysterical opposition expressed to the highlighting of similarities and affinities between the racist authoritarianism of Nazi Germany and that of the British Empire. The latter-day British imperialists jumping to defend the empire's historical representation are horrified by comparisons and analogies. They instead insist on the fundamental differences between the British Empire and Nazi Germany (and fascism more broadly) as a means of laundering the historical reputation of the former.

In arguing against the tendency of present-day imperial nostalgists towards British exceptionalism, this chapter looks back to the writings and activism of the British-based black anti-colonial activists of the interwar period who witnessed the rise of fascism first-hand and understood it through the prism of the wider struggle against European colonialism. It considers what exactly they were trying to say in drawing parallels between imperialism and fascism, why the fact that they did so is important, and what insights the history of their anti-colonial activism can bring to today's polarised public debates over Britain's colonial past. For instance, George Padmore was a leading political intellectual within a broader black activist community who theorised about the relationship between imperialism and fascism in the journal he edited, *The Negro Worker*, and then within the ranks of the anti-colonial organisation, the International African Service Bureau, of which he was a prominent member.

Ultimately, the political thought of black activists in the interwar period invites us to think more critically about Britain, its history, and its role in the present—one that reckons with the atrocities and injustices of our past instead of attempting to deny, disavow, or explain them away.

Fascism and the contemporary defenders of empire

The defenders of Britain's imperial legacy and historical reputation assert that none of the British Empire's atrocities or injustices are legitimately comparable to the policies of Nazi Germany or worthy of the label 'fascist'. The indignant disavowals of such comparisons have only intensified since the resurgence and international spread of Black Lives Matter in the summer of 2020 prompted fresh conversations and renewed critical introspection about the legacy of colonial and racist injustices. The online event, 'The Racial Consequences of Mr Churchill', held on 11 February 2021, represented one such conversation. This event took place as part of a programme of events organised under the title '*Churchill, Race and Empire*' by the University of Cambridge's Churchill College.[3] The purpose of the programme was to explore the life and views of its founder, Winston Churchill. Involving a panel of several academics—including Professor Priyamvada Gopal, Professor Kehinde Andrews, Dr Madhusree Mukerjee, and Dr Onyeka Nubia—the event aimed to examine the national narrative around Churchill and to go beyond the quasi-mythical renditions of his reputation. The event attracted the opprobrium of sections of the British press. Several of the commentators and letter-writers did not see this as an exercise in critical thinking but as a politically motivated attack.[4] They were particularly horrified by any suggestion that Churchill's views should be considered within the context of the same history of race and racism as Nazism.

Andrew Roberts, author of several popular history books on Churchill and the Second World War, was particularly incensed by comparisons between the British Empire and Nazi Germany made by Andrews, Professor of Black Studies at Birmingham City University.[5] Under the auspices of the conservative think-tank the Policy Exchange, Roberts co-authored a review of the event. Roberts and his co-author, Zewditu Gebreyohanes, dismissed Andrews' claims as 'puerile invective more befitting the playground than the seminar hall'.[6] They further argued that in terms of its duration, intensity, intentions, and effects, 'there is not a single metric by which the British Empire can be compared with Nazism'. They classified Nazism and the Holocaust as historical and moral outliers that it was both inappropriate and inaccurate to consider within the same analytical frame as British imperialism.[7]

Roberts' apparent ire at these perceived attacks on Churchill and, by extension, the British Empire, is by no means exceptional. Vehement reactions against such comparisons speak to the enduring power of what historian Kennetta Hammond Perry has called 'the mystique of British anti-racism'—a series of mythic narratives about the British nation and (former) empire that portray it as uniquely tolerant, liberal, and progressive both in the contemporary context and in its exceptional history.[8] Those who promote such narratives have historically reinforced them by comparing Britain with illiberal, intolerant, and reactionary 'others' including apartheid South Africa, America (especially its 'Deep South'), and Nazi Germany.

This 'mystique' has even shaped the imperial 'history wars' in the present. For instance, throughout his *Colonialism: A Moral Reckoning* (2023), author Nigel Biggar asserts an ennobled image of the British Empire as a system fundamentally run along Christian, humanitarian, and liberal lines by frequently contrasting it against Nazi Germany. Indeed, it would not be an exaggeration to say that, for Biggar, fascism functions as the moral foil of British imperialism. Where the Nazi regime killed intentionally and industrially, for Biggar, British imperial violence was largely accidental, tragic, and regrettable—'natives' (Biggar's choice of term, not mine) are massacred almost in a fit of absent-mindedness.[9] Where the Nazis revelled in pseudo-scientific fantasies of biological racism, in Biggar's view, British imperialists were guilty of no more than a bit of cultural chauvinism, apparently understandable and excusable in light of their technological and infrastructural superiority.[10] Where the Nazis were guided by the *Führerprinzip* and ideals of Aryan supremacy, according to Biggar, British imperialists were humanitarian Christian liberals who held out the possibility that, one day, their black and brown subjects would reach the appropriate threshold of cultural development to be treated as rights-bearing human beings.[11]

He returns to this theme in the book's conclusion, using the demonstrably systemic injustice of the Third Reich to argue that, by contrast, the British Empire 'was systematically just ... more or less'.[12] Biggar remarks: 'It is no accident that the contemporary enemies of European and, especially, British colonialism try to assimilate or identify it with Nazism. For then we can all be sure that it was basically, essentially evil—notwithstanding all the colonial building of bridges and railways.'[13] In concluding, Biggar maintains that on these grounds 'it is entirely inappropriate to liken [the British Empire] to Nazism', and that the empire was not '*essentially* racist or disproportionately violent' nor '*essentially* exploitative'. By disavowing racist violence and oppression, displacing it on to essentially foreign exemplars, and asserting a fundamental difference between fascism and imperialism, Britain can, Pilate-style, wash its historical hands clean.

Part of this historical sleight of hand in which pro-empire 'culture warriors' are engaged involves the erasure by omission of anti-colonialism and decolonisation as political projects with a history. They treat anti-colonial comparisons between the British Empire and Nazi Germany as shallow mudslinging, a kind of moral and intellectual shortcut to make denunciations of empire easier, born of recent debates over the history and legacy of the empire. In other words, they imagine that people only make such comparisons *retrospectively* in the heat of the present moment and did not do so at the time. The reality is that political thinkers of African and Asian descent have thought about empire with reference to fascism, and vice-versa, ever since the emergence of fascism in the interwar period.

EMPIRE IN BLACK POLITICAL THOUGHT

This partial understanding of history reflects broader problems with the state of public and academic history in Britain, problems resulting from the erasure of the voices, experiences, and intellectual contributions of people of colour from British history. For instance, the few occasions on which people of colour feature in Biggar's *Colonialism* and speak directly, they do so mostly to pay glowing compliments to the British Empire. This is with the noted exception of some out-of-context quotations from Frantz Fanon. Here, Biggar misreads excerpts of Fanon's famous work *The Wretched of the Earth*. He presents Fanon's political and psychoanalytical analysis of the deleterious effects of colonialism on colonised peoples, and of how these effects condition the early stages of the process of decolonisation, as a call by Fanon for an 'authoritarian' abandonment of the idea of objective truth and an embrace of 'native' barbarism.[14] However, the erasure of the voices, experiences, and intellectual contributions of people of colour is not peculiar to the work of pro-empire 'cultural warriors' nor only to discussions of history beyond the work of professional academic historians. Indeed, it is still relatively common to encounter scholarly studies of racism and colonialism within the academic field of British history that feature very limited engagement with the perspectives or experiences of black Britons.[15]

It is worth returning here to Andrews' comparisons between the British Empire and Nazism and placing them into their proper historical context. For Andrews, the mythological misremembering of Churchill is directly connected to the forgetfulness about the history of empire in Britain. Far from brandishing such comparisons as 'playground' insults, in placing imperialism and fascism in the same analytical frame, Andrews was advancing an argument rooted in a long tradition of anti-colonial critique, such as the one identified by Cedric Robinson mentioned at the opening to this essay. In his contribution to the online event, he also cited Césaire directly. Andrews further cautioned against regarding the Nazis as 'the bad guys of history... [a] kind of evil outlier'—the villain to Churchill's 'hero', referring to this as 'a really terrible way to understand racism or to understand the Nazis'. The Nazis were not, he added, again echoing Robinson, 'an aberration'.[16]

Empire and fascism in black political thought

British colonial subjects of African descent engaged in the political struggle against imperialism first drew attention to the similarities between imperialism and fascism years before the Nazis' rise to power. Much of the avowedly anti-imperialist political activity among colonial subjects in this period took place under the auspices of the Communist International (Comintern). The ideals and activities of the Moscow-based Comintern and its international affiliates attracted colonial subjects because of their unequivocal and active opposition to imperialism. George Padmore, born Malcolm Nurse in 1903, was drawn into communist political organising during his time studying in America.[17] Originally from Trinidad, Padmore came to the United States in 1925 to attend university. By 1928, Padmore was actively involved in the Communist Party of the United States of America, and, by the end of 1931, he arrived, after a short stint in Moscow, in the port city of Hamburg in Germany.[18] There he worked for the Comintern to help assist and encourage communist and trade union activity in Africa, and especially in South Africa.

During these years, the Comintern was increasingly turning its attention and efforts towards anti-colonial activity. Padmore became editor of *The Negro Worker*, the journal of the International Trade Union Committee of Negro Workers, itself part of the Comintern. This publication had an international circulation and, although banned in several British colonies for its incendiary contents, was smuggled throughout the world by black workers in the shipping industry, who disguised copies as Bibles and other religious literature.[19]

Padmore and other black communist activists repeatedly likened European imperialism to fascism and, moreover, even asserted that Britain and other imperial powers were 'fascist' in their character and conduct. Throughout *The Negro Worker* and *The Life and Struggles of the Negro Toilers*, a Comintern pamphlet authored by Padmore and published in 1931, they applied the term to a range of political phenomena.[20] In the years and months leading up to the Nazis' seizure of power in early 1933, black communist activists located fascism not in Europe but in South Africa and other parts of the British Empire.

The Negro Worker followed the Comintern line strictly, breathless in its uncritical praise for the Soviet Union. Unsurprisingly, then, Padmore and his comrades' use of the term fascism is partly reflective of political debates and discussions taking place within the Communist International. During the early 1930s, the broadly accepted definition of fascism within the Comintern held that fascism represented a counter-revolutionary response to the final crisis of capitalism.[21] However, black communist anti-colonialists gradually and unevenly developed their own more nuanced and independent analysis of empire, race, and capitalism. Their use of the term 'fascism' reflected this, as it was inflected by their experiences of colonial subjects across Africa and the Caribbean. Fascism, for them, did not refer solely to a development out of capitalism in crisis, but the precise manifestation that this form of 'crisis' capitalism adopted in the context of colonial rule.

Though the articles and editorials of *The Negro Worker* never offered a concise or precise definition of 'fascism' in the abstract, the consistent ways in which they deployed and applied the term conveyed their idiosyncratic and expansive political understanding. The ruling white settler government of the Union of South Africa, in particular, featured regularly in *The Negro Worker* and was vilified as 'fascist' as early as the very first issue of the publication that later became *The Negro Worker*.[22] In South Africa, a self-governing dominion of the empire, the late 1920s and early 1930s was a time of increasing African resistance to racial segregation. General J. B. M. Hertzog, National Party Prime Minister from 1924, and his draconian Minister of Justice, Oswald Pirow, were committed to repressing black political activity, especially forms suspected of being under communist influence. The Communist Party of South Africa, founded by white labour activists in 1921, aimed to increase its African membership from 1925, in line with Comintern initiatives on the so-called 'Negro Question'. In response to their activities and other efforts at black political organising outside of the Communist Party, the South African state 'developed the most sophisticated apparatus of state repression in Africa'.[23]

During the early 1930s, several contributors to *The Negro Worker* identified the South African state as a 'fascist dictatorship'.[24] Meanwhile Padmore characterised renegade black demonstrations against South African white supremacy as 'demonstrations against fascism'.[25] Elsewhere in *The Negro Worker* and related publications, black activists began referring to Pirow, as 'the *Mussolini of South Africa*'.[26]

In *The Negro Worker*'s coverage of South Africa, fascism became a byword for the maintenance and assertion of white supremacy, both by the state apparatus and wider society. The cast of 'fascists' included not only Pirow in his role as the Afrikaner *Il Duce* but also armed white citizens assisting the police and military. In focusing on the broader mobilisations of white power, black communist activists understood fascism specifically as 'racial capitalism'—to borrow the term later popularised by Robinson—in crisis mode.[27] With an intimate understanding of capitalism as racial, black radicals conceived of 'fascism' as the desperate defence of a system where the negative consequences of capitalism were displaced not just on to the working class in general but chiefly on to the non-white members of this class. They understood 'fascism' in action as the white community acting both as an economic class and as a racial group to keep black workers in a subordinate social and political position both as workers *and* as black people.

The 'fascist' Union of South Africa was by no means an exception, and contributors to *The Negro Worker* also attacked colonialism elsewhere in the British Empire as 'fascist'. Much of the coverage in *The Negro Worker* during Padmore's editorship in the early 1930s also focused on the West Indies. During the early 1930s, British colonies in the West Indies faced spiralling unemployment and economic stagnation relating to a crisis in the sugar industry and agriculture exacerbated by the Great Depression. At the time, colonial government in the British West Indies was an ossified institution essentially committed to 'the maintenance of a climate conducive to the well-being of investors in London and their agents in the colonies'.[28] As historian Cary Fraser wrote, '[t]he emergence of a modern democratic state in London had bypassed the West Indies'.[29] With slavery long since abolished, the white economic ruling class in these territories was keen to devise a means of suppressing and subordinating the West Indian working class.

Though British imperialists, then and since, articulated the empire as a liberal project, freedom of assembly and freedom of the press were precisely the kinds of things colonial governments were keen to suppress. The communist politics of *The Negro Worker*, coupled with the forthright political critiques it published from Caribbean correspondents, saw it outlawed in Trinidad in 1932. One Trinidadian correspondent lambasted Governor Sir

THE TRUTH ABOUT EMPIRE

Alfred Claud Hollis as 'the Mussolini of Trinidad'. This expansive invocation of 'fascism' was more than mere name-calling. When it came to colonial politics in the Caribbean, it was part of a political argument about the nature of crown colonies, that is, colonies under direct British rule run by an appointed governor on behalf of the monarch. In calling Hollis and other crown colony governors and governments 'fascist', black activists drew attention to the authoritarianism at the heart of the British Empire and throughout its colonies from the West Indies to West Africa. With their talk of 'Crown Colony Dictatorship' or 'Fascist Dictatorship' in the West Indies or in their arguments that the West Indies was a region in which '[u]nbridled colonial fascism prevails', these activists were insisting that the British Empire was acting as a hothouse for a variety of fascism.[30]

They continued to theorise along these lines in the context of the Nazis' seizure of power in early 1933. With *The Negro Worker*'s editorial offices in Hamburg, Padmore experienced these authoritarian shifts first-hand and at close range. He soon found himself rounded up and deported by the new regime and, as British colonial subject, sent to London. Over the rest of 1933, and still under Padmore's editorship, *The Negro Worker* sought to convey to its readers that 'fascism' represented 'the most hostile movement against the Negro race' and did so with repeated reference to its similarity to European colonialism. *The Negro Worker* even made early attempts to appeal to the fledgling anti-fascist movement in Europe, encouraging them to oppose the ascendance of authoritarianism within Europe and beyond in its colonial territories. The same issue contained an open letter addressed to European anti-fascists that affirmed its solidarity with the 'white proletariat' but also entreated them to direct their anti-fascist outrage at the 'fascism' of European colonialism in Asia and Africa.[31] In reminding anti-fascist workers in Europe that the struggle for black liberation was part of the struggle against fascism, they noted: 'The Negro peoples of the world realize only too well the full meaning of fascism. For centuries we have been the victims of the most inhuman, brutal, and barbarous fascist methods at the hands of various imperialist powers.'

Padmore's insistence on the importance of race and class as intersecting factors in world politics meant that he soon fell afoul of Comintern's single-minded Stalinism, which paid lip service to but showed little practical solidarity with the struggles of black workers. He resigned his position as editor of *The Negro Worker* in late 1933 and was shortly afterwards expelled from the Comintern.[32] Padmore also fell out of step with Comintern's line on fascism, which altered during the early to mid-1930s to make a distinction between *democratic* imperialists—Britain, America, and France—who could act as potential allies, and enemy *fascist* imperialists (Germany, Italy, and Japan). Now in Britain, where he remained for much of the rest of his life, and outside of the international Communist movement, Padmore published two more books on colonial affairs and world politics. *How Britain Rules Africa* (1936) was a detailed indictment of British colonialism in Africa, in which Padmore attacked the governments of South Africa, South West Africa, Southern Rhodesia, and Kenya as reminiscent of Nazi rule. The following year, his *Africa and World Peace* (1937) further explored the world situation in the context of fascist expansionism.

'Colonial fascism' on the eve of the Second World War

Alongside and in addition to his writing, Padmore immersed himself in the black and anti-colonial political networks based in Britain. The imperial ambitions of fascist Italy and Nazi Germany meant that the struggle against colonialism in the 1930s also entailed a struggle against fascism. Padmore soon became involved in the black movement in Britain campaigning against increasing aggression by Benito Mussolini's Italy towards Ethiopia, which culminated in a full-scale Italian invasion in October 1935. The invasion of Ethiopia, one of the few black-ruled nations in the world at this time and thus an incredibly important symbol of black sovereignty, enraged and engaged black people throughout the world. Padmore was a member of the group the International African Friends of Ethiopia (IAFE), founded in July 1935 by Amy Ashwood Garvey, an energetic anti-colonial activist and first wife of black nationalist Marcus Garvey, and C. L. R. James, the Trotskyist, historian, and a childhood friend of Padmore's from back in Trinidad. IAFE organised support for the independence and self-determination of Ethiopia, holding meetings in Trafalgar Square and promoting the Ethiopian cause at Hyde Park's Speakers' Corner.

Padmore, Ashwood Garvey, James, and several other anti-colonial activists later widened IAFE's remit beyond Ethiopia to focus on the broader struggle for the liberation of Africans and people of African descent, converting it into the International African Service Bureau (IASB) in late April 1937. IASB's founders conceived of it as an organisation that would support the mass struggle against colonialism across the world, to help stimulate and shape the political consciousness of the black diaspora, and to promote the cause of the black 'masses' in Britain. During 1938 and early 1939, they published a journal, *International African Opinion*, which continued to explore the relationship between imperialism and fascism in the context of increasing diplomatic tensions in Europe and colonial rebellion in parts of Africa and the Caribbean.

International African Opinion stands as an important record of the voices of dissent in the years leading up to the much-memorialised Second World War. This conflict is popularly remembered variously as a war against fascism and/or Nazi atrocities and a war for democracy and human rights. The contents of *International African Opinion* are a reminder of the aspects of Britain's past that do not quite fit into these more triumphalist narratives. The contributors to IASB's journal wrote angrily of what they perceived as Britain's betrayal of democracy in favour of imperialism and their embrace of fascism via appeasement during the late 1930s. They wrote with the memory of the Italian conquest of Ethiopia bitterly fresh in their minds, particularly appalled at the role played by Britain and France in reaching settlement agreements with Italy. Moreover, Padmore, James, and the other members of its editorial board made important connections and drew comparisons between the political situation in Europe and the situation in Africa and the Caribbean. They were keenly aware that appeasement, as well as fascism, had its colonial dimensions—and not only when it came to Ethiopia.

During the late 1930s, in the pages of their journal and in demonstrations on the streets of London, IASB protested against South African demands for the annexation of British protectorates neighbouring the Union of South Africa, known as the High Commission Territories—Bechuanaland, Swaziland, and Basutoland (modern-day Botswana, Eswatini, and Lesotho). The Afrikaner community—including the South African Prime Minister, Hertzog, and his deputy, Jan Smuts—had long nursed ambitions to expand into these territories and create a 'Greater South Africa'.

Over the course of several decades between the late nineteenth and early twentieth century, each of these territories had come under British protection from designs of Afrikaner expansionists as a result of negotiations, requests from African leaders, or more straightforward imposition. During the negotiations that combined the Boer republics into the Union of South Africa over 1908 and 1909, Britain had stated its intention to eventually transfer the territories to South Africa, governed by its white settler population, but also pledged to pay attention to African wishes and interests. This created a bind that, especially by the 1930s, turned the issue of the High Commission Territories into an 'exceedingly troublesome' matter for British politicians, 'second only to Ireland as the major Dominions Office headache in Commonwealth affairs, and second to none in its intractability'.[33]

Discussions of a transfer reached their peak between 1935 and 1937 and featured in the first issue of *International African Opinion*. The article in this issue expressed shock and disappointment at the British government's repeated consideration of the idea of ceding African territories to a country that IASB considered 'openly Fascist'.[34] They interpreted this as a sign that '[i]mperialism, whatever its high pretensions to philanthropy, cannot be anything else but Fascist in its actual operation'. They further maintained that '[t]he history of the proposals for the transfer of the Protectorates is an illustration of this; it shows how the real meaning of the British Empire was gradually unveiled'. IASB used the issue of the transfer of the protectorates to expose this 'real meaning'. They drew from these events the lesson that '[e]mpire and Democracy are not compatible: in the end one must give way to the other'. For all of Britain's liberal imperial pretensions, IASB argued that by recognising South African demands they were giving in to fascism, as they had given in to fascism when Germany annexed Austria and when Mussolini invaded Ethiopia.

The IASB returned to this issue in the spring of 1939. During this time, fierce debate raged within South Africa over whether the country would support Britain in a future war with Germany or adopt a position of neutrality. Some Afrikaner nationalists, including Hertzog and Pirow, favoured neutrality. *International African Opinion* warned that in order to placate these essentially pro-German elements, '[q]uietly and sinisterly ... steps for appeasement within the British Empire itself are being taken'.[35] They reported that the Duke of Devonshire, Under-Secretary of

State for the Dominions, had been sent to discuss the question of a transfer with Hertzog's government and that several remarks by British statesmen indicated that the government believed that South Africa 'apparently has an equal privilege with Hitler to annex bountiful or strategic territories to advance its imperialist ambitions'. In the event, the protectorates remained under British control until they won their independence in the 1960s—the issue of annexation definitively settled by apartheid South Africa's 1961 withdrawal from the Commonwealth.

The IASB were also concerned that the former German colonies held by Britain as League of Nations' mandated territories since the end of the First World War would be used as bargaining chips to appease the Nazis as well. And they had cause for this concern. Hitler was initially openly disinterested in colonial expansion beyond the quest for greater *Lebensraum* (meaning literally 'living space') for ethnic Germans in Central and Eastern Europe. However, by the middle of the 1930s, he changed his tactics.[36] Though they still ultimately remained less interested in Germany's former colonies in Africa than in future expansion within Europe, Hitler and other Nazi diplomats used the colonial question to get British diplomats to take Germany's broader foreign policy ambitions more seriously. In the late 1930s, the British government gave this issue serious consideration. In late 1937, *The Times* carried letters and reports of speeches from several prominent British politicians, as well as editorials, sympathetic to Germany's colonial claims.[37] While, in the end, the Nazis abandoned any serious interest in regaining Germany's African colonies around the time of the Austrian Anschluss in March 1938, from this point on, public anxiety within Britain and its empire about their return reached its height.[38] This anxiety clearly registers in the pages of *International African Opinion*.

In the first issue of their journal after the Munich Crisis and subsequent Munich Agreement in late September 1938, which ceded part of Czechoslovakia to Nazi Germany, IASB expressed their solidarity with Czechoslovakia.[39] Fearing both further concessions involving giving African colonies back to Germany and a future war in which colonial subjects would be conscripted into a war to defend European empires, IASB issued a 'Manifesto against War'. They rejected imperialists—'democratic' or fascist—and called on black people 'everywhere' to fight only for independence. As another article in *International African Opinion* ran:

> Nothing is sacred to those who put imperial interests before any other consideration. Yesterday the victim of their treachery was Ethiopia, to-day Czechoslovakia. To-morrow it may easily be that some portion of black Africa will be thrown to the Nazi wolves in order to maintain the infirm foundations of British imperialism.[40]

The article further insisted that opposition among Conservative die-hard imperialists and certain colonial administrators 'on the spot' to giving British territories to Germany was overblown, noting '[i]t is not Fascist methods to which these men are opposed, but Fascist annexation'. They continued: 'Fascism is not a monopoly of Mussolini and Hitler but is employed by the "democratic" nations throughout their colonies.' The point they repeatedly made as the diplomatic situation darkened in the closing years of the 1930s was that Britain's National Government—a coalition of Conservative, Labour, and Liberal politicians—was both fully prepared to appease fascist regimes by admitting them into the ranks of colonial powers and was itself incubating a form of fascism within its own empire.

'Colonial fascism' was thriving, they maintained, in the repression of the widespread unrest throughout the British West Indies during the mid- to late 1930s. Workers throughout the Caribbean were moved to rebellion by deepening economic problems and unemployment. Colonial governments in Trinidad, British Guiana, Jamaica, and elsewhere responded with military force and martial law, deploying marines, raising local militias, and routinely firing upon strikers. The use of extraordinary violence and other measures including the imposition of harsh prison sentences, suppression of the press, suspension of rights of assembly, and so on represented, as expressed in the columns of *International African Opinion*, the highest stage of 'Colonial Fascism'.

Throughout 1938 and 1939, IASB highlighted Britain's hypocrisy as it used without qualm or complaint the very measures it viewed with suspicion and horror when employed by fascist regimes in Europe. When the British government eventually appointed an all-white Royal Commission in 1938, under Lord Moyne, to investigate the causes of the unrest in the West Indies, the IASB submitted a joint memorandum with other black political organisations in Britain to ensure that views of West Indians were represented. It is unclear how much difference their representations made to the Moyne Commission's findings or final report, but it is worth noting that when the Commission published their report in 1939, it was suppressed due to fears that it painted such a damning picture of British imperial rule that the Nazis might well use it as propaganda.[41]

In the final issue of *International African Opinion* before the outbreak of the Second World War, one editorial—styled as an open letter to West Indian intellectuals—offered its definition of fascism:

> In the present break-down of world economy, wide-spread poverty in the midst of plenty, millions of unemployed, the relentless drive to war, [the property-owning class] see the capitalist system threatened by the wrath of the masses. In defiance of any constitution, law and order they subsidise armed bands of mercenaries and smash down the leaders and organisations of the workers, set up a new ideology of their own, and reduce the workers and all men with liberal ideas to a state of mute vassalage which is unparalleled in human history. This is Fascism.[42]

They understood fascism as a worldwide problem, representing the most brutal and illiberal form of imperialism, operating within Europe and beyond, in Africa and the West Indies. And, they maintained, it was present in Britain, too, in 'the classic home of parliamentary democracy' and in the Chamberlain government's all-too-conciliatory dealings with fascist powers. In the face of fascism, in its colonial and metropolitan variants, they encouraged West Indian intellectuals to throw themselves into the mass struggle for democratic freedoms and workers' rights to organise, to a free press, to free assembly, and to receive an education—rights and values claimed as 'British' but suppressed as seditious in British colonies.

Conclusion: rendering fascism familiar

Those seeking to rescue and champion the British Empire from the wreckage of its history insist that to make comparisons between the empire and fascism is simplistic. Comparisons of this kind, made by black political activists in Britain and its empire during the 1930s, constitute much more than a simplistic or crude accusation that imperialism and fascism were both as bad as each other. Padmore and comrades, first at *The Negro Worker* and then in the IASB, did indeed wish a plague on both houses but misunderstood neither the threat of fascism nor the injustices of empire. They argued that imperialism could never decisively defeat fascism because it contained the germ of fascism within it. They insisted on a family resemblance between the two political systems and on the presence of something in the metaphorical gene pool that meant that the meaningful survival of democracy was incompatible with the survival of imperialism.

Thus, to demonise Hitler but excuse Churchill not only lets 'colonial fascism' off the hook but represents a poor effort at historical enquiry. To think about the history of imperialism and of fascism relationally is not to engage in the crude ethics of comparative calculations, of working out how many Bengalis starved to death against how many Jews were gassed but about contemplating the ways in which Britain—past and present—is not so different, not so exceptional, and no more inoculated against committing atrocities than any other nation.

The black colonial subjects of Britain's empire found fascism familiar precisely because they had experienced a state of affairs they struggled to meaningfully distinguish from fascism as they understood it. Looking at the interwar history of colonialism and anti-colonialism through the lens of their theoretical engagements with 'fascism', understood in expansive terms, renders Britain's history ordinary, rather than exceptional, characterised by the same ideological and material forces as the rest of Western Europe, if not the wider world, forming part of the same history of colonialism, of racism, and of fascism as Germany, Italy, and elsewhere. The black radical voices of dissent speaking truth to the imperial powers of the 1930s are a reminder that history is more complicated than a didactic narrative of national pride. If we embrace, rather than seek to avoid, this complexity, history can be a resource for critical thinking about how the world was, is, and could yet be.

Further reading

Fryer, Peter, *Staying Power: The History of Black People in Britain*, London: Pluto, 2018, especially Chapter 10.

Gopal, Priyamvada, *Insurgent Empire: Anticolonial Resistance and British Dissent*, London: Verso, 2019, especially Chapters 8 and 9.

Robinson, Cedric, *Black Marxism: The Making of the Black Radical Tradition*, London: Penguin, 2021, especially Chapter 10.

Williams, Theo, *Making the Revolution Global: Black Radicalism and the British Socialist Movement before Decolonisation*, London: Verso, 2022.

10

ESCAPE FROM EMPIRE

DECOLONISATION AS DISENTANGLEMENT, ERASURE, AND EVASION

Erik Linstrum

No figure illustrates Britain's transition from empire-state to nation-state more dramatically than Enoch Powell. He was, famously, devastated by the independence of India, where he was stationed during the Second World War and dreamed of someday becoming viceroy. In 1951, he could still declare that "without the Empire, Britain would be like a head without a body."[1] Within a few years, however, Powell's conversion to a constricted vision of territorial and ethnic nationalism was underway. Rather than clinging to the globe-spanning illusions fostered by the Commonwealth of Nations, which he saw as a confused dilution of sovereignty, he advanced the ideal of a smaller but indivisible and homogenous Britannic realm. Shoring up the post-imperial nation—a status which he believed had irretrievably arrived with the 1954 agreement to withdraw British troops from the Suez Canal Zone—required what he called a "clean break" with the past.[2] Powell urged his countrymen to reject airy cosmopolitan visions in favor of the rooted patriotism of blood and soil, a kind of homecoming after "years of distant wandering."[3]

The insistent note in Powell's rhetoric might be read as evidence that he was fighting a determined reluctance among his fellow Britons to sever imperial connections. After all, the Commonwealth did serve as a focal point for various fantasies of projecting power after empire: the Angloworld counterweight to the American and Soviet superpowers; the resource bank for postwar reconstruction; and, above all, the platform for continued moral leadership on the world stage. By the early 1960s, self-flattering contrasts between the rogue apartheid state in South Africa and the multiracial ideal of the Commonwealth—symbolized by Asian and African heads of state dining with the queen at Buckingham Palace—were commonplace.[4]

The sense of post-imperial British benevolence operating on a global scale coursed through other channels as well. Aid organizations like Oxfam, Save the Children, and Christian Aid—many of them staffed by veteran colonial officials and targeting former colonized territories—rivaled state-funded development programs in scope. As they shifted their focus from short-term crisis relief to long-term campaigns against the chronic social problems of hunger, ignorance, and poverty, these groups anchored new relationships of moral involvement with the rest of the world.[5] "Ruling" and "caring" had been decoupled: the British people may have lost an empire but remained motivated by the desire to alleviate suffering in distant lands.[6]

Did Powell, then, lose the argument? Did Britain after empire remain suffused with a cosmopolitan paternalism forged over centuries of imperial dominance? If decolonization in practice entailed a "reconfiguration rather than a severing of connections," it was always a project of "disentanglement" at its core.[7] Great expectations for the Commonwealth proved exceedingly short-lived. Officials came to resent the indignities inflicted, and the development funds consumed, by what many saw as Lilliputian postcolonies now elevated to the status of coequal partners.[8] The shift from Commonwealth to Europe, meanwhile, could itself be seen as a homecoming: a rejection of inherited obligations to different "races" on multiple continents in favor of elective affinity with a more ethnically homogenous community across the English Channel.[9] If Powell himself rejected this new form of international involvement, other right-wing champions of the nation-state embraced it, braiding Britain's imperial history into the spiritual legacy of Christendom which it shared with the continent.[10]

By the same token, the flourishing of the postcolonial aid industry is best understood neither as a continuation nor an expansion of an empire's obligations but as a slimmed-down and hollowed-out replacement for them. As historian Anna Bocking-Welch has argued, the promise of humanitarian activism after empire was "the promise of making a difference" without "the burdensome liability of colonial responsibility."[11] Perhaps the quintessential humanitarian cause of the postcolonial era, the Biafra crisis of the late 1960s, was driven by sensational imagery of starving African children which eclipsed the concrete legacies of British rule. Less than a decade after Nigerian independence, the federal system engineered by colonial officials—which broadly aligned regional government boundaries with ethnic blocs—had devolved into civil war. Yet civilian British activism to "save" Biafra was predicated less on any sense of national responsibility than on the elective affinity of Christians moved by the plight of their coreligionists and ordinary people disturbed by the spectacle of emaciated bodies.[12] A voluntarist and ephemeral "politics of pity," preoccupied with postcolonial wars and natural disasters for which Britain bore no obvious blame, took the place of more durable connections.[13]

At the same time, actual legal obligations to British subjects overseas—specifically, the rights of entry into and residence within the United Kingdom—were whittled away by legislation in 1962, 1968, 1971, and 1981. This process of ethnic exclusion, which Powell conspicuously encouraged, fell especially hard on South Asian populations in East Africa targeted by postcolonial regimes for discrimination and expulsion. Even as British volunteers were raising funds to support refugees in some parts of the world, their state was creating new populations of refugees elsewhere, by withdrawing the rights conferred by a British passport. Indeed, British officials took pains to redefine British citizens in Kenya and Uganda as stateless refugees, hoping to share the burden of absorbing migrants with other nations rather than bearing it alone.[14] Provincializing Britishness—narrowing the pool of people who could make claims on British identity as well as the geographic remit of those claims—was central to the process of decolonization.[15]

Historians have observed that the pageantry accompanying independence for British colonies was intended to telegraph a peaceful, deliberative, and willing "transfer of power." As the Union Jack was hauled down and the new national standard run up the flagpole, representatives of the British state—including, most of the time, members of the royal family—looked on benignantly. The handover of sovereignty was staged to represent the culmination of a civilizing mission, signaling that the paternalistic work of preparing formerly backward societies for self-government was complete at last.[16] Less often remarked is that the rhetoric and ceremony of independence served not only to put a happy face on the potentially embarrassing retreat of British power, "dressing up a defeat as a victory," but to insulate

British officials as far as possible from the chaotic and often violent consequences of their withdrawal.[17]

The ethnic violence provoked by the Partition of India, in which hundreds of thousands and perhaps millions died, offers a case in point. It was not until two days after the Independence Day fanfare, on 17 August 1947, that British officials disclosed the boundaries running between the new states of India and Pakistan. Sir Cyril Radcliffe, the jurist who oversaw the boundary-drawing process, made a hasty exit in anticipation of an angry response, flew back to Britain on the same day, and later burned all his papers on the Partition. As the death toll mounted precipitously in the late summer and fall, the last viceroy, Lord Mountbatten, would come to regret staying on in the figurehead role of governor-general of India for another year. Yet Mountbatten's savvy management of British newspaper and newsreel coverage helped to ensure that the bloodshed did not tarnish his reputation at home. Some commentators claimed that communal violence was being exaggerated to discredit the decolonizing process; others cast the strife as confirmation that the Raj had long served as a stabilizing and pacifying presence. In either case, the British could simultaneously feel pride in the imperial legacy and relief at having escaped an ugly quagmire. A Leslie Illingworth cartoon which appeared in *Punch* in May 1947 set the tone. Titled "The Rope Trick," it showed a khaki-clad figure representing the Raj climbing a rope into the sky as four menacing tigers circled each other on the ground. The none-too-subtle implication was that the proper British response to animalistic conflict on the subcontinent was a disappearing act.[18]

Already in the run-up to independence, officials responded to outbreaks of communal violence less with determination to maintain order than impatience to be free of their responsibilities. Punjab governor Sir Evan Jenkins reported in June 1947 that "the behavior of Punjab people in the recent disturbances had been so revolting that very few British officials were now prepared to stay on ... [They] are also tired of being told that they are to blame."[19] Back in Britain, even Conservatives who publicly bashed the Attlee government for a policy of "scuttle" privately acknowledged that Britain might be fortunate to escape from the subcontinent. Arch-imperialist Winston Churchill was among them: influenced by calculations of declining economic benefit as well as a belief that territorial control mattered less in an age of air power, he had come to see India as a "very great" and "very heavy burden."[20] One reason that Conservative accusations of shirking imperial duty failed to carry the day in 1947 was that ordinary Britons were just as eager to shed the expense and risk of governing a massive, increasingly hostile population on the other side of the globe. As a Sheffield housewife noted in her diary for the Mass-Observation social research project in August 1947: "I swear most folks couldn't care less [about independence for India] ... Most folk are simply glad to be shot of them."[21]

In later years, many veteran Raj officials expressed shame about what they saw as a cowardly retreat. They felt that Britain had betrayed loyal Indian subjects by leaving them exposed to the horrors of ethnic cleansing. Yet these administrators pinned the blame on decisions made elsewhere, by the Labour government and its appointee Mountbatten above all, while portraying themselves as powerless captives of a state whose authority suddenly collapsed.[22] A variation on this rhetoric of displacement held that the American and Soviet superpowers, pursuing their own cynical agendas in the guise of colonial liberation, forced Britain to leave.[23]

Mountbatten and his allies, for their part, maintained that it was the act of voluntarily surrendering power—rather than the subsequent carnage—that should define Britain's legacy. Even in 1948, with millions still in refugee camps, the viceroy's top aide could tell a London audience: "It may be said of the British Raj, as Shakespeare said of the Thane of Cawdor, 'Nothing in his life became him like the leaving of it.'"[24] From this perspective, which long remained the standard narrative on the British left, the transfer of power represented both a noble expression of the liberal-imperial ideal and an immediate transfer of moral responsibility. Mountbatten himself clung to an implausibly low-end estimate of deaths in Partition as a way of downplaying the catastrophe.[25]

In many ways, the British retreat from India set the template for imperial exits as projects of escaping accountability. Alongside the rhetoric of deflection, decolonization reactivated a long history of shielding imperial agents from legal liability for their actions. The suspension of habeas corpus, a recurring practice in Ireland through the mid-nineteenth century, was routinely followed by passage of Indemnity Acts which granted officials retrospective immunity from prosecution.[26] Likewise, the imposition of martial law, a standard response to colonial insurrections through the early twentieth century, brought indemnity legislation in its wake almost as a matter of course. This was the case with Jamaica in 1865, Ceylon (Sri Lanka) in 1915, South Africa in 1916, and, notoriously, India in 1919, when officials muscled an Indemnity Bill through the Legislative Council even before an inquiry into the Amritsar massacre reported its findings.[27] As this final example suggests, anxieties about liability intensified at the end of empire because the suppression of dissent which so often accompanied it involved violence of questionable legality.

So it was in India in 1946–7, when the highest echelons of the Raj worried that officials might be prosecuted for their brutal suppression of the Quit India movement in 1942. The concern was not that accusations of excessive force, as well as bribery and theft, leveled by nationalist politicians and their press allies, were false: on the contrary, Secretary of State for India Lord Pethick-

Lawrence conceded that "actions taken by individuals in 1942 ... were clearly unjustifiable." But he and others feared that a sweeping inquiry into official misconduct would "have a most devastating effect on the morale of the Services."[28] Behind the scenes, the British pressured leaders of the main nationalist party, the Indian National Congress, to pull back on their demands for investigations in exchange for pensioning off the officials implicated in wrongdoing. Among themselves, meanwhile, Raj administrators discussed the possibility of forcing through Indemnity Acts if gentler methods failed.[29]

Another strategy for thwarting accountability at the end of empire was the destruction and removal of government documents. In India, this process began as early as 1937, when Congress politicians for the first time held ministerial positions at the provincial level. In the anti-colonial hub of Bombay, officials were particularly worried that colleagues previously involved in cracking down on Congress campaigners could be targeted by the machinery of state power once it passed out of their hands. The imperative, they argued, was to "protect officers from victimization." While their counterparts elsewhere objected that tampering with official archives would sow mistrust with Congress politicians and impede them from governing effectively, Bombay officials won authorization to stash a selection of files in British-controlled offices and to destroy others. Dossiers on individual political activists and the correspondence of "very high officials" were marked as priorities for this kind of special handling.[30]

Less than ten years later, as national independence for India approached, the procedure pioneered in Bombay was being put into practice more widely, systematically, and urgently. From London, the India Office wrote officials in Delhi seeking assurance that "all necessary measures are in train to prevent documents in the archives of the Government of India that would be likely to cause embarrassment if they were to fall into the hands of a 'political,' and particularly an independent, Indian government, falling into such hands."[31] The archives of the Political Department—covering relations with the nominally independent princely states and "including reports of those murky and squalid occasions when Princes had had to be rebuked or disciplined for their excesses"—aroused particular concern. Aside from the scandalous behavior of Indian royals, these documents risked exposing the seamy reality of British wire-pulling behind the fictitious veneer of their sovereignty. An estimated 4 tons of files were relegated to the flames.[32]

Principled hesitation about the wholesale sanitization of archives, expressed by many British officials in 1937, came under pressure in the final months of imperial rule. It was not just the threat of individual prosecutions, but the danger of reputational damage to the whole imperial enterprise, which loomed now. As one administrator put it, "there is an immense amount of material in the various [other] departments which could be used to document a malicious history of British exploitation of India."[33] Nehru wrote repeatedly to Viceroys Archibald Wavell and Lord Mountbatten in the spring of 1947 pleading for a stop to the destruction of documents and suggesting that a historian oversee the process of sorting them. "Delay in weeding out papers will not injure anybody," he pointed out, "but if paper is once destroyed, it cannot be replaced."[34] British officials responded with contradictory explanations of their document policy, sometimes asserting a right to dispense with certain files as they saw fit and sometimes claiming that only files which "possess no historical interest" and "are patently valueless for purposes of future reference" were being weeded out.[35] While the scale of destruction remains unclear, it was extensive enough that journalists noticed "a pall of smoke" over government ministries in New Delhi in the final weeks of British rule.[36]

THE TRUTH ABOUT EMPIRE

India's 1949 entry into what was then restyled the Commonwealth of Nations seemed to confirm the triumph of British reputational management. Over the objections of Australians, Canadians, and New Zealanders who bemoaned the abandonment of "kinship and kingship" as unifying values, Britain cemented ties of friendship with its largest former colony and embraced the mantle of multicultural modernity.[37] Yet this soft-power makeover was made possible in part by the twin tactics of legal evasion and document removal, which averted potentially inflammatory dramas of accountability and disclosure at a delicate political moment. These tactics would be employed repeatedly as decolonization accelerated in the 1950s and 1960s.

The bloody uprisings which broke out in Malaya, Kenya, Cyprus, and other British colonies posed another kind of challenge to the objective of avoiding moral quagmires. In moving to suppress these insurgencies, British authorities employed methods—including torture, collective punishments, and summary executions—which troubled consciences as knowledge about them circulated through British society. This knowledge circulated widely: soldiers wrote letters home about atrocities; journalists covered them; missionaries and aid workers debated their complicity in them; stage plays and television programs even dramatized them. As a result, the effort to disengage from colonial violence at home was not fought on the terrain of ignorance or denial, but rather with the language of hard choices and outright justifications. If Britons were unsettled by brutality in defense of empire, many—and perhaps most—who participated in these debates were prepared to defend it as a necessary evil.[38]

While changes in mass media, the introduction of mass conscription, and an increase in colonial immigration were among the factors that made brutality harder to ignore at home in the 1950s, British officials overseas clung to tried-and-true methods of evading accountability.

Along one track, they moved to place themselves and their agents beyond the reach of the law. In Malaya, after British troops massacred around two dozen rubber tappers at Batang Kali in 1948, the government hastily rewrote its Emergency Regulations to shield soldiers from criminal liability.[39] In Kenya, the general amnesty declared on 18 January 1955 was ostensibly a means of inducing insurgents to surrender; in fact, officials saw it as an opportunity to immunize themselves and their African foot soldiers, the Kikuyu Home Guard, from prosecution for atrocities. Twenty-six murder cases pending before the amnesty date, including three implicating European district officers, were summarily dropped afterwards. Administrators in subsequent years cited the amnesty as a blanket justification for refusing even to open investigations of misconduct.[40] In Cyprus, the law was changed to make government officials virtually immune to lawsuits by making complainants subject to prosecution if their allegations were not upheld in court.[41] Ethnic Greek insurgents in Cyprus did enjoy a major legal advantage over other insurgent groups: the backing of a sovereign state, Greece, which enabled access to the European Court of Human Rights (ECHR) in Strasbourg. But a condition of the independence agreement negotiated in 1958–9 was Greek withdrawal of the ECHR complaint, short-circuiting an investigation into more than a dozen cases of torture and sealing the case files in perpetuity.

Elsewhere, bureaucratic foot-dragging and conflicts of interest achieved the same effect as statutory loopholes and negotiated settlements. The Royal Ulster Constabulary (RUC), a significant actor in the counterinsurgency waged in Northern Ireland, also held the responsibility for prosecuting criminal cases of excessive force by security forces. Unsurprisingly, it used this power sparingly, with roughly a dozen cases brought against military personnel in the more than three-decade history of the Troubles—out of more than 250,000 soldiers who served—and even fewer resulting in convictions. The much-heralded Good Friday Agreement of 1998 made no provision for bringing to justice the soldiers or police officers who perpetrated abuses. It was instead the ECHR that provided the impetus for change, ruling in a series of cases brought by victims' families from 2001 that authorities in Northern Ireland had failed to fulfill their legal obligations to prosecute misconduct. But the new investigative body established to comply with these rulings, the Historical Enquiries Team in the Police Service of Northern Ireland, was itself stocked with RUC veterans and later accused by a government watchdog of applying a gentler double standard to police and military suspects.[42] A budget-strapped successor agency managed to file six cases against military suspects after its creation in 2014, but several collapsed on procedural grounds, and only one so far has produced a conviction.[43]

Even this fitful and long-delayed measure of accountability was enough to anger veterans' groups and prompt the Conservative government to interfere in the legal process. Over the objections of every major political party in Northern Ireland, the families of victims, and the governments of Ireland, Europe, and the United States, the UK Parliament in September 2023 passed the Legacy and Reconciliation Act. This legislation removed all criminal and civil cases concerning the Troubles from the judicial system, diverting them to a newly created commission tasked with "information recovery" rather than prosecution. Most controversially of all, the commission will be empowered to grant amnesties to perpetrators who cooperate with its investigations.

In contrast to the pursuit of legal impunity, which evolved through a patchwork of ad hoc measures, the sanitization of government archives was systematized and routinized in the years after Indian independence. On the eve of independence for Ceylon in 1948, the Colonial Office instructed local British officials that sensitive documents "should either be destroyed or sent home" rather than transferred to the new Ceylonese national archives.[44] This was the origin of what would later be named "Operation Legacy." While weeding archives and preserving relatively few documents was standard procedure in the British civil service, Operation Legacy was different. Its goal was not bureaucratic efficiency but reputational protection; the decisive criterion for transmitting documents to postcolonial states was not historic significance but lack of political sensitivity. By the time of independence for the Gold Coast (Ghana) in 1957, British policy was explicitly targeting documents which "might embarrass members of Her Majesty's Government" for special handling.[45]

The existence of a document destruction program was not itself a secret. In 1961, a British Academy committee on historical preservation voiced concern about the destruction of African colonial archives, followed a few months later by a *Guardian* report on "a bonfire of documents" in Kenya.[46] Postcolonial leaders were sometimes informed about the practice, too, if often misled about its scale. Yet implementation of the policy in private revealed the depth of British anxieties about exposing the inner workings of their administration. Sometimes, papers slated for transfer to postcolonial states were marked "clean," while those intended for destruction or migration were labeled "dirty."[47] In a few colonies, at least, the process of selecting and handling documents was carried out in accordance with a strictly racialized division of labor. Only British subjects "of European descent" could participate; even trusted junior officials of other racial backgrounds were excluded despite time pressures and manpower shortages. Given the need for discipline and discretion as well as the scale of the logistical challenge, the British military often performed the final work of destruction: sometimes burning files in incinerators, sometimes loading them with weights and dumping them in the ocean.[48]

THE TRUTH ABOUT EMPIRE

Altogether, roughly 8,800 files were removed from thirty-seven colonies and transported to Britain. Because they were created outside the United Kingdom, the Public Records Act of 1958 did not cover them, and National Archives staff refused to take custody of them. This was the legal gray zone that made it possible for the files to remain at an intelligence facility known as Hanslope Park, in the Buckinghamshire countryside, for more than three decades. Only in 2011 did the existence of this archive become public knowledge—not on the initiative of the British government, but as a result of a lawsuit filed against it by five elderly Kenyans victimized during the counterinsurgency of the 1950s. The tactics of legal and documentary evasion, always entangled, helped to undo one another in the end.[49]

The extraordinary spectacle of the British government called to account for late colonial crimes in a British courtroom inevitably felt like the culmination of a long-suppressed history. In some ways, it was. The academic discipline of British imperial history was shifting in ways that bore directly on the case of *Mutua and Others v. Foreign and Commonwealth Office*. A field born in the patriotic purpose of late Victorian settler colonialism gave way in the second half of the twentieth century to the fragmentation of area studies and a collective disengagement from moral questions.[50] It was not until 2005 that pathbreaking books by historians David Anderson and Caroline Elkins on the Kenya Emergency moved colonial violence to the top of the scholarly agenda.[51] Although the research underlying these books began many years earlier, the post-9/11 context powerfully shaped their reception—particularly in the United States, where Elkins, an American, was awarded the Pulitzer Prize. The parallels between Kenya, on the one hand, and Afghanistan and Iraq, on the other, were impossible to overlook: in each case, nominally liberal empires had seemingly lost their way in wars against "terrorists." If the British Empire was on trial in London's High Court, so was the newly critical imperial historiography, with Anderson, Elkins, and historian Huw Bennett serving as expert witnesses for the plaintiffs.

Other forces conspired to make *Mutua* the vehicle for thwarting a long history of moral evasion. In Kenya, the Mau Mau legacy had been politically contentious for decades after independence, and the grievances of former insurgents were suppressed by the state in the interest of stabilization. Even their ability to meet and organize as Mau Mau veterans was proscribed by law. But after the 2002 presidential election brought decades of undemocratic rule to an end, these constraints relaxed, and activists at the Kenya Human Rights Commission—who themselves embraced Mau Mau as a dissenting tradition—mobilized in support of the lawsuit.[52] In Britain, meanwhile, the common law had long placed limits on employers' liability for wrongs committed by their employees. But tort rules on so-called "vicarious liability" had recently been loosened in a series of cases on sexual abuse in the Catholic Church.[53] Then too, the piecemeal British approach to indemnity and amnesty legislation—a contrast to France and the Netherlands, which passed sweeping amnesties in the age of decolonization—left the state vulnerable to litigation from former colonial subjects once the political and legal contexts changed.

Legal representatives of the British government nonetheless tried to have the lawsuit dismissed on a series of technicalities. Perhaps most strikingly, they argued that any liabilities of the British colonial government in Kenya passed onto the postcolonial state of Kenya after independence in 1963. Justice Richard McCombe rejected this attempted displacement of responsibility in an impassioned 2011 ruling which noted "the revulsion with which English law regards torture" as well as the central involvement of the Colonial Office, the British Army, and other unquestionably British institutions in prosecuting the counterinsurgency. Soon afterward, the Foreign and Commonwealth Office settled the suit, establishing a nearly £20 million fund for the benefit of the survivors and financing a memorial in downtown Nairobi. Foreign Secretary William Hague expressed regret for abuses by British authorities, but did not explicitly apologize for them, in the House of Commons in 2013.[54]

Whether this outcome represented a turning point or an endpoint for post-imperial accountability remains an open question. A lawsuit brought by Cypriot torture victims resulted in a 2019 settlement of £1 million and another regretful non-apology from the British government.[55] A lawsuit brought by a larger group of Kenyan survivors was dismissed by a judge in 2018 on the grounds that too much time had elapsed.[56] The High Court likewise rejected a 2012 suit that would have forced the British government to hold a public inquiry into the Batang Kali massacre.[57] Has the "juridification" of the past inaugurated a sustained process of memorialization in Britain or merely substituted for it? One thing, at least, is clear. The limits of the human lifespan mean that lawsuits brought by survivors of seven-decade-old wars do not represent a durable strategy for the future.

Decolonization has been conceptualized in many different ways: as a heroic story of liberation; as a world-historical process of demographic inevitability; as a shrewd strategy for maintaining Western dominance by subtler means. But the British experience of retreating from empire must also be seen as a project of shedding moral burdens, dissolving relationships of obligation, and evading mechanisms of accountability. To be sure, a "clean break" from empire could not be willed into existence quite so easily as Powell hoped. It was nonetheless a powerful ideal, the longstanding pursuit of which continues to distort and obscure the imperial past.

11

NO END OF A RECKONING

Stuart Ward

Skirmishing over the moral legacies of empire is by no means a recent trend. Running disputes about official apologies, colonial reparations, school curricula and what to do with redundant monuments and anniversaries have a complex pre-history. The combative tone may have scaled new heights, befitting an age when the trenches of the culture wars run deep. But the battle lines were drawn long ago.

This is easily overlooked. Whatever one makes of Nigel Biggar's *Colonialism: A Moral Reckoning*, few seem to dissent from the view that it marks a new departure. Favourable reviewers recorded their 'acute subversive delight' in encountering a work so attuned to its turbulent times, guaranteed to 'grate with the throng for whom anticolonialism is a stock-in-trade'.[1] A string of dust jacket endorsements heralded a 'timely riposte' to the distortions of 'fashionable condemnation', commending the author for displaying rare courage 'in these days of academic group think'. By going fearlessly 'where few other scholars now venture to tread', Biggar had provided 'welcome relief from the polemicists'—'as necessary at the present time as it is persuasive'.[2]

Even Biggar's detractors largely concurred that 'opinion about empire has never been as deeply divided', and that historical scholarship is 'now politicised in ways that most of us could never have imagined just a few years ago'.[3] For or against, enamoured or incensed, Biggar's intervention seemed to arise out of a uniquely vexed moment in the politics of historical truth-telling. The author himself signalled his intent precisely in these terms. In taking up the cudgels in a dispute that was really 'about the present, not the past', he also staked his claim to originality.[4] Describing how he had stumbled 'blindly, into the Imperial History Wars', oblivious to the polemical minefield strewn in his path, Biggar surmised that such 'naivety has its advantages', enabling him to see the problem with 'fresh eyes'.

This chapter puts that core assumption to the test. How 'fresh' are the controversies that have erupted in recent years, and what deeper fissures are overlooked by insisting on their novelty? Has our broader comprehension of the 'truth' about the British Empire moved forward, even as the warring parties have moved further apart? Taking a broader view of the moral imperatives that have always infused public engagement with these issues, we would do well to treat claims of a great 'moral reckoning' with a healthy scepticism. Very little of what passes for informed debate about the ethics of empire has not been said before—and indeed long before.

What follows, then, is an exploration of the earliest moral reckonings that attended Britain's postwar imperial retreat. As the empire itself was gradually wound up, the first of many 'empire retrospectives' began to appear, tentatively weighing up Britain's imperial track record in the light of posterity. All manner of techniques were employed to insulate the country from overly harsh judgement, not just about the empire's evident moral shortcomings but also the wider culpability of the British people themselves. Most prominently, the 'colonial balance-sheet' was pioneered in these years as a reasoned, methodical and dispassionate way of finding definitive answers to disturbing questions. But 'balance', as we shall see, was not always what it seemed, bound up as it was in the very liberal conundrums it was meant to resolve.

* * *

'The flaw is an incurable one.' Jeremy Bentham was far from the first to raise objections to 'the sort of colony that has been obtained by conquest'—in this case, the colony of New South Wales, which had been sanctioned by no treaty or diplomatic exchange with the prior Indigenous owners. But his 1803 pamphlet, 'A Plea for the Constitution', remains significant for its exhaustive catalogue of every conceivable infringement of moral principle 'for oppressive as well as anti-constitutional purposes' in the founding of Botany Bay. Historians frequently refer to his complaint about the unlawful treatment of the Aborigines as evidence of an early twitch in the imperial conscience. As it happens, Indigenous dispossession ran a very distant second in Bentham's priorities to the 'enormities committed to British subjects', namely the hapless convicts condemned to 'that land of exile in a state of bondage'.[5] Nevertheless, by including colonized peoples as part of a broader liberal indictment, he reduced to essentials the age-old dilemma of a 'free though conquering people'.[6]

Throughout the nineteenth century, liberal reformers grappled with the moral tension around an empire of presumptive liberty incorporating an illiberal chain of overseas conquests. And not just reformers. Even the chief proselytizer for the

'Expansion of England'—Regius Professor of History at Cambridge J. R. Seeley—baulked at the 'oriental despotism' Britain had come to preside over in India. 'We cannot', he ventured in 1883, 'on looking more closely into the phenomenon, reconcile ourselves to it.'[7] Though contemporaries generally proved quite adept at reconciling the anomalies, their task was complicated by the rising clamour among colonized peoples themselves, condemning the 'un-Britishness' of imperial rule and asserting their constitutional rights in terms far more radical than anything in Bentham's pamphlets.[8] These early interventions from South Asia, the Caribbean and Africa pushed for a more racially inclusive conception of English constitutionalism that was all the more confronting for being 'articulated as a *demand*'.[9]

'England was by no means unanimous in her imperialism', as Bernard Porter noted more than half a century ago, and this was particularly true of the early decades of the twentieth century.[10] The disputes that arose out of the Anglo-Boer War and Irish Home Rule provided fertile ground for protest, often springing from heartfelt disenchantment at the yawning gap between liberal principle and imperial practice. For the three young authors of *Liberalism and the Empire* (1900), all dedicated to 'the policy of non-interference, to the studied avoidance of aggression, to toleration and generous amity between conflicting creeds and diverse races, to Liberal principles and Liberal ideas', the unfolding tragedy in South Africa raised genuine moral qualms:

> There is at present grave danger of these higher considerations being almost forgotten, and of force and aggression becoming not only too often employed as means towards good or tolerable ends, but actually worshipped and glorified as ends in themselves. ... The greatness of Greater Britain lies not in these things, and is not compatible with these things. Our conceptions of it must be utterly freed from the false atmosphere that has clogged and blinded them.[11]

NO END OF A RECKONING

But precisely how the empire might be 'utterly freed' from the stigma of force and aggression was left unresolved. It was one thing to raise objections but another matter entirely to disentangle the sordid means from the hallowed ends.

The early discipline of imperial history emerged in a political climate that pitted pride in imperial achievement against 'bedrock moral and legal sensibilities'.[12] When H. E. Egerton, the first occupant of the Beit Chair of Colonial History at Oxford University, produced a pamphlet in 1914 called 'Is the British Empire the Result of Wholesale Robbery?', his spirited rebuttal only accentuated the charge.[13] The volley of recrimination aroused by General Dyer's infamous slaughter of innocent Punjabis at Amritsar in 1919 raised similar questions about the appalling human cost of defending Britain's global coordinates. Opinion may have been deeply divided about Dyer, but there could be no doubt that imperial authority 'rested as firmly on a set of moral relations as it did on bayonets and bullets'.[14]

Into the interwar years, a remarkably wide range of opinions about the ethics of empire permeated the public sphere, neatly distilled into the diverse cast of characters in George Orwell's *Burmese Days* (1934). 'Everyone knows', proclaimed the dust jacket of the first edition, 'that behind the glamorous front of the white man's rule in the East there are things so evil, so shocking, so dangerous that all officialdom tries to cover them up.'[15] Though such murmurings never gained the upper hand politically, they provided a hazy backdrop of moral ambiguity and a creeping uncertainty about the empire's long-term prospects.

At some point after 1947, the whole tenor of the conversation changed as recognition dawned that the empire itself was entering its final days. When that moment arrived cannot be discerned with any precision, but within five years of Indian Independence, *The Times* was waxing nervously about a 'state of flux' in imperial nomenclature. Lamenting that it 'would be more than a pity if the name of Empire were to be driven out', it had nevertheless become clear that the gradual 'extension of the word Commonwealth' was leaving little room to talk about the 'British empire' as a going concern.[16]

One measure of the transition is the emergence of the 'empire retrospective'—a distinct genre of writing dedicated to weighing the historical scales of the empire's net moral worth. The empire itself might have been fading into obscurity, but it remained saddled with unresolved questions about its liberal credentials. Any attempt to survey its record of achievement, then, was bound to generate polarizing sentiments.

Take, for example, two books published in 1950. For the veteran left-wing radical R. Palme Dutt, the tipping point of decolonization marked a rare opportunity for Britain to renounce capitalism, racism and exploitation in all its forms. In *Britain's Crisis of Empire*, his verdict was unequivocal, condemning outright an empire project that had 'begun to stink in the nostrils of mankind and become a term of abuse'.[17] Meanwhile, the Cambridge historian, Charles Carrington, was equally convinced that the empire was 'in full retreat'—so much so that its history 'could now be written'. But in his monumental *The British Overseas*, he was at pains to dispel any notion that 'the mission of the British is concluded' or that 'the race' had become 'decadent'. For all the strategic setbacks and moral brickbats of recent years, he remained convinced that Britain and the self-governing 'dominions' would 'retain their moral unity and may retain the moral leadership of the world'.[18]

Viewed together, these works offer an early glimpse of the gulf of historical understanding that would widen in the years ahead. For Dutt, a founding member of the British Communist Party and wartime conscientious objector, the empire had left nothing but the most shameful legacy, useful only as a spur to reform Britain from within. But for Carrington (who revealed his sympathies early by relishing his 'good fortune to be born into one of those middle-class families whose members, for a hundred years, have moved freely about the Empire') it was an admirable record of disseminating liberal principle and robust institutions from which a prosperous postwar order might be fashioned.[19] The only question was whether Britain might continue to exercise 'moral leadership' in lieu of strategic primacy and economic clout. Then, as now, it was 'about the present, not the past'.[20]

It was the Labour Party's John Strachey who first published a major title with *The End of Empire* unambiguously rendered in the past tense. Appearing in 1959, it was also the first fully fledged 'empire retrospective'—or as the author termed it, 'the first book to face up to the situation in which Britain finds herself as the result of the voluntary dissolution of her Empire'.[21] His timing could not have been more opportune, arriving on the cusp of the 'wind of change' that would shortly be signalled by Harold Macmillan only months later in February 1960.

Part historical survey of the empire's origins and evolution, and part stocktaking of the material and moral implications for the British themselves, Strachey's book was steeped in Marxist convictions about the intricate connections between imperialism and capitalism. But unlike Dutt, he allowed his more moderate left-wing sympathies to take him in a different direction entirely, absolving the British people of any culpability for the empire whatsoever.

It would be a mistake, Strachey argued, to consider the East India Company's ascendancy in India 'as marking the moment in history when a daemonic will to conquer and to rule seized the British, an imperial will which possessed them for the next two centuries'. Such motivations acted 'powerfully on a few key individual figures' only, for the exclusive benefit of a 'narrow class of investors'.[22] By magnifying the connections between colonialism and venture capitalism, Strachey was able to minimize the social repercussions. At no stage, he insisted, did the people at large become caught up in any kind of collective imperial 'fixation'.[23]

The lopsided economic returns also helped to explain why, when it came to imperial retrenchment, there was 'enough sanity amongst us to make it possible for Britain to avoid destroying itself in the attempt to retain the untenable'. The long tradition of anti-imperial sentiment in the Liberal and Labour movements had insulated 'the most independently minded' of the lower and middle social orders 'from the pervasive imperialist mental climate of the day'. He gave the example of the accelerated retreat from India in the 1940s, which 'no government could have done' had the people been truly wedded to the Raj. Indeed, the 'most politically conscious' segments of working-class opinion even 'felt a sympathy and identification with the colonial peoples as, to some extent, joint victims of the exploitation of the imperialist system'. Hence the 'steady march of a voluntary, or at least largely non-violent dis-imperialism' since the Second World War.[24]

Here was moral accounting of a different kind. It was not so much a refusal to acknowledge the regrettable record of colonial exploitation, more a matter of selectively apportioning blame. Strachey revelled in Britain's 'lucky escape' (as he termed it) from any deeper or lasting moral taint. But when it came to the pattern of imperial withdrawal, he sought to have it both ways. For him, it had become 'an irresistible subject of self-congratulation' that the British had managed 'peacefully to relinquish their rule over nearly a quarter of the entire human race'.[25] This was 1959, yet the recent conflagrations of Malaya, Kenya, Palestine and the Partition of India had somehow evaded his notice. In this scheme of things, the 'British visitor to present-day India' could be permitted a certain 'pride in the mighty legacies' which 'his countrymen have left'.[26]

The reasoning seems erratic, but Strachey was no eccentric. His conviction that the general public had few material or moral investments in the empire became a soothing tonic in the years ahead. A. J. P. Taylor went so far as to excise the empire entirely from his 1965 volume for the *Oxford History of England* on the grounds that it was of no great concern to ordinary English men and women ('The British Empire declined, the position of the people improved').[27] Other prominent historians of the day overwhelmingly endorsed Strachey's claim that the British had never really been 'imperially-minded'; that the empire had 'little or no meaning to working-class life and society'; and that the 'great British public viewed the dissolution of their Empire with disinterest. They thought it was a bit of a joke.'[28]

One leading historian of the end of empire elaborated on this theme in the early 1960s. Originally from Glasgow, A. P. Thornton had established his reputation with *The Imperial Idea and Its Enemies*—also published in 1959. Among the empire's enemies, he included the vast majority of ordinary Britons themselves, who 'had always been indifferent to the future of the British Empire, mainly because they knew so little about its past and had so little to do with its present'. They had neither designed the structures nor staffed the administrative organs; they had never instigated the major initiatives nor planned imperial strategy. 'Such business was not their business, nor did they share the assumptions of those whose business it was.' This posed the most debilitating challenge of all to the British Empire as it entered the postwar world:

> It was the paternalists' loss of grip on the allegiance of their own people, indeed their failure to retain the latter's attention, that weakened the assurance with which they faced the world, and made the precariousness of the imperial structure plain for all to see ... The Empire and its concerns were reckoned an irrelevance, and the concept of the Commonwealth never impinged on the general outlook at all. The imperialists were forced on to the retreat, to the far Right of the Conservative party, to the pages of *The Round Table* and to the letter-columns of *The Times*.[29]

THE TRUTH ABOUT EMPIRE

There is no need to rush to the opposite judgement—that the British people were somehow perpetually drunk on imperial ambition, uniformly and universally swept up in its romance and wonder—to see an element of special pleading at work here. Each of these historians took it entirely for granted that the empire had left behind a substantial moral burden—why else invest so much energy in the procedures of unburdening? But to write off the entire enterprise as the plaything of a mere 10 per cent of the population ('at most', according to Strachey) was to stretch all credibility.[30]

All of which suggests a more troubling disturbance that could neither be precisely named, nor easily quelled. Even as Strachey and Thornton poured their energies into minimizing the moral implications, neither could resist talking up the stakes. Thus, Thornton proceeded unwittingly to demolish his own argument, expounding at length on how the loss of empire had 'deprived Britain herself of her long-standing assumptions', along with an abiding sense of moral purpose. The people may not have cared much about the empire's inner workings, but they knew it was there—as a 'monument to British convictions, British exuberance, British abilities, British institutions and above all to British power and influence in the world'. Its passing thus left Britain 'a somewhat draughty place, politically and morally, to live in'.[31] Thornton would soon take himself off to the West Indies, and later Toronto, for the remainder of his long career.

Strachey became even more vexed, pivoting from 'irresistible self-congratulation' to an irrepressible foreboding that is worth quoting at length:

> The morale, the spirit, the mental health even, of all of us in Britain are deeply involved in the question of the dissolution of our empire. The whole tone of our national life will partly depend on whether we can comprehend the process in the perspective of history ... many people in Britain feel a sense of personal loss—almost of amputa-

NO END OF A RECKONING

tion—when some colony or semi-colony, Burma or the Soudan for example, becomes independent. The hauling down of the Union Jack in yet another part of the world has a depressing effect. This feeling of personal loss from the fact that the writ of the parliament of Westminster no longer runs in some territory is all the more difficult to deal with because it is essentially irrational ... So tremendous an imperial tradition could not but have profound effects upon the national psychology. To a considerable degree (though never quite wholeheartedly) the British people became an imperial people, with the characteristic faults and virtues of such peoples. The moral and psychological shock of the rapid dissolution, whether voluntarily or involuntarily, must inevitably be great.[32]

This, from a man who had been treated for a nervous breakdown in the 1930s now sharing his intimacy with the novel procedures of psychoanalysis. And indeed, from the same Strachey who had just devoted hundreds of pages to debunking the merest suggestion of residual hankerings in a country that had 'been saved from the fate which has overtaken most nations which have lost their empires'.[33] Much, indeed, seemed to hinge on 'whether we can comprehend the process in the perspective of history'.

Perhaps it was this that Thornton was driving at when he enigmatically concluded: 'The death of British imperialism left a curious void.'[34]

* * *

Into the void stepped Margery Perham in November 1961. The sixty-six-year-old Fellow of Nuffield College Oxford had been asked to deliver the BBC's prestigious Reith Lectures that year, the first time the honour had been bestowed on a woman. As the country's leading expert on colonial administration, with half a century of direct personal experience traversing the empire, particularly in Africa, she seemed the perfect choice to take in the full meaning and significance of the wind of change. Coming towards the end of her career, it was a time when Perham 'was ready to think over all I had been working upon, and generalize about it at what was, probably, the right historical moment'.[35]

Indeed, the timeliness of her intervention became apparent in the opening lines of the first lecture:

> "Colonialism". This is a new word, or at least a word that has been used in new ways during the last few years. It is generally used in contexts which do not leave us in much doubt that it is a word of abuse.

Perham signalled from the outset her inclination to push back on the voguish 'cult of anti-colonialism' that had so roundly condemned 'our past record'. Equally, however, she voiced a readiness to confront her own assumptions, as someone who had been 'taught from their schooldays that our empire was a splendid achievement, conducted as much for the good of its many people as for our own'. Her abiding question thus combined a combative irony with an element of genuine self-examination: 'How, we ask, has "colonialism" suddenly, as it seems, become such a term of abuse? Have we been utterly blind?' In dubbing the lectures 'The Colonial Reckoning', she fashioned a two-edged sword—checking the momentum of the empire's trenchant critics while creating a space for a certain confessional for career colonialists such as herself—perhaps even a path to redemption.[36]

It is worth staying with Perham, because her five lectures—later published as a short but influential book in 1962—would set the template for a certain mode of ethical stocktaking for decades to come. Her presence looms large in Biggar's *Colonialism: A Moral Reckoning*, right down to his subtitle, which serves as a silent tribute. Biggar borrowed freely from Perham's observations, not least her conviction that the pace of decolonization in Britain's African colonies had been rushed through far too quickly, long before the new democracies were ready for the demands of self-government.[37]

NO END OF A RECKONING

Above all, Biggar shared Perham's preoccupation with the idea of balancing the historical ledger—tallying up the empire's positives and negatives to discern its moral attributes. The late 1950s had witnessed the emergence of 'cost–benefit analysis', pioneered by economists in the UK civil service to devise a more capacious way of quantifying the net worth of public investments.[38] In a similar vein, Macmillan had directed Whitehall in 1957 to prepare 'something like a profit and loss account' for each of Britain's remaining colonies, to see whether 'we are likely to gain or lose by its departure'.[39] Something of the spirit of this seems to have influenced Perham, who surmised in her opening lecture that, by examining Britain's colonial record 'through the eyes of her critics, we shall be able to draw up, for their benefit and for our own, a very rough and ready political and moral colonial balance-sheet'.[40]

Perham was undoubtedly the first to frame the *moral* economy of empire in these terms—certainly the first to do so from a retrospective vantage point. Indeed, it was the presumptive endpoint of decolonization that made the moment and the method seem so opportune. For Biggar, her efforts remained a source of inspiration sixty years on. 'Instead of indiscriminate condemnation', he recalled, 'she sought to offer a discriminating judgement ... I shall seek to do the same here.'[41]

Several things need be said to place Perham in her proper context, none of which suggest that her 'discriminating judgement' can be taken at face value. The first is her own deep personal investments at a time when the subject at hand—colonial administration—was rapidly becoming obsolete. This helps to account for some of her more wayward observations.

For example, there was nothing at all 'sudden' about the pejorative connotations of the word 'colonialism' in 1961. Perham's own career was punctuated by frequent reflection on the empire's many moral setbacks over the years—from the perspective of a committed 'progressive' who was quick to call out antiquated thinking. Twenty years earlier, for example, with the eviction of the British from Southeast Asia at the hands of the Japanese in 1942, she experienced the first of many 'reckonings'—recorded in her personal correspondence with the Labour Party's Arthur Creech Jones. 'Don't you somehow begin to think that the old imperialism has received a blow in the Far East, moral as well as physical?', ran one of her missives. The whole 'time-spirit' had changed irrevocably, 'and if we do not rapidly adjust ourselves ... I do not see how we can go on having an Empire.'[42] She aired these views publicly in two prominent articles in *The Times*, calling for a major rethink of colonial structures and assumptions in the light of the 'Malayan disaster'.[43]

What evidently troubled Perham in the early 1960s was not the adverse ideological climate for colonialism so much as the sense that a long-anticipated denouement was finally coming to pass. Though she had always encouraged policies geared to that very end, the reality nevertheless seemed to catch her uncharacteristically off guard. In a revealing passage in her Reith Lectures, Perham recalled a recent visit to Lagos to attend Nigeria's independence ceremony, staged at midnight on 1 October 1960. It was when the Union Jack fluttered down the flagpole that Perham

> felt a wholly unexpected, almost physical shock. It may have been that, having made some study of Nigeria's history, I realized just what it was that was being brought to an end, all the hopes and fears, the achievements and mistakes, all the work of hundreds of British lives, many of which ended in this country.

Her composure returned when the Nigerian flag was raised amid general euphoria from the assembled crowd.[44] But the whole episode was remarkably reminiscent of John Strachey, pointing to the underlying apprehensions of a career colonialist in the anteroom of empire's end. As David Fieldhouse once pithily observed: 'Her subject died before she did.'[45]

NO END OF A RECKONING

It might be said that for Perham, the passing of empire doubled as a great personal reckoning and an occasion for genuine introspection. This is borne out by the extensive handwritten notes she compiled in preparation for the lectures, now housed in her manuscript collection in Oxford. 'The failure of gradualism' reads one heading, followed by 'the failure of white liberalism' and the 'suddenness of the change'. Herself an outspoken advocate of gradualism as well as liberalism, such jottings suggest more than a hint of enquiry into her own personal failings. 'Why did we give up?' starts a new page, and further down: 'Why did we give way?', followed by a stream of consciousness: 'Psychological—a sense of disenchantment about empire ... a kind of "what the hell—if they hate us so much and want to be rid of us—let her go. We shall be well rid of them."'[46]

A sense of deflated purpose and perhaps even dented confidence also hampered Perham's efforts to balance up the moral ledger. She boiled the difficulty down to one fundamental dilemma: 'What criteria should we use?'[47] Spreading the 'benefits of civilization' could no longer carry the day, given the inroads of anti-colonial critique in puncturing the universal projection of Western values. Perham's response was to charge the empire's critics in turn with imposing anachronistic moral categories, measuring the entire historical sweep of the colonial encounter against 'quite new and difficult' standards of altruism that had 'only lately' been applied to colonial administration, and imperfectly so.[48] It was Perham's way of saying 'don't judge the past by the moral standards of the present', but it was unclear exactly what she meant. Liberal and humanitarian objections to the empire's coercive, autocratic tendencies had been 'standard' fare for generations—a theme that Perham herself explored in her final lecture.[49]

In the end, Perham demurred when it came to casting final judgement. Though the final lecture was dubbed 'The Colonial

Account', she was quick to inform listeners that she was not 'going to draw up an imperial balance-sheet with all our beneficent acts upon one side and all our errors on the other, and then see if we end up with a moral credit or debit'. She had evidently come to recognize the futility of her own rhetorical device, opting instead for some very general, unstructured remarks on either side of the ledger.

On the debit side, she listed the 'unimaginable sufferings' of slavery (a 'long ante-dated cheque ... which we still ought to try to honour') and the serial transgressions of unrestrained settlers (proving the adage that 'once out of sight of Britain, the white man could not be trusted to deal justly with the black man').[50] With her intricate network of personal contacts throughout the African settler world, it was a genuine wrench for Perham to cast judgement on 'these countrymen of ours', who had 'given all their hearts and their hopes to that glorious land'. But she held firm to her conviction that white minority rule must come to an end.[51]

On the credit side, Perham again echoed Strachey in extolling the transfer of power across so many former colonial territories 'with so little bloodshed or even disorder'.[52] And she could not bring herself to find fault with her own lifelong project, the officers of the Colonial Service, to whom she dedicated a heartfelt tribute. Their ideals of selfless service, devotion to duty, tolerance, team spirit, courage and physical prowess were all duly lionized, mixed with an undisguised contempt for the 'fashionable reaction today' against these much-maligned qualities and the men who embodied them.[53] An abundance of supporting anecdotes from friends, relatives and former students in the field left little room for doubt that, on this score at least, Perham was anything but an independent witness.[54]

The upshot of Perham's intricate display of even-handedness was the underwhelming conclusion: 'Britain's record is mixed. She could be slow, neglectful, unimaginative. She could, however, have done much more if the sudden growth of African nationalism had not prematurely cut short her slow and steady work on the foundations of the new states.'[55] Perham may have been grappling inwardly with a great reckoning, but in the final analysis she was unable to distil it on to the page.

This is entirely understandable, and the point is not to demand more of someone of Perham's professional background and life experience. But it does raise questions about the inherent slant of the 'empire retrospective' as a framing device, particularly the sober invocation of 'balance' as the indispensable quality for any fair-minded assessment. No reasonable person could raise objections to judiciously weighing the issue from all sides. How, then, were Perham's efforts received, and what can this tell us about the rhetorical purchase of the colonial 'balance-sheet'?

Reviewers were quick to latch on to the 'colonialism' libel, with *The Daily Telegraph* leading a chorus of unvarnished relief at the way Perham—with 'vision, authority and understanding'—had coolly rebutted the claims of those who 'revile us as Colonialists'. In the final analysis, only when it came to the matter of slavery had 'these lectures damned our own colonial record. Otherwise, they have left the balance on the credit side, with due praise for the unselfish services of the men in the field.'[56] *The Listener* drew attention to Perham's commendable sense of proportion, and her ability to 'admire the ideals of men like Cecil Rhodes, Lord Cromer, and Lord Lugard' while at the same time 'weigh impartially the problems of the imperial aftermath'.[57] *The Sunday Telegraph*'s review was titled 'Maturity or Just Pride?' (both qualities anchored conspicuously on the 'credit' side of the ledger), congratulating Perham for exploding 'the fiction, not only that colonialism is essentially evil, but that it is still alive and must be fought'.[58] For *The Spectator*, Perham was the perfect choice to deliver the lectures as someone 'quite rightly unharassed by guilt complexes about British colonialism'.[59]

THE TRUTH ABOUT EMPIRE

What, then, of the avalanche of private mail Perham received from grateful listeners throughout the United Kingdom and beyond? One might have thought that an avowedly 'balanced' account of a 'mixed' colonial record would generate responses from both sides of the moral divide. But that is not what we find in Margery Perham's mailbag.

The tone was set from the very first lecture in a letter from a Mr Francis Curtler: 'I had expected a lot of dreary cliché stuff about the iniquities of our former Empire and a lot of "liberal" affectations and pretensions. Quite the reverse!'[60] A leading Northern industrialist chimed in with the hope that Perham's lectures might 'actually set alive a force which would destroy the malevolent influences of the false interpretation of "colonialism" now being force-grown in Africa'.[61] Sandy Fraser from the YMCA thanked Perham for the 'fresh light' she had cast, which 'will have persuaded all but the most incorrigible of your listeners to re-examine their prejudices'.[62] He evidently did not have to spell out what those prejudices were. One well-wisher from the London School of Economics simply commended Perham for her 'cogent apologia for colonialism'.[63]

By Perham's own account, her 'very large mail' contained 'only two abusive letters so I suppose I ought to be pleased'.[64] Neither of those writers complained that she had erred on the credit side of the ledger.[65] She was also showered with attention from several prominent figures such as the evolutionary biologist Julian Huxley, who had the 'feeling that anti-colonialism is a kind of escape mechanism' that allowed the empire's newly liberated peoples to 'project their frustrations onto something outside themselves'.[66] His cousin, Michael Huxley (founder of the *Geographical Magazine*), queried whether Perham was right to place all of the blame for the institution of slavery at the feet of Europeans, urging: 'Might we not be a little fairer to ourselves in this matter?'[67] Other prominent letter-writers included the elderly political economist Moritz J. Bonn, who had first coined the term 'decolonization' in the 1920s as a way of rationalizing the dispiriting loss of Germany's status and prestige as an imperial power—now witnessing the same dilemmas affecting Britain.[68] And none other than John Strachey appears among Perham's many well-wishers, thanking her for sending a copy of the published lectures.[69]

Strachey's appearance in Perham's in-tray points to a shared surface tension. Just as Strachey presented himself as the dispassionate intellect, bent on deflecting certain moral misgivings, so too Perham's posture of impartial judge seems unconvincing in retrospect. In a way, the influx of fan-mail failed to do her justice, freighted as it was with an unalloyed contempt for 'radicals' and a self-vindicating righteousness. Perham herself was more open, and more genuinely perplexed by the ethical dilemmas of empire's end. In her replies to well-wishers, she sometimes corrected their more overwrought assertions (politely so, to the point where they may not themselves have noticed). She also knew full well that her perspective could only ever be partial: 'To profess complete impartiality, as a Chinese sage once said, is itself a kind of partiality.'[70] But she also knew instinctively how to *perform* the role of the detached expert, and in this regard her 'colonial balance-sheet' furnished the perfect vehicle. In Perham's hands, the very practice of balancing the historical scales became imbued with an unacknowledged bias.

* * *

If even an aborted attempt like Perham's to weigh up the pros and cons could produce a listener response so uniformly aligned with the 'credit' side of the ledger, it is no small wonder that the device has been redeployed for similar ends ever since. Within a few years of Perham, the Stanford-based duo of L. H. Gann and Peter Duignan presented their own moral accounting in *Burden of Empire: An Appraisal of Western Colonialism in Africa South of the Sahara*. The preliminaries were now becoming familiar, with the opening page calling for a 'reexamination of some of the major assumptions' that now governed the study of modern imperialism, some of which had 'acquired the prestige of well-established doctrine'.[71] Though the 'smug moralizing' of the old 'gunpowder and grapeshot' view of empire had rightly been overturned, there remained a nagging sense that 'the pendulum has swung too far the other way'.[72] Specifically, an 'unduly philanthropic approach to world affairs' had produced distortions of its own, tending to 'regard overseas imperialism as the main culprit' of too many of the world's contemporary ills.[73] Over the course of some 400 pages, Gann and Duignan tallied their way to a resounding endorsement of the British Empire in Africa:

> Historical balance sheets are always hard to draw up. They involve their accountants in problems of extreme complexity, of differing standards of comparison, and of making value judgements. But the imperialists can plead that, even within their critics' own unspoken terms of reference, the colonial record involved tremendous achievements for good as well as ill. In our view, the imperial system stands out as one of the most powerful engines for cultural diffusion in the history of Africa; its credit balance far outweighs its debit account.[74]

How they arrived at this startlingly clear verdict, or by what 'standard of comparison', need not delay us here; suffice it to say that the outcome never seemed in doubt. What distinguished these authors from Perham was not only their supreme confidence in their findings but also the absence of any real reservations about the method they employed.

Since that time, the resort to moral balance sheets has become a frequent accompaniment to the 'empire retrospective'. Politicians, polemicists and public moralists have reached for the scales whenever the colonial record has been subjected to what they regard as excessively harsh judgement. Into the 1970s, high school textbooks began to employ the 'cost–benefit analysis' as a means of engaging students in 'healthy debate' about empire.[75] By the time Niall Ferguson devoted a six-part television series to 'whether the Empire was a good or bad thing' in 2003, the rhetorical procedures had become as conventional as they were predictable.[76] Notably, they are rarely deployed by the empire's critics to make the case for a colonial deficit. 'Balance', it seems, is monopolized by the credit side.[77]

Biggar charted his course midway between Perham and Gann/Duignan, citing both with unqualified approval. For him, there could be no doubt that 'whatever the debit column of British colonialism, there is a credit column, too, of which any fair ethical assessment must take account'. He thus embarked on his own elaborate exercise in 'drawing up a tally'—with considerably more conviction than Perham.[78] Yet he, too, pulled back when it came to whether the British Empire did '*more* good than evil', for the perfectly valid reason that the two sides of the ledger 'are incommensurable'. This led him to the surprisingly open verdict (surprising, because it goes against the polemical slant of much of the book) that 'to ask these questions is immediately to expose their absurdity ... a utilitarian calculation cannot be conducted rationally'.[79] Elsewhere, he has trenchantly denied ever having 'argued that the sins of empire are outweighed by its benefits'. No doubt—but from its very inception, the colonial balance-sheet was generically structured to insinuate just that, without explicitly saying so.[80]

Quite apart from the skewed premise, there are other reasons to be wary of the moral sage waving the latest imperial audit. As Priya Satia argues, the very notion that the empire can be evaluated *neutrally* confers an aura of political legitimacy. It also assumes that we have reached the point when 'the story is over, the accounts are closed, and we can actually tot up the balance'.[81] As we have seen, that aspect was integral to Perham's thinking—the sense of an ending, and the attendant need for moral certainty as she closed her own personal account. To this day, framing the question in these terms tends to screen out the myriad ways in which colonial empires remain unfinished business.

Above all, the logic of moral accounting is inherently disingenuous. By separating out the sordid from the salutary (distributing them to 'either side' of the ledger), the moral taint is expressly placed at one remove, allowing a space where residual pride can cleave to the surplus credit. Thus, the 'incurable flaw' of liberal imperialism is circumvented. But as conscientious objectors to the Anglo-Boer War were to find more than a century ago, the 'good and the bad' could never entirely be disaggregated. Malevolent means were all too frequently harnessed to presumptively beneficial ends, and no honest moral accounting can get past this impacted state of affairs. The tangled legacies endure—which is why the colonial balance-sheet is such a singularly ill-fitting metaphor. Its persistence speaks to a lasting urge to rescue liberal intentions from tragic consequences—a tell-tale symptom of the moral conundrum it purportedly dissects.

Which is not to say that it should be of no interest to historians. In the shower of accolades bestowed on Perham's *Colonial Reckoning* in the early 1960s, one observer—Anthony Hartley of *The Spectator*—offered a few lines of gentle but revealing critique:

> Miss Perham does not deal with the effect of the loss of empire on ourselves, and this is a pity. For it is my belief that this inevitable process of divesting ourselves, not so much of power—that came before—but of connections with the world outside the British Isles, has been bad for us in a number of ways. If we owe a debt for colonial errors and misdeeds, it seems likely to be paid in frustration and provincialism at home rather than in any more dramatic form. This too is part of the colonial reckoning, and it contains figures which we have hardly yet begun to count.[82]

This is where the empire retrospective becomes particularly instructive—as a window into the moral world, not of the empire per se, but of its protracted aftermath in contemporary Britain. While often visceral debates have festered in other parts of the former British Empire—from Canada to Australia, New Zealand and elsewhere—they tend to revolve around these countries' own, more immediate colonial legacies (with the moral balance-sheet always close to hand).[83] Only in Britain, it seems, is the vast complex of the imperial past presented as a consolidated, macro-moral accounting. Here, the sense of onetime 'ownership' of the entire imperial enterprise invites a seemingly endless moral reckoning.

What ultimately distinguishes the empire retrospective as a genre is the outward show of wrestling with the moral implications, while working subtly to wrest them from a weary conscience. The attendant strategies of displacement and deflection, rationalization and rhetorical evasion, and the persistent urge to defend the indefensible have a history of their own that persists to the present day. The commotion surrounding Biggar ultimately has more to do with the extremes of polarization that structure contemporary politics than the inherent novelty of his intellectual—or indeed ethical—contribution. Though Perham never endured anything like the wholesale denunciation of her Oxford colleagues that awaited her latter-day champion, there is nevertheless every reason to read the two as part of a much wider arc. Not a 'moral reckoning' in any honest sense, but a much deeper, concerted effort to reconcile modern Britain to its ambivalent past at a minimal moral cost.

Further reading

Doble, Josh, Liam J. Liburd and Emma Parker (eds), *British Culture after Empire*, Manchester: Manchester University Press, 2023.
Faught, C. Brad, *Into Africa: The Imperial Life of Margery Perham*, London: I. B. Tauris, 2012.

THE TRUTH ABOUT EMPIRE

Gopal, Priyamvada, *Insurgent Empire: Anticolonial Resistance and British Dissent*, London: Verso, 2019.

Perham, Margery, *The Colonial Reckoning*, London: Collins, 1962.

Satia, Priya, *Time's Monster: History, Conscience and Britain's Empire*, London: Penguin, 2022.

Smith, Alison and Mary Bull (eds), *Margery Perham and British Rule in Africa*, London: Frank Cass, 1991.

Strachey, John, *The End of Empire*, London: Victor Gollancz, 1959.

12

COLONIALISM

A METHODOLOGICAL RECKONING

Margot Finn

Nigel Biggar's 2023 *Colonialism: A Moral Reckoning* raises a host of thorny methodological issues for historians. In this chapter, I assess textual evidence that illuminates the book's approach to historical research and historical argumentation. Focusing predominantly, but not exclusively, on the author's arguments about British colonial history in the heyday of the East India Company (EIC), I explore the ways in which selection biases in the choice and use of primary and secondary sources in turn produce interpretative skews that undercut the hefty book's analytical rigour. In keeping with its ambitious chronological and geographical remit, *Colonialism* cites hundreds of authors who have written on a capacious range of historical topics. But it also ignores large and distinctive swathes of the historiographical landscape. The book's argumentation and referencing, indeed, are shot through with exclusions that map in significant ways onto authorial gender, geography and generation. Attention to the genres and contexts in which chosen historical examples—often borrowed from other secondary authors—are embedded is similarly highly selective. These patterns of usage have implications for our understanding of both how empire in Britain worked and upon whom it exerted its sway, notably with respect to women and racialised colonial populations. The evidence considered here suggests that the selection choices informing *Colonialism* are neither historiographically nor morally neutral. In short, *Colonialism*'s methods, which depart significantly from twenty-first-century disciplinary conventions, distort both the historical record and our interpretation of it. To understand the ethics of both *Colonialism* and colonialism, we need to make a methodological reckoning.

Before assessing *Colonialism*'s arguments, it is worth asking whether this volume is intended as a work of history, and thus amenable to historical methodologies and disciplinary expectations. The author himself initially appears to answer this question in the negative. Describing himself as the victim of 'online denunciation by a group of students' after stumbling 'blindly, into the Imperial History Wars', Biggar comments that '[h]ad I been a professional historian, I would have known what to expect, but being a mere ethicist, I did not'.[1] Notwithstanding these demurs, *Colonialism* nevertheless claims roots in historical soil, invoking historical evidence and adducing the arguments of named historians to support its claims. Appeals to the use of data and reason punctuate *Colonialism*'s pages. Noting in his Introduction that he has 'consigned most of my skirmishes with historians to the endnotes', Biggar observes that he has however offered critical appraisals of the secondary literature in key sections of the text: 'The purpose in each case is the same: to lay bare the gap between the data and reasons given on the one hand, and the anti-colonialist assertions and judgements made on the other.'[2] Appeals to 'the data' of the historical record align with the book's professed determination to anatomise the 'historical truth', a phrase that runs like a leitmotif through the volume and is offered as a striking contrast to the ostensibly polemical, politically motivated texts and actions of *Colonialism*'s opponents. For student activists and their anti-colonialist and postcolonial tutors, Biggar asserts, an 'unscrupulous indifference to historical truth indicates that the controversy over empire is not really a controversy about history at all. It is about the present, not the past.'[3]

What are the historical data upon which *Colonialism*'s arguments depend? Stretching over thirty-three pages, its extensive bibliography cites 664 printed and web-based works.[4] Of these, eighty-nine (or 13 per cent) are examples of recent journalism—predominantly articles and opinion pieces in *The Guardian*, *The Daily Telegraph*, *The Times* and the like that lack scholarly references. Many are positioned to contribute to one side or the other of the Anglo-American 'culture wars'.[5] Primary sources dating from the periods of imperialism under scrutiny make a relatively modest contribution to *Colonialism*'s evidence base in terms of their numerical representation in the bibliography: ninety-seven (or 15 per cent) of all entries fall into this category. Printed texts that date predominantly from the nineteenth and twentieth centuries, they typically convey the sentiments of white Britons (chiefly men) in positions of power within the empire or in Parliament or offer fictional accounts of colonialism based on the lived experiences of settlers. Works by Edmund Burke, the Earl of Cromer, Rider Haggard, Elspeth Huxley, T. E. Lawrence, David Livingstone, Frederick Lugard, Sir John Malcolm and Alfred Milner exemplify these prevailing perspectives.[6] In a field of enquiry in which photography, film, media and material culture studies have for over two decades provoked novel research questions and set new research agendas, the book remains resolutely based in longer-form text publications. Biggar deploys no images to illustrate his arguments—even when, as with controversies over statuary representations of Cecil Rhodes or museum collections of Benin Bronzes, images and objects are centrally at issue. Nor does he appear to have sampled the hundreds of colonial and imperial newspapers, dating from the eighteenth century through decolonisation, that are now available and readily, systematically searchable online. Instead, secondary works—comprising both popular and scholarly studies of imperialism and cognate topics—account for the great bulk of his bibliographical entries, providing 478 sources or 72 per cent of the total works cited. Chronologically, these secondary works span from 1943 to 2022, with a median publication date of 2003.[7]

Examined simply in terms of representation in *Colonialism*'s bibliography, this list of authors and titles displays interesting patterns of inclusion and exclusion. Overwhelmingly Anglophone, it tilts strongly toward Biggar's undergraduate alma mater and former place of employment: Oxford researchers feature conspicuously in the bibliography, as they do in the text and endnotes. Scholarship emanating from Cambridge and Manchester (much less Belfast, Cardiff, Glasgow and Edinburgh) makes only fleeting appearances. References to the multi-volume *Oxford History of the British Empire* (1998–9) and to the *Oxford Handbooks* (established 2001) abound, contrasting sharply with the complete absence of any engagement with any volume in the *New Cambridge History of India* or with the more than 100 volumes published in Manchester University Press's Studies in Imperialism series.[8] Historians of South Asia will be surprised to find no Indian representatives of the Subaltern Studies school cited in either the bibliography or text: Dipesh Chakrabarty, Partha Chatterjee, Ranajit Guha, Gyanendra Pandey and Gayatri Spivak, among other scholars who have fundamentally transformed research on British colonialism in India since the 1980s, garner no notice. Turning from India to the Atlantic Ocean world, experts will likewise be surprised to encounter so few of the black intellectuals whose work catalysed this vibrant area of study: C. L. R. James, Stuart Hall and Paul Gilroy, for example, are nowhere referenced. These lacunae are as striking as the looming presence of Biggar's two especial bêtes noirs: Marxists stalk the pages of *Colonialism* together with the allegedly misguided 'disciples' of Edward Said's 1978 *Orientalism*, animating and guiding the book's contentious historiographical encounters with postcolonialism.[9]

Of course, a bibliography indicates only which works have been consulted. How they have been deployed by the author is another matter. Drilling down into *Colonialism*'s arguments, and the endnotes that document their claims, allows us to assess modes and preponderances within its analyses in ways that bibliographical statistics alone cannot. How are historical 'data' and reasoning manifest in *Colonialism*'s pages? By beginning with *Colonialism*'s use of primary sources as factual evidence and then moving to a historiographical assessment of its deployment of secondary works and its engagements with these publications' authors, we can add qualitative dimensions to a bald bibliographical analysis of this volume.

Biggar educes British colonial aspirations, attitudes and policies both directly, from printed primary sources, and indirectly, from primary citations recycled from other secondary authors. In both cases, he eschews discussions—now normative in postcolonial history—of how colonial archives are formed and how their distinctive origins, purposes and configurations shape and limit their sources' available interpretations.[10] Biggar offers essentially flat readings of his primary 'data', typically taking textual assertions by interested imperialists at face value with at most a passing reference to their generic identity and specificity of context.

Novels, for example, feature in *Colonialism* as primary sources whose evidential value is rendered unproblematic by the authority of their authors' experiences as men (or, less often, women) on the spot. Minor caveats, relegated to the endnotes, acknowledge that these sources are works of fiction, only to bat this observation aside. Having cited David Livingstone's 1857 assessment, in his *Missionary Travels and Researches in South Africa*, of African character (a primary source quoted via a 1998 essay by the Nigerian Chinua Achebe), Biggar thus makes a seamless transition to the '[s]imilar sentiments ... expressed a century later by David Lovatt Smith, who served as a field intelligence officer during the Mau Mau uprising in colonial Kenya in the 1950s'. He supports this analogy with a reference to Lovatt Smith's fictional character George Harris, and an extensive quotation from this author's 2000 Mau Mau novel, *My Enemy: My Friend*.[11] In the accompanying endnote, he justifies his elision between fact and fiction over this extended chronological and geographical sweep by appealing to the veracity of Lovatt Smith's colonial experiences. In this interpretation, the novelist's status as a witness, bolstered by his assertion that his fiction is based on historical records and has been affirmed by other 'people with whom I was associated at the time', corroborates his memories notwithstanding his text's status as a novel and the fact that 'more than forty years ... elapsed' between its publication and the sentiments it purports to represent.[12]

Fictional works cited directly or borrowed from other secondary authors are not the only types of primary 'data' that Biggar deploys with limited attention to genre or context in *Colonialism*. This type of methodological slippage is also repeatedly manifest in his discussions of British India. Having hailed the rise of a new 'Christian, humanitarian, "improving" spirit' among British imperialists on the subcontinent in the aftermath of the 1784 India Act, for example, Biggar cites the private diary of the first marquess of Hastings—who served as governor general of India from 1813 to 1823—as clear evidence that the reforming zeal of Hastings' predecessor, the marquess Cornwallis, had by the early nineteenth century produced colonial leaders 'expressly dedicated ... to promoting the "happiness of the vast population of this country"'.[13] Putting to one side the notorious financial exigencies that drove Hastings to India and his involvement in a scandalous princely loan at Hyderabad which earned him the EIC's formal censure in 1825,[14] what can examination of this quotation from the governor general's diary tell us about Biggar's historical methodology? As the direct observation of a historical agent in EIC India—albeit a source published posthumously decades later in an edition edited by Hastings' daughter—his diary entries arguably offer more immediate evidence of British attitudes than do retrospective works of fiction. Yet tracing the evidentiary trail through *Colonialism*'s references to their original sources exposes issues of provenance and context that undercut their ability to support Biggar's dominant lines of argument.

The quoted snippet, in which Hastings declared his desire to promote the 'happiness of the vast population of this country', is documented in Biggar's corresponding endnote by references to two separate publications. The first portion of the endnote refers the reader to three pages, located in two separate volumes, of the posthumous 1858 edition of Hastings' private diary; the second cites a popular history book published by Lawrence James in 1997, in which the Hastings quotation deployed by Biggar was originally cited.[15] Biggar's endnote offers a somewhat circuitous route to the Hastings quotation itself. Initially referring the reader to volume 1, page 35 in Hastings' diary, it then cites volume 2 pages 101–2. This second reference indeed includes the quoted snippet, found on page 101 of the diary and expressing the governor general's desire to promote the 'happiness of the vast population of this country'. However, looks can be deceiving. In the original source, the quoted phrase forms part of a more substantial diary entry, beginning before and extending beyond the cited material. Here Hastings mused on his imperial purposes at the start of a new year. Writing on 1 January 1816, he contemplated the efficacy of his role (and rule) in India, drawing on his Christian faith to bolster his faltering spirits as he faced the imminent departure for Britain of his wife and children:

> Never before did a year open to me with such chilling prospects ... I at times endeavour to arouse myself with the hope that I may succeed in establishing such institutions, and still more such dispositions, as will promote the happiness of the vast population of this country; but when the thought has glowed for a moment it is dissipated by the austere verdict of reason against the efficacy of exertion from an atom like me.

Cited by Biggar to underline the newly reform-minded zeal of Britain's ruling class in India, this passage (when read in context) instead underlines the humility and personal despair that compelled the governor general to reflect that 'the notion of being useful is only one of those self-delusions with which one works oneself through the essentially inept vision of life'. Where Biggar highlights the governor general's public-minded devotion to the Indian population, the diary entry instead expatiates on the private considerations that shaped Hastings' reflections on his role in India, forcibly reminding us of the presence of British women and children not only in the empire but in imperialists' justifications of their colonial lives. Reading beyond the short fragment quoted at second hand by Biggar, we find that Hastings—rather than elaborating his imperial duty—instead recorded his marital motivations for remaining in India notwithstanding the departure of his family: 'We perceive an indispensable duty to our children which enjoins it', he observed of his and his wife's colonial calculations.[16]

COLONIALISM

Biggar's initial reference in this endnote, to page 35 of volume 1 of Hastings' published private diary, is curious, for it does not correspond to the short phrase he quotes.[17] Indeed, the text on the cited page in Hastings' diary, as well as the pages that precede it, could reasonably be interpreted to run directly counter to Biggar's argument about colonial leaders' predominantly beneficent attitudes and intentions toward the Indian population in the last half century of EIC rule. The page in the first volume of Hastings' diary which Biggar includes in his reference derives from a much longer entry for 2 October 1813 in the 1858 edition of Hastings' diary, extending there from page 29 to page 35. This entry was penned very shortly after his arrival at Diamond Harbour, en route to the seat of government at Calcutta. Here the governor general, 'divesting myself as far as is practicable of opinions gathered from reading', offered his immediate impressions of the Indian population. 'The survey is not favourable to the natives', he began, before turning to describe the population over which he had come to rule. 'The Hindoo appears a being nearly limited to mere animal functions, and even in them indifferent', Hastings opined, asserting that Hindu craftsmen exerted 'little more than the dexterity which any animal with similar conformation, but with no higher intellect than a dog, an elephant, or a monkey, might be supposed capable of attaining'. Ascribing their 'debility of race' to the fact that Hindus chose to 'marry in absolute infancy', Hastings remarked that '[t]he great mass of the natives have no consideration of pride or other sentiment as to who governs them, provided their superstitions and nearly vegetative comforts be not outraged'. In this context, he concluded, '[a]n army, therefore ... must rule India'.[18] Given the tenor, content and context of Hastings' diary entry, it is difficult to reconcile his words with Biggar's assertion that Hastings was predominantly guided by his concern for the 'happiness' of the Indian population. Nor do Hastings' words align with Biggar's immediately previous direct quotation—words that he again cites from James' 1997 book, asserting that Hastings and his ilk 'saw themselves not as India's conquerors but as its emancipators'.[19]

Extracting pithy quotes from primary sources mined by previous authors is a problematic methodology, prone to strip historical evidence of its textual as well as social, cultural, political and economic context and thus to render up ahistorical analyses. In the pages of Biggar's volume, selective citation repeatedly blurs the vital boundaries between interpretation, casuistry and colonialist apologetic. This analytical flaw is conspicuous in his quotations from secondary as well as primary sources. Biggar's use of James' book to channel the spirit of Hastings is itself a case in point. Turning from his citations of short phrases from James' *Raj* to examine that author's original statements reveals a different, far more rounded, version of the governor general—one that specifically references (and also contextualises) his political and military leadership in the Third Anglo-Maratha War (1817–19). Having quoted from Hastings' diary to attest his desire to benefit 'the vast population' of India, James notes that this goal 'included the extension of civil peace to areas which had hitherto lacked it'. He then proceeds to describe the governor general's 'expansionist inclinations' and 'aggressive spirit', observing in the context of Anglo-Maratha warfare that his 'aspirations ran against the grain of his instructions, which were to continue the peaceful policies of his immediate predecessors'.[20] Absent from Biggar's representation, these excluded passages yield a far more balanced assessment of British imperial power, one in which colonial violence and humanitarian reform are seen to occupy a shared analytical frame.

Is this detailed example a rogue instance of skewed citation practices? Scrutiny of a wider range of authors cited by Biggar suggests not. Like Hastings, his reform-minded predecessor as governor general, the first marquess Cornwallis figures in

Colonialism's pantheon of right-minded imperialists of the EIC era as a public servant of overwhelming rectitude and probity, the architect of a colonial civil service 'widely regarded as incorruptible and just' into the nationalist era, as Biggar quotes historian David Gilmour asserting in his recent *British in India*.[21] Like James, however, Gilmour offers a far more rounded image of Cornwallis in his popular study of British imperialism than this citation of his words suggests. In assessing how Cornwallis' policies 'irrevocably altered the tone and nature of British government on the Subcontinent',[22] the two authors use different starting points and reach different conclusions. Biggar leads with Gilmour's assertion that Cornwallis 'helped create a civil service that became widely regarded as incorruptible'; Gilmour himself on the previous page, however, had specifically highlighted the need to examine the impact of the governor general's policies in India 'for good *and* bad'. Gilmour's analysis begins by observing that Cornwallis' 'decision to exclude Indians from all senior positions in the army and military naturally widened racial and cultural divides and helped foster British attitudes of haughtiness, aloofness and superiority'.[23] Biggar declines to note either this policy or the well-known long-term racial consequences of Cornwallis' exclusion from the EIC's covenanted services—and their income streams—of the sons of British men born to Indian women.[24] Here as so often in *Colonialism*, selective citation works to obscure the miasma of imperial racism from readers' view.[25]

Women and racialised colonial subjects, already habitually underrepresented in the colonial archive, prove especially prone to disappear from the historical record through *Colonialism*'s citation practices. Tracing the narrative line that the book constructs from the public-spirited reforms of Lord Cornwallis to the twentieth-century professional civil servants Biggar lauds as exemplars of imperial humanitarianism illustrates this point. The author rarely hesitates to leap from one century, colony or phenomenon to the next and to find continuity among 'famous examples of official probity in the British Empire'. From a brief paeon to Cornwallis' later eighteenth-century reform campaign, it is thus but a short hop (within the same paragraph) to the sterling qualities of the Indian civil service in the early 1920s and thence to the exemplary service in Ceylon in 1905 of Leonard Woolf.[26] Borrowing his quotations from Gilmour's *British in India* and from Fred Leventhal and Peter Stansky's biography of this colonial civil servant, Biggar—paraphrasing Gilmour and then quoting Woolf via Gilmour, Leventhal and Stansky—asserts that in Ceylon

> Woolf found himself rarely able to think 'of anything else except the District and the people, to increase their prosperity, diminish the poverty and disease, start irrigation works, open schools. I did not idealise or romanticise the people or the country; I just liked them aesthetically and humanly and socially.'[27]

Untangling, and tracing to their points of origin, the references that accompany this portion of Biggar's text highlights again the perils of selection bias in his citations. Gilmour does indeed cite the first sentence of Woolf's quoted statement, words that underscore the district officer's commitment to Ceylon's colonised population. The cited text appears in Woolf's memoir *Growing*, written decades after his colonial service had ended and published in 1964. Unlike Biggar, Gilmour continues his analysis of Woolf's reflections after citing these words by acknowledging, in his next sentence, that colonial civil servants' 'zeal could sometimes be overdone', and then observing that '[t]he idea of enlightened despotism, so long as it was benevolent, appealed to district officers' such as Woolf.[28] A page later, Gilmour revisits this theme, locating Woolf's ideals of service within a wider framework that includes race, gender and marriage. Such men,

Gilmour states, 'had the Tennysonian fantasy of the perpetual paternalist putting down his roots and never stirring them'. Had he not married Virginia Stephen, Gilmour quotes Woolf musing in his 1964 memoir, he would instead have returned to Ceylon to administer a district and make 'a final withdrawal, a final solitude, in which, married to a Sinhalese' he would create 'the most efficient, the most prosperous place in Asia'.[29] Where Biggar presents the course of colonialism as a Whiggish progression of British men bearing a triumphal arc of Western values, Gilmour instead presents us with a complex historical canvas, cross-cut by good intentions, overzealous officials and retrospective nostalgia—an imperial world animated by indigenous women as well as by white men.

Consulting Leventhal and Stansky's biography of Woolf adds further dimensions to this convoluted evidence trail and reinforces the salience in Biggar's quoted sources (in contrast to his interpretation of them) of colonial gender and race relations. Leventhal and Stansky quote both the sentences from Woolf's 1964 memoir that Biggar cites, words that affirm Woolf's single-minded commitment to his imperial duties in Ceylon. Like Gilmour, Leventhal and Stansky also elaborate upon Woolf's retrospective comments, locating them within wider contexts and acknowledging their internal contradictions. Observing that Woolf had 'a deserved reputation as a severe administrator, sparking complaints about him to his immediate supervisor', they record that a senior officer accompanying Woolf about his duties 'was greeted with a demonstration against' him.[30] Earlier in their chapter, moreover, Leventhal and Stansky quote not from his retrospective 1964 memoir but instead from a contemporary letter, written by Woolf to Lytton Strachey in 1905. This source offers a very different perspective on his putatively single-minded pursuit of colonial enlightenment on behalf of the Sinhalese. Describing the aftermath of a night spent with his

'Burgher' (mixed-race) concubine, Leventhal and Stansky note, Woolf observed to Strachey, 'I am worn out or rather merely supine through a night of purely degraded debauch. The pleasure of it is of course grossly exaggerated certainly with a halfcaste whore.' A month later, Woolf's private correspondence described domestic life with his concubine in his bungalow by the lagoon, his time 'divided between reading Voltaire on the immense verandah & copulating in the vast & empty rooms'.[31] Present and conspicuous on the pages of primary and secondary sources that he cites, sexuality, gender and race—like the forms of colonial violence historically associated with them—are persistently erased from Biggar's *Colonialism*.

The patterns of selective citation that mark this volume form part of a wider tapestry of bibliographic and historiographical exclusion that shapes and skews its argumentation. Of the bibliography's 664 entries, a binary authorial gender ascription can be made for 632 (or 95.2 per cent of the total).[32] Of these 632 items, 552 (or 87.3 per cent) have only male authors; twenty-one (or 3 per cent) have male and female authors; and fifty-nine (or 9 per cent) have only female authors. Thus overall, eighty (or just under 13 per cent) of the works cited in the bibliography to which an authorial gender can be ascribed were composed in whole or in part by women authors. For the 478 secondary works in the bibliography, a gender ascription can be made for 477 titles. Of these, fifty-nine (or 12 per cent) have a female author.[33] This gender profile offers a significant contrast to women's representation in the academic discipline of history in both the UK and the United States, the authorial provenance of the great majority of Biggar's cited secondary sources. In the UK in 2018, for example, 41.6 per cent of academic historians were women (up from 38.5 per cent in 2013), while at senior level 26.2 per cent of UK history professors were female in 2018 (up from 20.8 per cent in 2013).[34]

COLONIALISM

Searching for authors of colonial histories in the online Bibliography of British and Irish History strongly suggests that Biggar's bibliography and references reflect neither the gender profile of authors in this field nor its full topical range.[35] Indeed, even very basic historiographical knowledge would suggest an extensive list of obvious omissions from *Colonialism*'s bibliography of works written by women—absences that in turn feed into and enable this book's significant silences on the play of race and gender in the colonial past. For EIC-era India, a few of the many notable absences include any publications at all by Clare Anderson, Priya Atwal, Antoinette Burton, Indrani Chatterjee, Nandini Chatterjee, Durba Ghosh, Catherine Hall, Elizabeth Kolsky, Andrea Major, Lata Mani, Priya Satia and Radhika Singha—all authors of work with immediate relevance to themes addressed by Biggar.[36] Like representatives of the Cambridge and Manchester 'schools' of South Asian and imperial history, Indian historians (of any gender) based on the subcontinent are especially thin on the ground, further exacerbating this selection bias. These gendered and geographical bibliographical gaps complement and reinforce the citation lapses in *Colonialism*'s analyses. As noted above, *Colonialism* writes British and indigenous women out of the primary sources in which their presence is documented when it discusses Lord Hastings and Leonard Woolf; so too the disproportionate absence from its bibliography of women historians and women's historical lives under colonialism skews Biggar's reading list. Older secondary works, composed in an era when white men overwhelmingly governed the Anglo-American academic discipline and predominantly composed colonial histories in their own images, dominate his narratives and his historiographical frame.

When invoked, moreover, the work of female academics appears to have a particular propensity to attract *Colonialism*'s ire. Given their disproportionate absence from the bibliography and endnotes and the author's avowed commitment to avoid cluttering *Colonialism* with historiographical debates, the prominence of female authors in sections of the book devoted to criticism of other scholars is perhaps surprising. Jennifer Hart, and her 'seminal claim' that Charles Trevelyan viewed the Irish famine as God's retribution on a feckless nation, is taken to task at some length, notwithstanding her cited article having been published as long ago as 1960 within a hotly contested field of historiography which continues to defy easy consensus.[37] As Sean Carleton, Omeasoo Wahpasiw and Adele Perry also show in this volume, Biggar also extensively rebukes the academic, lawyer and indigenous rights activist Tracey Lindberg and the prize-winning Canadian historian of gender, race and property Sarah Carter in the body of his text, critiquing these authors' failure to understand that—presumably in contrast to sources he deploys, such as Western memoirs and novels—'oral testimony is not always reliable'.[38] He draws particular attention to Lindberg's use of 'present-day testimony' to support her claim that British colonial treaties failed to recognise 'the impossibility of cession of land by Indigenous peoples'.[39] Readers of Lindberg's cited chapters will be interested to find that her 370 footnotes predominantly cite colonial treaties, legal treatises and academic studies such as professional law reviews (one of which, a 1986 volume that quotes Blackfoot legal scholar Leroy Little Bear, represents Biggar's example of 'present-day testimony'), and that her assessment of 'the impossibility of cessation of land by Indigenous peoples' reads very differently if quoted both in full and in context.[40] Biggar's dismissal of Elleke Boehmer, 'whose departmental webpage presents her as "a founding figure in the field of colonial and postcolonial studies"' is likewise arguably partial. The paragraph of Boehmer's work Biggar cites to deride her and other postcolonial scholars' historical accuracy is in fact co-authored with Tom Holland, an author who intriguingly fails to attract Biggar's condemnation.[41]

Boehmer earns Biggar's censure predominantly as an exemplar of the 'disparate bunch' of academic 'anti-colonialists', a group 'whose bible is Edward Said's *Orientalism* (1978) and who tend to inhabit university departments of literature rather than those of history'.[42] Among scholars of British colonialism in India, Priyamvada Gopal stands at the forefront of Biggar's sustained critique of postcolonialism. Dubbing these postcolonial scholars 'disciples' of Saidian Orientalism, Biggar asserts that he attaches this label 'advisedly, since sometimes their faith in Said is blind'. He instances Gopal's 2019 *Insurgent Empire* to evidence his claim, accusing her of methodological naivety in clinging to the hollow thrall of Said's *Orientalism* 'without any hint of awareness that his thesis has attracted considerable criticism'. Citing seven pages of *Insurgent Empire* to attest Gopal's allegedly indiscriminate, unreconstructed allegiance to *Orientalism*, Biggar buttresses his condemnation of this foundational postcolonial text with references to a litany of right-minded (male) scholars who dissent from it.[43] Examining the cited pages of *Insurgent Empire*, however, the reader again encounters obvious lapses in Biggar's referencing. None of the seven cited pages in Gopal's text in fact references Said's 1978 *Orientalism*. Instead, Gopal specifically cites later works that refined Said's arguments, in part in response to criticism of *Orientalism*. Thus, her endnotes—in obvious contrast to Biggar's perfervid imaginations of them—cite Said's 1993 *Culture and Imperialism*, his 1994 *Representations of the Intellectual* and his posthumously published 2004 *Humanism and Democratic Criticism*.[44]

What can account for *Colonialism*'s narrow bibliographical purview with regard to colonial and postcolonial histories, notably those written by and about women? The author's habit of borrowing pithy citations from favoured male secondary authors cannot in itself explain this pattern of exclusion, for these historians' works do not invariably exhibit this pattern of gender bias.

The sections of *Colonialism* that detail British history in India, for example, rely heavily on popular works by David Gilmour. An author who cannot credibly be accused of postcolonial tendencies, Gilmour nonetheless devotes substantial attention to women and colonial families in his work, braiding these topics into his interpretation of how British colonialism (and its racialised forms of power) unfolded on the subcontinent.[45] His references reflect wide reading in the secondary literature, including a broad spectrum of works by and about women absent from *Colonialism*.[46] Yet Biggar's citations from Gilmour selectively erase passages in his book that highlight racial conflict and its gendered contexts. 'In India, relations between imperial Britons and native populations changed over time and became more aloof', Biggar writes, in a rare passage acknowledging the historical presence and function of women in EIC India:

> During the eighteenth century and well into the following one, it was not uncommon for the British to mix with native people socially, even to the point of taking Indian women as mistresses or wives, having children with them and sometimes bringing their Indian families back to live in Britain.

A reference to the absence of racial exclusivity at the Bengal Club established in Calcutta in 1827, citing Gilmour's *British in India* as his source, immediately follows.[47]

Gilmour's text and endnote indeed confirm the absence of a colour bar at the Bengal Club in 1827. But the wider tenor of his sub-section 'Mixed Marriages' (pages 309–14), set within an extensive discussion of this subject in Chapter 9 'Intimacies' (pages 283–336), diverges significantly from Biggar's interpretation. Drawing on a wide array of primary and secondary sources, Gilmour argues that class considerations largely outweighed British racial prejudices in EIC India prior to the arrival of evangelical missionaries, but he nonetheless recognises and details overt examples of gendered racism in this period. Discussing the Calcutta diarist William Hickey's reflections on his sexual impotence in 1783 Bengal, Gilmour quotes from Hickey's diary to register his 'horror' at the prospect of 'a connection with black women', observing that '[t]he horror receded when he realized that some Indian ladies were in fact "very lovely" and that it was not "correct to call them black"; those from the Upper Provinces were actually "very fair"'.[48] Biggar's assessment, that 'the rising influence of evangelical Christianity and modernising utilitarianism in the early nineteenth century' meant that 'social mixing declined and the two peoples became generally more estranged', contrasts significantly with Gilmour's corresponding text.[49] Reflecting on the 'eclipse of the Indian mistress' in EIC family life as missionary activity gained pace, Gilmour observes that '[e]vangelicals may have been enthusiasts for the abolition of slavery, but they were not enthusiasts for cohabiting with other races or even sympathizing with their cultures'. He notes that when John Kaye published his 1854 biography of the senior EIC civil servant Sir Charles Metcalfe, 'he suppressed the fact that his subject had an Indian wife and three half-Indian sons'. Commenting on Kaye's rewriting of Metcalfe's history, Gilmour concludes that '[i]t seemed that the whole idea of interracial physical relationships was so appalling that people had to pretend not just that they had stopped but that they had not even happened'.[50] So much for the Victorians' supposed commitment to cultural assimilation, a vital component of Biggar's argument that their belief in fundamental human equality overwhelmingly trumped their imperial racisms.[51]

If a pattern of selective citation from secondary sources that do include British and indigenous women in the history of colonialism is one salient element of Biggar's research methodology, another is reliance on a small cohort of trusted male elders to select his preferred readings and guide his historical interpretations. *Colonialism* offers important signposts to its author's bibliographical decision-making, seemingly unaware (or unconcerned) that his mode of adoption might reflect either conscious or unconscious bias. Other academic writers might turn to substantial historiographical reviews in peer-reviewed journals or to scholarly tools such as the Bibliography of British and Irish History to identify the full range of relevant and up-to-date readings. *Colonialism*'s author, instead, turns to an inner circle drawn from his own generation of academics, augmenting their guidance with the received alchemy of status-based credentialism. Acknowledging that Chapter 6, 'Free Trade, Investment and "Exploitation"', relies 'quite heavily' on David Fieldhouse's 1999 *The West and the Third World*, Biggar explains that 'the imperial historian John Darwin, the economic historian Tirthankar Roy and the development economist Paul Collier all recommended [it] to me as authoritative'.[52] The twenty-one references to Fieldhouse's book in this chapter are in fact exceeded by the twenty-six references to Roy's arguments, including no fewer than eight references to Roy's highly critical three-page book review of Shashi Tharoor's 2017 *Inglorious Empire*, from which Biggar borrows repeatedly.[53] He affirms Roy's analytical rigour, like that of many other academic authors he relies upon extensively, through professional and political credentialisation: Roy is 'the Bengali-born, liberal economic historian' and 'professor of economic history at the London School of Economics'.[54] Implicit in the text but rendered conspicuous in *Colonialism*'s endnotes is Roy's perceived allyship as a doughty fellow warrior in Biggar's battle against the supposedly pervasive threat of Marxism. Tilting at this decrepit windmill, Biggar deploys Roy's quantitative analyses, bolstered by Fieldhouse's strictures in his 1999 publication, to expose to view the dogmatic claims of 'pessimistic' Marxists on colonial economics, dispatching them expeditiously with Roy's borrowed sword of statistics and citations.[55]

COLONIALISM

Colonialism's is a backward-looking historiographical vision, informed by paradigms that have undergone successive reformulations since their articulation in the heyday of the Cold War. Tested and transformed by abundant and variegated new historical data—and by new conceptual toolkits, novel digital methodologies and sustained attention to hitherto underexamined populations—in the decades that have elapsed since Biggar's undergraduate studies in history, our knowledge and understanding of the British Empire has now moved on. By placing undue reliance on a narrow spectrum of later twentieth-century scholarship, *Colonialism* repeatedly rehearses past debates and perpetuates the exclusion of previously marginalised historical actors and analysts—including but by no means only women. In his acknowledgements, Biggar notes that he wrote this book in under six months and dates his intellectual formation to Oxford University five decades ago. Fondly recalling his tutor in modern history, he observes that '[o]f all the end-of-term reports I received, he wrote the only one I remember, since he urged "Mr Biggar to cease arriving at tutorials with ink dripping from his fingers."'[56] Sadly, *Colonialism* bears many of the characteristic hallmarks of hasty undergraduate composition: primary research poached from other secondary sources and quoted out of context, reliance on a small cluster of familiar authors (and topical journalism) to the detriment of consideration of a more robust, wide-ranging and recent peer-reviewed literature, and a lack of sophisticated conceptual or methodological engagement. The 'truth' about colonialism is now widely sought by academic, popular and family historians alike. We will be sorely tested to find its traces here.

NOTES

FOREWORD

1. Mark Bridge, 'Don't Be Bullied by Left on Statues, Oliver Dowden Tells Museums', *The Times*, 3 March 2021, https://www.thetimes.co.uk/article/dont-be-bullied-by-left-on-statues-oliver-dowden-tells-museums-wrdfq262k, accessed 29/11/23.
2. 'The Commission for Diversity in the Public Realm', Mayor of London, London Assembly, https://www.london.gov.uk/programmes-strategies/arts-and-culture/commission-diversity-public-realm, accessed 29/11/23.
3. Bridge, 'Don't Be Bullied'.
4. 'Mayor Announces Members of New Landmark Commission', Mayor of London, London Assembly, 9 February 2021, https://www.london.gov.uk/press-releases/mayoral/mayor-announces-members-of-landmark-commission#:-:text=The%20Commission's%20role%20is%20to,over%20the%20removal%20of%20statues, accessed 29/11/23.
5. Steph Cockcroft, 'Boris Johnson Vows to "Resist" Attempts to Remove Winston Churchill Statue and Brands Racism Charges "height of lunacy"', *The Standard*, 15 June 2020, https://www.standard.co.uk/news/uk/boris-johnson-winston-churchill-statue-a4468906.html, accessed 29/11/2023.
6. Tom Haines, 'Metropolitan Police under Fire for Protecting Churchill Statue after Protestors Leave', My London, 14 March 2021, https://www.mylondon.news/news/zone-1-news/metropolitan-police-under-fire-protecting-20154598, accessed 29/11/23.
7. Aaron Robertson, 'Defenders of a George Eliot Statue Had No Idea What They Were Doing and I'm Here for It', Literary Hub, 16 June 2020, https://lithub.com/defenders-of-a-george-eliot-statue-had-no-idea-what-they-were-doing-and-im-here-for-it/, accessed 29/11/23; Danyal Hussain, '"Are they worried

about Jane Austen fans?"': Statue Defenders Draw Scorn as They Stand in Front of Sculpture of Writer George Eliot during Black Lives Matter Protest', 16 June 2020, https://www.dailymail.co.uk/news/article-8426005/Statue-defenders-stand-sculpture-writer-George-Eliot-Black-Lives-Matter-demo.html, accessed 29/11/23.

8. 'A Crowd-Sourced Map of UK Statues and Monuments That Celebrate Slavery and Racism', Topple the Racists, https://www.toppletheracists.org/, accessed 29/11/23.

9. Jason Hickel, 'How Britain Stole $45 Trillion from India and Lied about It', Al Jazeera, 19 December 2018, https://www.aljazeera.com/opinions/2018/12/19/how-britain-stole-45-trillion-from-india, accessed 29/11/23; 'The First African World Reparations and Repatriation Truth Commission Conference', School of Languages, Literatures and Cultures, University of Edinburgh, https://www.inosaar.llc.ed.ac.uk/en/timelinefirst-african-world-reparations-and-repatriation-truth-commission-conference, accessed 29/11/23.

10. Brian Cathcart, 'The Right-Wing Bid to Capture the National Trust Exposed', *Byline Times*, 27 October 2022, https://bylinetimes.com/2022/10/27/the-right-wing-bid-to-capture-the-national-trust-exposed/, accessed 29/11/23; 'Tufton Street: Shine a Light on Dark Money', Good Law Project, https://goodlawproject.org/case/tufton-street-shine-a-light-on-dark-money-in-politics/, accessed 29/11/23.

11. Nick Duffy, 'Gavin Williamson Rejects Calls to "Decolonise" History Curriculum, Saying Britons Should Be "proud of our history"', *iNews*, 19 June 2020, https://inews.co.uk/news/education/gavin-williamson-british-history-decolonise-blm-reject-empire-451290, accessed 29/11/23.

12. Numbers from Saul Dubow's essay in this volume.

13. Angus Cochrane, 'Rees-Mogg Compares Concentration Camp Death Rate to Glasgow Mortality Figures', *The National*, 15 February 2019, https://www.thenational.scot/news/17436773.rees-mogg-compares-concentration-camp-death-rate-glasgow-mortality-figures/, accessed 29/11/23.

14. 'Tories Bet on Culture Wars to Unite Disparate Voters', *The Economist*, 18 February 2021, https://www.economist.com/britain/2021/02/18/tories-bet-on-culture-wars-to-unite-disparate-voters, accessed 29/11/23.

15. Tim Shipman, 'How the Tories Weaponised Woke', *The Times*, 13 June 2021, https://www.thetimes.co.uk/article/how-the-tories-weaponised-woke-jlmwh0p36, accessed 29/11/23.

16. Michael Taylor, 'The Gammoning of British History', Medium, 27 March 2021, https://mhtaylorhome.medium.com/the-gammoning-of-british-history-bd05668e2f4f, accessed 29/11/23.

17. Aletha Adu, 'Rishi Sunak Refuses to Apologise for UK Slave Trade or to Pledge Reparations', *The Guardian*, 26 April 2023, https://www.theguardian.com/world/2023/apr/26/rishi-sunak-refuses-to-apologise-for-uk-slave-trade-or-to-pledge-reparations, accessed 29/11/23.

18. William Dalrymple and Anita Anand, 'Queen Elizabeth II & Empire (with David Olusoga)', Empire podcast, 13/09/2022, https://open.spotify.com/episode/5fvidV68X1ddQrNLfdJOaz?si=879ddc1fb23f4c18&nd=1, accessed 29/11/2023.
19. Peter Walker, 'Abuse Has Led Sathnam Sanghera to "more or less stop" Doing Book Events in UK', *The Guardian*, 9 June 2023, https://www.theguardian.com/books/2023/jun/09/abuse-has-led-sathnam-sanghera-to-more-or-less-stop-doing-book-events-in-uk, accessed 29/11/23.
20. 'Written evidence submitted by Professor Corinne Fowler, School of Museum Studies, University of Leicester (OSB57)', Online Safety Bill, 2 June 2022, https://publications.parliament.uk/pa/cm5803/cmpublic/OnlineSafetyBill/memo/OSB57.htm, accessed 29/11/23.
21. Corinne Fowler, 'Public Debate Is Important: Waves of Press and Political Attacks Damage It', Hacked Off, 11 March 2021, https://hackinginquiry.org/public-debate-is-important-waves-of-press-and-political-attacks-damage-it/, accessed 29/11/23.
22. Corinne Fowler, 'Inclusive Histories: Responding to the "Culture War" through Engagement and Dialogue', Museums Association, https://www.museumsassociation.org/campaigns/decolonising-museums/inclusive-histories-responding-to-the-culture-war/, accessed 29/11/23.
23. Niall Ferguson, *Empire: How Britain Made the Modern World*, London: Penguin Books, 2003, 108–9.
24. Jan Morris, *Heaven's Command: An Imperial Progress*, vol. 1 of the Pax Britannica trilogy, London: Faber & Faber, 2012, 447.
25. Robert Hughes, *The Fatal Shore: A History of the Transportation of Convicts to Australia, 1787–1868*, London: Vintage, 2003, 120.
26. Ann Curthoys, 'Raphaël Lemkin's "Tasmania": An Introduction', *Patterns of Prejudice*, 39, 2, 2005, 162–9, https://www.tandfonline.com/doi/abs/10.1080/00313220500106212, accessed 29/11/23.

INTRODUCTION: THE TRUTH ABOUT COLONIAL HISTORY

1. My sincere thanks to the colleagues who have helped me with comments on drafts of this introduction, especially Sean Carleton, Adele Perry, Sathnam Sanghera, Stuart Ward, Catherine Hall and Michael Taylor.
2. See James Davison Hunter, *Culture Wars: The Struggle to Control the Family, Art, Education, Law, and Politics in America*, New York: Basic Books, 1992.
3. See Alan Lester, *Deny and Disavow: Distancing the Imperial Past in the Culture Wars*, 2nd edn, London: SunRise, 2023.
4. Gareth Bacon, 'What Is Wokeism and How Can It Be Defeated?', in 'Common Sense: Conservative Thinking for a Post-Liberal Age', 19, https://www.mar-

colonghi.org.uk/sites/www.marcolonghi.org.uk/files/2021–05/Common-Sense. pdf, accessed 26/1/24.

5. Nigel Biggar, *Colonialism: A Moral Reckoning*, London: William Collins, 2023, 291, n. 14, 427, 295.
6. Ibid., 1–19; J. R. Seeley, *The Expansion of England: Two Courses of Lectures*, Cambridge: Cambridge University Press, 2010; Richard Drayton, 'Where Does the World Historian Write From? Objectivity, Moral Conscience and the Past and Present of Imperialism', *Journal of Contemporary History*, 46, 3, 2011, 371–85. Priya Satia's *Time's Monster: How History Makes History*, Cambridge, MA: Harvard University Press, 2020, shows how History as a discipline was shaped in large part around the justification of imperialism.
7. Biggar, *Colonialism*, xiii–xiv, 1–10.
8. It should be pointed out that neither of what Biggar describes as the 'denunciations ... manned by professional academics, the first comprising fifty-eight colleagues at Oxford, the second, about two hundred academics from around the world' (ibid., 1), called for his work to be terminated. The letter from Biggar's Oxford colleagues was clear that 'Professor Biggar has every right to hold and to express whatever views he chooses or finds compelling, and to conduct whatever research he chooses in the way he feels appropriate': 'Ethics and Empire: An Open Letter from Oxford Scholars', The Conversation, 19 December 2017, https://theconversation.com/ethics-and-empire-an-open-letter-from-oxford-scholars-89333, accessed 27/2/24. That from the 200 academics around the world concluded: 'We call upon Oxford University to clarify the nature of its support for the project, the source of its funding, the research protocols that will be put in place to ensure that its outputs are subject to due peer scrutiny, and what measures will be taken to safeguard principles of equality, inclusivity and diversity': 'A Collective Statement on "Ethics and Empire"', Medium, 21 December 2017, https://medium.com/oxfordempireletter/a-collective-statement-on-ethics-and-empire-19c2477871a0, accessed 27/2/24. However social media commentary from other academics was less measured, and it is this which Biggar emphasises in *Colonialism* (299, endnote 5).
9. For the anonymous threats which led the editor to withdraw the article with Gilley's agreement, see Bruce Gilley, 'The Case for Colonialism', Third World Quarterly, 2017, 1–17, https://www.tandfonline.com/doi/abs/10.1080/01436 597.2017.1369037. For an example of academic objections to its contents, see Joseph McQuade, 'Colonialism Was a Disaster and the Facts Prove It', The Conversation, 27 September 2017, https://theconversation.com/colonialism-was-a-disaster-and-the-facts-proveit-84496, accessed 27/2/24.
10. Such accusations seem to be made especially against people of colour and/or women. Samira Shackle, 'The Backlash: How Slavery Research Came under Fire', *The Guardian*, 1 June 2023, https://www.theguardian.com/news/2023/

jun/01/cotton-capital-legacies-of-slavery-research-backlash-cambridge-university, accessed 8/12/23.

11. The most vocal of these were never historians of colonialism. Mark Edmonds, 'Does This Look "Unpleasant"? Academic Signed Up by the National Trust to Lecture Us on the Evils behind Our Most Glorious Estates Says GARDENING Has Its Roots in Racial Injustice', *The Daily Mail*, 16 January 2021, https://www.dailymail.co.uk/news/article-9153499/Academic-says-GARDENING-roots-racial-injustice.html, accessed 10/12/23; Simon Osborne, 'National Trust in Woke Row after Children Lecture Staff on Colonialism—"Out of touch!"', https://www.express.co.uk/news/uk/1382074/national-trust-woke-row-children-country-house-colonialism-slavery-black-lives-matter, accessed 10/12/23; Robert Tombs, 'The Rewriting of History Has Taken a Sinister Turn', *The Daily Telegraph*, 25 September 2023, https://www.telegraph.co.uk/news/2023/09/25/the-rewriting-of-history-has-taken-a-sinister-turn/; Tombs, 'The "Anti-racist" Mission to Destroy Britain Is Working—and We Have Surrendered', *The Daily Telegraph*, 10 April 2023, https://www.telegraph.co.uk/news/2023/04/10/the-anti-racist-mission-to-destroy-britain-is-working/; David Abulafia, '"Colonialism" Is More Complex than Woke Historians Would Have You Believe', *The Daily Telegraph*, 25 September 2021, https://www.telegraph.co.uk/news/2021/09/25/colonialism-complex-woke-historians-would-have-believe/; Abulafia, 'Time for Historians to Fight Back against the Ideologues Who Want to Tear Down the Past', *The Daily Telegraph*, 29 August 2021, https://www.telegraph.co.uk/news/2021/08/29/time-historians-fight-back-against-ideologues-want-tear-past/; Abulafia, 'Woke Activists, Take Note: There Is No Public Appetite for Erasing British History', *The Daily Telegraph*, 4 December 2021, https://www.telegraph.co.uk/news/2021/12/04/woke-activists-take-note-no-public-appetite-erasing-british/, all accessed 8/12/23.

12. Jenny Bulstrode, 'Black Metallurgists and the Making of the Industrial Revolution', *History and Technology*, 39, 1, 2023, 1–41, DOI: 10.1080/07341512.2023.2220991; Hannah Devlin, 'Industrial Revolution Iron Method "was taken from Jamaica by Briton"', *The Guardian*, 5 July 2023, https://www.theguardian.com/science/2023/jul/05/industrial-revolution-iron-method-taken-from-jamaica-briton, accessed 4/01/24; Amy E. Slaton and Tiago Saraiva, 'Editorial', *History and Technology*, 39, 2, 2023, DOI: 10.1080/07341512.2023.2275357

13. Alan Lester (@aljhlester), Twitter/X post, 16 November 2023, https://twitter.com/aljhlester/status/1725161655019929659, and comments, accessed 4/1/24.

14. Alan Lester, 'The British Empire Rehabilitated?', Bella Caledonia, March 2023, https://bellacaledonia.org.uk/2023/03/07/the-british-empire-rehabilitated/; Lester, 'The British Empire in the Culture War: Nigel Biggar's Colonialism: A Moral Reckoning', *The Journal of Imperial and Commonwealth History*, 51,

4, 2023, 763–95, DOI: 10.1080/03086534.2023.2209947; 'Nigel Biggar (2023) on Colonialism: A Moral Reckoning; A Reply to Alan Lester', *The Journal of Imperial and Commonwealth History*, 51, 4, 2023, 796–824, DOI: 10.1080/03086534.2023.2209948 and Alan Lester, 'On *Colonialism*: A Response to Biggar's Reply', https://blogs.sussex.ac.uk/snapshotsofempire/2023/06/02/on-colonialism-a-response-to-nigel-biggars-reply/, accessed 8/12/23; Gordon's School (@GordonsSch), Twitter/X post, 6 October 2023, https://twitter.com/GordonsSch/status/1710335443479269837, accessed 27/2/24.

15. Hilary Mantel, 'Why I Became a Historical Novelist', *The Guardian*, 3 June 2017, https://www.theguardian.com/books/2017/jun/03/hilary-mantel-why-i-became-a-historical-novelist, accessed 5/12/23.
16. This renders the idea of a 'replicability' crisis in the humanities suspect: Alan Lester (@aljhlester), Twitter/X post, 22 November 2023, https://twitter.com/aljhlester/status/1727244097830666585, accessed 27/2/24.
17. Ann Laura Stoler, *Along the Archival Grain: Epistemic Anxieties and Colonial Common Sense*, Princeton, NJ: Princeton University Press, 2009.
18. Antoinette Burton, 'Archive Stories: Gender in the Making of Imperial and Colonial Histories', in Philippa Levine (ed.), *Gender and Empire*, Oxford History of the British Empire Companion Series, Oxford: Oxford University Press, 2007, 291.
19. J. R. Seeley, *The Expansion of England: Two Courses of Lectures*, Cambridge: Cambridge University Press, 2010. British historians also assumed, at least until the mid-twentieth century, that it was entirely natural to desire continued British global power. See Richard Drayton, 'Where Does the World Historian Write From? Objectivity, Moral Conscience and the Past and Present of Imperialism', *Journal of Contemporary History*, 46, 3, 2011, 671–85.
20. Burton, 'Archive Stories'.
21. Gayatri Chakravorty Spivak, 'Can the Subaltern Speak?', in Cary Nelson and Lawrence Grossberg (eds), *Marxism and the Interpretation of Culture*, Basingstoke: Macmillan, 1988, 271–313. Another respondent to Antoinette Burton's survey reported: 'It is often hard to find even the mediated voices of African women in the colonial archives, because Colonial and Foreign Office representatives generally did not interview African women and seldom reproduced their translated testimonies in correspondence, let alone reports. British officials privileged the opinions of male representatives of African communities': Burton, 'Archive Stories'.
22. Email correspondence, 23/1/24.
23. 'Among UK-national staff, 96.1% of university historians are White, a figure ... higher than in most other subjects. Underrepresentation is particularly stark for Black historians, who make up less than 1% of UK university-based History staff': Royal Historical Society, 'Race, Ethnicity & Equality Report', https://

royalhistsoc.org/racereport/#:-:text=Among%20UK%2Dnational%20 staff%2C%2096.1,UK%20university%2Dbased%20History%20staff, accessed 26/1/24.

24. E. P. Thompson, *The Making of the English Working Class*, London: Penguin, 2013, 12.
25. My thanks to Stuart Ward for this phrase in personal correspondence, and to Richard Huzzey for helping clarify the argument.
26. Caroline Elkins, *Legacy of Violence: A History of the British Empire*, New York: Bodley Head, 2022, 7, 8, 680.
27. Catherine Hall, *Lucky Valley: Edward Long, Slave Owner and Historian of Jamaica*, Cambridge: Cambridge University Press, 2024, 4.
28. C. E. Callwell, *Small Wars: Their Principles and Practice*, London: HMSO, 1906, 31–2, 23–5, 148. Such systematic distinctions between acceptable tactics deployed against Europeans and non-Europeans, even for the same kinds of guerrilla warfare, seem to contradict the conclusion that Biggar reaches, after sampling just six colonial conflicts, that 'culpable violence or negligence was not symptomatic of a consistent, characteristically racist, colonial "logic". It was not essential or systemic': Biggar, *Colonialism*, 272.
29. Gareth Knapman in this volume.
30. Nigel Biggar, 'Dan Hicks, the Brutish Museums: The Benin Bronzes, Cultural Violence and Cultural Restitution', History Reclaimed, 12 August 2021, https://historyreclaimed.co.uk/dan-hicks-the-brutish-museums-the-benin-bronzes-cultural-violence-and-cultural-restitution, accessed 5/12/23.
31. Alan F. C. Ryder, *Benin and the Europeans 1485–1897*, London: Longmans, 1969; Dan Hicks, *The Brutish Museums*, London: Pluto, 2020; Evo Ekpo, 'The Dialects of Definitions: "Massacre" and "Sack" in the History of the Punitive Expedition', *African Arts*, 30, 3, Summer 1997, 34–5; James D. Graham, 'The Slave Trade, Depopulation and Human Sacrifice in Benin History: The General Approach', *Cahiers d'études Africaines*, 5, 18, 1965, 317–34.
32. N. Etherington, P. Harries and B. K. Mbenga, 'From Colonial Hegemonies to Imperial Conquest, 1840–1880', in C. Hamilton, B. K. Mbenga and R. Ross (eds), *The Cambridge History of South Africa*, vol. 1, *From Early Times to 1885*, Cambridge: Cambridge University Press, 2009, 383.
33. British Parliamentary Papers, C. 2220, No. 105, Frere to Hicks Beach, 30 September 1878.
34. One of the three invading columns suffered the greatest military defeat of this unceasing series of colonial wars at Isandlwana, while the ensuing defence of Rorke's Drift was immortalised in the film *Zulu*. Frances Colenso, the Archbishop's daughter, wrote of the war as 'one of the most needless and disastrous campaigns that ever disgraced our British arms … There are few now … who will maintain that the British invasion of Zululand in 1879 was either just,

necessary, or "expedient"': Frances Colenso, *The Ruin of Zululand: An Account of British Doings in Zululand since the Invasion of 1879*, vol. 1, London: William Ridgway, 1884, xiv–xv.

35. Neil Parsons, *King Khama, Emperor Joe, and the Great White Queen: Victorian Britain through African Eyes*, Chicago, IL: University of Chicago Press, 1998.
36. A. J. Christopher, *The British Empire at Its Zenith*, London: Routledge, 1988, 29; James Belich, *Replenishing the Earth: The Settler Revolution and the Rise of the Angloworld*, Oxford: Oxford University Press, 2011.
37. See the discussion in Biggar, *Colonialism*, 103–8.
38. Lyndall Ryan, this volume.
39. 'Colonial Frontier Massacres, Australia, 1788 to 1930', https://c21ch.newcastle.edu.au/colonialmassacres/map.php, accessed 27/2/2024.
40. Tom Lawson, *The Last Man: A British Genocide in Tasmania*, London: I. B. Tauris, 2014; Jonathan Richards, *The Secret War: A True History of Queensland's Native Police*, St Lucia, Queensland: University of Queensland Press, 2008; Alan Lester, 'The Sydney Morning Herald's Apology for Myall Creek and the Culture War over Colonialism', *History*, Royal Australian Historical Society, 26–35: https://www.rahs.org.au/wp-content/uploads/2023/12/The-Sydney-Morning-Heralds-Apology-for-Myall-Creek-and-the-Culture-War-over-Colonialism.pdf, accessed 27/2/2024.
41. Lyndall Ryan, this volume; Jane Lydon and Lyndall Ryan (eds), *Remembering the Myall Creek Massacre*, Sydney: New South Publishing, 2018.
42. Belich, *Replenishing the Earth*.
43. Alan Lester and Fae Dussart, *Colonization and the Origins of Humanitarian Governance: Protecting Aborigines across the Nineteenth-Century British Empire*, Cambridge: Cambridge University Press, 2014.
44. Testimony recorded for the Stolen Generations exhibition, https://museumsvictoria.com.au/bunjilaka, accessed 11/12/23.
45. 'Bringing Them Home: The "Stolen Children" Report', 1997, https://humanrights.gov.au/our-work/aboriginal-and-torres-strait-islander-social-justice/publications/bringing-them-home, accessed 11/12/23.
46. Sean Carleton, Omeasoo Wahpasiw and Adele Perry in this volume.
47. Ibid. For reconciliation in New Zealand, which many see as something of a model for other settler societies, see Malcolm Mulholland, 'New Zealand's Indigenous Reconciliation Efforts Show Having a Treaty Isn't Enough', The Conversation, 11 May 2016, https://theconversation.com/new-zealands-indigenous-reconciliation-efforts-show-having-a-treaty-isnt-enough-49890, accessed 6/12/23.
48. 'Slave Voyages', https://www.slavevoyages.org, accessed 12/12/23.
49. James Walvin, *A World Transformed: Slavery in the Americas and the Origins of Global Power*, Berkeley, CA: University of California Press, 2023; Maxine Berg

and Pat Hudson, *Slavery, Capitalism and the Industrial Revolution*, Cambridge: Polity, 2023.
50. Bronwen Everill in this volume. Arab trafficking of African captives had operated across much of the eastern side of the continent for a millennium, providing enslaved people for domestic, sexual and military service rather than mainly for commercial plantation production: Paul E. Lovejoy, *Transformations in Slavery: A History of Slavery in Africa*, 3rd edn, Cambridge: Cambridge University Press, 2012.
51. Eric Williams, *Capitalism and Slavery*, London: Penguin, 2022 [1944]; Berg and Hudson, *Slavery, Capitalism and the Industrial Revolution*.
52. Olaudah Equiano, *The Interesting Narrative of the Life of Olaudah Equiano*, London: Hodder, 2021; Mary-Antoinette Smith (ed.), *Thomas Clarkson and Ottobah Cugoano: Thoughts and Sentiments on the Evils of Slavery (1787–8)*, New York: Broadview, 2010; David Turley, *The Culture of English Antislavery, 1780–1860*, London: Routledge, 1991; Christopher Leslie Brown, *Moral Capital: Foundations of British Abolitionism*, Chapel Hill, NC: University of North Carolina Press, 2006.
53. See the contributions from Bronwen Everill and Richard Huzzey in this volume.
54. Jake Christopher Richards, 'Anti-slave-Trade Law, "Liberated Africans" and the State in the South Atlantic World, c.1839–1852', *Past & Present*, 241, 1, 2018, 179–219, https://doi.org/10.1093/pastj/gty020, accessed 27/2/2024; Padraic X. Scanlan, *Freedom's Debtors: British Antislavery in Sierra Leone in the Age of Revolution*, New Haven, CT: Yale University Press, 2017; Richard Anderson and Henry B. Lovejoy (eds), *Liberated Africans and the Abolition of the Slave Trade, 1807–1896*, Rochester, NY: University of Rochester Press, 2020; Lisa Ford and Naomi Parkinson, 'Legislating Liberty: Liberated Africans and the Abolition Act, 1806–1824', *Slavery & Abolition*, 42, 2021, 827–46.
55. Seymour Drescher, *The Mighty Experiment: Free Labor versus Slavery in British Emancipation*, Oxford: Oxford University Press, 2004; Padraic X. Scanlan, review of *Advocates of Freedom: African American Transatlantic Abolitionism in the British Isles* by Hannah-Rose Murray, and *The Ties That Bind: Transatlantic Abolitionism in the Age of Reform, c.1820–1865* by J. R. Oldfield, *Victorian Studies*, 65, 2, 2023, 309–12.
56. 'Centre for the Study of the Legacies of British Slavery', https://www.ucl.ac.uk/lbs, accessed 6/12/23.
57. William Dalrymple, *The Anarchy: The Relentless Rise of the East India Company*, London: Bloomsbury, 2019; John Keay, *The Honourable Company: A History of the English East India Company*, London: HarperCollins, 1993; Nick Robins, *The Corporation That Changed the World: How the East India Company Shaped the Modern Multinational*, London: Pluto Press, 2006; Jon Wilson, *India*

Conquered: Britain's Raj and the Chaos of Empire, London: Simon & Schuster, 2017.
58. Walvin, World Transformed. Aside from textiles, the British armaments trade was significant in linking multiple sites of conflict across the globe during this period of almost continual warfare. Its contribution to the Industrial Revolution is a topic that warrants further research: Priya Satia, Empire of Guns: The Violent Making of the Industrial Revolution, London: Duckworth, 2018; Judy Stephenson, 'Empires, Guns and Economic Growth: Thoughts on the Implications of Satia's Work for Economic History', Journal of Global History, 14, 3, 2019, 456–8.
59. Madhavi Kale, Fragments of Empire: Capital, Slavery, and Indian Indentured Labor in the British Caribbean, Philadelphia, PA: University of Pennsylvania Press, 1998; Gaiutra Bahadur, Coolie Woman: The Odyssey of Indenture, Chicago, IL: University of Chicago Press, 2014.
60. Philip Harling, Managing Mobility: The British Imperial State and Global Migration, 1840–1860, Cambridge: Cambridge University Press, forthcoming.
61. Keletso E. Atkins, The Moon Is Dead! Give Us Our Money! The Cultural Origins of an African Work Ethic, Natal, South Africa, 1843–1900, London: Pearson, 1993; Frederick Cooper, Decolonization and African Society: The Labor Question in French and British Africa, Cambridge: Cambridge University Press, 1996.
62. Max Siollun, What Britain Did to Nigeria: A Short History of Conquest and Rule, London: Hurst, 2021, 313.
63. Quoted in A. R. Dilley, 'The Economics of Empire', in Sarah Stockwell (ed.), The British Empire: Themes and Perspectives, Oxford: Blackwell, 2008, 112.
64. Shashi Tharoor, Inglorious Empire: What the British Did to India, London: Hurst, 2017; Patnaik and Patnaik calculated the original $45 trillion drain by estimating the import surplus into Britain from Asia and according it a present value at 5 per cent interest rates. They later updated the figure, arguing that 'cumulated up to 2020, it is $64.82 trillion ... much higher than the combined 2020 GDP' of the United Kingdom, the United States and Canada. Slightly different assumptions and estimates lead to widely varying cumulative figures. But even in 1840, Montgomery Martin estimated the overall 'drain' from India to Britain between 1803 and 1833 at £724 million, noting that such 'a drain even on England would soon impoverish her', while George Wingate wrote that 'The tribute paid to Great Britain is by far the most objectionable feature in our existing policy. Taxes spent in the country from which they are raised are totally different in their effects from taxes raised in one country and spent in another': Utsa Patnaik and Prabhat Patnaik, 'The Drain of Wealth Colonialism before the First World War', Monthly Review, February 2021, https://monthlyreview.org/2021/02/01/the-drain-of-wealth/.
65. Tirthankar Roy, An Economic History of India 1707–1857, 2nd edn, London:

Routledge, 2021, 12, 1; See Romesh Chunder Dutt, The Economic History of India, vol. I, Government of India, 1960, and Sven Beckert, Empire of Cotton: A New History of Global Capitalism, London: Penguin, 2015. Priya Satia notes that 'through deskilling, deindustrialization, displacement, and expropriation' Indian artisans, communal farmers and pastoralists were actively turned into 'peasants and laborers in the first place'. Thus the new inequalities acknowledged by Roy, 'were the result of colonialism. It's not just that poorer subjects didn't gain much, or that they were exploited, but that so many subjects became poor and landless and thus vulnerable to exploitation and neglect. That's what the inequality is about.' (personal correspondence). The share of the Indian population living in extreme poverty is thought to have increased dramatically under British rule, from less than 23 per cent to over 50 per cent: Robert C. Allen, 'Poverty and the Labor Market: Today and Yesterday', Annual Review Of Economics, 12, 2020, 107–34: https://doi.org/10.1146/annurev-economics-091819-014652.

For debates over the causes and alleviation of the famines which cost tens of millions of lives during the period of British rule, see Mike Davies, Late Victorian Holocausts: El Niño Famines and the Making of the Third World, London: Verso, 2017; Amartya Sen, Poverty and Famines: An Essay on Entitlement and Deprivation, Oxford: Oxford University Press, 1990; Tirthankar Roy, 'Were Indian Famines "Natural" Or "Manmade"?', London School Of Economics And Political Science Department Of Economic History Working Papers, 243, June 2016, https://www.lse.ac.uk/Economic-History/Assets/Documents/WorkingPapers/Economic-History/2016/WP243.pdf; Tirthankar Roy, 'Colonialism Did Not Cause the Indian Famines', History Reclaimed, 18 January 2023: https://historyreclaimed.co.uk/colonialism-did-not-cause-the-indian-famines/#_edn5; Tamoghna Halder, 'Colonialism and the Indian Famines: A response to Tirthankar Roy', Developing Economics: A Critical Perspective On Development Economics, 20 February 2023, https://developingeconomics.org/2023/02/20/colonialism-and-the-indian-famines-a-response-to-tirthankar-roy/#more-6949, and Jason Hickel, 'On The Mortality Crises In India Under British Rule: A Response To Tirthankar Roy', 7 January 2023, https://www.jasonhickel.org/blog/2023/1/7/on-the-mortality-crises-in-india-under-british-rule-a-response-to-tirthankar-roy

66. Richard Temple, '"The General Statistics of the British Empire": The Address of the President of Section F, "Economic Science and Statistics", of the British Association at the Fifty-Fourth Meeting, Held at Montreal, in August, 1884', *Journal of the Statistical Society of London*, 47, 3, September 1884, 468–84, https://doi.org/10.2307/2979250, accessed 7/12/23. See Gurminder K. Bhambra, 'Imperial Revenue and National Welfare: The Case of Britain', in Gurminder K. Bhambra and Julia McClure (eds), *Imperial Inequalities: The Politics of*

Economic Governance Across European Empires, Manchester: Manchester University Press, 2022, https://manchesteruniversitypress.co.uk/9781526166142/.

67. Alan Lester, Kate Boehme and Peter Mitchell, *Ruling the World: Freedom, Civilisation and Liberalism in the Nineteenth-Century British Empire*, Cambridge: Cambridge University Press, 2021.

68. The Arab trade in captives up the East African coast, over the Red Sea and across the Sahara came to be associated with the exclusive enslavement of darker-skinned Africans as it became entangled with the trans-Atlantic trade. Other forms of slavery had never distinguished free and unfree in racial terms: Lovejoy, *Transformations*; Walvin, *World Transformed*.

69. David Hume, 'Of National Characters', in T. H. Green and T. H. Grose (eds), *The Philosophical Works of David Hume*, 4 vols, London, 1882 [1753], 3, 252, cited in Hall, *Lucky Valley*, 19.

70. Nancy Stepan, *Idea of Race in Science: Great Britain, 1800–1960*, London: Palgrave, 1982, 1.

71. Richard Huzzey, personal correspondence and in this volume.

72. Catherine Hall, *Civilising Subjects: Metropole and Colony in the English Imagination 1830–1867*, Chicago, IL: University of Chicago Press, 2002; Thomas C. Holt, *The Problem of Freedom: Race, Labor, and Politics in Jamaica and Britain, 1832–1938*, Baltimore, MD: Johns Hopkins University Press, 1991.

73. Frederick Douglass, 'West India Emancipation', speech delivered at Canandaigua, New York, 3 August 1857, on the occasion of the anniversary of the American Abolition Society, https://rbscp.lib.rochester.edu/4398, accessed 7/12/23.

74. Jane Lydon, *Imperial Emotions: The Politics of Empathy across the British Empire*, Cambridge: Cambridge University Press, 2019.

75. Philip D. Curtin, *The Image of Africa: British Ideas and Action, 1780–1850*, vol. 2, Madison, WI: University of Wisconsin Press, 1964; Felix Driver, *Geography Militant: Cultures of Exploration and Empire*, Oxford: Blackwell, 2000.

76. Douglas Lorimer, *Science, Race Relations and Resistance: Britain, 1870–1914; A Study of Late Victorian and Edwardian Racism*, Manchester: Manchester University Press, 2013.

77. This legislation continued to blight the lives of members of these 'tribes' right up to independence in 1947, and the stigma remained. Sanjay Nigam, 'Disciplining and Policing the "Criminals by Birth", Part 1: The Making of a Colonial Stereotype—The Criminal Tribes and Castes of North India', *The Indian Economic & Social History Review*, 27, 2, 1990, 131–64, https://doi.org/10.1177/001946469002700201, accessed 4/3/24.

78. Stepan, *Idea of Race in Science*.

79. Victor Kiernan, *The Lords of Human Kind: European Attitudes to Other Cultures in the Imperial Age*, New York: Serif, 1995.
80. 'The White Man's Burden', Kipling Society, https://www.kiplingsociety.co.uk/poem/poems_burden.htm, accessed 7/12/23.
81. Sadiah Qureshi, *Peoples on Parade: Exhibitions, Empire, and Anthropology in Nineteenth-Century Britain*, Chicago, IL: University of Chicago Press, 2011.
82. Thomas Packenham, *The Scramble for Africa*, London: Abacus, 1992.
83. Alan Lester, 'Empire and the Place of Panic', in Robert Peckham (ed.), *Empires of Panic: Epidemics and Colonial Anxieties*, Hong Kong: Hong Kong University Press, 2015, 23–34.
84. Fae Dussart, *In the Service of Empire: Domestic Service and Mastery in Metropole and Colony*, London: Bloomsbury, 2022.
85. Elizabeth Kolsky, *Colonial Justice in British India: White Violence and the Rule of Law*, Cambridge: Cambridge University Press, 2010.
86. Brooke Newman, *A Dark Inheritance: Blood, Race, and Sex in Colonial Jamaica*, New Haven, CT: Yale University Press, 2018.
87. Lester et al., *Ruling the World*.
88. Aparajita Mukhopadhyay, *Imperial Technology and 'Native' Agency: A Social History of Railways in Colonial India, 1850–1920*, Abingdon: Routledge, 2018, 28.
89. G. H. Pirie, 'Racial Segregation on South African Trains, 1910–1928: Entrenchment and Protest', *South African Historical Journal*, 20, 1, 1988, 75–93, DOI: 10.1080/02582478808671637
90. Saul Dubow, *Racial Segregation and the Origins of Apartheid in South Africa, 1919–1936*, Basingstoke: Palgrave, 1989; Adam Ashforth, *The Politics of Official Discourse in Twentieth-Century South Africa*, Oxford: Oxford University Press, 1990.
91. Saul Dubow, *Apartheid, 1948–1994*, Oxford: Oxford University Press, 2014; Alan Lester, Etienne Nel and Tony Binns, *South Africa Past, Present and Future*, London: Prentice Hall, 2000.
92. Robert Bickers (ed.), *Settlers and Expatriates: Britons over the Seas*, Oxford History of the British Empire Companion Series, Oxford: Oxford University Press, 2010.
93. Eric Stokes, *The English Utilitarians and India*, Oxford: Clarendon, 1959; Uday Singh Mehta, *Liberalism and Empire: A Study in Nineteenth-Century British Liberal Thought*, Chicago, IL: University of Chicago Press, 1999; Jennifer Pitts, *A Turn to Empire: The Rise of Imperial Liberalism in Britain and France*, Princeton, NJ: Princeton University Press, 2006; Lester et al., *Ruling the World*.
94. Catherine Hall, Keith McClelland and Jane Rendall, *Defining the Victorian Nation: Class, Race, Gender and the British Reform Act of 1867*, Cambridge: Cambridge University Press, 2010.

95. Lester et al., *Ruling the World*, Part III.
96. Paul Smith, 'Cecil, Robert Arthur Talbot Gascoyne-, Third Marquess of Salisbury (1830–1903), Prime Minister', *Oxford Dictionary of National Biography*, 2011, https://www.oxforddnb.com/view/10.1093/ref:odnb/9780198614128.001.0001/odnb-9780198614128-e-32339, accessed 28/10/19.
97. Earl Grey, *The Colonial Policy of Lord John Russell's Administration*, vol. 1 (1853), Cambridge: Cambridge University Press, 2010, 27.
98. C. A. Bayly, *Recovering Liberties: Indian Thought in the Age of Liberalism and Empire*, Cambridge: Cambridge University Press, 2012; Lester et al., *Ruling the World*.
99. Jeremy Martens, 'A Transnational History of Immigration Restriction: Natal and New South Wales, 1896–97', *The Journal of Imperial and Commonwealth History*, 34, 3, 2006, 323–44, DOI:10.1080/03086530600825969; Marilyn Lake and Henry Reynolds, *Drawing the Global Colour Line: White Men's Countries and the International Challenge of Racial Equality*, Cambridge: Cambridge University Press, 2012.
100. 'Laura Trevelyan Quits BBC to Campaign for Reparative Justice for Caribbean', *The Guardian*, 16 March 2023, https://www.theguardian.com/world/2023/mar/16/laura-trevelyan-quits-bbc-to-campaign-reparative-justice-slavery-caribbean, accessed 27/2/24.
101. Berg and Hudson, *Slavery, Capitalism and the Industrial Revolution*.
102. Alan Lester, 'Indians in Eastern Africa: Sir Henry Bartle Frere's Vision and the Networks of Empire', University of Sussex, 1 November 2022, https://blogs.sussex.ac.uk/snapshotsofempire/2022/11/01/indians-in-eastern-africa-sir-henry-bartle-freres-vision-and-the-networks-of-empire/; Robert E. Washington, 'Brown Racism and the Formation of a World System of Racial Stratification', *International Journal of Politics, Culture, and Society*, 4, 2, 1990, 209–27, http://www.jstor.org/stable/20006991, accessed 27/2/24.
103. Michèle Barrett, 'Subalterns at War', *Interventions*, 9, 3, 2007, 451–74, DOI: 10.1080/13698010701618703, and David Lambert, *Soldiers of Uncertain Rank: The West India Regiments in British Imperial Culture*, Cambridge: Cambridge University Press, 2024.
104. The chaperoning of the soldiers so that they would not meet local White women was one aspect of British hospitality that the censors were keen to suppress in letters home: Samuel Hyson and Alan Lester, '"British India on Trial": Brighton Military Hospitals and the Politics of Empire in World War I', *Journal of Historical Geography*, 38, 1, 2012, 18–34, https://doi.org/10.1016/j.jhg.2011.09.002, accessed 27/2/24.
105. Sunil Amrith, 'Political Culture of Health in India: A Historical Perspective', *Economic and Political Weekly*, Aspects of the Social History of Medicine, 13 January 2007, 114–21, https://ruralindiaonline.org/en/library/resource/political-culture-of-health-in-india-a-historical-perspective, accessed 27/2/24.

106. Chinua Achebe, *Things Fall Apart*, London: Penguin, 2006.
107. Bruce Gilley, 'Chinua Achebe on the Positive Legacies of Colonialism', *African Affairs*, 115, 461, 2016, 646–63. Gilley's argument is rehearsed again in Biggar, *Colonialism*, 90–1, 199–202.
108. Gilley, 'Chinua Achebe', 652, 646.
109. Quoted in ibid., 652.
110. Quoted in ibid., 649.
111. Chinua Achebe, *There Was a Country*, London: Penguin, 2013; Kwasi Kwarteng, *Ghosts of Empire: Britain's Legacies in the Modern World*, London: Bloomsbury, 2012; Siollun, *What Britain Did to Nigeria*.
112. Achebe, *There Was a Country*, 99.
113. Ibid., 243, 244.

1. WHAT ABOUT SLAVERY?

1. This chapter is derived from research previously published in my book, *Not Made by Slaves*, Cambridge, MA: Harvard University Press, 2020, and "African Leaders in Sierra Leone Played a Key Role in Ending the Transatlantic Slave Trade," The Conversation, 2023, https://theconversation.com/african-leaders-in-sierra-leone-played-a-key-role-in-ending-the-transatlantic-slave-trade-207382, accessed 16/10/23.
2. Robin Pearson and David Richardson, "Social Capital, Institutional Innovation and the Slave Trade before 1800," *Business History* 50, 6, 2008, 765–80, https://doi.org/10.1080/00076790802420336, accessed 27/02/24.
3. Madge Dresser and Andrew Hann (eds), *Slavery and the British Country House*, Swindon: English Heritage, 2013; "National Trust Report on Slavery and Colonialism," National Trust, https://www.nationaltrust.org.uk/who-we-are/research/addressing-our-histories-of-colonialism-and-historic-slavery#rt-our-collections-and-slavery, accessed 16/10/23.
4. Maxine Berg and Pat Hudson, *Slavery, Capitalism, and the Industrial Revolution*, Cambridge: Polity, 2023; Barbara Solow, *The Economic Consequences of the Atlantic Slave Trade*, Lanham, MD: Lexington Books, 2014; Bonnie Martin, "Neighbor-to-Neighbor Capitalism: Local Credit Networks and the Mortgaging of Slaves," in *Slavery's Capitalism: A New History of American Economic Development*, eds Sven Beckert and Seth Rockman, Philadelphia, PA: University of Pennsylvania Press, 2016, 107–21; Jessica M. Lepler, *The Many Panics of 1837: People, Politics, and the Creation of a Transatlantic Financial Crisis*, New York: Cambridge University Press, 2013; Joseph Inikori, "The Credit Needs of the African Trade and the Development of the Credit Economy in England," *Explorations in Economic History*, 27, 2, 1990, 197–231; Inikori, *Africans and the Industrial Revolution in Britain*, Cambridge: Cambridge University Press, 2009.

5. Thomas Clarkson, *Letters on the Slave Trade*, London: C. Wheeler, 1791, 81. See also Rudolph T. Ware III, *The Walking Qur'an*, Chapel Hill, NC: University of North Carolina Press, 2014.
6. José Lingna Nafafé, *Lourenço da Silva Mendonça and the Black Atlantic Abolitionist Movement in the Seventeenth Century*, Cambridge: Cambridge University Press, 2022.
7. Walter Hawthorne, *Planting Rice and Harvesting Slaves*, Portsmouth, NH: Heinemann, 2003; Christopher DeCorse (ed.), *West Africa during the Atlantic Slave Trade: Archaeological Perspectives*, London: Leicester University Press, 2001.
8. An African Merchant, *A Treatise upon the Trade from Great-Britain to Africa; Humbly Recommended to the Attention of Government*, London: R. Baldwin, 1772, 27.
9. Huntington Library, MSS MY 418, Folder 28, 11 December 1798.
10. Huntington Library, MSS MY 418 Box 20 Folder 20, 8 May 1797.
11. Joseph J. Bangura, *The Temne of Sierra Leone*, Cambridge: Cambridge University Press, 2017.
12. Padraic Scanlan, *Freedom's Debtors*, New Haven, CT: Yale University Press, 2017.
13. Robin Law (ed.), *Dahomey and the Ending of the Transatlantic Slave Trade*, Oxford: Oxford University Press, 2012; Bronwen Everill, "Bridgeheads of Empire? Liberated African Missionaries in West Africa," *Journal of Imperial and Commonwealth History*, 40, 5, 2012, 789–805, https://doi.org/10.1080/03086534.2012.730833, accessed 27/2/24; Dan Hicks, *The Brutish Museums*, Cambridge: Polity, 2020; Richard Huzzey, *Freedom Burning*, Ithaca, NY: Cornell University Press, 2012.

2. TASMANIA AND THE QUESTION OF GENOCIDE IN THE BLACK WAR, THE HISTORY WARS AND THE CULTURE WAR

1. Geoffrey Blainey first adopted the term 'Black Armband historians' in his 1993 Sir John Latham Memorial Lecture.
2. Government notice, 29 November 1826, 'Van Diemen's Land Copies of All Correspondence between Lieutenant-Governor Arthur and His Majesty's Secretary of State for the Colonies on the Subject of the Military Operations Lately Carried on against the Aboriginal Inhabitants of Van Diemen's Land', *British Parliamentary Papers*, 19, 259, 1831, 20–1.
3. For population statistics, see Lyndall Ryan, *Tasmanian Aborigines: A History since 1803*, Sydney: Allen & Unwin, 2013, 74.
4. *Colonial Times*, 15 December 1826.
5. Proclamation, 15 April 1828, 'Military Operations', 5–7.

NOTES pp. [57–61]

6. Ibid., 6.
7. Ryan, *Tasmanian Aborigines*, 79–83.
8. Ibid., 87–93.
9. Memorandum by Arthur, 20 November 1830; Arthur to Sir George Murray, 'Military Operations', 72–5.
10. Ryan, *Tasmanian Aborigines*, 138–41.
11. Charles Darwin, *The Voyage of the Beagle*, London: J. M. Dent, 1961, 430.
12. *The Times* (London), 2 January 1828; A. G. L. Shaw (ed.), *Van Diemen's Land: Copies of All Correspondence between Lieutenant-Governor Arthur and His Majesty's Secretary of State for the Colonies, on the Subject of the Military Operations Lately Carried on against the Aboriginal Inhabitants of Van Diemen's Land*, Paper No. 259 (originally published by the House of Commons, 23 September 1831; facsimile edition, Hobart, Tasmania: Tasmanian Historical Research Association, 1971); House of Commons, 'Report from the Select Committee on Aborigines (British Settlements) with Minutes of Evidence, Appendix and Index' (1836); 'Copy of Despatch from Colonel Arthur to Lord Glenelg Dated the 29th October 1836' (1837); 'Report of the Parliamentary Select Committee on Aboriginal Tribes (British Settlements)' (1837).
13. Sir George Murray to Lieut-Governor Arthur, 23 April 1830, in P. Chapman (ed.), *Historical Records of Australia Resumed Series III*, vol. ix, Melbourne: Melbourne University Press, 2006, 311.
14. J. Bonwick, *The Last of the Tasmanians, or, The Black War in Van Diemen's Land*, London: Sampson, Low, Son & Marston, 1870, 371 (facsimile edition, Adelaide, Libraries Board of South Australia, 1969).
15. N. Biggar, *Colonialism: A Moral Reckoning*, London: William Collins, 2023, 136.
16. K. Windschuttle, *The Fabrication of Aboriginal History: Volume One; Van Diemen's Land 1803–1847*, Sydney: Macleay Press, 2002, 3; L. Ryan, *The Aboriginal Tasmanians*, Brisbane: University of Queensland Press, 1981; L. Robson, *A History of Tasmania: Volume I; Van Diemen's Land from the Earliest Times to 1855*, Melbourne: Oxford University Press, 1983, Chapter 11, 'Destruction of the Aborigines', 210–53; H. Reynolds, *Fate of a Free People: A Radical Re-examination of the Tasmanian Wars*, Ringwood, Victoria: Penguin Books Australia, 1995; Robson died in 1991 and thus was unable to defend his argument.
17. Ryan, *Aboriginal Tasmanians*, 1–6.
18. N. J. B. Plomley (ed.), *Friendly Mission: The Tasmanian Journals of G. A. Robinson, 1829–34*, Sydney: Angus & Robertson, 1966; Tasmanian Archive and Heritage Office (TAHO), Hobart, CSO 1/316/7578/1–17.
19. Plomley, *Friendly Mission*, 217–19; Ryan, *Aboriginal Tasmanians*, 139.
20. Reynolds, *Fate of a Free People*, 122.
21. H. Reynolds, *An Indelible Stain? The Question of Genocide in Australia's History*, Ringwood, Victoria: Viking, 2001, 'Tasmania', 49–86.

22. R. Jones, 'The Demography of Hunters and Farmers in Tasmania', in D. J. Mulvaney and J. Golson (eds), *Aboriginal Man and Environment in Australia*, Canberra: ANU Press, 1971; N. J. B. Plomley, 'The Aboriginal Tribes in Tasmania', Appendix 5, in *Friendly Mission*, 2nd edn, Launceston: Queen Victoria Museum & Art Gallery, 2008, 1006–13.
23. Windschuttle, *Fabrication of Aboriginal History*, 386.
24. Ibid., 160–2, 387–97.
25. Ibid., 404.
26. *The Australian*, 6, 12, 14, 28–9 December 2002; 10, 11 January; 12 February, 5 April, 7 May 2003.
27. Quoted in R. Manne (ed.), *Whitewash: On Keith Windschuttle's Fabrication of Aboriginal History*, Melbourne: Black Inc. Agenda, 2003, 'Introduction', 9.
28. G. Blainey, *The Australian*, 14 April 2003.
29. H. Reynolds, 'Terra Nullius Reborn', in *Whitewash*, 109–38.
30. J. Boyce, 'Fantasy Island', in *Whitewash*, 19.
31. L. Ryan, 'Who Is the Fabricator', in *Whitewash*, 230–57.
32. Quoted in Windschuttle, *Fabrication*, 403; Boyce, 'Fantasy Island', in *Whitewash*, 46.
33. See J. Semelin, 'In Consideration of Massacres', *Journal of Genocide Research*, 3, 10, 2000, 377–89.
34. Ryan, *Tasmanian Aborigines*, xxv.
35. J. Boyce, *Van Diemen's Land*, Melbourne: Black Inc., 2008; T. Lawson, *The Last Man: A British Genocide in Tasmania*, London: I. B. Tauris, 2014; L. Ryan et al., digital online map: https://c21ch.newcastle.edu.au/colonialmassacres, accessed 27/2/24.
36. Biggar, *Colonialism*, 136.
37. Ibid.
38. Ibid., 142.
39. Ibid., 136.
40. Ibid.
41. Ibid.
42. Ibid., 137, quote from Blainey.
43. Ibid.
44. J. Campbell, *Invisible Invaders: Smallpox and Other Diseases in Aboriginal Australia 1780–1880*, Melbourne: Melbourne University Press, 2002.
45. Van Diemen's Land, 'Register of Deaths, 1803–20', Mitchell Library, State Library of New South Wales, Sydney, ML C 190; Ryan, *Aboriginal Tasmanians*, 2nd edn, Sydney: Allen & Unwin, 1996, 175.
46. Biggar, *Colonialism*, 138.
47. Reynolds, *Fate of a Free People*, 122–3.
48. Biggar, *Colonialism*, 138.

NOTES

49. Plomley, *Aboriginal/Settler Clash*, 82.
50. Biggar, *Colonialism*, 138.
51. Windschuttle, *Fabrication*, 366–71.
52. Windschuttle, cited in Biggar, *Colonialism*, 139.
53. Reynolds, *Indelible Stain*, 76.
54. Biggar, *Colonialism*, 139.
55. Reynolds, *Indelible Stain*, 71–2, cited in Biggar, *Colonialism*, 140–1.
56. Biggar, *Colonialism*, 146.
57. Boyce, *Van Diemen's Land*, 308.
58. *The Examiner*, 2 October 1847.
59. Biggar, *Colonialism*, 142.
60. Windschuttle, cited in Biggar, *Colonialism*, 142.
61. Ryan, *Tasmanian Aborigines*, 198–218.
62. Biggar, *Colonialism*, 144.
63. Ibid., 145.
64. Ibid.
65. Ryan, *Tasmanian Aborigines*, 47–52.
66. https://c21ch.newcastle.edu.au/colonialmassacres, accessed 5/3/24.
67. C. Darwin, *The Voyage of the Beagle*, London: J. M. Dent, 1961, 430.

3. THE MISUSE OF INDIGENOUS AND CANADIAN HISTORY IN *COLONIALISM*

1. Chinua Achebe, *Things Fall Apart*, 50th anniversary edn, Toronto: Anchor Canada, 2009, 208–9.
2. We are paraphrasing Frantz Fanon, *The Wretched of the Earth*, New York: Grove Press, 2004, 15. Nigel Biggar cites *Things Fall Apart* (Nigel Biggar, *Colonialism: A Moral Reckoning*, London: William Collins, 2023, 86, 87) but pays most attention to Achebe's later work. Following Bruce Gilley, as Alan Lester notes in the Introduction to this volume, this is misrepresented as favoring colonial rule (Bruce Gilley, 'Chinua Achebe on the Positive Legacies of Colonialism', *African Affairs*, 115, 461, 2016, 646–63; Biggar, *Colonialism*, 199–202).
3. See, for example, Ian Cobain and Richard Norton-Taylor, "Sins of Colonists Lay Concealed for Decades in Secret Archive," *The Guardian*, 18 April 2012, https://www.theguardian.com/uk/2012/apr/18/sins-colonialists-concealed-secret-archive, accessed 27/2/24. In terms of imperialists writing justificatory historical accounts in the Canadian context, see George R. Parkin, *The Makers of Canada: Sir John A. Macdonald*, vol. 12, Toronto: Morang & Company, 1908.
4. Biggar's *Colonialism* indicates its objective in reverse. In castigating the "anti-colonials," it says: "One important way of corroding faith in the West is to denigrate its record, a major part of which is the history of European empires. And

of all those empires, the primary target is the British one, which was by far the largest and gave birth to the United States, Canada, Australia and New Zealand." Turned around and put another way, *Colonialism* thus seeks to shore up faith in the West and its institutions by praising the record of European empires, specifically the British Empire. See Biggar, *Colonialism*, 6.

5. See Terry Cook, "A Reconstruction of the World: George R. Parkin's British Empire Map of 1893," *Cartographica: The International Journal for Geographic Information and Geovisualization*, 21, 4, 1984, 53–65.
6. Biggar, *Colonialism*, 43.
7. Ibid., 127.
8. On Flanagan, see Mitchell Thompson, "Fraser Institute Fellow Tom Flanagan: Stories about Residential School Graves are 'Fake News,'" Press Progress, 21 January 2022, https://pressprogress.ca/fraser-institute-fellow-tom-flanagan-news-stories-about-residential-school-graves-are-fake-news, accessed 4/3/24.
9. *Colonialism* fawns over Canadian politics professor Patrice Dutil's counting of "native deaths attributable to starvation on the Canadian plains from 1879–1883" as being "somewhere in the region of forty-five. No, that is not a typographical error." Biggar, *Colonialism*, 192.
10. We have assembled to confront far-right selective representations of Canadian history before. See Omeasoo Wahpasiw, Adele Perry, and Sean Carleton, "Nostalgia and the Politics of Selective Remembering," ActiveHistory.ca, 5 May 2021, https://activehistory.ca/blog/2021/05/05/nostalgia-and-the-politics-of-selective-remembering, accessed 4/3/24.
11. See Alan Lester, "The British Empire in the Culture War: Nigel Biggar's *Colonialism: A Moral Reckoning*," *The Journal of Imperial and Commonwealth History*, 51, 4, 2023, 763–95.
12. See, for accessible biographies, Lewis H. Thomas, "RIEL, LOUIS (1844–85)," in *Dictionary of Canadian Biography*, vol. 11, Toronto: University of Toronto/Université Laval, 2003–, http://www.biographi.ca/en/bio/riel_louis_1844_85_11E.html, accessed 4/3/24.
13. See Darren O'Toole, "Métis Claims to 'Indian' Title in Manitoba, 1860–1870," *The Canadian Journal of Native Studies*, 28, 2, 2008, 241–70; Adam Gaudry, "Fantasies of Sovereignty: Deconstructing British and Canadian Claims to Ownership of the Historic North-West," *Native American and Indigenous Studies*, 3, 1, 2016, 48–50.
14. See Sarah Carter, *Aboriginal People and Their Colonizers in Western Canada to 1900*, Toronto: University of Toronto Press, 1999, Chapter 8; Bill Waiser and Blair Stonechild, *Loyal till Death: Indians and the Northwest Rebellion*, Markham, Ontario: Fifth House, 1997.
15. M. Max Hamon, "Re-presenting Riel: 100 Years in the *Canadian Historical Review*," *Canadian Historical Review*, 102, 1, 2021, S3.

16. Biggar, *Colonialism*, 104.
17. Ibid., 332, n. 24.
18. Thomas Flanagan, *Riel and the Rebellion: 1885 Reconsidered*, Toronto: University of Toronto Press, 2000, 94.
19. Nigel Biggar, "On *Colonialism: A Moral Reckoning*; A Reply to Alan Lester," *The Journal of Imperial and Commonwealth History*, 51, 4, 2023, 803.
20. See, especially, *Imperial Plots: Women, Land the Spadework of British Colonialism on the Canadian Prairies*, Winnipeg, Manitoba: University of Manitoba Press, 2016; *The Importance of Being Monogamous: Marriage and Nation Building in Western Canada*, Edmonton, Alberta: University of Alberta Press, 2008; *Aboriginal People and Colonizers of Western Canada*, Toronto: University of Toronto Press, 1999; *Capturing Women: The Manipulation of Cultural Imagery in Canada's Prairie West*, Montreal: McGill–Queen's University Press, 1997; *Lost Harvests: Prairie Indian Reserve Farmers and Government Policy*, Montreal: McGill–Queen's University Press, 1990.
21. Biggar, *Colonialism*, 116–17.
22. Ibid., 330–1; 189–92, 290.
23. John L. Tobias, "Canada's Subjugation of the Plains Cree, 1879–1885," *Canadian Historical Review*, 64, 4, 1983, 519–48; Maureen Lux, *Medicine That Walks: Disease, Medicine and the Canadian Plains People, 1880–1940*, Toronto: University of Toronto Press, 2001.
24. Biggar, *Colonialism*, 190–1.
25. Ibid., 330, n. 31.
26. Robert Alexander Innes, "Historians and Indigenous Genocide in Saskatchewan," Shekon Neechie: An Indigenous History Site, 21 June 2018, https://shekon-neechie.ca/2018/06/21/historians-and-indigenous-genocide-in-saskatchewan, accessed 16/10/23.
27. Gina Starblanket and Dallas Hunt, *Storying Violence: Unraveling Colonial Narratives in the Stanley Trial*, n.p.: ARP, 2020.
28. See, for example, Arthur Manuel and Grand Chief Ronald Derrickson, *The Reconciliation Manifesto: Recovering the Land, Rebuilding the Economy*, Toronto: Lorimer, 2017; Paulette Regan, *Unsettling the Settler Within: Indian Residential Schools, Truth Telling, and Reconciliation in Canada*, Vancouver: UBC Press, 2010.
29. For a full list of prizewinners, see the CHA's website: https://cha-shc.ca/prize-winners/?table_filter=The%20Indigenous%20History%20Best%20Article%20, accessed 4/3/24. Since 2003, the following books have been awarded the CHA's best book prize: 2003 winner—Cole Harris, *Making Native Space: Colonialism, Resistance, and Reserves in British Columbia*, Vancouver: UBC Press, 2002; 2005 winner—Dominique Deslandres, *Croire et faire croire: Les missions françaises au XVIIe siècle, 1600–1650*, Paris: Fayard, 2003; 2013 winner—

William C. Wicken, *The Colonization of Mi'kmaw Memory and History, 1794–1928: The King v. Gabriel Sylliboy*, Toronto: University of Toronto Press, 2012; 2014 winner—James Daschuk, *Clearing the Plains: Disease, Politics of Starvation, and the Loss of Aboriginal Life*, Altona: University of Regina Press, 2013; 2015 winner—Jean Barman, *French Canadians, Furs, and Indigenous Women in the Making of the Pacific Northwest*, Vancouver: UBC Press, 2014; 2017 winner—Sarah Carter, *Imperial Plots: Women, Land, and the Spadework of British Colonialism on the Canadian Prairies*, Winnipeg, Manitoba: University of Manitoba Press, 2016; 2021 winner—Brittany Luby, *Dammed: The Politics of Loss and Survival in Anishinaabe Territory*, Winnipeg, Manitoba: University of Manitoba Press, 2020; 2022 winner—Benjamin Hoy, *A Line of Blood and Dirt: Creating the Canada–United States Border across Indigenous Lands*, Oxford: Oxford University Press, 2021; 2023 winner—Lianne C. Leddy, *Serpent River Resurgence: Confronting Uranium Mining at Elliot Lake*, Toronto: University of Toronto Press, 2022. The CHA Indigenous History Group also awards a best book prize. Biggar only cites one prizewinner since 2010, Daschuk's book. Prizes, of course, are not the only indicator of merit, but it will be obvious to any serious scholar that a lack of meaningful engagement with recent notable scholarship to construct one's argument is a red flag.

30. Such studies are not only published by scholars that Biggar might denounce as "anti-colonials." For example, P. Whitney Lackenbauer has recently sided with right-wing commentators to defend Canada's reputation in culture wars, but his work is not a straightforward apology for Canada's colonial policy regarding Indigenous peoples. See Yale D. Belanger and P. Whitney Lackenbauer (eds), *Blockades or Breakthroughs? Aboriginal Peoples Confront the Canadian State*, Montreal: McGill–Queen's University Press, 2014. Similarly, J. R. Miller, whom Biggar cites more than any other Canadian historian, has also joined a consortium of right-wing voices arguing Canada's treatment of Indigenous peoples does not meet the definition of genocide, but his recent work does not suggest that colonialism was beneficial. J. R. Miller, *Residential Schools and Reconciliation*, Toronto: University of Toronto Press, 2017.

31. See, for example, Waiser and Stonechild, *Loyal till Death*; Kenton Storey, *Settler Anxiety at the Outposts of Empire: Colonial Relations, Humanitarian Discourses, and the Imperial Press*, Vancouver: UBC Press, 2018; and Sarah Nickel, *Assembling Unity: Indigenous Politics, Gender, and the Union of BC Indian Chiefs*, Vancouver: UBC Press, 2019.

32. Biggar, *Colonialism*, 100.

33. Ibid., 100.

34. Ibid., 101.

35. Tracey Lindberg, "The Doctrine of Discovery in Canada," in Robert J. Miller, Jacinta Ruru, Larissa Behrendt, and Tracey Lindberg (eds), *Discovering*

Indigenous Lands: The Doctrine of Discovery in the English Colonies, Oxford: Oxford University Press, 2010, 89.

36. Ibid., 90.
37. Biggar, *Colonialism*, 329.
38. Ibid., 101.
39. Lindberg, "Doctrine of Discovery," 91.
40. Biggar, *Colonialism*, 124.
41. Ibid.
42. Katherine L. Reedy-Maschner and Herbert D. G. Maschner, "Marauding Middlemen: Western Expansion and Violent Conflict in the Subarctic," *Ethnohistory*, 46, 4, 1999, 703–43.
43. Biggar, *Colonialism*, 103.
44. Kerry Sloan, "'A New German-Indian World' in the North-West: A Métis Deconstruction of Rhetoric of Immigration in Louise Riel's Trial Speeches," in Hans V. Hanson (ed.), *Riel's Defence: Perspectives on His Speeches*, Montreal: McGill–Queen's University Press, 2014, 176, 195.
45. Canada, Department of the Secretary of State, Sessional Papers, No. 43, Saturday, 1 August 1885, *Epitome of Parliamentary Documents in Connection with the North-West Rebellion, 1885*, Ottawa: Maclean, Roger & Co., 1886, 218.
46. See, for example, the Truth and Reconciliation Commission of Canada, *Volume One: Summary: Honouring the Truth, Reconciling for the Future*, Toronto: Lorimer, 2016; Andrew Woolford, *This Benevolent Experiment: Indigenous Boarding Schools, Genocide, and Redress in Canada and the United States*, Winnipeg, Manitoba: University of Manitoba Press, 2015.
47. See Richard Raycraft, "MPs Back Motion Calling on Government to Recognize Residential Schools Program as Genocide," CBC News, 27 October 2022, https://www.cbc.ca/news/politics/house-motion-recognize-genocide-1.6632450, accessed 4/3/24.
48. Ka'nhehsí:io Deer, "Pope Says Genocide Took Place at Canada's Residential Schools," CBC News, 30 July 2022, https://www.cbc.ca/news/indigenous/pope-francis-residential-schools-genocide-1.6537203, accessed 4/3/24.
49. Tristin Hooper, "Vast Majority of Canadians Support Reconciliation, Even if They Differ on the Details: Poll," *National Post*, 30 September 2022, https://nationalpost.com/news/canada/vast-majority-of-canadians-support-reconciliation-even-if-they-differ-on-the-details-poll, accessed 4/3/24.
50. Erin Millions and Mary Jane Logan McCallum, "Toppling Colonialism: Historians, Genocide, and Missing Indigenous Children," *Prairie History*, Summer 2021, 4.
51. For more on residential school denialism and the use of false balance, see Sean Carleton, "'I don't need any more education': Senator Lynn Beyak, Residential

School Denialism, and Attacks on Truth and Reconciliation," *Settler Colonial Studies*, 11, 4, 2021, 446–86.
52. "*A National Crime* Makes Top 100 List," Trent University, 15 December 2005, https://www.trentu.ca/newsarchive/daily/archive/051215jmilloy.html, accessed 4/3/24. For the new edition, see John Milloy, *A National Crime: The Canadian Government and the Residential School System*, 2nd edn, with foreword by Mary Jane Logan McCallum, Winnipeg, Manitoba: University of Manitoba Press, 2017.
53. "Historians Rally vs. 'Genocide' Myth," *The Dorchester Review*, 9 August 2021, https://www.dorchesterreview.ca/blogs/news/historians-rally-vs-genocide-myth, accessed 4/3/24. For a response, showing how Canada's treatment of Indigenous peoples does, in fact, meet the definition of genocide, see Sean Carleton and Andrew Woolford, "Ignore Debaters and Denialists, Canada's Treatment of Indigenous Peoples Fits the Definition of Genocide," The Conversation, 25 October 2021, https://theconversation.com/ignore-debaters-and-denialists-canadas-treatment-of-indigenous-peoples-fits-the-definition-of-genocide-170242, accessed 4/3/24.
54. Biggar, *Colonialism*, 350, n. 67.
55. Peter Shawn Taylor, "Reckoning with Canada's Colonial Past: In Conversation with Nigel Biggar," C2C, 6 April 2023, https://c2cjournal.ca/2023/04/reckoning-with-canadas-colonial-past-in-conversation-with-nigel-biggar, accessed 24/3/24.
56. Peter Shawn Taylor, "Colonialism Contained 'good things as well as bad': Why Can't We Just Accept That?," *The National Post*, 3 May 2023, https://nationalpost.com/opinion/colonialism-contained-good-things-as-well-as-bad-why-cant-we-just-accept-that, accessed 5/3/24.
57. Taylor, "Reckoning with Canada's Colonial Past."
58. Biggar, *Colonialism*, 90. Taylor, "Reckoning with Canada's Colonial Past."
59. Achebe quoted in Nasrin Pourhamrang, "*Things Fall Apart* Now More Famous Than Me, Says Chinua Achebe," Daily Trust, 8 September 2012, https://dailytrust.com/things-fall-apart-now-more-famous-than-me-says-chinua-achebe, accessed 4/3/24.
60. Achebe, *Things Fall Apart*, 209.
61. Achebe quoted in "*Things Fall Apart* Now More Famous Than Me, Says Chinua Achebe."

4. 'WHEN MEN BURN WOMEN ALIVE, WE HANG THEM': SATI AND 'CIVILISING MISSION' IN COLONIAL INDIA

1. Sati literally translates as 'virtuous women' but was used by the British in the nineteenth century (often transliterated as suttee) to denote the rare and controversial Hindu practice of burning widows on their husband's funeral pyre.

NOTES

2. William F. P. Napier, *History of General Sir Charles Napier's Administration of Scinde*, London: Chapman and Hall, 1851, 35. Sindh, which includes the city of Karachi, is in the south-eastern region of modern-day Pakistan and has borders with the Indian states of Rajasthan and Gujarat. Until 1988, it was spelled Sind and can also be found transliterated as Scind or Scinde in nineteenth-century British sources.
3. Ibid.
4. Michael Gove, 'Trafalgar Square Plinth Should Be the Public's Decision', *Times*, 19 February 2008, https://www.thetimes.co.uk/article/trafalgar-square-plinth-should-be-the-publics-decision-mkr870k8r7h, accessed 2/11/2023. The pun was the work of sixteen-year-old schoolgirl Caroline Winkworth, who sent it to the satirical magazine. For a detailed discussion of the pun, its origins, and subsequent meanings, see Wendy Doniger, '"I Have Scinde": Flogging a Dead (White Male Orientalist) Horse', *Journal of Asian Studies*, 58, 4, 1999, 940–60.
5. Gove 'Trafalgar Square Plinth Should Be the Public's Decision'.
6. Jeremy Paxman, *Empire: What Ruling the World Did to the British*, London: Penguin, 2012, 86.
7. Jacob Rees-Mogg, *The Victorians: Twelve Titans Who Forged Britain*, London: W. H. Allen, 2019, 107.
8. Polly Toynbee, 'Limp Liberals Fail to Protect Their Most Profound Values', *Guardian*, 10 October 2001, https://www.theguardian.com/world/2001/oct/10/afghanistan.politics1, accessed 2/11/2023.
9. Matthew Parris, 'Williams Is Dangerous: He Must Be Resisted', *Times*, 10 February 2008, https://www.thetimes.co.uk/article/williams-is-dangerous-he-must-be-resisted-zrx9zqz3mh0, accessed 2/11/2023.
10. Jonah Goldberg, 'The Napier Doctrine', *The National Review*, 2 November 2015, https://www.nationalreview.com/magazine/2015/11/02/napier-doctrine, accessed 2/11/2023.
11. 'Rhodes Not Taken', *The New Criterion*, 42, 3, February 2016, https://newcriterion.com/issues/2016/2/rhodes-not-taken, accessed 2/11/2023.
12. Chris McGovern, 'The Harry Potter Publisher and the Cancelled Professor', Conservative Woman, 1 February 2023, https://www.conservativewoman.co.uk/the-harry-potter-publisher-and-the-cancelled-professor, accessed 2/11/2023.
13. Nigel Biggar, *Colonialism: A Moral Reckoning*, London: William Collins, 2023.
14. See, for example, Prachi Priyanka, 'Cultural Syndromes in India: Understanding Widow Burning in Sati and Jauhar through Indian Literature', in Cringuta Irina Pelea (ed.), *Culture-Bound Syndromes in Popular Culture*, Abingdon: Routledge, 2023, 83–105 and Saumya Saxena, 'Policing Sati: Law, Order, and Spectacle in Postcolonial India', *Law and History Review*, 41, 2, 2023, 1–23, for two examples from this year alone. For a recent high-profile example of its cultural resonance, see its role as a pivotal plot point in the blockbuster series *Game of Thrones* (HBO).

15. Anand Yang, 'Whose Sati? Widow-Burning in Nineteenth Century India', *Journal of Women's History*, 1, 2, 1989, 22.
16. Christopher Bayly, 'From Ritual to Ceremony: Death Ritual and Society in Hindu North India since 1600', in Joachim Whaley (ed.), *Mirrors of Mortality: Social Studies in the History of Death*, Abingdon: Routledge, 1981, 173.
17. The last woman to be burned at the stake for witchcraft in Britain was Janet Horne of Dornoch, Sutherland, in 1727. Burning alive remained a form of execution for women in Britain until 1790, with the last recorded case being that of counterfeiter Catherine Murphy in 1789, although from the mid-seventeenth century onwards the custom was to strangle the condemned before lighting the fire. Between 1735 and 1789, at least thirty-three women suffered this fate, mostly for the crime of murdering their husbands, which was deemed petty treason.
18. See Kumkum Sangari and Sudesh Vaid, 'Institutions, Beliefs, Ideologies: Widow Immolation in Contemporary Rajasthan', in Kumari Jayawardena and Malathi De Alwis (eds), *Embodied Violence: Communalising Women's Sexuality in South Asia*, New Delhi: Kali for Women, 1996, 240–96; Mala Sen, *Death by Fire: Sati, Dowry Death and Infanticide in Modern India*, London: Weidenfeld & Nicolson, 2001, for just two examples.
19. The tendency for Western observers to exoticise certain forms of violence against women, such as sati, while ignoring or normalising forms of patriarchal oppression in their own culture has been commented on extensively by postcolonial feminists. Given that in England and Wales alone 1.7 million women suffered domestic abuse in the year to March 2022 (nearly 7 per cent of the female population over sixteen), with incidents of domestic violence increasing by up to 38 per cent during major football tournaments, and Refuge reporting that on average two women a week are killed by a current or former partner in England or Wales, it is obviously deeply problematic to exoticise violence against women or present it as exclusively the problem of other cultures, either in the past or the present.
20. Carey Watt, 'The Relevance and Complexity of Civilising Missions c.1800–2010', in Carey Watt and Michael Mann (eds), *Civilizing Missions in Colonial and Postcolonial South Asia: From Improvement to Development*, London: Anthem Press, 2011, 1.
21. Ibid.
22. Partha Chatterjee, *The Nation and Its Fragments: Colonial and Postcolonial Histories*, Princeton, NJ Princeton University Press, 1993, 16.
23. A good example of this is EIC reluctance to intervene to suppress caste-based slavery in South India. Despite vocally espousing anti-slavery sentiments and ideals, colonial officials repeatedly demurred when it came to doing anything about slavery in their districts on the basis that it would disrupt the collection

of the land tax. See Andrea Major, *Slavery, Abolitionism and Empire in India, 1772–1843*, Liverpool: Liverpool University Press, 2012, 199.
24. Biggar, *Colonialism*, 90, 83. Biggar's arguments are largely based on uncritical acceptance of nineteenth-century British assessments of the characters and aptitudes of 'the natives'. His failure to pay proper attention to the views, experiences, and identities of these groups is reinforced by his lazy use of this pejorative term. His argument that the term can equally be applied to 'native Britons', and thus should not be considered offensive, demonstrates a marked lack of understanding of both the history of the term and the moral and methodological reasons why homogenising the diverse groups that came under colonial sway is actively unhelpful.
25. Biggar, *Colonialism*, 83. Biggar admits that 'the imperial government was often reluctant to interfere' on social reform issues such as slavery, female infanticide, and child marriage, a reticence which for some reason he thinks 'should attract the approval of contemporary anti-colonialists, but does not'. Biggar, *Colonialism*, 84.
26. Lata Mani, *Contentious Traditions: The Debate on Sati in Colonial India*, Berkeley, CA: University of California Press, 1998; Ania Loomba, 'Dead Women Tell No Tales: Issues of Female Subjectivity, Subaltern Agency and Tradition in Colonial and Post-colonial Writings on Widow Immolation in India', *History Workshop*, 36, 1993; Vasudha Dalmia-Lüderitz, '"Sati" as a Religious Rite: Parliamentary Papers on Widow Immolation, 1821–30', *Economic and Political Weekly*, 27, 4, 1992, PE58–64.
27. Christopher Bayly compares the focus on sati to the more muted response to famine deaths, arguing that while sati became a matter of EIC concern, the 'mortality that derived from the working of the grain market was treated as a law of nature, in no way amendable to intervention by the state'. Bayly, 'From Ritual to Ceremony', 173.
28. John MacDonald, *Memoirs of an Eighteenth Century Footman, Travels 1745–1779*, New York: Harper, 1790, 160.
29. John Zephaniah Holwell, 'The Religious Tenets of the Gentoos', in P. J. Marshall (ed.), *The British Discovery of Hinduism in the Eighteenth Century*, Cambridge: Cambridge University Press, 1970, 96.
30. Andrea Major, *Pious Flames: European Encounters with Sati 1500–1830*, New Delhi: Oxford University Press, 2006.
31. Parliamentary Papers, 18, 1821 (749), Extract Bengal Judicial Consultations, 7 February 1805, 24–6.
32. Ibid.
33. Ibid.
34. Parliamentary Papers, 18, 1821 (749), Extract Bengal Judicial Consultations, 17 April 1813, 32–4.

35. Lata Mani, 'Production of an Official Discourse on "Sati" in Early Nineteenth Century Bengal', *Economic and Political Weekly*, 21, 17, 1986, WS32–40.
36. Ashis Nandy, 'Sati: A Nineteenth Century Tale of Women, Violence and Protest', in *At the Edge of Psychology: Essays in Politics and Culture*, Delhi: Oxford University Press, 1980.
37. Andrew Porter, 'Religion, Missionary Enthusiasm, and Empire', in Andrew Porter (ed.), *The Oxford History of the British Empire*, Oxford: Oxford University Press, 1999, 230; Sydney Smith, *The Works of Sydney Smith*, London: Longmans, Green, Reader, and Dyer, 1859, 120.
38. *Asiatic Journal*, 13, 1822, 447.
39. Cited in V. N. Datta, *Sati: A Historical, Social and Philosophical Enquiry into the Hindu Right of Widow Burning*, New Delhi: Manohar, 1987, 146.
40. Byron Farwell, *Queen Victoria's Little Wars*, London: W. W. Norton & Co., 1985, 34.
41. Doniger, '"I Have Scinde"', 940.
42. Farwell, *Queen Victoria's Little Wars*, 36.
43. Sarah Ansari, 'The Sind Blue Books of 1843 and 1844: The Political "Laundering" of Historical Evidence', *The English Historical Review*, 120, 485, 2005, 35–65.
44. Farwell, *Queen Victoria's Little Wars*, 35.
45. Ibid., 34–5.
46. Napier, *History*, 33–4.
47. Ibid., 34.
48. Ansari, 'Sind Blue Books', 41.
49. William Napier Bruce, *Life of General Sir Charles Napier*, London: Murray, 1885.
50. G. C. Spivak, 'Can the Subaltern Speak?', in Patrick Williams and Laura Chrisman (eds), *Colonial Discourse and Post-colonial Theory: A Reader*, Hemel Hempstead: Harvester, 1993, 93.
51. National Archives of India, Home Department Records, POLICE: No. 44–6, 18 June 1870.
52. National Archives of India, Home Department Records, JUDICIAL: No. 31, 3 September 1870.
53. National Archives of India, Home Department Records, Public: No. 260, 12 July 1904, PART B.
54. National Archives of India, Home Department Records, Public: No. 260, July 1904, PART B.
55. National Archives of India, Home Department Records, Public: No. 120–1, December 1903, PART B.
56. National Archives of India, Home Department Records, Public: No. 108–9, December 1904, PART B.

57. National Archives of India, Home Department Records, Public: No. 120–1, December 1903, PART B.
58. For an extended discussion of narratives of the miraculous sati and intersections between this and revivalist/nationalist defences of sati, see Andrea Major, 'The Burning of Sampati Kuer: Sati and the Politics of Imperialism, Nationalism and Revivalism in 1920s India', *Gender & History*, 20, 2, 2008, 228–47.
59. National Archives of India, Home Department Records, Public: No. 120–1, December 1903, PART B.
60. National Archives of India, Home Department Records, Police: File No. 132/30, 1930.
61. Ibid.
62. R. J. Hirst, 'Suttee: A Modern Instance', *The Police Journal*, 2, 2, 1929, 309.

5. 'UNENCUMBERED BY THE SCRUPLES OF JUSTICE AND GOOD FAITH': THE COLONIAL ACHIEVEMENTS OF RAFFLES IN SOUTH-EAST ASIA

1. Nigel Biggar, *Colonialism: A Moral Reckoning*, London: William Collins, 2023, 2.
2. Ibid., 323.
3. Ibid., 76.
4. Ibid.
5. Ibid., 66.
6. Ibid., 61. As his main source, Biggar used Victoria Glendinning, *Raffles and the Golden Opportunity*, London: Profile, 2012, xv, 45, 121, 198–9.
7. Gareth Knapman, 'Settler Colonialism and Usurping Malay Sovereignty in Singapore', *Journal of Southeast Asian Studies*, 52, 3, 2021, 418–40, DOI: 10.1017/S0022463421000606
8. Original orders issued to the Java expedition—'conquer Java, destroy French military installations and hand the island over to the Javanese'. Peter Carey, *The Power of Prophecy: Prince Dipanagara and the End of an Old Order in Java, 1785–1855*, n.p.: KITLV Press, 2008, 36; Major William Thorn, *The Conquest of Java*, n.p.: T. Egerton, Military Library, 1815.
9. C. E. Wurtzburg, *Raffles of the Eastern Isles*, London: Hodder and Stoughton, 1954, 117.
10. John Bastin, 'Palembang in 1811 and 1812 (Part II)', *Bijdragen tot de taal-, land- en volkenkunde/Journal of the Humanities and Social Sciences of Southeast Asia*, 110, 1, 1954, 64–88, at 66, https://doi.org/10.1163/22134379-90002392
11. Ahmat Adam, *Letters of Sincerity: The Raffles Collection of Malay Letters (1780–1824)*, Kuala Lumpur: Malaysian Branch of the Royal Asiatic Society, 2009, 251.

12. Ibid.
13. Ibid., 254.
14. Ibid.
15. Ibid., 259.
16. Bastin, 'Palembang in 1811 and 1812', 65.
17. Adam, *Letters of Sincerity*, 263.
18. 'Java Factory Records', India Office Records IOR G/21/65, British Library, 89 (251).
19. 'Java Factory Records', India Office Records IOR G/21/64, British Library, 26–9.
20. IOR G/21/64, 26–9.
21. John D. Grainger, *Lieutenant General Sir Samuel Auchmuty, 1756–1822: The Military Life of an American Loyalist and Imperial General*, Barnsley: Casemate Publishers, 2018, 237; *Java Government Gazette*, Batavia, Saturday, 18 July 1812, 2, lists the Lieutenant Colonel's share of the prize from Yogyakarta as 16,984 Spanish dollars.
22. 'Five Ways to Compute the Relative Value of a U.K. Pound Amount, 1270 to Present', MeasuringWorth, 2022, www.measuringworth.com/ukcompare
23. *Java Government Gazette*, Batavia, Saturday, 4 July 1812, 8.
24. 'Copies of Mr. Fox and Mr. Pitt's East-India Bills', in *The Parliamentary Register of History of the Proceedings and Debates of the House of Commons; Containing an Account of the Most Interesting Speeches and Motions; Accurate Copies of the Most Remarkable Letters and Papers; Of the Most Material Evidence, Petitions, &c. Laid Before and Offered to the House, during the Fourth Session of the Fifteenth Parliament. 1784-01-24–1784-03-24*, 1784, 325.
25. Nicholas B. Dirks, *The Scandal of Empire: India and the Creation of Imperial Britain*, Cambridge, MA: Belknap Press of Harvard University Press, 2006; Gareth Knapman, *Race and British Colonialism in South-East Asia, 1770–1870*, New York: Routledge, 2017, 18.
26. Sankar Muthu, *Enlightenment against Empire*, Princeton, NJ: Princeton University Press, 2003; Jennifer Pitts, *A Turn to Empire: The Rise of Imperial Liberalism in Britain and France*, Princeton, NJ: Princeton University Press, 2005; Dirks, *Scandal of Empire*.
27. 'Copies of Mr. Fox and Mr. Pitt's East-India Bills', 325.
28. IOR G/21/64, 33–5.
29. Thorn, *Conquest of Java*, 166.
30. Quoted in Bastin, 'Palembang in 1811 and 1812 (Part II)', 67.
31. Report of Phillips, Wardenaar and Hare, [6] December 1811, Bengal Civil Colonial Consultations, Range 167, vol. 42. Consultations of September 4, 1813; cited in Bastin, 'Palembang in 1811 and 1812 (Part II)', 67.
32. IOR G/21/65, 89 (251).

33. Thorn, *Conquest of Java*.
34. Ibid., 122–3.
35. Crawfurd's first draft of the account leading up to war is contained in IOR G/21/64. This was redrafted and improved in IOR G/21/65. Both accounts are technically anonymous. We know the account in IOR G/21/64 is written by Crawfurd because of his distinctive handwriting style. See IOR G/21/64, 63–4.
36. Thorn, *Conquest of Java*, 123.
37. IOR G/21/65, 39/200.
38. Marinus Lodewijk van Deventer, *Het Nederlandsch gezag over Java en onderhoorigheden sedert 1811: Verzameling van onuitgegeven stukken uit de koloniale en andere archieven, Volume 1, Het nederlandsch gezag over Java en onderhoorigheden sedert 1811: verzameling van onuitgegeven stukken uit de koloniale en andere archieven*, S'Gravenhage: M. Nijhoff, 1891, 318.
39. Thorn, *Conquest of Java*, 123, 177.
40. IOR G/21/65, 144.
41. Ibid.
42. Ibid.
43. 'The Sultan of Djocjocarta', *The Examiner*, 269, Sunday, 21 February 1813, 121.
44. Hyde Villiers, 'Report from the Select Committee on the Affairs of the East India Company; With Minutes of Evidence in Six Parts, and an Appendix and Index to Each', *Parliamentary Papers*, 1831; 'Letter from John Crawfurd, Esq., to Thomas Hyde Villiers, Esq. 24 February 1832', Appendix No. 8, page 93. The office of 'Resident' was a political office in the Company that facilitated indirect rule. It operated as a form of diplomatic post; however, the Resident controlled all communication between the native ruler and the Company. The Resident was also meant to advise the native ruler on political matters; Michael H. Fisher, *Indirect Rule in India: Residents and the Residency System 1764–1857*, Oxford: Oxford University Press, 1991, 60–3.
45. Villiers, 'Report from the Select Committee', Appendix No. 8, Crawfurd lists 'Hydrabad, Oude and Mysore, or the Guicowar' as examples of princely states.
46. Ibid., 93.
47. A translation of the 'Babad Bĕdhah ing Ngayogyakarta' is the subject of Peter Carey, *The British in Java, 1811–1816: A Javanese Account*, Oxford: Oxford University Press, 1992.
48. Carey, *Power of Prophecy*, 85.
49. Raffles, *Memoir*, 130.
50. C. U. Aitchison (ed.), *A Collection of Treaties, Engagements, and Sunnuds, Relating to India and Neighbouring Countries*, vol. 1, London: Longmans, Green, Reader, and Dyer, 1862, 291.
51. Thomas Stamford Raffles, 'Arrangements with the Sultan and Toomoongong',

7 June 1823, in J. R. Logan (ed.), 'Singapore Notices', *Journal of the Indian Archipelago*, 1853, 344.
52. Abdullah bin Abdul Kadir, *Hikayat Abdullah*, Oxford: Oxford University Press, 1970, 159.
53. H. Eric Miller, 'Extracts from the Letters of Col. Nahuijs', *Journal of the Malayan Branch of the Royal Asiatic Society*, 19, 2, 1941, 196.
54. Ibid., 196
55. Villiers, 'Report from the Select Committee', Appendix No. 8, 98.
56. Raffles, *History of Java*, I, vi.
57. Ibid., 232.
58. James Brooke and John C. Templer, *The Private Letters of Sir James Brooke, K.C. B Rajah of Sarawak*, vol. 1, London: Richard Bentley, 1853, 9, 11–12.
59. Raffles minute on land tenure in Java, 267.
60. Ibid., 268.
61. Bastin, 'Palembang in 1811 and 1812 (Part II)', native policies of Raffles, 58.
62. Ibid., 69.
63. Ibid., 118–19 and Knapman, 'Settler Colonialism'.
64. 'J Crawfurd to G Swinton 10 January 1823', reproduced in J. R. Logan (ed.), *The Journal of the Indian Archipelago and Eastern Asia*, 9, Singapore: Jacob Baptist, 1855, 461.
65. Biggar, *Colonialism*, 61.
66. Thomas Stamford Raffles, 'Report to the Bengal Government on the Laws and Regulations of Singapore', 29 March 1823, in Sophia Raffles (ed.), *Memoir of the Life and Public Services of Sir Thomas Stamford Raffles*, London: James Duncan, 1835, 543–4.
67. The geographical imagery of India was much greater than it is today. For the Company officials, India extended into Southeast Asia, and the presence of Hindu statues in Java represented a claim for Raffles that Java should be part of Britain's Indian empire.
68. Raffles, 'Letter to the Rev. Dr Raffles', in ibid., 548–9.
69. Shawana Herzog, *Negotiating Abolition: The Antislavery Project in the British Straits Settlements, 1786–1843*, London: Bloomsbury Academic, 2021, 87.
70. Adam, *Letters of Sincerity*, 168, 198, 328, 329, 335, 349.
71. Ibid., 328.
72. Tim Hannigan, *Raffles and the British Invasion of Java*, Singapore: Monsoon Books, 2012, 129.
73. 'Extract, Bengal Civil Colonial Consultation, 17 October 1812, Government of Java to the Right Honourable Gilbert Lord Minto, Governor General, etc. Fort William', *Correspondence on State of Slavery in Territories under Rule of East India Company, and Slave Trade* (Nineteenth-Century House of Commons Sessional Papers: 24, 125), 160.

74. Ibid., 157.
75. Kadir, *Hikayat Abdullah*, 182–4.
76. Herzog, *Negotiating Abolition*, 2.
77. Free trade is actually rarely mentioned in *The Wealth of Nations*, although Smith in his frequent criticisms of mercantilism supports it by implication. Free trade in Smith is usually not positively defined so much as espoused by the absence of such things as excise duties, tariffs and other government restrictions on trade. For a discussion of this and the few instances where Smith articulated the virtues of free trade, see Mary Quilty, 'British Economic Thought and Colonization in Southeat Asia, 1776–1850', PhD thesis, University of Sydney, 2001, 89–90.
78. John Bastin, 'Introduction', in Sophia Raffles and John Bastin (eds), *Memoir of the Life and Public Services of Sir Thomas Stamford Raffles; With an Introduction by John Bastin*, Oxford: Oxford University Press, 1991 [1835].
79. See Tze Shiung Ng, 'The Ideological Origins of the Founding of Singapore', in Gareth Knapman, Anthony Milner and Mary Quilty (eds), *Liberalism and the British Empire in Southeast Asia*, n.p.: Routledge, 2019, 68–95, at 65, his source material for the quotations are: Stamford Raffles, 'On the Administration of the Eastern Islands in 1819', in Raffles, *Memoir*, Appendix 16; Raffles to Peter Auber, 6 December 1821, Raffles, *Memoir*, 503.
80. See Tze Shiung Ng, 'Ideological Origins'; his source material is Stamford Raffles, 'On the Administration of the Eastern Islands in 1819', in Raffles, *Memoir*, Appendix 16; Raffles to Peter Auber, 6 December 1821, Raffles, *Memoir*, 503; Raffles to Minto (Raffles' 'Malay policy' paper), 10 June 1811, revised 20 September 1811, British Library, 'Raffles–Minto Papers', MSS Eur F148/7.
81. Timothy Barnard, 'Commemorating Raffles: The Creation of an Imperial Icon in Colonial Singapore', *Journal of Southeast Asian Studies*, 50, 4, 2019, 579–98, at 581, DOI: 10.1017/S0022463420000077
82. Ibid., 582.
83. 'Stamford Raffles', Westminster Abbey, www.westminster-abbey.org/abbey-commemorations/commemorations/stamford-raffles
84. 'William Wilberforce & Family', www.westminster-abbey.org/abbey-commemorations/commemorations/william-wilberforce-family#i15160
85. *The Straits Times* ran a column called 'An Anecdotal History of Singapore' along with a few articles in the *Straits Branch of the Royal Asiatic Society*. Excluding Sophia Raffles' biography of her husband, the first biography was not until 1897.
86. The Hotel was called Emerson's Hotel after its owner founder, Charles Emerson. It closed in September 1887 and reopened in December 1887 with the new name Raffles Hotel. Joanna H. S. Tan, 'Raffles Hotel', https://eresources.nlb.gov.sg/infopedia/articles/SIP_37_2005-01-05.html; Timothy Barnard, 'Com-

memorating Raffles: The Creation of an Imperial Icon in Colonial Singapore', *Journal of Southeast Asian Studies*, 50, 4, 2019, 579–98, at 594, DOI: 10.1017/S0022463420000077
87. Frederick Weld, 'Speech by Frederick Weld: The Straits Settlements and British Malaya', *The Straits Times Weekly Issue*, 16 July 1884, 9.
88. Ibid.
89. Ibid., 9.
90. Hugh Egerton, *Sir Stamford Raffles: England in the Far East*, London: T. F. Unwin, 1900, 1; Demetrius Boulger, *The Life of Sir Stamford Raffles*, London: Horace Marshall & Son, 1897, 1.
91. The 1972 label was a modernised version of an early statue of Raffles erected in 1919 outside the Victoria Theatre which stated: 'This tablet to the memory of Sir Stamford Raffles to whose foresight and genius Singapore owes its existence and prosperity was unveiled on February 6th 1919 the 100th Anniversary of the Foundation of the Settlement.'
92. Glendinning, *Raffles and the Golden Opportunity*, 12.

6. MY EMPIRE, RIGHT OR WRONG: RHODES, MILNER AND THE SOUTH AFRICAN WAR

1. 'South African Muddles', *Financial Times*, 31 January 1889.
2. Nigel Biggar, *Colonialism: A Moral Reckoning*, London: William Collins, 2023, 1–2. My own small contribution to this debate can be found in 'Rhodes Must Fall, Brexit, and Circuits of Knowledge and Influence', in S. Ward and A. Rasch (eds), *Embers of Empire in Brexit Britain*, London: Bloomsbury, 2019, 111–20.
3. Andrew Manson, *The Valiant Englishman: Christopher Bethell, Montshiwa's Barolong and the Bechuanaland Wars 1878–1886*, Pretoria: UNISA Press, 2021, 46.
4. Kevin Shillington, *Charles Warren: Royal Engineer in the Age of Empire*, Pretoria: Protea, 2021, 203, 238, vii.
5. Ibid., 259; See also Alan Lester, 'Christopher Bethell, Charles Warren and the Colonisation of the Southern Batswana', *South African Historical Journal*, 74 (2), 2022, 392–398.
6. J. Van der Poel, *The Jameson Raid*, Oxford: Oxford University Press, 1951, 35. See also D. Schreuder and J. Butler (eds), *Sir Graham Bower's Secret History of the Jameson Raid and the South African Crisis, 1895–1902*, Cape Town: Van Reibeeck Society, 2002.
7. Van der Poel, *Jameson Raid*, 201–2.
8. Ibid., 207, 231; Jeffrey Butler, *The Liberal Party and the Jameson Raid*, Oxford: Clarendon, 1968, 12–13; Rotberg, *The Founder*, 548–50.
9. A. Milner to G. Parkin, 28 April 1897, Milner to Chamberlain, 23 February 1898, in C. Headlam (ed.), *The Milner Papers: South Africa 1899–1905 Vol. 1*, London: Cassell, 1931, 42, 222.

10. Milner to Chamberlain [confidential], 2 August 1897 in Headlam, *Milner Papers Vol. 1*, 72–3.
11. Biggar, *Colonialism*, 119–22.
12. Milner to Asquith 18 November 1897, in Headlam, *Milner Papers Vol. 1*, 178.
13. A. Milner to P. Fitzpatrick, 28 November 1899 [Very Confidential], in C. Headlam (ed.), *The Milner Papers: South Africa 1899–1905 Vol. 2*, London: Cassell, 1933, 35.
14. D. Lowry, 'Introduction: Not just a "Teatime" War', in D. Lowry (ed.), *The South African War Reappraised*, Manchester: Manchester University Press, 2000, 2.
15. G. Cuthbertson, 'Pricking the "nonconformist conscience": Religion against the South African War', in Lowry, *South African War Reappraised*, 172–3, 174.
16. Heloise Brown, *'The Truest Form of Patriotism': Pacifist Feminism in Britain, 1870–1902*, Manchester: Manchester University Press, 2003, 174–6; Biggar, *Colonialism*, 261–2, 406–7.
17. P. Bridgen, *The Labour Party and the Politics of War and Peace, 1900–1924*, Woodbridge: Boydell, 2009, 23, 35, 41; Stephen Koss (ed.), *The Pro-Boers: The Anatomy of an Antiwar Movement*, Chicago, IL: University of Chicago Press, 1973, 54.
18. A. S. Thompson, 'The Language of Imperialism and the Meanings of Empire', *Journal of British Studies*, 36, 1997, 148.
19. Heartfield, *Aborigines' Protection Society*, 280, 282
20. R. T. Steam, 'War Correspondents and Colonial War, c.1870–1900', in J. M. MacKenzie (ed.), *Popular Imperialism and the Military 1850–1950*, Manchester: Manchester University Press, 1992, 139, 141.
21. P. J. Cain, *Hobson and Imperialism: Radicalism, New Liberalism, and Finance 1887–1938*, Oxford: Oxford University Press, 2002, 7, 92–3.
22. J. A. Hobson, *Imperialism: A Study*, New York: Cambridge University Press, 2010 [London, 1902], 85.
23. In the South African context, these themes are explored in Hobson's *The War in South Africa: Its Causes and Effects*, London: Nisbet, 1900. See especially Chapters 2 and 3.
24. P. J. Cain and A. G. Hopkins, *British Imperialism: Innovation and Expansion 1588–1914*, London: Longman, 1993, 16–17.
25. This much-quoted pronouncement (including by Lenin in his *Imperialism, the Highest Stage of Capitalism*) is reported to have been said by Rhodes to W. T. Stead in 1895.
26. Hobson, *War in South Africa*, 231, 61.
27. L. Curtis, 'The Place of Subject People in the Empire', 9 May 1907, 11, 13, 25, in 'Fortnightly Club' papers, A146, Historical Papers, University of the Witwatersrand.

28. Biggar, *Colonialism*, xiv–xv, 254–6, 408.
29. Eric Stokes, 'The British Moment in South Africa', *The Journal of African History*, 7, 3, 1966, 528.
30. Biggar, *Colonialism*, 322, n. 17.
31. See e.g. Mae Ngai, 'Trouble on the Rand: The Chinese Question in South Africa and the Apogee of White Settlerism', *International Labor and Working Class History*, 91, Spring 2017, 59–78.
32. Biggar, *Colonialism*, 158. He offers the term 'overwrought' elsewhere to deflect moral criticisms.
33. Ibid., 261.
34. Ibid., 406–7.
35. See, for example, Cain and Hopkins, *British Imperialism*.
36. Ibid.
37. These theories were propounded by E. Belfort Bax, H. M. Hyndman and Robert Blatchford, for example. See J. Davis, 'Pro-Boers (act. 1899–1902)', *Oxford Dictionary of National Biography*, 24 May 2008, https://www.oxforddnb.com/view/10.1093/ref:odnb/9780198614128.001.0001/odnb-9780198614128-e-95545, accessed 29/1/24.
38. Biggar might have remembered this Webb quote from his undergraduate tutorials. It appears on p. 29 of Le May's *British Supremacy*.
39. Biggar, *Colonialism*, 252–3.
40. See Brian Willan, *Sol Plaatje: A Life of Solomon Tshekisho Plaatje 1876–1932*, Auckland Park: Jacana Media, 2018.
41. See for example C. Gerdov, 'A Scandinavian "Magna Charta"? The Scandinavian Corps and the Politics of Memory in South Africa (1899–1927)', *Historia*, 61, 2, 2016, 54–78; A. Davidson, and I. Filatova, *The Russians and the Anglo-Boer War*, Cape Town: Human & Rousseau, 1998; D. McCracken, *Forgotten Protest: Ireland and the Anglo-Boer War*, Belfast: Ulster Historical Foundation, 2003; D. Cammack, *The Rand at War 1899–1902*, London: J. Currey, 1990.
42. Biggar, *Colonialism*, 71. See Alan Lester, 'The British Empire in the Culture War: Nigel Biggar's Colonialism: A Moral Reckoning', *The Journal of Imperial and Commonwealth History*, 51, 4, 2023, 763–95, DOI: 10.1080/03086534.2023.2209947
43. Speech by Rhodes cited in W. Beinart, 'Cecil Rhodes: Racial Segregation in the Cape Colony and Violence in Zimbabwe', *Journal of Southern African Studies*, 48, 3, 2022, 583.
44. Biggar, *Colonialism*, 372, n. 27.
45. Farai Nyika and Johan Fourie, 'Black Disenfranchisement in the Cape Colony, c.1887–1909: Challenging the Numbers', *Journal of Southern African Studies*, 46, 3, 2020, 462.
46. See also Lester, 'British Empire in the Culture War'.

47. S. Trapido, 'The Origins of the Cape Franchise Qualifications of 1853', *Journal of African History*, 5, 1, 1964, 53. See also my *Commonwealth of Knowledge: Science, Sensibility and White South Africa 1820–2000*, Oxford: Oxford University Press, 2006.
48. See e.g. M. Tamarkin, *Cecil Rhodes and the Cape Afrikaners: The Imperial Colossus and the Colonial Parish Pump*, n.p.: London, 1996.
49. See Jeff Guy, *The Destruction of the Zulu Kingdom: The Civil War in Zululand, 1879–1884*, Pietermaritzburg: University of KwaZulu-Natal Press, 1999; Alan Lester, Kate Boehme and Peter Mitchell, *Ruling the World: Freedom, Civilisation and Liberalism in the Nineteenth Century British Empire*, Cambridge: Cambridge University Press, 2021.
50. Biggar, *Colonialism*, 119–20.
51. See for example Shula Marks and Stanley Trapido, 'Lord Milner and the South African State', *History Workshop Journal*, 8, 1979, 50–80, http://www.jstor.org/stable/4288258, and Saul Dubow, 'Colonial Nationalism, the Milner Kindergarten and the Rise of "South Africanism", 1902–10', *History Workshop Journal*, 43, 1997, 53–85, http://www.jstor.org/stable/4289491, accessed 5/3/24.
52. Margery Perham, *The Colonial Reckoning: The Reith Lectures, 1961*, London: Collins, 1961; See also C. Brad Faught, *Into Africa: The Imperial Life of Margery Perham*, London: I. B. Tauris, 2011.
53. Biggar, *Colonialism*, 275, 286–7.
54. Beinart, 'Cecil Rhodes', 581–603; Biggar, *Colonialism*, 320–1, 331–2.
55. Biggar, *Colonialism*, 340, 402, 407.
56. I am not, as it happens, a proponent of the Hobson thesis of underconsumption, but I do recognise its significance.
57. See articles such as 'Measuring the Elephant: The Morality of the British Empire' on the History Reclaimed website, https://historyreclaimed.co.uk/measuring-the-elephant-the-morality-of-the-british-empire, accessed 5/3/24.

7. WRITTEN ON THE CITY: IMPERIAL BRITAIN AND CHINA

1. For some surveys, see English Heritage, 'London Statues and the History of Empire', https://www.english-heritage.org.uk/visit/london-statues-and-monuments/london-statues-empire/; Alan Lester, 'London's Imperial Statues, Black Lives Matter and the Culture War', https://blogs.sussex.ac.uk/snapshotsofempire/2021/04/28/londons-imperial-statues-black-lives-matter-and-the-culture-war/; 'Sculptures at the Foreign and Commonwealth Office', Statues: Hither and Thither, https://statues.vanderkrogt.net/object.php?webpage=CO&record=gblo035, all accessed 29/10/23; G. Alex Bremner, 'Nation and Empire in the Government Architecture of Mid-Victorian London: The Foreign and India Office Reconsidered', *The Historical Journal*, 48, 3, 2005, 703–42; see also

Caroline Dakers, 'Sigismund Goetze and the Decoration of the Foreign Office Staircase: "Melodrama, Pathos and High Camp"', *Journal of the Decorative Arts Society*, 21, 1997, 54–66.

2. Here and throughout, I draw on my books *The Scramble for China: Foreign Devils in the Qing Empire, 1832–1914*, London: Allen Lane, 2011, and *Out of China: How the Chinese Ended the Era of Foreign Domination*, London: Allen Lane, 2017; see also: Matthew Heaslip, *Gunboats, Empire, and the China Station: The Royal Navy in 1920s East Asia*, London: Bloomsbury, 2020; and on military intelligence: James L. Hevia, *The Imperial Security State: British Colonial Knowledge and Empire-Building in Asia*, Cambridge: Cambridge University Press, 2012.

3. The charge routinely made by the Chinese was that the *Amethyst* had fired on the ill-fated vessel and that hundreds of passengers died. This was not true, but by following it the British had drawn communist fire on to the civilian ship. *Amethyst* had also run into and sunk a junk. Lives were lost. *Ta Kung Pao* (Hong Kong), 3 August 1949, 1; Nanking No. 1152, 2 August 1949, The National Archives (hereafter TNA), FO 371/75895; stimulating analysis of the impact of the episode can be found in Malcolm H. Murfett, 'A Pyrrhic Victory: HMS Amethyst and the Damage to Anglo-Chinese Relations in 1949', *War and Society*, 9, 1, 1991, 121–40, and more widely in his *Hostage on the Yangtze: Britain, China and the Amethyst Crisis of 1949*, New York: Naval Institute Press, 1991.

4. Nigel Biggar, *Empire: A Moral Reckoning*, London: William Collins, 2023, 220.

5. Biggar quotes Sun, at length, extolling colonial Hong Kong as an exemplar for China (ibid., 198–9). But in this speech, given at the University of Hong Kong in February 1923, Sun was trying to flatter the British, whose support would have been useful, and to appease some in his coalition of supporters. Nothing came of it, and instead Sun cemented his alliance with the Soviets, which was already developing: Marie-Claire Bergère, *Sun Yat-sen*, Stanford: Stanford University Press, 1998, 311–14.

6. T. G. Otte, *The China Question: Great Power Rivalry and British Isolation, 1894–1905*, Oxford: Oxford University Press, 2007.

7. Complexities: Jürgen Osterhammel, 'Semi-colonialism and Informal Empire in Twentieth-Century China: Towards a Framework of Analysis', in Wolfgang J. Mommsen and Jürgen Osterhammel (eds), *Imperialism and After: Continuities and Discontinuities*, London: Allen & Unwin, 1986, 290–314. Qing Empire: Peter Purdue, *China Marches West: The Qing conquest of Central Asia*, Cambridge, MA: Harvard University Press, 2005.

8. Essential analyses can be found in: Rana Mitter, *A Bitter Revolution: China's Struggle with the Modern World*, Oxford: Oxford University Press, 2004; Dong Wang, *China's Unequal Treaties: Narrating National History*, Lanham, MD: Rowman & Littlefield, 2005; William A. Callahan, *China: The Pessoptimist*

Nation, Oxford: Oxford University Press, 2009; Zheng Wang, *Never Forget National Humiliation: Historical Memory in Chinese Politics and Foreign Policy*, New York: Columbia University Press, 2012.

9. Various episodes are discussed in: Paul A. Cohen, *China and Christianity: The Missionary Movement and the Growth of Chinese Antiforeignism, 1860–1870*, Cambridge, MA: Harvard University Press, 1963; Henrietta Harrison, '"A Penny for the Little Chinese": The French Holy Childhood Association in China, 1843–1951', *American Historical Review*, 113, 1, 2008, 72–92; Mary Backus Rankin, 'The Ku-t'ien Incident (1895): Christians versus the Ts'ai-Hui', *Papers on China*, 15, 1961, 30–61; Songchuan Chen, '"Shame on you!": Competing Narratives of the Nation in the Laoxikai Incident and the Tianjin Anti-French Campaign, 1916–1917', *Twentieth Century China*, 37, 2, 2012, 121–38.

10. Paul A. Cohen, *Discovering History in China: American Historical Writing on the Recent Chinese Past*, New York: Columbia University Press, 1984; good examples include: Pär Cassel, *Grounds of Judgment: Extraterritoriality and Imperial Power in Nineteenth-Century China and Japan*, Oxford: Oxford University Press, 2012; Ruth Rogaski, *Hygienic Modernity: Meanings of Health and Disease in Treaty-Port China*, Berkeley, CA: University of California Press, 2004.

11. See the accompanying book: Jessica Harrison-Hall and Julia Lovell (eds), *China's Hidden Century: 1796–1912*, London: British Museum, 2023.

12. Capt. Adrian Jones, *Memoirs of a Soldier Artist*, London: Stanley Paul & Co., 1933, 109–10. A useful short survey of the politics of the monument's creation and history can be found in John Bolt, 'The Battle of Graspan and the Royal Marines', *Topmasts: The Quarterly Newsletter of the Society for Naval Research*, 30, May 2019, 10–13. The monument is also known as the 'Graspan Memorial'.

13. Here I draw on Alexandra Gerstein's introduction to her edited volume, *Display and Displacement: Sculpture and the Pedestal from Renaissance to Post-modern*, London: Courtauld Institute of Art Forum and Paul Holberton Publishing, 2007, 11.

14. *The Daily Telegraph*, 27 April 1903, 7.

15. Peter Donaldson, *Remembering the South African War: Britain and the Memory of the Anglo-Boer War, from 1899 to the Present*, Liverpool: Liverpool University Press, 2013, 66–7.

16. Bolt, 'The Battle of Graspan and the Royal Marines'. Bolt provides fuller context in 'The Sons of Neptune and of Mars: Organisational Identity and Mission in the Royal Marines, 1827–1927', unpublished PhD dissertation, University of Portsmouth, 2020.

17. This paragraph draws on Bolt, 'The Sons of Neptune and of Mars', 108–16; the quotation from Conan Doyle is on 111.

18. The best narrative remains Paul A. Cohen, *History in Three Keys: The Boxers as Event, Experience and Myth*, New York: Columbia University Press, 1997, which also places Boxer beliefs in comparative perspective; Lanxin Xiang is useful on the outbreak of the war: *The Origins of the Boxer War: A Multinational Study*, London: RoutledgeCurzon, 2003.
19. Robert Coltman, *Beleaguered in Peking: The Boxer's War against the Foreigner*, Philadelphia, PA: F. A. Davis Company, 1901, 96–8.
20. On De Normann, see my blog post 'Lost Monuments and Memorials: Shanghai's De Normann Cross', https://robertbickers.net/2023/08/08/lost-monuments-and-memorials-shanghais-de-normann-cross, accessed 8/8/23.
21. See, for example, Jan Stuart, *The Admonitions Scroll*, London: British Museum, 2014, 56–7. James Hevia provides a striking account of the journeys of loot into British museums and galleries in *English Lessons: The Pedagogy of Imperialism in Nineteenth-Century China*, Durham, NC: Duke University Press, 2003, 74–118.
22. Ashley Jackson, *Buildings of Empire*, Oxford: Oxford University Press, 2013, 242; Tori Smith, '"A grand work of noble conception": The Victoria Memorial and Imperial London', in Felix Driver and David Gilbert (eds), *Imperial Cities: Landscape, Display and Identity*, Manchester: Manchester University Press, 2017, 21–39; Lt General A. French, Chairman, Royal Marines Memorial Committee to Deputy Adjutant, Royal Marines, 31 October 1901, in TNA, WORK 20/55; Trafalgar Square statuary: Sue Lavern, 'The Fourth Plinth or the Vicissitudes of Public Sculpture', in Gerstein, *Display and Displacement*, 132–7.
23. This controversy can be followed in articles, editorials and letters in *The Times*: 28 October 1939, 7; 3 September 1940, 9; 10 October 1940, 5; 13 October 1940, 5; 17 December 1940, 5; 24 December 1940, 5; 30 January 1941, 2; 1 September 1945, 10; weeping and wailing: *Aberdeen Evening Express*, 17 February 1941, 2; Berkhamsted: *The Illustrated London News*, 12 July 1941, 5; 26 September 1942, 17. For a stimulating essay on the history of the problem of statues and memorials in London, see Durba Ghosh, 'When Rhodes Was Not Built', Historical Transactions, https://blog.royalhistsoc.org/2021/06/13/when-rhodes-was-not-built, accessed 29/10/23.
24. Minutes, 13 and 28 December 1940, 8 May 1943, 19 June 1946, in TNA WORK 20/239; Cmnd. 7698. 'Summary Report of the Ministry of Works for the Period 1st January 1948 to 31st December 1948', London: HMSO, 1949, 19; *The Daily Telegraph*, 20 November 1948, 2; see also *The Times*, 11 August 1949, 10.
25. *The Times*, 26 November 1925, 13; Adjutant General, Royal Marines, to Secretary, H.M. Office of Works, 22 November 1929: TNA: WORK 20/138. There is one record of an attempt to hold a small ceremony to mark the 'gallantry of our late comrades' in the Boxer War in August 1909, on the anniver-

sary of the relief of the siege. The request, from the honorary secretary of a newly formed Royal Marines Old Comrades Association, was turned down by civil servants as a side effect of a standing rule to thwart attempts to use monuments in the royal parks for sectarian religious purposes: TNA, WORK 20/55, letter from W. M. P. Cochrane, June 1909 and minutes.

26. The Royal Marines Charity, 'Our History', https://rma-trmc.org/about-us/charity-history, accessed 30/10/23.
27. William de Burgh Whyte to Secretary of State, February 1927: TNA, WORK 20/138; *The Tatler*, 5 February 1941, 28.

8. MORALITY AND THE HISTORY OF ABOLITION AND EMPIRE

1. Robert Tombs, 'Today's History Wars: Ideology, Propaganda, Careerism', History Reclaimed, 16 April 2023, https://historyreclaimed.co.uk/todays-history-wars-ideology-propaganda-careerism, accessed 16/10/23.
2. John Oldfield and Mary Wills, 'Remembering 1807: Lessons from the Archives', *History Workshop Journal*, 90, 2020, 253–72.
3. David Brion Davis, *Slavery and Human Progress*, New York: Oxford University Press, 1984; Seymour Drescher, *Abolition: A History of Slavery and Antislavery*, Cambridge: Cambridge University Press, 2009.
4. Thomas Clarkson, *History of the Rise, Progress, and Accomplishment of the Abolition of the African Slave Trade by the British Parliament*, 2 vols, Cambridge: Cambridge University Press, 1808; Priya Satia, *Time's Monster: How History Makes History*, Cambridge, MA: Belknap Press of Harvard University Press, 2020, 47.
5. W. E. H. Lecky, *The Natural History of European Morals*, 2 vols, n.p.: London, 1869, i, 161. For a subtle consideration of Lecky's dictum, see David Brion Davis, *Inhuman Bondage: The Rise and Fall of Slavery in the New World*, Oxford: Oxford University Press, 2006, 234.
6. Eric Williams, *Capitalism and Slavery*, New York: Russell & Russell, 1944.
7. Thomas Bender (ed.), *The Antislavery Debate: Capitalism and Abolitionism as a Problem in Historical Interpretation*, Berkeley, CA: University of California Press, 1992; Seymour Drescher, *Capitalism and Antislavery: British Mobilization in Comparative Perspective*, Oxford: Oxford University Press, 1987.
8. Criticism quoted and response provided in Nigel Biggar, *Colonialism: A Moral Reckoning*, London: William Collins, 2023, 8.
9. See, for example: David Turley, *The Culture of English Antislavery, 1780–1860*, London: Routledge, 1991; Kinga Makovi, 'The Signatures of Social Structure: Petitioning for the Abolition of the Slave Trade in Manchester', *Social Science History*, 43, 2019, 625–52; J. R. Oldfield, *The Ties That Bind: Transatlantic Abolitionism in the Age of Reform, c.1820–1865*, Liverpool: Liverpool University Press, 2020.

10. Christopher Leslie Brown, *Moral Capital: Foundations of British Abolitionism*, Chapel Hill, NC: University of North Carolina Press, 2006, 437–46.
11. See, for example, Catherine Hall, Nicholas Draper, Keith McClelland, Katie Donington, and Rachel Lang, *Legacies of British Slave-Ownership: Colonial Slavery and the Formation of Victorian Britain*, Cambridge: Cambridge University Press, 2014; Kathleen Paugh, *The Politics of Reproduction: Race, Medicine, and Fertility in the Age of Abolition*, Oxford: Oxford University Press, 2017; Aaron Graham, 'The Colonial Sinews of Imperial Power: The Political Economy of Jamaican Taxation, 1768–1838', *Journal of Imperial and Commonwealth History*, 45, 2017, 199. The present author is indebted to the late Aaron Graham for discussion of this point, as well as his exemplary scholarship on the topic.
12. Gelien Matthews, *Caribbean Slave Revolts and the British Abolitionist Movement*, Baton Rouge, LA: Louisiana State University Press, 2006.
13. Biggar, *Colonialism*, 54–5.
14. Katharine Gerbner, *Christian Slavery: Conversion and Race in the Protestant Atlantic World*, Philadelphia, PA: University of Pennsylvania Press, 2018.
15. David Richardson, *Principles and Agents: The British Slave Trade and Its Abolition*, New Haven, CT: Yale University Press, 2022.
16. John Coffey, '"Tremble, Britannia!": Fear, Providence and the Abolition of the Slave Trade, 1758—1807', *English Historical Review*, 127, 527, 2012, 844–81; Richard Huzzey, *Freedom Burning, Antislavery and Empire in Victorian Britain*, Ithaca, NY: Cornell University Press, 2012.
17. Lawrence Goldman, 'The British Campaigns against Slavery', History Reclaimed, 21 January 2023, https://historyreclaimed.co.uk/the-british-campaigns-against-slavery, accessed 29/10/2023.
18. Paugh, *Politics of Reproduction*.
19. Matthews, *Caribbean Slave Revolts*.
20. Roger Anstey, 'A Re-interpretation of the Abolition of the British Slave Trade, 1806–1807', *English Historical Review*, 87, 343, 1972, 304–32.
21. Biggar, *Colonialism*, 29.
22. Ibid., 13.
23. *Reading Mercury*, 19 March 1792, 2.
24. Seymour Drescher, *The Mighty Experiment: Free Labor versus Slavery in British Emancipation*, Oxford: Oxford University Press, 2004, 32–3.
25. Olaudah Equiano, *The Interesting Narrative and Other Writings*, ed. Vincent Carretta, London: Penguin, 2003 [1789], 235.
26. J. R. Oldfield, *Popular Politics and British Anti-slavery: The Mobilisation of Public Opinion against the Slave Trade 1787–1807*, Manchester: Manchester University Press, 1998; Richard Huzzey, 'A Microhistory of British Antislavery Petitioning', *Social Science History*, 43, 3, 2019, 599–623; Kinga Makovi, 'The Signatures of Social Structure: Petitioning for the Abolition of the Slave Trade in Manchester',

Social Science History, 43, 3, 2019, 625–52; Sami Pinarbasi, 'Manchester Antislavery, 1792–1807', *Slavery and Abolition*, 41, 2, 2020, 349–76.

27. Seymour Drescher, 'People and Parliament: The Rhetoric of the British Slave Trade', *Journal of Interdisciplinary History*, 20, 1990, 561–80.
28. Davis, *Slavery and Human Progress*.
29. Tombs, 'Today's History Wars'.
30. Biggar, *Colonialism*, 66.
31. Huzzey, *Freedom Burning*.
32. Richard Huzzey, 'Moral Geography of British Anti-slavery Responsibilities', *Transactions of the Royal Historical Society*, 22, 2012, 111–39.
33. Tombs, 'Today's History Wars'.
34. Thomas Holt, *The Problem of Freedom: Race, Labor, and Politics in Jamaica and Britain, 1832–1938*, Baltimore, MD: Johns Hopkins University Press, 1992.
35. Huzzey, *Freedom Burning*, 185.
36. Biggar, *Colonialism*, 7.
37. Jake Subryan Richards, 'Anti-slave-Trade Law, "Liberated Africans" and the State in the South Atlantic World, c.1839–1852', *Past & Present*, 241, 1, 2018, 179–219; Mary Wills, *Envoys of Abolition: British Naval Officers and the Campaign against the Slave Trade in West Africa*, Liverpool: Liverpool University Press, 2019; Lindsay Doulton, '"The Flag That Sets Us Free": Antislavery, Africans, and the Royal Navy in the Western Indian Ocean', in Robert Harms et al. (eds), *Indian Ocean Slavery in the Age of Abolition*, New Haven, CT: Yale University Press, 2013, 101–9.
38. Richard Huzzey, 'Politics of Slave-Trade Suppression', in Robert Burroughs and Richard Huzzey (eds), *The Suppression of the Atlantic Slave Trade: British Policies, Practices and Representations of Naval Coercion*, Manchester: Manchester University Press, 2015, 17–53.
39. Richards, 'Anti-slave-Trade Law'. I am grateful to Jake Subryan Richards for the chance to read his forthcoming book expanding on the topic.
40. Biggar, *Colonialism*, 62; Chaim D. Kaufmann and Robert A. Pape, 'Explaining Costly International Moral Action: Britain's Sixty-Year Campaign against the Atlantic Slave Trade', *International Organization*, 53, 4, 1999, 631–68.
41. Richards, 'Anti-slave-Trade Law'; Richard Anderson and Henry B. Lovejoy (eds), *Liberated Africans and the Abolition of the Slave Trade, 1807–1896*, Rochester, NY: University of Rochester Press, 2020.
42. Jenny Martinez, *The Slave Trade and the Origins of International Human Rights Law*, Oxford: Oxford University Press, 2012; Huzzey, *Freedom Burning*.
43. Robin Law, 'International Law and the British Suppression of the Atlantic Slave Trade', in Derek R. Peterson (ed.), *Abolitionism and Imperialism in Britain, Africa and the Atlantic*, Athens, OH: Ohio State University Press, 2010, 150–74.

44. Huzzey, *Freedom Burning*.
45. Biggar, *Colonialism*, 61–2.
46. Ibid., 5.
47. John Darwin, 'Imperialism and the Victorians: The Dynamics of Territorial Expansion', *English Historical Review*, 112, 447, 1997, 614–42.
48. Suzanne Miers, *Britain and the Ending of the Slave Trade*, London: Longman, 1975; Huzzey, *Freedom Burning*.
49. Miers, *Britain and the Ending of the Slave Trade*.
50. Amalia Ribi Forclaz, *Humanitarian Imperialism: The Politics of Anti-slavery Activism, 1880–1940*, Oxford: Oxford University Press, 2015; Christopher Gevers, 'Refiguring Slavery through International Law: The 1926 Slavery Convention, the "Native Labor Code" and Racial Capitalism', *Journal of International Economic Law*, 25, 2, 2022, 312–33.
51. Reginald Coupland, *The Anti-slavery Movement*, London: Oxford University Press, 1933.
52. Ribi Forclaz, *Humanitarian Imperialism*, 139–71.
53. Manisha Sinha, 'The Problem of Abolition in the Age of Capitalism', *American Historical Review*, 124, 1, 2019, 140–63, at 160.
54. Huzzey, *Freedom Burning*.
55. Robert Tombs, 'Are the History Wars Worth Fighting?', History Reclaimed, 4 October 2023, https://historyreclaimed.co.uk/are-the-history-wars-worth-fighting/, accessed 16/10/23.
56. Lawrence Goldman, 'The Royal Family and Slavery: Leave History to the Historians; Focus on the Future', History Reclaimed, 16 April 2023, https://historyreclaimed.co.uk/the-royal-family-and-slavery-leave-history-to-the-historians-focus-on-the-future/, accessed 10/10/23.
57. Tombs, 'Today's History Wars'.
58. Robert Tombs, 'The Rewriting of History Has Taken a Sinister Turn', *The Daily Telegraph*, 25 September 2023, https://www.telegraph.co.uk/news/2023/09/25/the-rewriting-of-history-has-taken-a-sinister-turn/, accessed 20/10/23.
59. Biggar, *Colonialism*, 7.
60. Tombs, 'Today's History Wars'.
61. Goldman, 'The British Campaigns against Slavery'.
62. Ibid.
63. Biggar, *Colonialism*, 7–8.
64. Ibid., 9.
65. Ibid., 14.
66. Ibid., 5
67. Robert Tombs, 'The "Anti-racist" Mission to Destroy Britain Is Working—and We Have Surrendered', *The Daily Telegraph*, 10 April 2023, https://www.

telegraph.co.uk/news/2023/04/10/the-anti-racist-mission-to-destroy-britain-is-working, accessed 31/10/23.
68. Robert Tombs and Alan Lester, 'Debating the British Empire', History Reclaimed, 1 February 2022, https://historyreclaimed.co.uk/debating-the-british-empire, accessed 31/10/23.
69. Goldman, 'Royal Family and Slavery'.
70. Brown, *Moral Capital*, 24–5; Huzzey, *Freedom Burning*, 136, 210–13. The latter author's frailties of expression must be responsible for the radical misapprehension of this point by Padraic X. Scanlan, 'Blood, Money and Endless Paper: Slavery and Capital in British Imperial History', *History Compass*, 14, 5, 2016, 218–30.
71. Aris Roussinos, 'How Liberals Made the British Empire', UnHerd, 20 September 2021, https://unherd.com/2021/09/how-liberals-made-the-british-empire, accessed 31/10/23.
72. Biggar, *Colonialism*, 9.
73. 'Should We Judge Historical Figures by the Morals of Today?', History Extra, 2018, https://www.historyextra.com/period/modern/historical-figures-statues-judge-morals-today, accessed 16/10/23.
74. As quoted by Fiona Parker, '"Brits feel guilt about the Empire because they know nothing about it", Oxford Don Tells Chalke Valley Festival', *The Daily Mail*, 1 July 2023, https://www.dailymail.co.uk/news/article-12254917/Brits-feel-guilt-Empire-know-Oxford-don-tells-festival.html, accessed 29/10/23.
75. *The Case of our Fellow-Creatures The Oppressed Africans*, n.p.: n.p., 1784, 4.
76. Joseph Woods, *Thoughts on the Slavery of the Negroes*, London: J. Phillips, 1784, 7–8, 23–4.
77. Biggar, *Colonialism*, 57.
78. Miranda Johnson, 'Decolonising Universities? Myth-Histories of the Nation and Challenges to Academic Freedom in Aotearoa New Zealand', *Transactions of the Royal Historical Society*, 1, 2023, 329–47.
79. 'About History Reclaimed', History Reclaimed, n.d., https://historyreclaimed.co.uk/about-history-reclaimed/, accessed 10/10/23.

9. A SHORT HISTORY OF A CONTROVERSIAL COMPARISON: EMPIRE AND FASCISM IN BLACK POLITICAL THOUGHT DURING THE 1930S

1. Aimé Césaire, *Discourse on Colonialism*, trans. Joan Pinkham, New York: Monthly Review Press, 2000, 36.
2. Cedric J. Robinson, 'Fascism and the Responses of Black Radical Theorists' [1990], in H. L. T. Quan (ed.), *Cedric J. Robinson: On Racial Capitalism, Black Internationalism and Cultures of Resistance*, London: Pluto Press, 2018, 152.

3. 'The Racial Consequences of Mr Churchill', Churchill College Cambridge, 12 February 2021, https://www.chu.cam.ac.uk/news/churchill-empire-and-race/racial-consequences-mr-churchill, accessed 3/10/23.
4. Craig Simpson, 'Churchill College Panel Claims Wartime PM Was a White Supremacist Leading an Empire "worse than the Nazis"', *The Daily Telegraph*, 11 February 2021, https://www.telegraph.co.uk/news/2021/02/11/churchill-white-supremacist-leading-empire-worse-nazis-claims, accessed 3/10/23; 'Times Letters: Churchill, Nazism and the British Empire', *The Times*, 13 February 2021, https://www.thetimes.co.uk/article/times-letters-churchill-nazism-and-the-british-empire-0vsm8lbvw, accessed 3/10/23.
5. Andrew Roberts, 'Why Race Warriors Who Hate Churchill Must Be Challenged, Says ANDREW ROBERTS', *The Daily Express*, 3 March 2021, https://www.chu.cam.ac.uk/news/churchill-empire-and-race/racial-consequences-mr-churchill, accessed 3/10/23.
6. Andrew Roberts and Zewditu Gebreyohanes, '"The Racial Consequences of Mr Churchill": A Review', London: Policy Exchange, 2021, 14.
7. Ibid., 13–14.
8. Kennetta Hammond Perry, *London Is the Place for Me: Black Britons, Citizenship, and the Politics of Race*, Oxford: Oxford University Press, 2015, 100–4.
9. Nigel Biggar, *Colonialism: A Moral Reckoning*, London: William Collins, 2023, 13, on imperial atrocities, see Chapter 5.
10. Ibid., Chapter 3.
11. Ibid., 71–2.
12. Ibid., 285.
13. Ibid., 286.
14. For colonial compliments, see ibid., 87, 167–70, 175–6, 198–200, 202, 205–6, 288, on Fanon, see 291–4.
15. Liam J. Liburd, 'The Politics of Race and the Future of British Political History', *The Political Quarterly*, 94, 2, 2023, 244–50.
16. 'The Racial Consequences of Mr Churchill', Churchill College, University of Cambridge, 13 February 2021, YouTube video, from 37:49 to 47:43, https://www.youtube.com/watch?v=wermPu-oG5w, accessed 3/10/23.
17. Leslie James, *George Padmore and Decolonization from Below: Pan-Africanism, the Cold War, and the End of Empire*, Basingstoke: Palgrave Macmillan, 2015, 17.
18. Ibid., 23–6.
19. Susan D. Pennybacker, *From Scottsboro to Munich: Race and Political Culture in 1930s Britain*, Oxford: Oxford University Press, 2009, 7, 31, 70.
20. James, *George Padmore*, 36.
21. David Beetham (ed.), *Marxists in the Face of Fascism: Writings by Marxists on Fascism from the Inter-war Period*, Manchester: Manchester University Press, 1983, 18.

22. 'Our Aims', *Negro Workers' Review*, 1, 1, January 1931, 4.
23. Barbara Bush, *Imperialism, Race and Resistance: Africa and Britain, 1919–1945*, London: Routledge, 1999, 161, 163.
24. George Padmore, 'The Revolutionary Movement in Africa', *The Negro Worker*, 1, 6, June 1931, 3; Padmore, *The Life and Struggles of Negro Toilers*, Hollywood, CA: Sun Dance Press, 1971 [1931], 78; Bransley R. Ndobe, 'Capitalist Terror in South Africa', *The Negro Worker*, 2, 4, April 1932, 15.
25. Padmore, *Life and Struggles of Negro Toilers*, 79.
26. Ibid., 82; Ndobe, 'Capitalist Terror in South Africa', 13–14; Otto F. Huiswood, 'The Economic Crisis and the Negro Workers', *The Negro Worker*, 2, 4, April 1932, 27.
27. In short, 'racial capitalism' refers to the way that racism as 'a material force' decisively shaped the development and nature of capitalism. See Cedric Robinson, *Black Marxism: The Making of the Black Radical Tradition*, London: Penguin, 2021, 2.
28. Cary Fraser, 'The Twilight of Colonial Rule in the British West Indies: Nationalist Assertion vs Imperial Hubris in the 1930s', *The Journal of Caribbean History*, 30, 1, 1996, 7.
29. Ibid.
30. Charles Alexander, 'Against Illusions in the West Indian Masses', *The Negro Worker*, 2, 7 July 1932, 14; 'Class War in the West Indies', *The Negro Worker*, 3, 2–3, February–March 1933, 23; George Padmore, 'Nationalist Movement in West Indies', *The Negro Worker*, 3, 1, January 1933, 6.
31. 'United Front against Fascism', *The Negro Worker*, 3, 6–7, June–July 1933, 30.
32. 'Au revoir', *The Negro Worker*, 3, 8–9, August–September 1933, 18; 'A Betrayer of the Negro Liberation Struggle', *The Negro Worker*, 4, 2, June 1934, 6–10.
33. Ronald Hyam and Peter Henshaw, *The Lion and the Springbok: Britain and South Africa since the Boer War*, Cambridge: Cambridge University Press, 2003, 107–8.
34. 'The Transfer of the Protectorates', *International African Opinion*, 1, 1, July 1938, 5.
35. 'Politics and the Negro', *International African Opinion*, 1, 7, May–June 1939, 14.
36. Andrew J. Crozier, *Appeasement and Germany's Last Bid for Colonies*, New York: St. Martin's Press, 1988, 140–1.
37. Ibid., 226–7.
38. Ibid., 265.
39. 'Editorial', *International African Opinion*, 1, 4, October 1938, 2.
40. 'Hitler and the Colonies', *International African Opinion*, 1, 5, November 1938, 2.
41. Leslie James and Daniel Whittall, 'Ambiguity and Imprint: British Racial

Logics, Colonial Commissions of Enquiry, and the Creolization of Britain in the 1930s and 1940s', *Callaloo*, 39, 1, 2016, 178.

42. 'Editorial: An Open Letter to West Indian Intellectuals', *International African Opinion*, 1, 7, May–June 1939, 2.

10. ESCAPE FROM EMPIRE: DECOLONIZATION AS DISENTANGLEMENT, ERASURE, AND EVASION

1. Simon Heffer, *Like the Roman: The Life of Enoch Powell*, London: Weidenfeld & Nicolson, 1998, 76, 169.
2. Camilla Schofield, *Enoch Powell and the Making of Postcolonial Britain*, Cambridge: Cambridge University Press, 2013, 99–102, 105–8, 143.
3. Ibid., 183.
4. Robert Saunders, "Brexit and Empire: 'Global Britain' and the Myth of Imperial Nostalgia," *Journal of Imperial and Commonwealth History*, 48, 6, 2020, 1140–74, at 1150–1; Wendy Webster, *Englishness and Empire, 1939–1965*, Oxford: Oxford University Press, 2005, 171–8.
5. Matthew Hilton, "Charity and the End of Empire: British Non-governmental Organizations, Africa, and International Development in the 1960s," *American Historical Review*, 123, 2, 2018, 493–517; Emily Baughan, *Saving the Children: Humanitarianism, Internationalism, and Empire*, Berkeley, CA: University of California Press, 2021.
6. Anna Bocking-Welch, *British Civic Society at the End of Empire: Decolonisation, Globalisation, and International Responsibility*, Manchester: Manchester University Press, 2019, 5.
7. Erik Linstrum et al., "Decolonizing Britain: An Exchange," *Twentieth-Century British History*, 33, 2, 2022, 274–303, at 283–4.
8. Saunders, "Brexit and Empire"; Ian Sanjay Patel, *We're Here Because You Were There: Immigration and the End of Empire*, London: Verso, 2022, 151–5.
9. David Edgerton, *The Rise and Fall of the British Nation: A Twentieth-Century History*, London: Allen Lane, 2018.
10. See, e.g., the Monday Club pamphlet *Europe, the Unguarded Legacy: A Conservative Approach to European Unity*, 1977.
11. Bocking-Welch, *British Civil Society*, 5.
12. Lasse Heerten, *The Biafran War and Postcolonial Humanitarianism: Spectacles of Suffering*, Cambridge: Cambridge University Press, 2017.
13. Hannah Arendt, *On Revolution*, Harmondsworth: Penguin, 2006.
14. Patel, *We're Here Because You Were There*, 250–78.
15. Stuart Ward, *Untied Kingdom: A Global History of the End of Britain*, Cambridge: Cambridge University Press, 2023.
16. David Cannadine, "Independence Day Ceremonials in Historical Perspective,"

Round Table, 398, 2008, 649–65; Robert Holland, Susan Williams, and Terry Barringer (eds), The Iconography of Independence: "Freedoms at Midnight", London: Routledge, 2010.

17. Williams, Holland, and Barringer, preface to Iconography of Independence, xi.
18. Chandrika Kaul, "'At the Stroke of the Midnight Hour': Lord Mountbatten and the British Media at Indian Independence," in Holland et al., Iconography of Independence.
19. "Note by Mr. Abell on a Discussion with Sir E. Jenkins (Punjab)," 7 June 1947, in Nicholas Mansergh (ed.), Constitutional Relations between Britain and India: The Transfer of Power, 1942–47, vol. 11, The Mountbatten Viceroyalty: Announcement and Reception of the 3 June Plan, London: HMSO, 1982, 177.
20. Nicholas Owen, "The Conservative Party and Indian Independence, 1945–47," Historical Journal 46, 2, 2003, 403–36, at 407–8.
21. Alex von Tunzelmann, Indian Summer: The Secret History of the End of an Empire, New York: Henry Holt, 2007, 221.
22. Catherine Coombs, "Partition Narratives: Displaced Trauma and Culpability among British Civil Servants in 1940s Punjab," Modern Asian Studies, 45, 1, 2011, 201–24.
23. Francis Tuker, While Memory Serves, Toronto: Cassell, 1950, 505–9.
24. Alan Campbell-Johnson, Mission with Mountbatten, Bombay: Jaico Publishing House, 1951, 1. Campbell-Johnson was quoting Herbert Samuels' remark from the House of Lords debate on the Indian Independence Act in 1947.
25. Von Tunzelmann, Indian Summer, 228.
26. A. W. B. Simpson, Human Rights and the End of Empire: Britain and the Genesis of the European Convention, Oxford: Oxford University Press, 2001, 57.
27. Ibid., 63; Christopher Roberts, "The Age of Emergency," Washington University Global Studies Law Review, 20, 1, 2021, 99–170.
28. Pethick-Lawrence to Wavell, 16 July 1946, in Mansergh (ed.), Transfer of Power, vol. 8, The Interim Government, London: HMSO, 1979, 70; Pethick-Lawrence to Attlee (draft), 15 July 1946, in Mansergh, Transfer of Power, vol. 8, 63.
29. Wavell to Pethick-Lawrence, 8 July 1946, vol. 8, 20.
30. David C. Potter, "Political Change and Confidential Government Files in India: 1937, 1947, 1967," Journal of Commonwealth Political Studies, 8, 2, 1970, 134–46.
31. Harris to Abell, 19 November 1946, in Mansergh (ed.), Transfer of Power, vol. 9, The Fixing of a Time Limit, London: HMSO, 1981, 113.
32. Potter, "Confidential Government Files," 135–6.
33. [G. E. B. Abell], "Notes on the Disposal of Records," n.d., in Mansergh, Transfer of Power, vol. 9, 357.
34. Nehru to Mountbatten, 1 May 1947, in Mansergh (ed.), Transfer of Power, vol. 10, The Mountbatten Viceroyalty: Formulation of a Plan, London: HMSO,

1981, 515. See also Nehru to Wavell, 6 March 1947, and Nehru to Wavell, 18 March 1947, in Mansergh, *Transfer of Power*, vol. 9, 873, 970–1.
35. Wavell to Nehru, 15 March 1947, in Mansergh, *Transfer of Power*, vol. 9, 958.
36. F. Mills to M. McMullen, 18 May 1963, FCO 141/19929, National Archives of the United Kingdom, Kew.
37. Ward, *Untied Kingdom*, 103–28.
38. Erik Linstrum, *Age of Emergency: Living with Violence at the End of the British Empire*, Oxford: Oxford University Press, 2023.
39. David French, *The British Way in Counter-Insurgency, 1945–1967*, Oxford: Oxford University Press, 2011, 166–8.
40. David M. Anderson, "Making the Loyalist Bargain: Surrender, Amnesty, and Impunity in Kenya's Decolonization, 1952–63," *International History Review*, 39, 1, 2017, 48–70; Juliana Appiah, Roland Mireku Yeboah, and Akosua Asah-Asante, "The Architecture of Denial: Imperial Violence, the Construction of Legal and Historical Knowledge during the Mau Mau Uprising, 1952–1960," *African Journal of Legal Studies*, 14, 2022, 3–27, at 17.
41. Robert Holland, *Britain and the Revolt in Cyprus, 1954–1959*, Oxford: Oxford University Press, 1999, 159.
42. HM Inspectorate of Constabulary and Fire & Rescue Services, "The Historical Enquires Team's Approach to Reviewing Deaths during 'The Troubles' Is Inconsistent, Has Serious Shortcomings and So Risks Public Confidence, HMIC Finds," 3 July 2013, https://hmicfrs.justiceinspectorates.gov.uk/news/releases/0182013-hmic-inspection-of-the-historical-enquiries-team, accessed 1/12/23.
43. Claire Mills and David Torrance, "Investigation of Former Armed Services Personnel Who Served in Northern Ireland," House of Commons Library Research Briefing, 18 May 2022, https://researchbriefings.files.parliament.uk/documents/CBP-8352/CBP-8352.pdf, accessed 1/12/23.
44. Shohei Sato, "'Operation Legacy': Britain's Destruction and Concealment of Colonial Records Worldwide," *Journal of Imperial and Commonwealth History*, 45, 4, 2017, 697–719, at 701.
45. Ibid.; Mandy Banton, "Destroy? 'Migrate'? Conceal? British Strategies for the Disposal of Sensitive Records of Colonial Administration at Independence," *Journal of Imperial and Commonwealth History*, 40, 2, 2012, 321–35.
46. Joel Hebert, "The Sun Never Sets: Rethinking the Politics of Late Decolonization, 1968 to the Present," PhD thesis, Chapel Hill, University of North Carolina, 2019, 55–6. See also Tim Livesey, "Open Secrets: The British 'Migrated Archives,' Colonial History, and Postcolonial History," *History Workshop Journal*, 93, 1, 2022, 95–116.
47. Sato, "'Operation Legacy,'" 706.
48. Hebert, "The Sun Never Sets"; Livesey, "Open Secrets."

49. Caroline Elkins, "Looking Beyond Mau Mau: Archiving Violence in the Era of Decolonization," *American Historical Review*, 120, 3, 2015, 852–68.
50. Richard Drayton, "Where Does the World Historian Write From? Objectivity, Moral Conscience, and the Past and Present of Imperialism," *Journal of Contemporary History*, 46, 3, 2011, 671–85.
51. David Anderson, *Histories of the Hanged: The Dirty War in Kenya and the End of Empire*, New York: W. W. Norton, 2005; Caroline Elkins, *Imperial Reckoning: The Untold Story of Britain's Gulag in Kenya*, New York: Henry Holt, 2005.
52. Marie-Emmanuelle Pommerolle, "Universal Claims and Selective Memory: A Comparative Perspective on the Culture of Opposition in Kenya," *Africa Today*, 53, 2, 2006, 75–93.
53. Mayo Moran, "The Problem of the Past: How Historic Wrongs Become Legal Problems," *University of Toronto Law Review*, 69, 4, 2019, 421–72.
54. Foreign and Commonwealth Office, "Statement to Parliament on Settlement of Mau Mau Claims," 6 June 2013, https://www.gov.uk/government/news/statement-to-parliament-on-settlement-of-mau-mau-claims, accessed 1/12/23.
55. *Athanasios Sophocleous and Others v. Secretary of State for the Foreign and Commonwealth Office and Another*.
56. *Kimathi and Others v. Foreign and Commonwealth Office*.
57. *Chong Nyok Keyu and Others v. Foreign and Commonwealth Office and Another*.

11. NO END OF A RECKONING

1. Tunku Varadarajan, "'Colonialism' Review: Empire without Apology', *Wall Street Journal*, 1 September 2023.
2. See the frontmatter to Nigel Biggar, *Colonialism: A Moral Reckoning*, London: William Collins, 2023, quotations selected from (in order of appearance): Zareer Masani, C. R. Hallpike, Ruth Dudley Edwards, Niall Ferguson, Vernon Bogdanor and Krishan Kumar.
3. David Arnold, 'In Defence of Empire', *Times Literary Supplement*, 3 March 2023; Alan Lester, 'The British Empire Rehabilitated?', *Bella Caledonia*, 7 March 2023: https://bellacaledonia.org.uk/2023/03/07/the-british-empire-rehabilitated, accessed 15/11/23.
4. Biggar, *Colonialism*, 3.
5. Jeremy Bentham, *Writings on Australia, VI. A Plea for the Constitution*, in T. Causer and P. Schofield (eds), pre-publication version, The Bentham Project, 2018, 38, 1, 10: https://discovery.ucl.ac.uk/id/eprint/10055304/1/6.%20Plea.pdf, accessed 15/11/23. On the use of Bentham as evidence of early pangs of liberal conscience about Indigenous dispossession, see for example Henry Reynolds, *This Whispering in Our Hearts*, Sydney: Allen & Unwin, 2018 [1998], x.
6. P. J. Marshall, *'A Free Though Conquering People': Eighteenth-Century Britain and Its Empire*, Farnham: Ashgate, 2003.

7. J. R. Seeley, *The Expansion of England: Two Courses of Lectures*, London: Macmillan, 1891 [1883], 296, 302.
8. John Darwin, *The Empire Project: The Rise and Fall of the British World-System, 1830–1970*, Cambridge: Cambridge University Press, 2009, 193.
9. Priyamvada Gopal, *Insurgent Empire: Anticolonial Resistance and British Dissent*, London: Verso, 2019, 85–8.
10. Bernard Porter, *Critics of Empire: British Radical Attitudes to Colonialism in Africa*, London: Macmillan, 1968, 1.
11. Francis W. Hirst, Gilbert Murray and J. L. Hammond, *Liberalism and the Empire: Three Essays*, London: R. Brimley Johnson, 1900, v–vi, xvi.
12. Rande W. Kostal, *A Jurisprudence of Power: Victorian Empire and the Rule of Law*, Oxford: Oxford University Press, 2005, 468, 20.
13. See Richard Drayton, 'Where Does the World Historian Write From? Objectivity, Moral Conscience and the Past and Present of Imperialism', *Journal of Contemporary History*, 46, 3, 2011, 671–85. Egerton cited on 676.
14. Derek Sayer, 'British Reaction to the Amritsar Massacre, 1919–20', *Past & Present*, 131, May 1991, 130–64, 140.
15. George Orwell, *Burmese Days*, New York: Harpers, 1934.
16. *Times*, 'Dominion and Empire', 15 January 1952.
17. R. Palme Dutt, *Britain's Crisis of Empire*, London: Lawrence & Wishart, 1950, 7.
18. C. E. Carrington, *The British Overseas: Exploits of a Nation of Shopkeepers*, Cambridge: Cambridge University Press, 1950, xviii–xix.
19. Ibid., xx.
20. Biggar, *Colonialism*, 3.
21. John Strachey, *The End of Empire*, London: Victor Gollancz, 1959, dustjacket.
22. Ibid., 23, 154.
23. Ibid., 213–14.
24. Ibid., 214–16.
25. Ibid., 214–15.
26. Ibid., 58.
27. A. J. P. Taylor, *English History, 1914–1945: The Oxford History of England, Vol. XV*, Oxford: Oxford University Press, 1965, 600.
28. Max Beloff, *Imperial Sunset, Vol. 1: Britain's Liberal Empire, 1897–1921*, London: Methuen, 1969, 19; Richard Price, *An Imperial War and the English Working Class*, London: Routledge and Kegan Paul, 1972, 241; James Morris, 'The Popularisation of Imperial History: The Empire on Television', *Journal of Imperial and Commonwealth History*, 1, 1973, 113–18, at 113.
29. A. P. Thornton, 'Decolonisation', *International Journal*, 19, 1, Winter 1963/4, 7–29, at 12–14.
30. Strachey, *End of Empire*, 215.

31. Thornton, 'Decolonisation', 24, 28.
32. Strachey, *End of Empire*, 204.
33. Ibid., 217. On Strachey's occasional forays 'into the seemingly fertile pastures of psychological speculation', see Noel Thompson, *John Strachey: An Intellectual Biography*, London: Macmillan, 1993, 114–15. On the effects of his breakdown and psychoanalysis on his political thought, see Michael Newman, *John Strachey*, Manchester: Manchester University Press, 1989, 50, 69–73.
34. Thornton, 'Decolonisation', 24.
35. Quoted in Prudence Smith, 'Margery Perham and Broadcasting: A Personal Reminiscence', in Alison Smith and Mary Bull (eds), *Margery Perham and British Rule in Africa*, London: Frank Cass, 1991, 197–200, at 199.
36. Margery Perham, *The Colonial Reckoning*, London: Collins, 1962, 9, 13, 14, 15.
37. 'Was she being patronising?', Biggar enquires, before answering in the negative. Biggar, *Colonialism*, 215.
38. Charles Troup's forthcoming work offers a penetrating account of the sheer novelty and rapid implementation of 'cost–benefit' reasoning in this period. See Troup, 'The Social Return on Capital in British Governance: Roads, Economic Reason, and the Emergence of Cost–Benefit Analysis, 1947–1964', unpublished manuscript. Sincere thanks to the author for sharing this original and fascinating work in draft.
39. Tony Hopkins, 'Macmillan's Audit of Empire, 1957', in Peter Clarke and Clive Trebilcock (eds), *Understanding Decline: Perceptions and Realities of British Economic Performance*, Cambridge: Cambridge University Press, 1997, 234–60, at 234.
40. Perham, *Colonial Reckoning*, 24.
41. Biggar, *Colonialism*, 275.
42. MS Perham Papers, 23/1, Perham to Arthur Creech Jones, 26 January 1942 and 21 June 1942, Bodleian Library Oxford.
43. *Times*, 13–14 March 1942. Roland Oliver describes this as the watershed in Perham's intellectual and indeed spiritual outlook. See Oliver, 'The Two Miss Perhams', in Smith and Bull, *Margery Perham*, 21–6.
44. Perham, *Colonial Reckoning*, 157.
45. Quoted in C. Brad Faught, *Into Africa: The Imperial Life of Margery Perham*, London: I. B. Tauris, 2012, 109.
46. MS Perham Papers, 349/2, wad of notes marked 'Poss. talk for BBC' (undated, but presumably 1961). Underlining in original. The ellipsis connotes an illegible portion of the passage.
47. Perham, *Colonial Reckoning*, 102.
48. Ibid., 22–3.
49. As she said of the anti-slavery and Aboriginal protection movements in the early nineteenth century: 'Here, then, was a new standard by which to judge the empire', ibid., 106.

50. Ibid., 104.
51. See especially Perham's fourth lecture, which is among her more considered attempts to view the matter from both sides of the racial divide: ibid., 81–101.
52. Ibid., 130.
53. Ibid., 124–5.
54. Though this would not restrain Nigel Biggar from citing her as such in his own moral accounting sixty years later, see Biggar, *Colonialism*, 200.
55. Perham, *Colonial Reckoning*, 134–5.
56. *The Daily Telegraph*, 'After Colonialism', 18 December 1961.
57. *The Listener*, 'Imperial Sunset?', 16 November 1961.
58. *The Sunday Telegraph*, 'Maturity or Just Pride?', 8 April 1962.
59. *The Spectator*, 'Account in Africa', 13 April 1962.
60. MS Perham Papers, 350/3, Francis Curtler to Perham, 13 November 1961.
61. MS Perham Papers, 350/3, Sir Raymond Streat (honorary fellow and colleague of Perham's at Nuffield from 1959) to Perham, 13 November 1961.
62. MS Perham Papers, 350/3, Sandy Fraser (Overseas Secretary, National Council of the YMCA) to Perham, 13 November 1961.
63. MS Perham Papers, 350/3, Letter from London School of Economic (name illegible) to Perham, 13 November 1961.
64. MS Perham Papers, 350/4, Perham to R. W. Sorensen, 30 January 1962.
65. To give something of the unhinged flavour, one gentleman was apoplectic that she had conceded far too much on the *debit* side: 'You are completely out of date, you stupid old hen. Don't you realize that the white races will be exterminated everywhere within 100 years? Is this what you want?', Aloysius Rappaport to Perham, 18 December 1961, MS Perham Papers, 350/4.
66. MS Perham Papers, 350/3, Sir Julian Huxley to Perham, 14 November 1961.
67. MS Perham Papers, 350/5, Michael Huxley to Perham, 20 January 1962.
68. MS Perham Papers, 350/3, Moritz J. Bonn to Perham, 21 November 1961. On Bonn's invention of 'decolonization' (of which he was quick to remind Perham), see Stuart Ward, 'The European Provenance of Decolonization', *Past & Present*, 230, February 2016, 227–60.
69. MS Perham Papers, 350/11, John Strachey to Perham, 31 July 1962.
70. Perham, *Colonial Reckoning*, 16.
71. L. H. Gann and Peter Duignan, *Burden of Empire: An Appraisal of Western Colonialism in Africa South of the Sahara*, London: Pall Mall Press, 1968, v.
72. Ibid., vi.
73. Ibid., vi, 79.
74. Ibid., 382.
75. Stephen Jackson's in-depth analysis of history textbooks in Texas high schools bears out the knock-on effects of the colonial balance-sheet among secondary school educators by the late 1970s; see *The Patchwork of World History in Texas*

High Schools, New York: Routledge, 2023, 124–5. The pedagogical practice has since become commonplace, as discussed by Priya Satia in 'One Tool of "Critical Thinking" That's Done More Harm Than Good', *Slate*, 22 March 2022.

76. Published as Niall Ferguson, *Empire: How Britain Made the Modern World*, London: Allen Lane, 2003, xii.
77. Although as Astrid Rasch perceptively notes, even trenchant critics of the 'moral balance-sheet' sometimes find themselves wading into its boggy foundations by stressing the overwhelming counterweight of the debit side of the ledger. See Astrid Rasch, 'Exemplar Empires: Battles over Imperial Memory in Contemporary Britain', in Josh Doble, Liam J. Liburd and Emma Parker (eds), *British Culture after Empire*, Manchester: Manchester University Press, 2023, 166–88, at 176.
78. Biggar, *Colonialism*, 283–4, 276.
79. Biggar, *Colonialism*, 285, emphasis in original.
80. Nigel Biggar, 'Don't Feel Guilty about Our Colonial History', *Times*, 30 November 2017.
81. Priya Satia, *Time's Monster: History, Conscience and Britain's Empire*, London: Penguin, 2022 [2020], 277.
82. Anthony Hartley, 'Account in Africa', *The Spectator*, 13 April 1962. Hartley was among the more astute diagnosticians of the first wave of 'declinism' in post-imperial Britain. His contribution is considered briefly in my *Untied Kingdom: A Global History of the End of Britain*, Cambridge: Cambridge University Press, 2023, 327–8.
83. In Australia, the leading practitioner was the conservative historian Geoffrey Blainey, who opposed the rush to judgement about Australia's colonial past in a highly influential 1993 essay, 'Drawing up a Balance Sheet of Our History', *Quadrant*, 37:7–8, July–August 1993, 10–15.

12. *COLONIALISM*: A METHODOLOGICAL RECKONING

1. Nigel Biggar, *Colonialism: A Moral Reckoning*, London: William Collins, 2023, 1, 2.
2. Ibid., 14. Appeals to historical 'data' recur: see for example p. 97, arguing against imperial racism—'as we have seen, that is not what the data have to say'—and p. 177, critiquing 'anti-colonialist' critiques of colonial capitalism: 'How does this account fare when it meets the historical data?'
3. Ibid., 3.
4. Ibid., 429–62.
5. Examples include William Dalrymple, 'Robert Clive Was a Vicious Asset-Stripper: His Statue Has No Place in Whitehall', *Guardian*, 11 June 2020 (Biggar, *Colonialism*, 436) and Zareer Masani, 'How British Orientalists Were Responsible

for Rediscovering Indian History', *The Wire*, 11 March 2018: https://thewire. in/history/how-british-orientalists-were-responsible-for-rediscovery-of-indian-history (Biggar, *Colonialism*, 449). The definitional lines between 'journalism' and both 'primary' and 'secondary' source are not fixed in stone; the figures in this paragraph are intended as indicative guidelines.

6. This is not to suggest that all of these primary sources are written by 'white' authors: a minority are penned by writers such as Chinua Achebe, Jomo Kenyatta and V. S. Naipaul, for example.
7. The mode is 2010 (twenty-seven items). Figures exclude journalism.
8. https://www.cambridge.org/core/series/new-cambridge-history-of-india/B52 6780B7DCEC98330410CD96B72233A: relevant volumes in the series include those by David Arnold, C. A. Bayly, Susan Bayly, Stewart Gordon, David Ludden, P. J. Marshall, Om Prakash and Barbara Ramusack; https://manchesteruniversitypress.co.uk/series/studies-in-imperialism/#:-:text=The%20 series%20has%20been%20a,education%2C%20culture%2C%20and%20 museums: the absence of any reference to the Manchester series' founding editor, John M. MacKenzie, is startling.
9. For Marxists, see for example Biggar, *Colonialism*, 119; 167; 280; 366–7, n. 81; 401 ns 175–6. Biggar's engagement with Edward Said is discussed below.
10. Antoinette Burton (ed.), *Archive Stories: Facts, Fictions, and the Writing of History*, Durham, NC: Duke University Press, 2005; Ann Laura Stoler, *Along the Archival Grain: Epistemic Anxieties and Colonial Common Sense*, Princeton, NJ: Princeton University Press, 2008. For the specific case of the Indian colonial archive, see Miles Ogborn, *Indian Ink: Script and Print in the Making of the English East India Company*, Chicago, IL: University of Chicago Press, 2007, and Patrick Joyce, *The State of Freedom: A Social History of the British State since 1800*, Cambridge: Cambridge University Press, 2013, Chapter 4.
11. Biggar, *Colonialism*, 70. The Livingstone reference, on page 319, n. 3, provides a page number for the Achebe but not the Livingstone quotation.
12. Lovatt Smith, cited by Biggar, *Colonialism*, 320, n. 4. This flattening of time, place and genre recurs later in the volume. Thus a reference to racist attitudes in India documented with a quotation from an officer in the Royal Indian Navy cited by Zareer Masani in his 1997 *Indian Tales of the Raj* is elaborated in the accompanying endnote as being 'sadly similar' to '[t]he story in Africa' as judged 'by fiction written by white authors with immediate experience of the colonial period', a statement underpinned by references to novels by Margery Perham, Lovatt Smith and Elspeth Huxley (323–4, n. 31). See also 87–8; 340, n. 104; 410, n. 233.
13. Biggar, *Colonialism*, 29–30 (citation 30).
14. Both aspects of Hastings' Indian career are well known, and documented in his *ODNB* entry, which offers a rather different overall assessment of his tenure

and the diary Biggar cites: 'In 1858 his daughter Lady Bute published a journal he kept in India until 1818 for family edification: it simplified public affairs, but showed a certain affection for India, where Hastings had interested himself in improving administration, justice, education, and freedom of the press: he valued publicity.' Roland Thorne, 'Hastings, Francis Rawdon, First Marquess of Hastings and Second Earl of Moira (1754–1826)', *Oxford Dictionary of National Biography*, 3 January 2008: https://www.oxforddnb.com/display/10.1093/ref:odnb/9780198614128.001.0001/odnb-9780198614128-e-12568?rskey=afsLXX&result=2

15. The relevant endnote (307–8, n. 31, cites vol. 1: 35 and vol. 2: 101–2 of Marchioness of Bute (ed.), *The Private Journal of the Marquess of Hastings, K.G., Governor-General and Commander-in-Chief in India*, London, 1858, as 'quoted by' Lawrence James, *Raj: The Making and Unmaking of British India*, London: Little, Brown and Company, 1997, 72. James, *Raj*, 672, n. 16 cites both vol. 1: 35 and vol. 2: 101–2 of the diary; the two references correspond to his points about Hastings on *Raj*, 71–2.
16. Bute, *Private Journal*, 2: 101–2.
17. His citation of the Hastings diary appears to have been lifted wholesale from James, *Raj*, 672, n. 16.
18. Bute, *Private Journal*, 1: 30, 31, 33, 35.
19. Biggar, *Colonialism*, 30, reference 307: n. 30, citing James, *Raj*, 151.
20. James, *Raj*, 72.
21. Biggar, *Colonialism*, 201; 380, n. 114, citing David Gilmour, *The British in India: Three Centuries of Ambition and Experience*, London: Penguin, 2019, 40.
22. Gilmour, *British in India*, 39.
23. Biggar, *Colonialism*, 201, 380, n. 114, citing Gilmour, *British in India*, 40; Gilmour, *British in India*, 40, 39.
24. In contrast to Biggar, C. A. Bayly and Katherine Prior conclude that '[h]e saw the world in stark colours of race and moral independency. Indians were corrupt ... Yet this was not the racism of high imperialism with its urge to "improve".' Bayly and Prior, 'Cornwallis, Charles, First Marquess Cornwallis (1738–1805)', *Oxford Dictionary of National Biography*, Oxford: Oxford University Press, 2011: https://www.oxforddnb.com/display/10.1093/ref:odnb/9780198614128.001.0001/odnb-9780198614128-e-6338?rskey=Oi0UON&result=9. Detailed assessments of the impact of this policy are found in Durba Ghosh, *Sex and the Family in Colonial India: The Making of Empire*, Cambridge: Cambridge University Press, 2006, and Christopher Hawes, *Poor Relations: The Making of a Eurasian Community in British India, 1773–1833*, London: Curzon, 1996.
25. Among other examples in which highly selective quotations from a secondary source lead Biggar to disavow colonial racisms and their legacies is his use of

the work of Krishan Kumar to substantiate his claim that '[t]he vicious racism of slavers and planters was not essential to the British Empire, and whatever racism exists in Britain today is not its fruit' (*Colonialism*, 66). The accompanying endnote (319, n. 74) cites Bernard Porter's *The Absent-Minded Imperialists: Empire, Society and Culture in Britain,* Oxford: Oxford University Press, 2004 to bolster this claim, further reinforcing this assertion by citing Kumar's argument on page 320 of his 2017 *Visions of Empire* that Porter's book is a valuable corrective to the 'sometimes mechanical assumptions' of 'postcolonial scholars' that empire exerted a powerful impact on Britons at home. Yet Kumar's next paragraph openly acknowledges the limits of Porter's arguments and concludes that 'it is simply wrong to think that ... the argument for the impact of the British Empire on British society rests on mere assertion or unsupported assumption. That position is as dogmatic and uninformed as the opposite claim.' Significantly, unlike Biggar, Kumar here both recognises and acknowledges 'the great influence of John MacKenzie's works in exploring the impact of empire on British society'. Krishan Kumar, *Visions of Empire: How Five Imperial Regimes Shaped the World*, Princeton, NJ: Princeton University Press, 2017, 320–1, 499, n. 8.
26. Biggar, *Colonialism*, 201.
27. Ibid., referenced at 380, n. 115, in which Biggar cites both Gilmour, *British in India*, 168 [the paraphrased and quoted material in fact is on 167–8] and Fred Leventhal and Peter Stansky, *Leonard Woolf: Bloomsbury Socialist*, Oxford: Oxford University Press, 2019, 42.
28. Gilmour, *British in India*, 167–8.
29. Ibid., 169.
30. Leventhal and Stansky, *Leonard Woolf*, 42. They also note (42–3) Woolf's more complex later reflections on his earlier unselfconscious imperialism.
31. Cited by Leventhal and Stansky, *Leonard Woolf*, 32. The original source they cite is Frederic Spotts (ed.), *Letters of Leonard Woolf*, London: Weidenfeld & Nicolson, 1990, 1 October 1905: 102, and 12 November 1905: 107.
32. Some websites and other materials cannot be ascribed a gender. In assigning gender identities, authors' names were checked against publisher, university or other websites to check usage of 'he' or 'she'.
33. Journalism was excluded. No gender identity was made for F. N. Howe (page 444). Women were the sole authors of forty-three secondary works; sixteen secondary items were co-authored by men and women.
34. Nicola Miller, Kenneth Fincham, Margot Finn, Sarah Holland, Christopher Kissane and Mary Vincent, *Promoting Gender Equality in UK History: A Second Report and Recommendations for Good Practice*, London: Royal Historical Society, 2018, 16. The representation of women is consistently higher at more junior levels: 45 per cent of history postgraduate research students in 2018 were

female while 55 per cent of undergraduates were women (ibid., 16–17). In the United States, just under 35 per cent of academic historians were female already in 2007: https://www.historians.org/research-and-publications/perspectives-on-history/april-2010/what-the-data-tells-us-about-women-historians

35. Readers can test this assertion by searching, for example, in the Bibliography of British and Irish History for 'colonialism Canada', 'colonialism India', 'colonialism Jamaica' or 'colonialism Kenya'. Likewise, the editorship and editorial boards of relevant peer-reviewed journals—a type of output poorly represented in Biggar's bibliography—suggests that female academics are well represented in British colonial history, even at senior levels. See for example *Comparative Studies in Society and History*, *Indian Economic and Social History Review*, *Journal of Colonialism and Colonial History*, *Journal of Imperial and Commonwealth History* and *Modern Asian Studies*.

36. Likewise, Biggar's discussion of Atlantic World slavery ignores foundational work on women by, among many other scholars, Henrice Altink, Marisa J. Fuentes, Catherine Hall, Cecily Jones, Natasha Lightfoot, Jennifer Lyle Morgan, Diana Paton, Katherine Paugh, Verene A. Shepherd and Christine Walker. The absence of any reference to Hall's work extends to Biggar's discussion of British compensation for the abolition of slavery in 1833, thus entirely ignoring the many publications and open access database produced by Hall's Legacies of British Slave-Ownership research team.

37. Biggar, *Colonialism*, 187–8, 374–5, n. 44. Biggar claims Paul Bew as his chief authority, but his reference departs significantly from experts' recent assessments. See Christophe Gillissen, 'Charles Trevelyan, John Mitchel and the Historiography of the Great Famine', *Revue française de civilisation britannique*, 19, 2, 2014, 195–212, and John Leazer, 'Politics as Usual: Charles Edward Trevelyan and the Irish and Scottish Fisheries before and during the Great Famine', *Irish Economic and Social History*, 49, 1, 2022, 47–59. These authors' relative indifference to the impact of either Hart's 'seminal' article or Bew's assessments is noteworthy.

38. Biggar, *Colonialism*, 116–18, citation 117. On page 117, he supports his strictures on the use of oral history by citing at length the Byzantine historian Mark Whittow, who deploys 'early medieval Arabic sources' before turning to Canadian anthropologists Bruce Trigger and Alexander von Gernet for further affirmation.

39. Ibid., 116.

40. Ibid., 337, ns 83 and 84, citing Lindberg's 'Contemporary Canadian Resonance of an Imperial Doctrine' (Chapter 5), 168, n. 221, and 'Doctrine of Discovery in Canada' (Chapter 4), 112, in Robert J. Miller, Jacinta Ruru, Larissa Behrendt and Tracey Lindberg, *Discovering Indigenous Lands: The Doctrine of Discovery in the English Colonies*, Oxford: Oxford University Press, 2012. The relevant

footnote for the re-quoted Leroy Little Bear citation (at fourth-hand by the time Biggar cites it) is in Miller et al., *Discovering*, 112–13, n. 83. The quoted passage from Lindberg's chapter, 168, n. 221, begins: 'This is not a condemnation of non-Indigenous laws or governance. It is not an indictment of Canadian legislators or judiciary. It calls upon all of us, as peoples in a shared territory, to acknowledge Indigenous legal and governmental orders, to question the notion of immediate Canadian sovereignty and the impossibility of immediate cessation of land by Indigenous peoples.'

41. Biggar, *Colonialism*, 5, 302, n. 14.
42. Ibid., 5.
43. Ibid., 26, 306–7, n. 16. He cites pages 3, 9, 18, 26, 27, 29, 30 of Gopal's *Insurgent Empire*, and contrasts her work to, for example, Bernard Lewis, Ibn Warraq, Sameer Rahim.
44. Priyamvada Gopal, *Insurgent Empire: Anticolonial Resistance and British Dissent*, London: Verso, 2019, 457, n. 4 (corresponding to page 3); 459, n. 21 (corresponding to page 9); 460, n. 57 (corresponding to page 18); 461, n. 86 (corresponding to page 26); 461, n. 91 and 462, n. 92 (corresponding to page 27); 462, ns 101–4, 107 (corresponding to pages 29–31). Gopal does subsequently, on a page not noted by Biggar, reference *Orientalism* specifically in the context of Christopher Herbert's critique of Said's text, a critique which she quotes: 51, 464, n. 42. The only work by Said included in Biggar's biography is *Orientalism* (*Colonialism*, 456).
45. See for example Gilmour, *British in India*, Chapters 2–3, 9–10.
46. Examples in Gilmour's bibliography include works by Elizabeth Buettner, Barbara Caine, Sudhir Chandra, Anne Chitty, E. M. Collingham, Anne de Courcy, Indira Ghose and Durba Ghosh: *British in India*, 560, 561, 562, 565.
47. Biggar, *Colonialism*, 74, referenced on 322, n. 18, citing Gilmour, *British in India*, 309.
48. Gilmour, *British in India*, 285.
49. Biggar, *Colonialism*, 74. The statement is not referenced, but the reference to evangelicalism and utilitarianism corresponds to the section in Gilmour's text cited below.
50. Gilmour, *British in India*, 289–90.
51. For example, 'The view that native peoples were essentially equal to Britons, possessed of the potential to become equally civilised, predominated in the imperial metropolis, even when some settlers on the colonial periphery doubted it.' Biggar, *Colonialism*, 124.
52. Ibid., 359, n. 1.
53. Ibid., 360–71. The book review is referenced at ns 3, 78, 79, 87, 88, 90, 91 and 93.
54. Ibid., 167; 366, n. 78. Cf. Biggar's more dismissive credentialisms of Gopal:

'Called to action by Dr (now Professor) Priyamvada Gopal of Cambridge University', and 'One example has been provided by Priyamvada Gopal, then reader in postcolonial and related literatures at the University of Cambridge, now promoted to professor': ibid., 299, n. 5; 425, n. 6. Professor Roy, one might surmise, in contrast, has perpetually written as a professor, having emerged from his doctorate fully-fledged, like Athena from Zeus's manly forehead.

55. Ibid., see esp. 366–7, n. 81, and 367–8, n. 84.
56. Ibid., xiv–xv.

INDEX

Note: Page numbers followed by '*n*' refer to notes.

Abdul Kadir, Abdullah bin, 135–6, 140
Abdurahman, 161
Abolition Act (1807), 198
Abolition Act (1833), 197
Aboriginal people Black War (1826–32), 55–9
    genocide, act of, 59–64
    and Tasmanian genocide, 64–72
Abyssinia, 201
Achebe, Chinua, 44, 73–4, 89–91
Acting Magistrate for Bihar, 106
Admiralty Citadel, 182
Afghanistan, 95, 112, 248
Africa, 21, 29, 34, 37, 50–1, 76, 90, 100, 195, 220, 224, 226–7, 254, 261–2, 270
    See also South Africa; South African War
Afrikaner Bond party, 152, 165, 167

Afrikaner nationalism, 162
Aglen, Francis, 175
Ahmad Khan, Syed, 40
America, 217, 220, 225
American Revolution (1776–83), 51, 192, 193
Amery, Leo, 157
Amritsar, 255
Amritsar massacre, 241
Anderson, Clare, 289
Anderson, David, 248, 249
Andrews, Kehinde, 216–17, 219
Anglo-Afghan War II, 22–3
Anglo-Boer War I, 22–3
Anglo-Boer War. *See* South African War (1899–1902)
Anglo-Maratha War III, 284
Ansari, Sarah, 112
Anstey, Roger, 194
anti-fascism, 214–15

INDEX

anti-fascist movement, 224
anti-imperialism, 155, 176
anti-slavery imperialism, 207–8
anti-slavery policies
   abolitionist moralities, 190–6
   morality of, 196–202
Anti-Slavery Society, 201
Arthur, George (Tasmania's Governor), 56–7, 60, 67, 68, 69
Aryan supremacy, 218
Ashwood Garvey, Amy, 226
Asia, 42, 103, 125, 175, 224
Asiatic Journal, 109
Atlantic Ocean, 279
Atlantic slavery, 49–50
Attlee government, 240
Attlee, Clement, 173
Atwal, Priya, 289
Austen, Jane, 5
Australasia, 26
Australia, 21–2, 26–8, 42, 55, 76, 100, 138, 228, 273
Australian, The (newspaper), 61–2

Backhouse, James, 69
Bacon, Gareth, 12, 14
Badaruddin, Ratu Mahmud (Palembang's Sultan), 126–7
   British colonial expansion, 127–34
Bali, 125
Balochi amirs, 112–14
Banjarmasin, 125
Banten, 125
Barbados, 21, 26

Barh, 119
Barkly West, 150
Bass Strait Islands, 59
Basutoland, 227
Batang Kali, 245
Batang Kali massacre, 250
Batavia Government Gazette, 128
Batavia, 127
Batswana, 150
Battersea, 182
Bayly, Christopher, 96–7, 104, 321n27
BBC (British Broadcasting Corporation), 261
Bechuanaland, 227
Beinart, William, 165, 168
Belgium, 175
Bencoolen, 121
Bengal Club, 292
Bengal, 22, 96, 114, 115, 139
   sati, British debate on, 104–11
Bengalis, 233
Benin Bronzes, 23, 278
Benin, 24, 52
Bennett, Huw, 249
Bentham, Jeremy, 253–4
Bentinck, Lord William (India's Governor General), 109–10
   @Index-sub1:*See also* sati (widow-burning)
Berlin conference, 200
Berrington, J. D., 116–18
Biafra crisis, 237
Biafran War, 44–5
Big River people, 68

INDEX

Big River, 57, 58
Biggar, Nigel, 13–14, 15, 51, 74–5, 88–90, 96, 149, 154, 188, 251–2, 271, 273, 279–88, 290–5
   abolitionist moralities, 190–6
   anti-slavery, morality of, 196–202
   China, British violence in, 174–6
   'civilising mission', 98, 99–104
   colonialism and Tasmanian genocide, 64–72
   colonialism, benefits of, 39–46
   Fascism and contemporary defenders of empire, 215–20
   historical research, past and present in, 202–9
   indigenous knowledge, refusing, 82–4
   indigenous leader, 77–9
   justifying colonialism, 84–6
   methodological reckoning, 275–7
   and Perham, 262–3
   on Raffles, 121–2, 138–9
   Rhodes' imperialism, 161–70
Bihar, 119
'Bill for Africa', 166
Birmingham City University, 216
'Black Armband', 55
Black Line, 58, 68–72
Black Lives Matter protests, 188, 216
Black War (1826–32), 55–9
   colonialism and Tasmanian genocide, 64–72

   genocide, act of, 59–64
Blainey, Geoffrey, 62, 66–7
'Blue Books', 112
Board of Inland Revenue, 153
Bocking-Welch, Anna, 237
Boehmer, Elleke, 199, 290–1
Boer republics, 227
Boer War II. *See* South African War
Boers, 150, 153–4, 164
   South African War, 154–9
Bolivarian republics, 30
Bombay, 242
Bonn, Moritz J., 269
Bonwick, James, 59
Botany Bay, 55
Botha, general Louis, 160
Bower, Graham, 151–2
Boxer uprising (1899–1901), 162, 178
Boyce, James, 63–4, 69
Brighton Pavilion, 44
Britain, 5–6, 11, 22, 56, 147, 152, 154, 158, 225
   abolitionist moralities, 190–6
   anti-slavery, morality of, 196–202
   colonial fascism and World War II, 225–32
   colonialism and Tasmanian genocide, 64–72
   colonialism, benefits of, 39–46
   fascism and contemporary defenders, 215–20
   fascism vs. Negro Workers, 220–5

361

INDEX

historical research, past and present in, 202–9
racial segregation, 159–61
Rhodes' imperialism, 161–70
British 'Khaki' election, 164
British Academy committee, 247
British colonial history
  colonialism and racism, 34–8
  economic exploitation, 28–34
  occupation, 25–8
  political control, 20–5
British Commonwealth Office, 45
British Communist Party, 172–7, 222 256–7
British Empire, 55, 73–5, 189
  abolitionist moralities, 190–6
  anti-slavery, morality of, 196–202
  British India, prosecuting sati in, 115–19
  'civilising mission', 98, 99–104
  colonial expansion, 127–34
  colonial fascism and World War II, 225–32
  colonial humanitarianism, 136–41
  colonialism and Tasmanian genocide, 64–72
  colonialism, benefits of, 39–46
  Fascism and contemporary defenders, 215–20
  historical research, past and present in, 202–9
  native states, assistance of, 125–7

racial segregation, 159–61
Rhodes' imperialism, 161–70
sati, abolition of, 93–9
sati, British debate on, 104–11
See also India; Canada
British Guiana, 230–1
British imperialism, 97, 98, 148, 164, 166–8
British India, 31, 96, 97, 111, 280
  prosecuting sati in, 115–19
British Isles, 26
British Library, 115
British military, 128, 247
British Museum, 23
British Nigeria, 200
British Protectorate of Nyasaland, 32
British South Africa Committee of Inquiry (1897), 152
British West Indies, 189, 230
  abolitionist moralities, 190–6
Brits, 154
Brooke, James, 137
Brown, Christopher Leslie, 192
Bruce, James, 171
Brussels conference, 200
Buckingham Palace, 172, 181
Buckinghamshire, 248
Bulstrode, Jenny, 14–15
Burke, Edmund, 277
Burma, 22
Burton, Antoinette, 16, 289
Buxton, Thomas Fowell, 36

C2C, 89

INDEX

Cain, Peter, 158, 163
Calcutta, 110, 292–3
Callwell, Colonel Charles Edward, 22–3
Cambridge, 278
Campbell-Bannerman, Henry, 156, 162
Canada, 26, 28, 41, 42, 74–5, 273
    Biggar's book on, 75–7
    Canada's Indian Act, 76
    Canada's Indian policy, 86
    Canadian troops, 155
    colonialism, justifying, 84–6
    colonialism, scholars on, 79–82
    indigenous authors, 82–4
    Riel and indigenous communities, 77–9
    schooling, 86–9
Canada–US border, 77
Canadian Historical Association, 81
Canton, 22
Cape Colony, 25, 39, 151–3, 159–60, 166–7
Cape parliament, 154
Cape Town, 30, 179
capitalism, 164, 221, 223
capitalist imperialism, 163
Captain General Royal Marines, 183–4
Carey, William, 108
Caribbean colonies, 21, 25–6, 30–1, 193, 196–7, 200, 221, 223–4, 254
    colonial fascism and World War II, 225–32

Carleton, Sean, 290
Carlyle, Thomas, 35
Carrington, Charles, 256–7
Carter, Sarah, 79, 290
Catherine Hall, 18, 21
Central Africa, 41
Césaire, Aimé, 213–14, 220
Cetshwayo, King, 24–5
Ceylon (Sri Lanka), 56, 241, 246, 286–7
Chakrabarty, Dipesh, 278
Chamberlain, Joseph, 152, 156–7, 161, 163, 232
Charity Commission, 8
Charles III, King, 206
Charter renewal, 31
Chartwell, 7
Chatham, 183
Chatterjee, Indrani, 289
Chatterjee, Nandini, 289
Chatterjee, Partha, 101, 278
Chiang Kai-shek, 172
China Station, 174
China, 22, 31, 123, 144, 184
    British invasion, 172–80
Chinese civil war (1949), 172
'Chinese Communist Party', 174, 176–7
'Chinese slavery', 162
Christian Aid, 236
Christianity, 100, 150, 237
Churchill, Winston, 4, 32, 157, 216, 219, 232, 240
Cirebon, 125
'civilising mission', 98, 99–104, 114, 149–50

INDEX

Clark, Chris, 166
Clarkson, Thomas, 30, 50, 191–4
Clive, Robert, 23, 171
Clyde River valley, 56
Cohen, Paul A., 177
Colenso, Archbishop, 25
Collins, William, 13
Colonial and War Offices, 20
Colonial Countryside (research project), 8
'Colonial fascism', 225–32
Colonial Office (London), 20
Colonial Times, The (newspaper), 57
colonialism, 11–13
   abolitionist moralities, 190–6
   anti-slavery, morality of, 196–202
   benefits of, 39–46
   Biggar's book on, 75–7
   Black War (1826–32), 55–9
   colonialism and racism, 34–8
   colonialism, justifying, 84–6
   colonialism, scholars on, 79–82
   economic exploitation, 28–34
   genocide, act of, 59–64
   historical research, past and present in, 202–9
   indigenous authors, 82–4
   Riel and indigenous communities, 77–9
   scholars on, 15–19
   schooling, 86–9
   and Tasmanian genocide, 64–72
See also British Empire; China; Egypt; imperialism; India; racism
'Common Sense Group', 7, 8, 12, 14
Commonwealth of Nations, 235, 244
Communist International (Comintern), 220–5
Communist Party of South Africa, 222
Conan Doyle, Arthur, 179–80
Congress of Vienna (1814–15), 198
Conrad, Joseph, 137
Conservative Party, 7
Corn Laws, 39
Cornwallis, Lord, 281, 284–6
Council of Bengal, 128
Coupland, Reginald, 201
CoventryLive, 5
Cowessess First Nation, 80
Crawford, John, 131–3, 134–6, 141
"Cree 'First Nation,'", 82, 84
Criminal Tribes Act (1871), 36
Cromer, Earl of, 277
Cromer, Lord, 103
Cugoano, Ottobah, 30, 194
Curthoys, Ann, 65
Curtis, Lionel, 161
Curtler, Francis, 268
Cyprus, 244, 245
Czechoslovakia, 230

INDEX

Dagu, 180
Daily Express, The (newspaper), 14
Daily Mail, The (newspaper), 8, 14
Daily Telegraph, The (newspaper), 8, 13, 14, 168, 267, 277
Dalmia, Vasudha, 104
Darwin, Charles, 58–9, 71
Darwinian evolution, 36
Daschuk, James, 79–81, 81–2
de Normann, William, 181
de Villiers, Henry, 160
'decolonization', 245–50, 269
  in India, 239–44
  postcolonial regimes, 235–8
Delhi, 115, 242
Demerara, 194
'The Depredations', 60
Deputy General of Police, 119
Devonshire, Duke of, 228–9
Dharma Sabha, 110
Diamond Harbour, 283
Dickens, Charles, 35
Discourse on Colonialism (pamphlet), 213
Distinguished Service Cross, 180
"District Commissioner", 73–4
District Superintendent of Police, 116
Dorchester Review, The (magazine), 80, 88
Douglass, Frederick, 35
Duignan, Peter, 269–71
Dutch fort, 129
Dutch, 125–7, 136
native states, assistance of, 125–7
Dutil, Patrice, 80
Dutt, R. Palme, 256–7
Dyer, General, 255

East Africa, 41, 43, 238
East Bay Neck, 58
East India Company (EIC), 7, 20–2, 23, 31, 94, 115, 123, 257, 275, 281–3, 285, 289, 321n23, 321n27
  sati, British debate on, 104–11
East India House, 123
East Indian Railway Company, 38
Eastern Africa, 26
ECHR. *See* European Court of Human Rights (ECHR)
Economist, The (Newspaper), 6
Edinburgh Review, The (magazine), 109
Edinburgh, Duke of, 183
Egerton, H. E., 255
Egypt, 76, 153
EIC India, 292–3
Elgin, Eighth Lord, 171, 181
Eliot, George, 4–5
Elkins, Caroline, 19, 248, 249
Elphinstone, Lord (Governor General), 112
Eltis, David, 199
England, 26, 56–7, 105, 124, 143–4, 184, 254
English Channel, 237
Equiano, Olaudah, 30, 51, 194, 195

INDEX

Erasmus, George, 85
Erastianism, 203
'Ethics and Empire' project, 191
Ethiopia, 226
   colonial fascism and World War II, 225–32
Europe imperialism, 158
Europe, 29, 34, 50, 100, 221, 224–5, 246
   colonial fascism and World War II, 225–32
   liberalism, 39
European colonialism, 224
European Court of Human Rights (ECHR), 245–6
European fascism, 214
European Marxists, 158
European Union, 7
Examiner (newspaper), 132

'Fallist' movement, 148
Fanon, Frantz, 13, 74, 219
Farquhar, William, 134–5
Farwell, Byron, 112
fascism, 214, 217, 220–3, 232
   colonial fascism and World War II, 225–32
   vs, Negro Workers, 220–5
Fawcett, Millicent Garrett, 156
feminism, 103–4
Ferguson, Niall, 9, 271
Fieldhouse, David, 264, 294
financial crisis (2008), 11
Financial Times, 147–8
First Anglo-Chinese. *See* 'Opium' War

Flanagan, Thomas, 76, 78
Flanagan, Tom, 65, 80, 82, 84–6
Flinders Island, 69–72
Foreign and Commonwealth Office, 171
Foreign Office, 20
Fourie, Johan, 165
Fowler, Corinne, 7–8, 14
France, 174, 203, 225, 226, 249
Franchise and Ballot Act (1892), 165
Fraser, Cary, 223
Fraser, Sandy, 268
Freetown, 30
Frere, Henry Bartle, 24
Futa Toro, 50

Gandhi, Mahatma, 161
Gann, L. H., 269–71
Gaya, 106, 116, 117–18
Gebreyohanes, Zewditu, 216
George V, King, 178–9
George, Lloyd, 156
Gerard Nahuys, Baron Huibert, 136
German South West Africa (Namibia), 25
Germany, 220, 225, 228–30, 233, 269
   See also Hitler, Adolf
Ghosh, Durba, 289
Gillespie, Major General, 124, 127–8
Gilley, Bruce, 14, 44–5, 74
Gilmour, David, 122, 285–7, 292, 294

INDEX

Gilroy, Paul, 279
Gladstone, William, 5, 157
Glasgow, 259
Glen Grey Act (1894), 166
Glendinning, Victoria, 144
God's Providence, 191–2
Gold Coast (Ghana), 247
Goldberg, Jonah, 95
Goldman, Lawrence, 194, 202–7
Good Friday Agreement (1998), 246
Gopal, Priyamvada, 216, 291
Gordon, General, 183
Gove, Michael, 94
Government of India, 33, 111, 115, 242–3
Governor of Bencoolen, 124
'Graspan Parade', 183–4
Graspan, 178–80
Graspan, Battle of, 183
Great Depression, 223
Great Leap Forward, 29
Great War (1914–18). *See* World War I
Griqua, 24–5
Guardian, The (newspaper), 247, 277
guerrilla war, 60–1
Guha, Ranajit, 278
Gujarat, 111
Guomindang, 172, 177

Haggard, Rider, 277
Haitian revolution, 194
Hall, Catherine, 289
Hall, Stuart, 279
Hamburg, 220, 224
Hamengkubuwono II (Yogyakarta's Sultan), 130–3
Hamon, Max, 77–8
Hanslope Park, 248
Hardie, Keir, 156
Harling, Philip, 31
Harries, Patrick, 166
Harris, George, 280
Hart, Jennifer, 290
Hartley, Anthony, 272
Hastings, Lord Warren, 124, 128, 280–4, 289
Hastings, marquess of, 280–1
Hazaribagh district, 119
Heading to Cape Town, 153
Hertzog, General J. B. M., 222, 227–9
Hickey, William, 293
High Commission Territories, 227–8
Hilferding, Rudolf, 163
Hindus, 100, 283
  sati, British debate on, 104–11
  See also India
Hirst, R. J., 119–20
Historical Enquiries Team, 246
History Reclaimed, 187–9, 209–10
  abolitionist moralities, 190–6
  anti-slavery, morality of, 196–202
  historical research, past and present in, 202–9
Hitler, Adolf, 232, 229

INDEX

See also Mussolini, Benito; Germany; Nazism
HMS *Amethyst*, 173
Hobart, 56, 60
Hobhouse, Emily, 156, 162
Hobson, J. A., 157–9, 163
Hofmeyr, J. H., 167
Holland, Tom, 290
Hollis, Governor Alfred Claud, 223–4
Holwell, John Zephaniah, 105
Home Department Records, 115
Hong Kong, 22
Hopkins, Tony, 158, 163
Hottentot, 167
House of Commons, 250
House of Lords, 132
The Hudson's Bay Company, 75–6, 77
Hughes, Robert, 9, 59
humanitarianism, 191
Hume, David, 34
Hunt, Dallas, 81
Hussein, Sultan, 134
Huxley, Elspeth, 277
Huxley, Julian, 268
Huxley, Michael, 268
Hyderabad, 281

Ignatius Sancho, 29–30
Illingworth, Leslie, 239
Illustrated London News, The, 182–3
imperialism, 74, 155, 177, 187, 218, 220

abolitionist moralities, 190–6
anti-slavery, morality of, 196–202
benefits of, 39–46
Biggar's book on, 75–7
Black War (1826–32), 55–9
colonialism and racism, 34–8
colonialism, justifying, 84–6
colonialism, scholars on, 79–82
economic exploitation, 28–34
genocide, act of, 59–64
historical research, past and present in, 202–9
indigenous authors, 82–4
Riel and indigenous communities, 77–9
schooling, 86–9
and Tasmanian genocide, 64–72
See also colonialism; racism
Indemnity Acts, 241
India Act (1784), 128–9, 133
India Office, 20
India, 20–2, 39–40, 44, 76, 138–9, 142, 144, 175, 235, 239–42, 254, 257, 279, 282, 292
'civilising mission', 98, 99–104
economic exploitation, 28–34
prosecuting sati in, 115–19
sati, abolition of, 93–9
sati, British debate on, 104–11
See also colonialism; racism
Indian National Congress, 242
Indian Ocean, 197–8
Indian Penal Code, 115–16, 117, 119

INDEX

'Indian policy', 28
Industrial Revolution (Britain), 15
"information recovery", 246
Innes, Robert Alexander, 80
International African Friends of Ethiopia (IAFE), 226
International African Opinion (journal), 226–32
International African Service Bureau (IASB), 215, 226–31, 232
International Labour Organization, 200
International Trade Union Committee of Negro Workers, 220–1
Iraq, 248
Ireland, 39, 76, 246
Irish Home Rule, 254
Italy, 225, 226, 233
 See also Mussolini, Benito

Jackson, Thomas, 178
Jamaica, 39–40, 194, 197, 230–1, 241
Jamaica, Taino of, 21
Jambi, 125
James Fox, Charles, 109
James, C. L. R., 226, 227, 279, 284–5
James, Lawrence, 281
Jameson, Leander Starr, 159–60
Japan, 174, 176–7
Java, 123–4
 British colonial expansion, 127–34

colonial humanitarianism, 136–41
native states, assistance of, 125–7
Java, Lieutenant Governor of, 121, 124, 139
Jenkins, Evan, 239–40
Jews, 233
Jim, Lord, 137
Johannesburg, 151
Johnson, Miranda, 209
Jones, Adrian, 178
Jones, Arthur Creech, 264
Jones, Rhys, 61, 68
Joseon, 175
Juxtaposing, 120

Kane, Abd al-Qadir, 50–1
Kat River rebellion (1851–2), 166
Kaye, John, 293
Kendall, E. A., 109
Kenya Human Rights Commission, 249
Kenya, 38–9, 225, 238, 244, 245, 247, 248, 249, 258
Kettle, Tilly, 105
'Khaki election', 155
Khama III, King, 25, 150
Khedivate government, 153
Kikuyu Home Guard, 245
Kimball, Roger, 62
Kimberley, 24, 149, 166, 179
Kipling, Rudyard, 37
Kitchener, General, 6
Knox, Robert, 36

INDEX

Kolsky, Elizabeth, 289
Korea, 175
Kris, 124
Kruger, Paul, 151, 152, 153, 163

Labour Party, 156, 257, 264
Lagos, 52, 264
Lake Echo, 58
lambadar (a powerful local estateholder), 116
Latin America, 59
Launceston, 56
Lawrence, T. E., 277
Lawson, Tom, 64, 70
Le May, G. H. L., 161
League of Nations, 200, 229
Lecky, William, 191
Legacy and Reconciliation Act, 246
Lemkin, Raphael, 9
Lenin, Vladimir, 158, 163
Lester, Alan, 76–7
Leventhal, Fred, 286–8
'Liberal Imperialism', 157
Liberal Party, 157
liberalism, 19, 39–42, 105, 265
Life and Struggles of the Negro Toilers, The (Comintern pamphlet), 221
Lindberg, Tracey, 82–3, 86, 290
Listener, The (magazine), 267
Livingstone, David, 150, 199–200, 277, 280
Lobengula (Matabele King), 147, 151

London, 41, 52–3, 124, 132, 142, 152, 173, 176, 180, 182, 223, 224, 227, 241
   abolitionist moralities, 190–6
   anti-slavery, morality of, 196–202
   benefits of, 39–46
   Biggar's book on, 75–7
   Black War (1826–32), 55–9
   colonialism and racism, 34–8
   colonialism, justifying, 84–6
   colonialism, scholars on, 79–82
   genocide, act of, 59–64
   historical research, past and present in, 202–9
   indigenous authors, 82–4
   Riel and indigenous communities, 77–9
   schooling, 86–9
   and Tasmanian genocide, 64–72
London's High Court, 248
Loomba, Ania, 104
Lovatt Smith, David, 280
Lugard, Lord Frederick, 200, 267, 277
Lux, Maureen, 80
Luxemburg, Rosa, 163

Macdonald, John A. (Canada's Prime Minister), 80, 89
MacDonald, John, 105
MacDonald, Ramsay, 156
Mackenzie, John, 150
Macmillan, Harold, 257, 263
Madura, 125

INDEX

Mahomet, Tunku Radin, 126
Major, Andrea, 289
Malacca Straits, 124
Malay rulers, 134–5
Malaya, 244, 245, 258
Malcolm, John, 277
Manchester Guardian, The (newspaper), 157
Manchester, 278
Manchester University Press, 278
Manchuria, 176
Mani, Lata, 104, 289
Manitoba, 77
Manne, Robert, 62–3
Mantel, Hilary, 15–17
Māori people, 209
Marathas, 22
Martin, Ged, 80
Marxism, 294
Mashona, 151
Matabele king, 147
Mataram, 125, 129, 130
Mataram, Sultan of, 131
Matthews, Gelien, 193
Mau Mau, 249, 280
Mauritius, 41
McCallum, Mary Jane Logan, 87
McCombe, Richard, 249
McGovern, Chris, 96
Medicine that Walks (monograph), 80
Melville, Henry, 63–4
Mercator map, 75
Merriman, John X., 160, 167
Metcalfe, Charles, 293

Mexico, 30
Miani, Battle of, 112
Miers, Suzanne, 200
Miller, J. R., 76, 88
Millions, Erin, 87
Milloy, 88
Milner, Alfred, 103, 153–6, 163, 277
  mining, 149–54
  racial segregation, 159–61
Milton, John, 182
Minto, Lord (Governor General), 123–4, 127, 134, 139–40, 144
Molteno, John, 167
Monty Pythonesque, 97
'moral capital', 192
moral imperialism, 49
Morant Bay rebellion, 39–40
Morris, Jan, 9
Moscow, 220
Mountbatten, Lord (India's Viceroy), 239, 240–1, 243
Moyne, Lord, 231
Mughal Empire, 22, 100
Mukerjee, Madhusree, 216
Munich Agreement, 229–30
Munich Crisis, 229
Murdoch press, 64
Murphy, Catherine, 320n17
Muslim rulers, 100
Muslims, 95, 114–15
'the Mussolini of Trinidad', 224
Mussolini, Benito, 201, 226, 228

Nairobi, 250

371

INDEX

Nandy, Ashis, 108
Nanjing, 22
Nanjing, Treaty of, 174
Napier Bruce, William, 114
Napier, Charles, 23, 100, 105–6, 119–20
    British India, prosecuting sati in, 115–19
    sati, abolition of, 93–9
    Sindh, conquest of, 111–15
Napier, William F. P., 113
Napoleonic Wars, 56, 123–4, 155, 194
Natal, 25
National Archives of India, 115
National Party, 222
National Post, The (newspaper), 89
National Review, The (magazine), 95
National Trust (2019), 7
National Trust Act (1907), 7–8
National Trust report, 14
Naval Brigade, 179
Nazi Germany, 215–18, 225, 230
Nazism, 216–19
Ndebele, 151
Negro Worker, The (journal), 215, 220–3, 232
Nehru, Jawaharlal, 243
Nelson, Lord, 4
Nepal, 22
Netherlands, 124, 249
New Criterion, The (magazine), 62, 95
New England, 26

New South Wales, 69, 253
New York, 176
New Zealand, 21, 42, 155, 209, 273
New Zealand Wars, 22
Newbury, 195
Nguyen dynasty, 175
Niger Coast Protectorate, 24
Niger Expedition (1841), 36
Nigeria, 45, 264
Nigerian flag, 264
9/11 terror attacks, 95
Nizamat Adalat, 106–8
Norfolk tombstone, 181
North America, 21, 26, 75, 100
North China, 174–5
North Midlands, 57
Northeast Asia, 175
Northern Batswana, 150
Northern Bechuanaland (Botswana), 25
Northern Ireland, 245–6
North-West Mounted Police, 77
Nova Scotia, 51
Nubia, Onyeka, 216
Nuffield College Oxford, 261
Nyika, Farai, 165

Oba, 24
Olusoga, David, 7
"Operation Legacy", 247
Opium War I, 39, 172, 174
Opium War II, 39, 172, 181
Orange River colonies, 159
Oriel College, 148

INDEX

Oriel College Commission, 168
Orwell, George, 255
Oxfam, 236
Oxford University, 148, 168, 255, 295
Oyster Bay, 57, 58

Padmore, 215, 220–5, 225–6, 227, 232
Pakenham, Thomas, 162, 167–8
Pakistan, 239
Pakubuwono IV, 133
Palawa, 58–9
Palembang, 125–30
Palembang, Sultan of, 126–7, 129
Palestine, 76, 258
Pandey, Gyanendra, 278
Panular, Pangeran Arya, 133
Parkin, George R., 75
Parris, Matthew, 95
Patna, Commissioner of, 118
Pax Britannica, 101
Paxman, Jeremy, 94
Pedi, 24–5
Peggs, James, 110
Peking, 178–80
Penang, 138–9
Perham, Margery, 168, 261–9, 270–3
Perry, Adele, 290
Perry, Kennetta Hammond, 217
Pethick-Lawrence, Lord, 241–2
Philip, Prince, 183
Philippines, 37
Phillips, James (Niger Coast Protectorate's Acting Consul General), 23–4
Pirie, Gordon, 38
Pirow, Oswald, 222–3, 228
Plaatje, Sol, 164
Plains Cree, 80
Plomley, Brian, 61, 64, 67–9
Police Service of Northern Ireland, 246
Pontianak, 125
Port Davey, 67–8
Porter, Bernard, 254
Porter, William, 166–7
Powell, Enoch, 235–8
Princely States, 20, 22, 111, 114–15, 243
Privy Council, 110
Public Records Act (1958), 248
Pulitzer Prize, 248
Punch (magazine), 94, 239
Punjabi Sikhs, 22

Qing dynasty, 22, 175
Quadrant (magazine), 62–3
Quakers, 69, 199, 209
Quebec, 26
Quit India movement, 241

'racial capitalism', 149, 222–3
racism, 13, 19, 43, 164–5, 189, 197, 216–20, 233, 256, 293
 anti-Black racism, 20
 anti-racism, 210
 colonialism and, 34–8
 imperial racism, 285

373

INDEX

Radcliffe, Cyril, 239
Raffles, Sophia, 137
Raffles, Stamford, 23
Raffles, Thomas Stamford, 23, 121–5, 134–6, 142–3
   British colonial expansion, 127–34
   colonial humanitarianism, 136–41
   native states, assistance of, 125–7
Raid, Jameson, 152, 153, 161–2, 167
Rajasthan, 114
Rann of Kutch, 111
Reclaimers, 187–90
   anti-slavery, morality of, 196–202
   historical research, past and present in, 202–9
Red River Resistance (1869–70), 77
Rees-Mogg, Jacob, 6, 7, 94
Reform Act (1832), 39
Reform Act (1867), 39
Regent, Prince, 136
Reith Lectures, 261, 264
Rendel, A. M., 38
Republic of China. *See* China
Reynolds, Henry, 59, 61, 62–4
   colonialism and Tasmanian genocide, 64–72
Rhodes Must Fall movement, 13
Rhodes Scholarship, 95
Rhodes, Cecil John, 13, 103, 148–9, 149–54, 158, 167–8, 278

simperialism, 161–70
Rhodesia, 39
Riau, Port of, 124
Riau–Johor Sultanate, 124
Riau–Lingga, 125
Ribeiro-Addy, Bell, 7
Richardson, David, 193
Riel, Louis, 77–9, 85–6
Risdon Cove, 71
River Congo, 51
Roberts, Andrew, 208, 216
Robin Law, 199
Robinson, Cedric, 151–2, 214, 219–23
Robinson, G. A., 60, 69
Robinson, Hercules, 151
Rodin, 182–3
"The Rope Trick", 239
Rosebery, Lord, 157
Rowlandson, Thomas, 110
Roy, Raja Rammohan, 40, 110
Roy, Tirthankar, 32–3, 294
Royal Commission, 231
Royal Hospital Chelsea, 183
Royal Marines National Memorial, 172, 178–9, 181–3
Royal Navy, 30, 173, 174
Royal Ulster Constabulary (RUC), 245–6
Rudd, Charles, 151
Rupert Murdoch, 61
Russia, 175, 176
Ryan, Lyndall, 8–9, 27

Said, Edward, 122, 279, 291

INDEX

Saint Helena, 30
Salisbury, Lord, 40–1
Samachar Chandrika (newspaper), 110–11
Sambas, 125
Sanghera, Sathnam, 14
Santayana, George, 95
Saskatchewan, 80
sati (widow-burning), 114, 319n1
  abolition, 93–9, 100
  British debate on, 104–11
  British India, prosecuting sati in, 115–19
  See also Roy, Raja Rammohan
Satia, Priya, 289, 300 n6
Save the Children, 236
Schreiner, Olive, 157, 167
Scott, C. P., 157
'Scramble for Africa', 25
Seeley, J. R., 18, 254
Sellar, W. C., 99
Serampore, 108
Settled Districts, 58, 70
Seven Years War (1756–63), 21–2
Shandong, 180
Shanghai, 181, 184
Shanghai Defence Force, 172, 177, 184
Sharia law, 95
Sharp, Granville, 51, 194
Shaw, Flora, 157
Sheffield, 240
Shillington, Kevin, 150
Shipman, Tim, 6
Siak, 125

Sierra Leone Company, 52
Sierra Leone, 51–2
Sikh policemen, 172
Sindh, 93
  conquest of, 111–15
Sindh, Commander of, 111
Singapore, 121, 123–5, 134–6, 138–41
Singha, Radhika, 289
Sino-Japanese War (1937), 176
Sitapur Division, Commissioner of the, 116
Sitaram, 116
slave trade abolitionist moralities, 190–6
Slave Trade Act (1807), 52
Smith, Adam, 141, 195
Smuts, Jan, 160, 227
Social Darwinism, 61
Solomon, Saul, 167
Sophia, 141, 142
South Africa Company mining, 149–54
South Africa fascism vs, Negro Workers, 220–5
South Africa, 6, 32, 76, 147–8, 178–9, 217–29, 236, 241, 254
  Rhodes' imperialism, 161–70
  See also South African War
South African Republic (Transvaal), 151
South African War (1899–1902), 6, 38, 148, 154–9, 180, 254, 272
  Rhodes' imperialism, 161–70
South Asia, 103, 254, 278

INDEX

South West Africa, 225
Southeast Asia, 123, 124–5, 138, 175, 264
    British colonial expansion, 127–34
Southern Africa, 23, 24, 26
Southern Batswana, 150
Southern Bechuanaland, 151
Southern Rhodesia, 225
Soviet Union, 221
Spectator, The (magazine), 13, 267, 272
Spivak, Gayatri, 18, 114, 278
Sri Lanka. *See* Ceylon (Sri Lanka)
Stalinism, 225
Stansky, Peter, 286–8
Starblanket, Gina, 81
Stead, W. T., 156, 157
Steevens, G. W., 157
Stepan, Nancy, 34–5
Stephen, Virginia, 287
Stewart, Oliver, 184
Stokes, Eric, 161
'Stolen Generation', 28
'Stop the War Committee', 156
Strachey, John, 257–61, 264, 266, 269
Strachey, Lytton, 287–8
Straits Times, The (Singaporean newspaper), 143
Strasbourg, 245
Sudan, 76
Suez Canal Zone, 236
Sumatra, 124, 126–7, 138
Sumenep, 125

Sun Yat-sen, 175
Sunak, Rishi, 7
Sunday Telegraph, The (newspaper), 267
Sunday Times, The (newspaper), 6
Surakarta, 125
Susu, 51–2
Susuhunan ('Emperor of Java'), 125
Swaziland, 227
Sydney, 27

Taiping Civil War (1850–64), 177
Tasman Peninsula, 58
Tasmania, 27, 55
    genocide, act of, 59–64
    and Tasmanian genocide, 64–72
Tasmanian Aboriginal people, 59–64
    Black War, 56–9
    colonialism and Tasmanian genocide, 64–72
Tasmanian genocide, 8–9
Tatler, 184
Taylor, A. J. P., 259
Taylor, Michael, 6–7
Taylor, Peter Shawn, 89, 90
Telegraph, The (newspaper), 169
Temenggong, 124, 134, 138
Temne, 51
Temple, Richard, 33
1066 And All That (seminal), 99
Thames, 182
Tharoor, Shashi, 32, 294
Things Fall Apart (novel), 44, 73
Third Reich, 218

INDEX

Third World Quarterly (journal), 14, 44
Thompson, E. P., 19
Thorn, Major William, 129–31
Thornton, A. P., 259–60
Tianjin, 175
Times, The (newspaper), 95, 182, 229, 255–6, 264, 277
Tobias, John, 80
Tombs, Robert, 168, 188, 196, 202, 207
Toronto, 260
Toynbee, Polly, 95
Trafalgar Square, 173, 181–3, 226
Transvaal, 153
Treaty Lands Entitlement, 80
Trevelyan, Charles, 290
Trinidad, 220, 223–4, 226, 230–1
Trotskyist, 226
Truth and Reconciliation Commission of Canada's (TRC), 88, 91
Turtle Island, 85
Turtle Island, Nations of, 82
Tze Shung, 141

Uganda, 238
Ukraine, 6
Umuofia, 73
Union of South Africa, 222–3, 227
United Kingdom (UK), 33, 89, 192, 195–6, 238, 268, 288
  document destruction program, 246–8
United Nations Charter (1945), 128

United States (USA), 11, 26, 30, 37, 62, 158, 246, 288
University of Calgary, 76
University of Cambridge, 216
University of Cape Town, 148
Upper Canada, 79
Upper Senegal River, 50

Van Diemen's Land, 56, 69
Victoria Cross, 180
Victoria, Queen, 60, 181
Vienna, Peace of, 124
Vietnam, 175

Wahpasiw, Omeasoo, 290
Waitangi, Treaty of (1840), 22, 209
Wales Island, Prince of, 123, 178
Walker, G. W., 69
Wang Jingwei, 176
Ward, Stuart, 168
Warren, Charles, 150–1
Watt, Carey, 100, 101
Weld, Frederick, 143–4
Wellington, Duke of, 198
Wesley, John, 193
West Africa, 51, 73, 224
West Indies, 49, 194, 196, 223–4, 231–2, 260
West River flotillas, 174
West, John, 69–70
Westminster, 152
Westminster Abbey, 142
White Britons, 15
Wilberforce, William, 30, 143
Williams, Eric, 191
Williams, Rowan, 95

377

INDEX

Williamson, Gavin, 5
Wilson, Sarah, 157
Windschuttle, Keith, 59, 61, 62–4, 74
   colonialism and Tasmanian genocide, 64–72
Witbooi, Hendrik, 25
Witwatersrand, 151
Woods, Joseph (Quaker), 209
Woolf, Leonard, 286–8, 289
World War I, 13, 44, 174, 200, 229
World War II, 9, 216, 225–32, 235, 258

Xhosa, 24–5, 167

Yang, Anand, 96
Yangtze, 173, 174
Yeatman, R. J., 99
YMCA, 268
Yogya ruler, 133
Yogyakarta, prince of the, 124, 128, 129, 130–3
YouGov polls, 99–100

Zambezi, 152
Zimbabwe (Rhodesia), 151
Zoffany, John, 105
Zulu kingdom, 24–5, 148
Zulu nation, 24–5, 167
'Zulu War', 25